The Aesthetic Turn in Political Thought

The Aesthetic Turn in Political Thought

EDITED BY

NIKOLAS KOMPRIDIS

BLOOMSBURY
NEW YORK • LONDON • NEW DELHI • SYDNEY

Bloomsbury Academic
An imprint of Bloomsbury Publishing Inc.

1385 Broadway
New York
NY 10018
USA

50 Bedford Square
London
WC1B 3DP
UK

www.bloomsbury.com

Bloomsbury is a registered trade mark of Bloomsbury Publishing Plc

First published 2014

Library of Congress Cataloging-in-Publication Data
The aesthetic turn in political thought / edited by Nikolas Kompridis.
pages cm
ISBN 978–1-4411-4995-4 (hardback)-- ISBN 978–1-4411-4834-6 (paperback) 1. Political science–Philosophy. 2. Aesthetics, Modern. I. Kompridis, Nikolas.
JA71.A47145 2014
320.01–dc23
2013042231

ISBN: HB: 978-1-4411-4995-4
PB: 978-1-4411-4834-6
ePub: 978-1-4411-8516-7
ePDF: 978-1-4411-9669-9

Typeset by Fakenham Prepress Solutions, Fakenham, Norfolk NR21 8NN

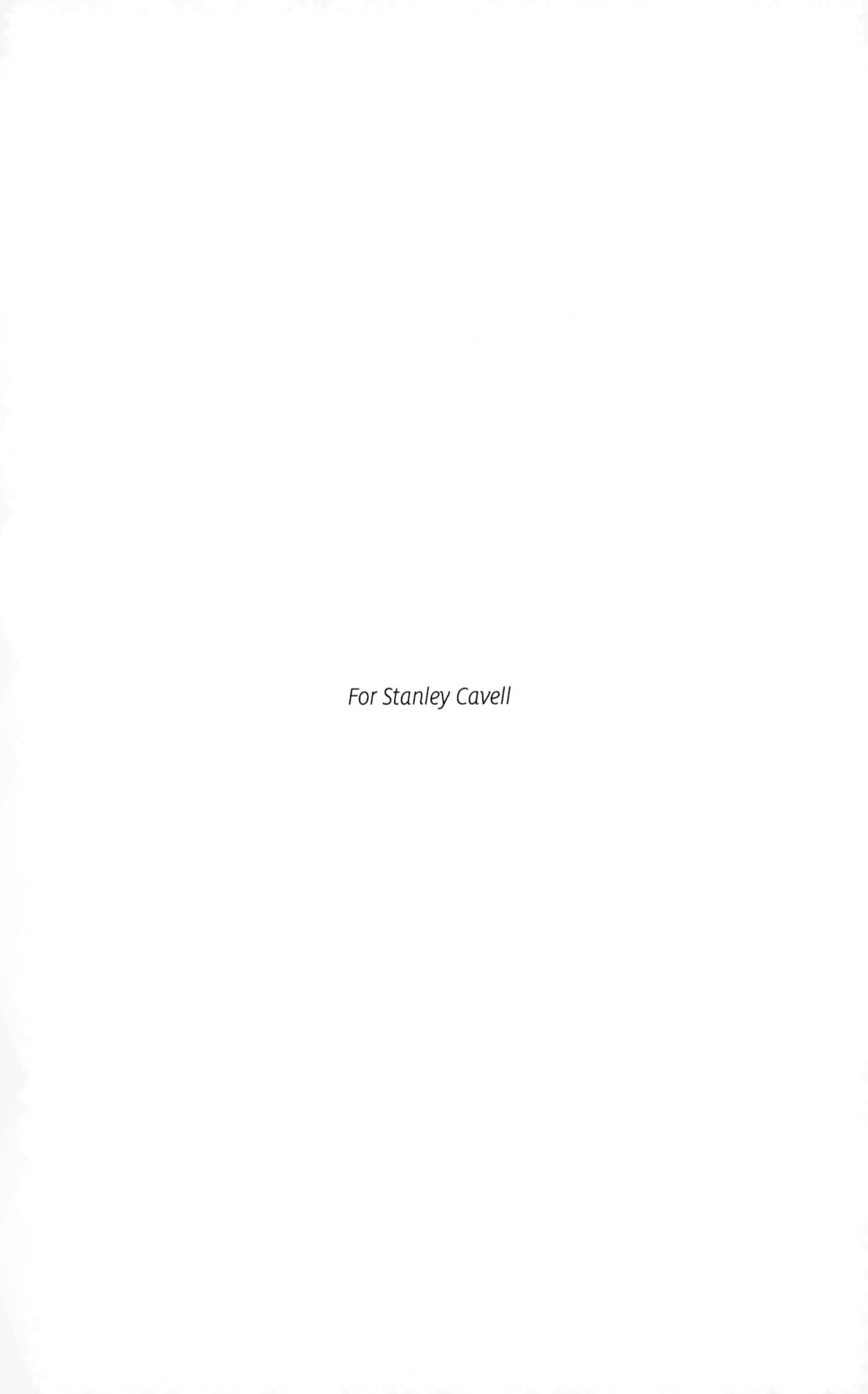

For Stanley Cavell

CONTENTS

ACKNOWLEDGMENTS

I would like to thank all the contributors for their terrific contributions to this volume, and for their forbearance and patience through its many twists and turns (pardon the pun), including the many interruptions that delayed its publication. I want also to thank all the people at Bloomsbury who helped along the way, and for their patience, too, not least, Matthew Kopel, Kaitlin Fontana, Dominic West, and James Tupper.

Finally, I want especially to thank Morton Schoolman for conceiving the APSA and WPSA panels on the "aesthetic turn," for drawing attention to it in the first place, and for various forms of intellectual support over the years.

The volume is dedicated to Stanley Cavell in recognition of all that I have learned from him about the aesthetic problems of philosophy, ethical and political, and in gratitude for the many paths he has opened to the still untapped and still unacknowledged resources of American and European romanticism.

***

Bloomsbury would like to thank the publishers of select works in this volume for granting permission to reproduce. Rights questions about these works should be directed to the original publishers.

"The aesthetic dimension: Aesthetics, politics, knowledge" by Jacques Rancière is reproduced by permission from *Critical Inquiry* 36, Autumn 2009 (Chicago: The University of Chicago Press, 2009). 0093-1896/09/3601-0006 © 2009 by the University of Chicago.

"Recognition and receptivity: Forms of normative response in the lives of the animals we are" by Nikolas Kompridis is reproduced by permission from *New Literary History,* (Baltimore: Johns Hopkins, 2013), 44: 1–24.

"We feel our freedom: Imagination and judgment in the thought of Hannah Arendt" by Linda M. G. Zerilli is reproduced by permission from Linda M. G. Zerilli, *"We Feel Our Freedom": Imagination and Judgment in the Thought of Hannah Arendt* (Thousand Oaks, CA: Political Theory, SAGE) 10.1177/0090591704272958.

"Writing a name in the sky: Rancière, Cavell, and the possibility of egalitarian inscription" by Aletta J. Norval is reproduced by permission from Aletta J. Norval, *"Writing a Name in the Sky": Rancière, Cavell, and the Possibility of Egalitarian Inscription* (American Political Science Review, 2012), 106 (4): 810–26.

LIST OF CONTRIBUTORS

Romand Coles
Northern Arizona University, USA

Romand Coles is the Frances B. McAllister Chair and Director of the Program for Community, Culture and Environment at Northern Arizona University where he is a leader in a movement for engaged democratic pedagogy. His books include *Beyond Gated Politics: Reflections for the Future of Democracy* (Minnesota, 2005), *Rethinking Generosity: Critical Theory and the Politics of Caritas* (Cornell, 1997), *Christianity, Democracy, and the Radical Ordinary: Conversations between a Christian and a Radical Democrat* (with Stanley Hauerwas) (Wipf and Stock, 2008), and *Self/Power/Other: Political Theory and Dialogical Ethics* (Cornell, 1992). He has recently completed a book tentatively titled *Radical Ecological Democracy: Receptive Resonance, Circulation, and the Dynamics of Transformation*, and is working on a co-authored book on the aesthetic dimension of politics with Lia Haro.

Jason Frank
Cornell University, USA

Jason Frank is Associate Professor of Government at Cornell University. He is the author of *Constituent Moments: Enacting the People in Postrevolutionary America* (Duke University Press, 2010), *Publius and Political Imagination* (Rowman & Littlefield, 2013), and editor of *A Political Companion to Herman Melville* (University Press of Kentucky, 2013). He has published widely in democratic theory and American political thought and is currently working on a project titled *The Democratic Sublime: Political Theory and Aesthetics in the Age of Democratic Revolution.*

Lewis R. Gordon
University of Connecticut, USA

Lewis R. Gordon is Professor of Philosophy and Africana Studies at the University of Connecticut; Europhilosophy Visiting Chair at Toulouse University, France; and Nelson Mandela Visiting Professor at Rhodes University, South Africa. His books include *Fanon and the Crisis of European*

Man: An Essay on Philosophy and the Human Sciences (Routledge) and *An Introduction to Africana Philosophy* (Cambridge). His website is: http://lewisrgordon.com

Lia Haro
Duke University, USA

Lia Haro is an anthropologist and literary theorist from Duke University. She is completing a manuscript on contemporary global development, poverty and utopianism entitled "The End(s) of the End of Poverty." She has done extensive direct action fieldwork in Africa and Latin America. She is also working on a co-authored book on the aesthetic dimension of politics with Romand Coles.

Nikolas Kompridis
Australian Catholic University

Nikolas Kompridis is Research Professor of Philosophy and Political Thought and Foundation Director of the Institute for Social Justice at the Australian Catholic University. He has published widely on a broad spectrum of topics in philosophy and political theory, and is the author of *Critique and Disclosure: Critical Theory between Past and Future* (MIT, 2006) and *Philosophical Romanticism* (Routledge, 2006). He is currently completing two new books, one on a normative theory of receptivity, and the other on the renewal of philosophical and political romanticism.

Patchen Markell
University of Chicago

Patchen Markell is Associate Professor of Political Science at the University of Chicago and the author of *Bound by Recognition* (Princeton University Press, 2003). He is currently completing a book on Hannah Arendt's *The Human Condition*, elements of whose argument also appear in articles and chapters in *The American Political Science Review* (2006), *College Literature* (2011), and *Radical Future Pasts: Untimely Political Theory*, ed. Mark Reinhardt, Rom Coles, and George Shulman (Kentucky, 2014).

Aletta J. Norval
University of Essex, United Kingdom

Aletta Norval is Professor in Political Theory in the Department of Government, University of Essex. Her monographs include *Aversive Democracy* (2007). *Inheritance and Originality in the Democratic Tradition* (Cambridge University Press), and *Deconstructing Apartheid Discourse* (Verso, 1996).

She is co-editor of *Practices of Freedom: Decentred Governance, Conflict and Democratic Participation* (Cambridge, 2014), *South Africa in Transition* (Macmillan, 1998) and *Discourse Theory and Political Analysis* (Manchester University Press, 2000). She is currently working on a book on Wittgenstein and Cavell. She is Consulting Editor of *Political Theory* and serves on the editorial boards of *Theory & Event*, *Acta Philosophica* and *Politikon*.

Melissa A. Orlie
University of Illinois, USA

Melissa Orlie teaches political theory at the University of Illinois, Urbana-Champaign (http://www.pol.illinois.edu/people/orlie). Her writing engages tensions and convergences among political, ecological, psychoanalytic and ethical concerns. She is currently finishing a long-term book project entitled "The Nietzsche we need now," from which the essay for this volume was drawn.

Davide Panagia
Trent University, Canada

Davide Panagia is a political and cultural theorist at Trent University (Canada). He is Co-Editor of the journal *Theory and Event* and a regular contributor to *The Contemporary Condition*. His research focuses on the historical and contemporary dimensions of an aesthetics of politics and theories of sensation, with an emphasis on citizenship studies, theories of solidarity, media ontologies and cultures of observation. He has published three books: *The Poetics of Political Thinking* (Duke University Press, 2006), *The Political Life of Sensation* (Duke University Press, 2009), and *Impressions of Hume: Cinematic Thinking and the Politics of Discontinuity* (Rowman & Littlefield, 2013).

Jacques Rancière
University of Paris-VII, France

Jacques Rancière is Emeritus Professor of Philosophy at the University of Paris-VIII. His books include *The Future of the Image* (Verso, 2007), *The Hatred of Democracy* (Verso, 2006), *The Politics of Aesthetics* (Continuum, 2004), *Dis-Agreement* (Minnesota, 1999), and *On the Shores of Politics* (Verso, 1995), *Aesthetics and its Discontents* (Polity Press, 2009).

Linda M. G. Zerilli
University of Chicago, USA

Linda M. G. Zerilli is the Charles E. Merriam Distinguished Service Professor of Political Science at the University of Chicago. She is also the current faculty director of the Center for the Study of Gender and Sexuality. She is the author of *Signifying Woman: Culture and Chaos in Rousseau, Burke, and Mill* (Cornell University Press, 1994) and *Feminism and the Abyss of Freedom* (Chicago University Press, 2005). Zerilli's latest book manuscript, *Towards a Democratic Theory of Judgment*, is forthcoming with Chicago University Press in 2014.

Introduction

Turning and returning: The aesthetic turn in political thought

Nikolas Kompridis

"Politics is aesthetic in principle."

JACQUES RANCIÈRE, *DISAGREEMENT*

A turn or a return?

It is nigh impossible to attend a professional meeting of political theorists or philosophers without coming across a significant number of papers that explore, often in systematic and unexpected ways, the connection between aesthetics and politics. Put more precisely, there is a widespread, ever-growing exploration of political life from an aesthetic perspective, a phenomenon that has become so prominent and persistent that we must speak of it as an *aesthetic turn* in political thought. But what does that signify for how we think about politics? What does it mean to turn to aesthetics to make sense of politics? In what sense is politics *aesthetic*? What is it about the aesthetic that it can *turn* political thought? Towards what in politics is it being turned? What is it about the aesthetic that politics itself might turn on it? All the papers collected in this volume deal with these questions, and each in its own way highlights different aspects of the aesthetic turn, while communicating directly and indirectly with each of the others.

No doubt there are those who might be understandably skeptical of talk that signals yet another "turn" in the humanities and social sciences. There have been so many "turns" of late—the cultural turn, the interpretive turn, the postmodern turn, the cognitive turn, the affective turn, and so forth—that it is difficult not to suspect that some of these "turns" might be more indicative of a fleeting academic fashion or academic opportunism than of a genuine sea change within or across academic disciplines. The so-called "linguistic turn," which began in philosophy and spread through the human sciences to become an orthodoxy of sorts, originally marked a fundamental break with methodologies and ontologies that for more than three centuries privileged the internal mental states of a disembodied knowing subject. Of course, there was not just one form of the linguistic turn, and it didn't happen overnight.[1] A half-century after its public emergence, the "linguistic turn" is now facing challenges of various sorts, most prominently by the "new materialism" or the "material turn." Turns can be overturned—some more easily than others.

Whatever the limitations of the linguistic turn, and the looming controversies over constructivism and anti-essentialism, it is very hard to imagine the displacement of language from *a* position of primacy in the inquiries we undertake and the ways we make sense of things and of ourselves. If we are to speak confidently of an aesthetic turn, we must show that this turn involves a consequential change in our understanding of politics and co-extensively a consequential change in our understanding of the aesthetic. But as with the linguistic turn, we need to appreciate that this did not happen overnight. In the history of Western political thought there is a long argument about the relation of aesthetics to politics, going back to Plato; an argument that remains unresolved, and when it flares up, as it has, again and again, unsettles and disturbs. There are signs that the terms of this long argument are finally changing, and it is in these changing terms that we can find something new in the aesthetic turn of our own time.

As the contributions in this volume demonstrate, aesthetics and politics have been overtly implicated and entangled with each other since the late eighteenth century, when one could already speak of an aesthetic turn in political thought, retrospectively, in the writings of European romanticism from Rousseau to Schiller and the Jena romantics, and in the framing of the debates about the meaning of the French Revolution. So what we may be speaking of is a return rather than a turn, or of a turn delayed and resisted until the emergence of more propitious conditions.

---

[1]One can tell a story about the linguistic turn that begins with Herder, Hamann and Humboldt, another that begins with Frege, Russell and the early Wittgenstein, or yet another that begins with Saussure and structuralism. There is hardly unanimity about the linguistic turn and its broader implications, but there is no going back to epistemologies and ontologies that bypass the constitutive role of language in making possible our access to the world and our understanding of ourselves.

It is obvious that there is growing dissatisfaction with the limits of conventional modes of normative political theorizing, and the truncated understanding of politics and political agency that they suppose and reproduce. But such dissatisfaction is only a necessary—not a sufficient—historical condition of the aesthetic turn. Another necessary condition is an enlarged conception of aesthetics as a normative and conceptual resource for making sense of political life. By the "aesthetic" or "aesthetics" we mean much more than a specialized inquiry into the nature of art, artworks, or beauty, grounded in a sensuous, usually non-cognitive, mode of perception. What is meant is something much wider in scope, something that is still being explored and mapped, something directly implicated in what counts as cognition, reason, experience, meaning and agency, as the rich tradition of philosophical thought I call *philosophical romanticism* has shown and continues to show.[2] It has been the case that much of what is excluded or marginalized in the debates over what counts as cognition, reason, experience, meaning and agency ends up in the aesthetic category, a massive refuse bin for what we cannot fit into our received categories of understanding. Our attempts to make sense of politics and of our own possibilities as political agents has been deeply impoverished by the failure to draw on the normative and conceptual resources of the aesthetic; resources we have tended to dismiss as either irrelevant or dangerous.

Just as certainly, the contemporary aesthetic turn emerges at a time when it is widely acknowledged that what counts as political theory or as the political is very much up for grabs. It may well be that the aesthetic turn is itself part of something bigger from which it draws and to which it contributes—call it, at the risk of "turn" proliferation, the "practical turn." There are different ways to characterize this practical turn. My own preference is for the Foucauldian and Wittgensteinian characterization given by James Tully: abandoning the genres of conventional normative theory, political theory turns into a species of practical philosophy, which is to say, "a philosophical way of life oriented toward working on ourselves by working on the practices and problematizations in which we find ourselves."[3] However, it is hard to make sense of this "practical turn" without recognizing, as Wittgenstein and Foucault did, that "working on ourselves by working on the practices and problematizations in which we find ourselves," involves an irreducibly aesthetic dimension.

Since romanticism, we have seen that each time modern theorists run up against the limits of extant modes of thinking about the possibilities of political life and the impediments to their realization, they turn to the aesthetic. The aesthetic turn is not a new turn that is happening just now,

---

[2]Nikolas Kompridis, *Philosophical Romanticism* (New York: Routledge, 2006).

[3]James Tully, "Political Philosophy as a Critical Activity," in *Public Philosophy in a New Key* (Cambridge: Cambridge University Press, 2008) pp. 15–38.

all of a sudden; it is a turning that is at once a returning and an overturning. In turning to the aesthetic, political thought is not only being turned by the aesthetic, it turns the aesthetic too, such that we also find ourselves thinking about the possibilities of the aesthetic differently, realizing that we do not really know its boundaries. Nonetheless, there is a view of aesthetics that presupposes that the boundaries of aesthetics and politics are well known and well established. According to the familiar Weberian/Habermasian narrative of modernity, ethics and politics have progressively split off from one another, and split off from science and from art, becoming institutionalized in autonomous expert cultures themselves split off from everyday life. On this basis, the aesthetic is itself just one more autonomous sphere of culture, constituted by specifically aesthetic activities and practices. If one accepts these premises, any talk of an "aesthetic turn" in political thought would be committing an egregious and potentially dangerous error about the character of modernity and the form of modern politics.

When in section 258 of *The Philosophy of Right* Hegel claims that "The state is no work of art," it is as if he is anticipating Walter Benjamin's well-known warning of what happens when aesthetics is introduced into politics: "All efforts to aestheticize politics culminate in one point. That one point is war."[4] Benjamin had no lack of empirical evidence to support this claim, and that very same evidence is still trotted out today in case any of us missed the connection. But for all Benjamin's insight, in this particular essay he is operating with much too narrow a conception of politics and aesthetics. The aestheticization of politics he accurately describes in the particular historical constellation of European fascism remains very misleading as an account of the relation between aesthetics and politics. As Jacques Rancière points out, partially in response to Benjamin and partially in response to Habermas,[5] "There has never been an aestheticization of politics in the modern age because politics is aesthetic in principle."[6] By this he means that politics is irreducibly aesthetic in so far as it involves a "framing of what is given and what we can see," and so involves a distribution or partition of the "sensible"—what is given to sense to make sense of, but also what already makes sense, what appears as already (unquestionably) intelligible.

A fascist aestheticization of politics is an ever-present possibility of modern politics, but it is not by any means a *necessary* consequence of politics being aesthetic in principle. If politics is also about what can appear

---

[4]Walter Benjamin, "The Work of Art in the Age of its Technological Reproducibility: Second Version," in *Selected Writings, Volume 3, 1935–1938*, edited by Howard Eiland and Michael W. Jennings (Cambridge, MA: Harvard University Press).

[5]In particular, to Habermas's *The Philosophical Discourse of Modernity*.

[6]Jacques Rancière, *Disagreement*, translated by Julie Rose (Minneapolis: University of Minnesota Press, 1999) p. 58.

and how it appears to sense, about what can be seen and heard and what can't be seen and heard; if it is about what we are able to see and hear and about what we are unable to see and hear, then *democratic* politics is about letting what could not be seen and heard *be* seen and heard by cultivating new ways of seeing and hearing. Put in slightly different language, politics takes place under given conditions of intelligibility and possibility that enable and disable the capacities of human agents to see what is at stake in what is seen and heard in the space of everyday appearance. It is the task of democratic politics to open up and re-disclose these conditions of intelligibility and possibility, creating alternative possibilities for thought and action. Such *reflective re-disclosure* requires much more than argument, as argument is traditionally conceived. It requires a transformation of perception and the conditions of perception, a transformation of sensibility as well as of rationality.[7]

Worries about an aestheticization of politics make sense only against a background understanding of politics and aesthetics as autonomous, purified domains. Instead of talking about "an aestheticization of politics in the modern age," we need to talk about the resistance or blindness to the ways in which "politics is aesthetic in principle." This may help to explain why on previous occasions an emergent aesthetic turn in political thought has been suppressed or deflected. Our conditions today are different. We are much more skeptical about our political institutions and political practices, and far less persuaded by the aims as well as the methods of conventional political theorizing. Thus our time may well be more inclined to taking seriously alternative conceptions of politics and political theorizing, and perhaps not quite as ready to be alarmed by the thought that there is an ineliminable aesthetic dimension to politics, and that among the tasks of political thought is conceptualizing that dimension as an aesthetics of politics.

While Hegel's repudiation of the state as a work of art may be read as an anticipation of Benjamin's worries about the aestheticization of politics, it can be more productively—and correctly—read as a rejection of the "classical" ideal of aesthetics as a model for modern political life. What is to be rejected is the idea of aesthetic perfection and purity at the heart of the Greek classical ideal, for perfection and purity require a definite departure from and defence against the mundane sphere of the everyday, the sphere in which the practice of politics resides. So in saying that the "state is not a work of art" Hegel is saying that politics cannot aim at perfection or perfect harmony. It exists in a sphere in which perfection cannot be achieved, a sphere in which human beings must contend with "contingency, arbitrariness, and error." It is the condition of politics to exist in a sphere of

[7]See Nikolas Kompridis, *Critique and Disclosure: Critical Theory Between Past and Future* (Cambridge, MA: MIT Press, 2006).

inescapable "contingency, arbitrariness and error," a sphere in which stuff happens all the time. The sphere in which stuff happens is also the sphere in which the novel and unexpected happen. If these are the inescapable conditions of politics then what should be its proper goal?

For Hegel, the goal of politics—the purpose of the state—is the "actualization of freedom," and it is the highest demand of reason that freedom should be achieved, for the fundamental principle of the modern world is "the freedom of subjectivity."[8] What does Hegel mean by this? Well, one thing he should mean is what Arendt means when she says that "the meaning of politics is freedom".[9] Freedom here does not refer to formal freedom or freedom of the will or of choice. It refers to the freedom to change how things are, to change ourselves by changing the circumstances in which we find ourselves—a change in conditions of intelligibility and possibility. Such change allows us to think and act differently in ways that would have previously been considered impossible or unintelligible. Freedom in this sense makes creativity and novelty central to our political practices and institutions, without which politics would be lifeless, rigid, caught in series of inalterable causes and effects. Thus freedom becomes identified with something traditionally thought of as "aesthetic"—an aesthetic process of change whereby, quoting Stanley Cavell, "You are different, what you recognize as problems are different, your world is different."[10] Instead of collapsing politics into aesthetics, the aesthetic turn in political theory demonstrates in myriad ways that much of what is essential to democratic politics can only by disclosed through "aesthetic" theorizing.

The aesthetic problems of modern political thought

Modern politics is understood conceptually in terms of a set of well-known problems—justice, liberty, legitimacy, constitution, sovereignty, and the like. And yet there are problems of politics that can appear *as* political problems only in an aesthetic dimension. Adapting a thought of Stanley Cavell's for our own purposes, we might say that the aesthetic turn consists in political thought's recognition of and response to the *aesthetic problems of modern politics*.[11] We can give them the following names: the

[8]G. W. F. Hegel, *Elements of the Philosophy of Right* (Cambridge: Cambridge University Press, 1991) p. 29.

[9]Hannah Arendt, *The Promise of Politics* (New York: Schocken, 2005) p. 108.

[10]Stanley Cavell, "The Aesthetic Problems of Modern Philosophy," in *Must We Mean What We Say?* (Cambridge: Cambridge University Press, 1976) p. 86.

[11]I derive the idea of the "aesthetic problems of modern politics" from Cavell's essay on the

problem of voice and voicelessness, the problem of the new, the problem of integrating (rather than dichotomizing) the ordinary and the extraordinary, the problem of judgment, the problem of responsiveness and receptivity, the problem of appearance, and of what is given to sense to make sense of, and, more generally, the problem of the meaning and scope of the aesthetic dimension of politics.

Edmund Burke was perhaps the first to recognize the peculiarly aesthetic problems of politics, and to grapple with them in all of their urgency. Jason Frank's opening contribution to the *Aesthetic Turn*, "'Delightful Horror:' Edmund Burke and the aesthetics of democratic revolution," illuminates not only the extent to which the aesthetic categories of beauty and the sublime were essential to Burke's conceptions of political authority and political community, but also to how Burke refashioned those categories in response to unexpected political events. Underscoring the point that the aesthetic turn is at once a turn to and a return of aesthetics to political thought, Frank draws attention to the frequency with which political events were framed in terms of aesthetic categories, most dramatically of course, in connection with the "insolent bloody theatre" of the French Revolution.

Long before his anti-revolutionary writings, Burke already realized that there were elements of political life that could not be captured in non-aesthetic categories, precisely because these elements were themselves aesthetic. He was perhaps the first to recognize that the possibility of politics was in some way staked to aesthetic experience and response; for instance, the possibility of enduring political community. As Frank demonstrates, Burke's early account of the sublime is essential to understanding "how Burke conceptualizes the complementary rather than antagonistic relationship between individual freedom and authority that he places at the center of his political thinking." In effect, Burke already *presupposed* what Rancière calls the distribution of the sensible, however differently Burke conceives of it. Distinctive to Burke, writes Frank, is "a vision of authority as a complex tapestry of social relations, sustained by aesthetic response." Burke's concern with the "fundamental question of how human attachments and political communities are engendered," led him to conclude that political belonging had a necessarily and ineliminably aesthetic dimension. Political community, "peoplehood," is "first and foremost a community of sense."

As much as Burke recoiled from the radical democratic sublime manifested in the revolutionary politics of his time, he did not abandon his commitment to making sense of politics aesthetically. Instead of rejecting aesthetics altogether, he shifted the conceptual and normative center of the sublime, as

"aesthetic problems of modern philosophy" (cited above). In order not to make too much of the difference between political theory and political philosophy I use the broader and less sectarian term "political thought."

Jason Frank explains, from a focus on "astonishment, novelty and productive or ennobling disorientation" to "the gravity of an immanent historical inheritance transmitted across time by the ancient constitution." We might say that Burke proposed to transform and not just moderate the sensibility of the sublime, which is to say, far from finding aesthetics inadequate to making sense of politics, he insisted on its indispensability, insisted on the link between sense and sensibility. He must have also come to recognize that aesthetic categories are just as contestable and contested as any other category of politics and political thought, and through the very same process came to recognize the plurality and depth of aesthetic political categories.

Burke's acute attunement to the aesthetic dimension of politics drew his attention—and ours—to another aesthetic problem of political thought, the multi-faceted problem Arendt was later to call the "the problem of the new." In the democratic revolutions of his time Burke came uncomfortably to see that his earlier account of aesthetic experience, especially his account of the sublime as rapture and rupture, was implicated in "a new and dangerous aesthetic sensibility: the radical democratic sublime" (Frank). The "power to begin the world over again," as Thomas Paine put it, represented a new, unprecedented power. Alarmingly for Burke, the power to begin the world over again signified the emergence of an "insolent" form of agency, an "unencumbered will freed from historical circumstance and contextual limitation" (Frank).[12]

The "radical democratic sublime" is one manifestation of this freedom and it represents a challenge to any idea of politics in which new beginnings, breaks in time and history, rupture and interruption, are construed as essential to politics, especially democratic politics. Arendt, another central figure of the aesthetic turn, regarded the freedom to begin anew as the most precious form of human freedom, the form of freedom through which human beings break free of something oppressive and debilitating in their relationships to one another, to their institutions, or their commonly shared world. A public space of freedom can open up and be sustained only so long as "new beginnings are constantly injected into the stream of things already initiated."[13] Indeed, freedom in this sense is identified with the

---

[12]Much of what Burke writes about the irreverence, desecration and iconoclasm of revolutionary aesthetic sensibility anticipates Nietzsche's critique of modernity, especially his later writings on Wagner. The following passage from *The Gay Science* would have had Burke nodding in emphatic agreement: "And as for our future, one will hardly find us again on the paths of those Egyptian youths who endanger temples by night, embrace statues, and want by all means to unveil, uncover and put into a bright light whatever is kept concealed for good reasons. No, this bad taste, this will to truth, to 'truth at any price,' this youthful madness in the love of truth, have lost their charm for us." Friedrich Nietzsche, *The Gay Science*, translated by Walter Kaufmann (New York: Vintage, 1974) p. 35.

[13]Hannah Arendt, "Freedom and Politics," in A. Hunold, ed., *Freedom and Serfdom* (Dordrecht: Riedel, 1961) p. 215.

very conditions of human natality, because we ourselves "are new beginnings and hence beginners."[14] Where Burke speaks of an "insolent form of agency" and of the devastating consequences that follow when political action is solely guided by the "mere pleasure of the beginner," Arendt speaks of the "proud privilege of being beginners of something altogether new."[15] How do proud beginners avoid becoming "insolent" beginners? How does the freedom to begin anew avoid becoming a wilful and arbitrary freedom?[16]

These Burkean questions are unavoidable. To take the problem of the new seriously is to take on the distinctive normative challenges these questions pose. In *On Revolution*, Arendt's response to one of those challenges, the challenge posed by Burke's critique of the "radical democratic sublime," was to distinguish those revolutionary acts that aim at "founding anew and building up" from those that aim at "rebellion and tearing things down."[17] That distinction, promising as it might be, does not remove all ambiguity, and there is indeed in any new beginning an element of unavoidable ambiguity as well as unavoidable risk. That comes with, as much as it partially defines, the normative territory of the new. The confrontation with the genuinely new is a confrontation with what is both unfamiliar to us and uncontrollable by us, and in that respect the new is also normatively distinctive, in virtue of which it demands a distinctive form of normative judgment, reflective judgment, the kind of judgment called forth by that which we cannot—and should not—subsume under our already available concepts and categories.

In her contribution to the volume, "'We Feel Our Freedom:' Imagination and judgment in the thought of Hannah Arendt," Linda M. G. Zerilli brings out some further aspects of the "problem of the new," related to questions of normativity and rationality, as well as to the question of which practices are most central to and most congruent with democratic politics. In our encounter with the problem of the new, the problem of making sense of something that challenges or eludes our available ways of making sense, we must "judge" in a context in which those familiar and reliable ways of making sense cannot make sense. We may be confronted by a "problem," the nature of which we are not yet able confidently and coherently to state, let alone to propose the solution it demands. Such a problem has to be newly formulated in language not already at our disposal. Getting it "right" here

---

[14]Hannah Arendt, "What is Freedom?," in *Between Past and Future* (New York: Penguin, 1993) p. 151.

[15]Hannah Arendt, *On Revolution* (New York: Penguin, 1990) p. 232.

[16]For a complementary analysis of Burke's remarkable reflections on revolution and its connections to colonialism, see Sunil M. Agnani's illuminating *Hating Empire Properly: The Indies and the Limits of Enlightenment Anticolonialism* (New York: Fordham University Press, 2013).

[17]Ibid., p. 234.

means more than correctly applying an existing concept to its corresponding object. Our concepts may need to be expanded, applied differently in this new context, and applied in new ways. Only then can whatever it is that confronts us in perplexing form start to mean something, to make sense, allowing us thereby to respond meaningfully and appropriately. Thus, before we can get to the point of justifying how we should respond or what we should do in such a case, we must first make sense of what it is we are dealing with, and achieve some kind of shared agreement about it. To get to that point will often require "an imaginative extension" of our political concepts, as Zerilli shows in connection with both Kant and Arendt: "to project a word like *beautiful* or a phrase like *created equal* into a new context in ways that others can accept, not because they (necessarily) already agree with the projection... but because they are brought to see something new, a different way of framing their responses to certain objects."

For this reason, the problem of the new calls for reflective judgment, oriented not to "knowledge but understanding," as Zerilli puts it. The normative orientation to "understanding" in the domain of political life is constitutively different from the normative orientation to validity, legitimacy, or justice. The latter are typically grounded in the normativity of rules or law, which is why practices grounded in rule-governed or law-like normativity can be proceduralized, can manifest the rationality of procedures. But reflective judgment, and the kind of arguments that must be made in support of it, cannot be proceduralized. For political philosophers such as Habermas, the rationality of procedures is the most morally and political significant manifestation of reason, and the only legitimate basis of normative validity. But when confronted with the problem of the new, the rationality of procedures is of no use for making sense of what we do not already understand or cannot already formulate in our conceptual vocabulary. There are no valid rules or procedures for making sense of the new. If there were such rules or procedures there could be nothing new to confront, nothing by which to be normatively perplexed or normatively challenged. And yet in spite of the fact that there is something always new to perplex or challenge us, something that eludes our inherited ways of making sense of things, our traditions of political thought have generally ignored the problem of the new, treating it as an abnormal case of politics, not a case of politics in its "normal," everyday form. Any turn to aesthetic sense-making is thus construed as a turn away from the everyday and a turn to the "extraordinary," and thereby portrayed as an implausible if not dangerous basis for politics.[18]

[18]For example, Habermas's portrayal of Castoriadis's work on the founding of new political institutions: "Castoriadis works out the normal case of the political from the limit case of the act of founding an institution; and he interprets this in turn from a horizon of aesthetic experience, as the ecstatic moment erupting from the continuum of time when something

To speak of the "normal case" of the political is profoundly misleading, since it takes for granted a world of shared agreement and understanding within which our various practices make sense and can be carried forward in intelligible, yet largely unquestioned ways. As Heidegger and later Wittgenstein showed, this background understanding of things is one we acquire pre-reflectively through various everyday practices, practices that disclose a world whose conditions of intelligibility they both manifest and which they inescapably presuppose.[19] Zerilli aptly summarizes the political significance of this Heideggerian and Wittgensteinian point: "Politics involves the exchange of arguments in the sense of opening up the world that has been disclosed to us through language, our criteria or concepts. However one understands the attempt to give reasons, it takes for granted a prior 'opening up of [the] world where argument can be received and have an impact,' as Jacques Rancière reminds us… Opening up creates the context in which a change in perspective may happen and things we may have known all along get counted differently." I call arguments that open up the world, that open new normative contexts in which arguments can be offered and received, *world disclosing arguments*.[20] Their "function" is not to win by the "non-coercive force of the better argument" (Habermas) but "to manifest for the other another way" (Cavell).[21] Argument functions differently in a language game of argumentation whose point is world-disclosure rather than justification. Zerilli rightly asks whether it is wise to reduce politics to a contest of better arguments. But why restrict argument to justification? Why not, as I have suggested, think of argument as *also* a practice of world-disclosure? [22] Why not let both "function" in an enlarged understanding of democratic politics and its possibilities? Surely democratic politics need *both* argument as a practice of justification *and* argument as a practice of world disclosure.

In so far as practices of judging and argument are also practices of "opening up" new contexts for "things [to] become public," they can alter what can count as public things (Zerilli). The ways in which aesthetic response and judgment help create a public space, in which things, everyday

absolutely new is founded." Habermas, *The Philosophical Discourse of Modernity*, trans. Frederick Lawrence (Cambridge: MIT Press, 1987) p. 329, translation altered. For an account of the similarities in Schmitt's and Habermas's views on the role of aesthetic experience in politics, see Nikolas Kompridis, "Political Romanticism" in Michael Gibbons (ed.), *The Encyclopedia of Political Thought* (Wiley Blackwell, 2014).

[19]For an extensive discussion of this, Nikolas Kompridis, *Critique and Disclosure*, pp. 30–148, and Charles Taylor, "Lichtung or Lebensform: Parallels between Heidegger and Wittgenstein," in *Philosophical Arguments* (Cambridge, MA: Harvard University Press, 1995) pp. 61–78.

[20]Kompridis, *Critique and Disclosure*, pp. 116–124.

[21]Stanley Cavell, *Conditions Handsome and Unhandsome. The Constitution of Emersonian Perfectionism* (Chicago: University of Chicago Press, 1990) p. 31.

[22]Kompridis, *Critique and Disclosure*.

things, can appear and endure, is a crucial point of contact and of possible convergence between Burke and Arendt. As Patchen Markell argues in his contribution to this volume, "Arendt, aesthetics, and 'The Crisis in Culture'," Arendt's account of the "crisis in culture" is an account of "the kind of attention and care required to sustain" that space in which things can appear and endure, neither as instrumentalizable objects nor as pure works of art. "Culture" in this sense is that "worldly in-between" around and within which the interrelation of work and action coalesce. Markell's careful reconstruction of the problem-contexts underlying Arendt's "The Crisis in Culture" shows that far from being some further iteration of the familiar elitist critique of mass culture, Arendt's essay was concerned most of all with the threatened "space of worldly appearance." Her concern was the way in which that space was being contracted and eroded by the conversion of "cultural objects into disposable consumer goods" (Markell). With the help of central ideas of Kant's *Third Critique*, namely, the ideas of purposiveness without purpose and of the "enlarged mentality," Arendt sought first and foremost to make sense of the conditions of worldly appearance, the "worldly conditions" to which both things and persons are subject. Rather than instancing a turn away from the everyday, the aesthetic turn instances a return to the everyday in and through its concern with the conditions of the worldly appearance of things. As Markell so appositely puts its:

> Rather than tie purposiveness without a purpose…to some feature of the object, Arendt locates it in the way in which an object – potentially *any* object – is treated: whenever we insulate an artefact from the immediate demands of use in order to encounter it differently, to linger (as Kant says) over the shape that it cannot help but display, to let the question of what the object is good for open out into the larger question of "how [the world] is to look, what kind of things are to appear in it" (Arendt, "Crisis in Culture"), we're establishing the conditions for an aesthetic experience – or, better, for an experience that is at once aesthetic and political.

If the "crisis of culture" is a crisis of attention and responsiveness to worldly appearance, the necessary conditions of which simply are that attention and responsiveness, then the aesthetic turn returns to the everyday its significance as the threatened and redemptive space of appearance—the space in which things public can appear, endure, and be experienced as such. In his contribution to *The Aesthetic Turn*, "Fanon's decolonial aesthetic," Lewis R. Gordon shifts the aesthetic and political problem of appearance to another register: the problem of the appearance, non-appearance or disappearance of the black writer. "If he or she writes exclusively to black readers, there is an immediate audience but a strange affirmation of seclusion and presuppositions of non-appearance. To write exclusively to the white reader is to erase the self and the world of blackness, since what is demanded from the white world is often a narcissistic reflection or affirmation of reality as that world prefers it" (Gordon).

Taking Frantz Fanon, *Black Skins, White Masks*, as his point of departure, Gordon pays close attention to the way in which Fanon thinks of writing as "a task of decolonizing knowledge." But this task also has a necessarily aesthetic dimension. If "decolonizing knowledge" requires "the liberation of the human mind being at the level of *how* she or he thinks," then what Fanon had to say as a black writer "needed to be said differently."

Therefore the problem Fanon had to confront was the problem of how to write in a way that makes possible a different, liberating way of thinking. This too is one of the aesthetic problems of modern political thought, the problem of voice and the threat of voicelessness, which Fanon helps us discover in relation to the ongoing process of decolonizing knowledge: "Understanding how black alienation was linked to that of the human being... Fanon outlined a more radical project as the *leitmotif* of *Black Skins, White Masks*—namely, the disalienation of the human being from the disaster of crushed relationships between one set of human beings and another" (Gordon).

Fanon does not propose to go down the path of modernist experimentation and formalism, as though the problem confronting the black writer is a matter of finding an appropriately radical aesthetic methodology; rather, as Gordon shows, it is a matter of connecting the problem of the black writer "to the question of lived reality, to voicing the question of what it means for human beings to organize a world in which they could actually live" (Gordon). This is of course a matter of imagining that world, projecting it from the present into the future, and from the future back into the present, which is to say: the problem of bringing into alignment poetics, theory and politics. Put another way, it is the problem of conjoining meaningfully and constructively utopian thinking and democratic politics. The time in which we live however is altogether inhospitable to such conjoining, for it is both skeptical towards utopian thinking and drained of utopian energies.[23] But what alternatives to the present state of things can we propose if we remain skeptical about the value of utopian thinking and incapable of regenerating utopian political energies?

Lia Haro and Romand Coles confront this question directly in their contribution to the volume, "Journeys to farther shores: Intersecting

---

[23]On the exhaustion of utopian energies see J. Habermas, *The New Obscurity* (Cambridge, MA: MIT Press, 1989) pp. 48–77; Wendy Brown, *Politics out of History* (Princeton: Princeton University Press, 2001) pp. 138–73; and Nikolas Kompridis, *Critique and Disclosure*, pp. 245–80.

movements of poetics, politics, and theory beyond Utopia." As they point out, "responses to events of the past two decades have declared the death of Utopia in discrepant ways that would seem to suggest we are somehow *beyond* Utopia. If we are truly beyond Utopia, how do we now imagine and actualize radical alternatives to what can now be said and thought?" What could politics be, what could it do, without, in Adrienne Rich's words: "the capacity to feel, see what we aren't supposed to feel and see, find expressive forms where we're supposed to shut up"? Rancière echoes this thought when he writes, "Politics means precisely this, that you speak at a time and in a place you're not expected to speak." Absent this capacity to speak when we are expected to "shut up," the "politics" we are left with is the politics of "dead power," or "normal politics," a contracting space of politics in which democratic politics is usurped by bureaucratized political parties and monopolized by political elites, depoliticized by technocrats and rendered unresponsive by rigid institutional processes and procedures, a politics that leads to stagnation, cynicism, passivity, and political fragmentation.[24]

Opposing resignation to the thought that there is no viable alternative to "normal politics," Haro and Coles persuasively argue for the need to rethink the richly complex and agonistic relation between aesthetics, theory, and politics, the separation of which "impoverishes our powers to move beyond merely carrying out the preordained business of the day." Following Adrienne Rich they argue that politics just as much as poetry demands from us an engagement "with states that themselves would deprive us of language and reduce us to passive sufferers" (Rich). But what states are those, politically speaking? Are they states we normally identify as political? If such states reduce us to passive sufferers, isn't it the case, then, that in politics it is our very agency, our freedom, that is at stake?

This is precisely what Arendt had in mind when she asserted that the "meaning of politics is freedom." Freedom in this sense is more and other than freedom from interference (negative) or freedom as self-legislation (positive); it is the "freedom to call something into being which did not exist before, which was not given, not even as an object of cognition or imagination, and which therefore, strictly speaking, could not be known."[25] To "call something into being which did not exist before" is not to create something out of nothing but rather to make sense of things in a new way, a way that didn't make sense before. This involves a struggle over

---

[24]I am here paraphrasing Andreas Kalyvas's description of "normal politics," in *Democracy and the Politics of the Extraordinary* (Cambridge: Cambridge University Press, 2008) p. 6. Kalyvas makes a concerted effort to overcome the dualism of the ordinary and extraordinary, but remains caught within its terms, partly because he does not draw on the resources of the aesthetic turn. For a different way of overcoming the dichotomy between the ordinary and the extraordinary, see Nikolas Kompridis, "The Idea of a New Beginning: A Romantic Source of Normativity and Freedom," in *Philosophical Romanticism*, pp. 32–59, especially pp. 40–7.
[25]Hanna Arendt, *Between Past and Future* (New York: Penguin, 1993) p. 151.

the meaning of things through an "engagement with states that themselves would deprive us of language." The deprivation of language is not to be understood as being in a state without language, but rather as being in a state where our language has become unresponsive to our needs, powerless to make sense of what has become obscure, elusive, oppressive. In this state we feel as though we have become voiceless, aphonic. It is the state in which we find ourselves deprived of language, the state in which our freedom to make sense of things is tested, when "dead power" seems to rule over us, and we are unable to articulate a different vision of things, opening up possibilities that could not previously appear and making them appear as genuine alternatives to the present order of things.

Freedom in this Arendtian sense is not capturable as a "right" or as something law-like in form or nature. When we are talking about freedom as a matter of our voice, we are talking about more than the right to have a voice in decisions about laws and policies to which we are to be subject; we are talking about bringing an end to a condition, a state of things, in which we are "reduced to passive sufferers." Bringing an end to this state requires bringing into being another way to make sense of things, of what and how things can mean. It involves giving voice to "an expanded sense of what is 'humanly possible'" (Rich), and articulating that in our voice, since it is our voice that is called for, if our situation is to be voiced at all. As Haro and Coles show in relation to the richly illustrative "politics of shit" staged as "Toilet Festivals" by Mumbai's slum dwellers, "toilets, which have been denied to slum dwellers, are powerful metaphors for class injustice on the one hand and for self-generated alternatives on the other." Arjun Appadurai, from whose work on the Mumbai toilet festivals Haro and Coles draw, reminds us that in India, the "distance from your own shit is the virtual marker of class distinction," which means that "the politics of shit is turned on its head, and humiliation and victimization are turned into exercises in technical initiative and self-dignification."[26] Framing the politics of shit as part of a political poetics, Haro and Coles liken it to what Rich calls "the truly revolutionary poem" through which "what is represented as intolerable – as crushing – becomes the figure of its own transformation." So, contrary to the mistaken but widely held assumption that the freedom to bring something into being that did not exist before is something that requires some heroic act of genius, artistic or otherwise, far removed from the concerns of everyday life, the inversion of the politics of shit brings something into being in a place where its very possibility was denied or dispossessed. The politics of shit transformatively restaged by Mumbai's Muslim slum dwellers thus compellingly demonstrates at the very most

[26]Cited by Haro and Coles in this volume. Original in Arjun Appadurai, "The Capacity to Aspire," in Vijayendra Rao and Michael Walton (eds), *Culture and Public Action* (Stanford: Stanford University Press, 2004), p. 79.

mundane level of everyday appearances, how reconnecting aesthetics, theory and politics can bring into appearance what could not intelligibly appear before.

In my contribution to the volume, "Recognition and receptivity: Forms of normative response in the lives of the animals we are," I offer a reading of J. M. Coetzee's novella, *The Lives of Animals*, whose central character, Elizabeth Costello, engages with states that threaten to deprive her of language and reduce her to passive suffering. Subjected to ongoing failures of recognition as much by the characters in the text as by the commentators chosen to respond to it, Costello's words and action are found bizarre and unintelligible. Her struggle is not a struggle for recognition in the sense relevant to political theories of recognition, but a struggle to make herself intelligible to others and to herself. It is a struggle for acknowledgment, in Stanley Cavell's sense, and her struggle for acknowledgment is similar if not parallel to Nora Helmer's in *A Doll's House*. Just as the case of Nora Helmer pointed to a lacuna in John Rawls's *Theory of Justice*, the case of Elizabeth Costello points to a lacuna in political theories of recognition, which similarly fail to acknowledge and make sense of a form of injustice and suffering that, as the young Marx famously put it, "lays claim to no particular right, because it is the object of no particular injustice but of injustice in general."[27]

Through the character of Elizabeth Costello and through its very form, *The Lives of Animals* poses again and again the question of how it is that we are "supposed to reply to something or to someone when it is not clear just what it is we are dealing with and what it is that is being asked of us. Can we speak meaningfully about responding rightly or wrongly in cases like this – as readers, as intimates, as citizens, as human beings? What can guide us, normatively speaking? How do we tell what form of response we owe an other when that other appears inscrutable to us or, as in the case of Elizabeth Costello, when the other appears as inscrutable to herself as she appears to us? Where do we begin? What might get in the way of a reply that is just, in every sense of just, not callous, insensitive, indifferent?" This is the central theme and the organizing principle of *The Lives of Animals*: "the question of how we should respond and reply, how we should answer and be answerable to others, the question of human responsiveness or lack of it in the face of suffering." I argue that this calls for a particular form of normative response that I call receptivity, and by which I mean a form of answerability: *receptivity as answerability*.[28]

---

[27]Karl Marx, "Towards a Critique of Hegel's Philosophy of Right," in *Karl Marx: Selected Writings*, ed. David McLellan (Oxford: Oxford Univ. Press, 1977) p. 72.

[28]For further elaboration of this idea of receptivity, see Nikolas Kompridis "Receptivity, Possibility, and Democratic Politics," in *Ethics and Global Politics*, 2011, Vol. 4, No. 4, pp. 255–72.

For Elizabeth Costello, who is calling on us to become receptive to what we have heretofore been unreceptive, it will mean becoming answerable to a call to change our lives. In drawing attention to the lives of animals as lives that can be lived well or badly, as lives that can be exchanged and shortchanged, Costello and Coetzee invite renewed reflection on how lives, human and non-human lives, should be lived—the very question Socrates poses in *The Republic*.

Whereas for Socrates and Plato only the lives of human animals are at stake, for Costello and Coetzee the time has come for us to see that the lives of human and nonhuman animals are *together* at stake in how we answer this question. Sometimes the kind of seeing that is called for is one that requires an engagement with what is not already intelligible, requires being somewhere where we are not already at home, requires struggling with accustomed ways of not seeing, and so struggling to see as if for the first time, and to see what was often already there. This kind of engagement might be awakened by literature's capacity to manifest for others another way, in ways both complex and ambiguous... [and] shoulder political theorists out of our assumptions about how best to make sense of things political, making us more alert to the inadequacy of our conceptual vocabularies. It might also make us capaciously less confident about the powers of academic forms of argument and practices of justification, and more sensitively attuned to the need for new ways of thinking and reasoning with others, ways that must themselves be newly cultivated.

The idea that we need to cultivate new forms of perception and responsiveness is also central to the argument of Melissa Orlie's "For the love of earthly life: Nietzsche and Winnicott between modernism and naturalism." Following Aldo Leopold's suggestion that we not only need to see better, we also need better "eyes" with which to see, Orlie draws out a reading of Nietzsche that emphasizes his call to bring "to conscious awareness of an ever-broadening range of affective experience. Broadened awareness of the affective reverberations flowing into our predominate perceptions and intentions, judgments and actions not only allows us to become more conscious of the roots of our perspectives on life. Such a broadening of affective awareness also allows competing perceptions and affects to enter our conscious life and, along with them, divergent possibilities of life, especially in those aspects of life which may evoke our ire and foster our hatred of life. Awakening to fuller affective experience first facilitates feeling, then taking up the task of affirming, a broader range of earthly life than we are readily inclined toward by birth or habit." It is a call, as Nietzsche put it, "to learn more and more to see as beautiful what is necessary in things." The kind of learning process this involves is aesthetic, in the broad and capacious sense. Positioning herself between naturalistic and modernist readings of Nietzsche, Orlie argues that "our love of this world and the discovery of its beauty depend upon aesthetic judgments and actions which are as much contrary to the ways of nature as they are continuous with it." If we are "to become able to be affected by what is in such a way that we come to love it," we are able to "make it beautiful rather than an object of scorn and resentment." Love in this sense, which one must learn, as Nietzche reminds us, is a diurnal practice of letting ourselves be affected, a practice of becoming receptive, making visible what was invisible, and audible what was inaudible.

The "task of affirming a broader range of earthly life than we are readily inclined toward by birth or habit" requires the capacity to embrace and sustain a set of paradoxes, identified by Donald Winnicott as necessary for the emergence of "transitional phenomena," such as transitional objects and transitional spaces. These in turn depend on a normative stance that allows them "to be perceived, rather than conceived of, to be felt there rather than only experienced conceptually in the mind. In short, one can accept paradox if one can bear to embody an attitude of 'not knowing.'" A normative stance towards things that is not driven by "fantasies of omnipotence and omniscience," but rather is guided by attentiveness and patience will be rewarded for its "hospitality," for "what is strange," as Nietzsche writes, echoing Emerson, will "shed its veil and turns out to be a new and indescribable beauty."

This self-unveiling of things, occuring when we offer our "hospitality," when we do not seize and grasp them but receive and answer them, is what Emerson refers to as our "mode of illumination."[29] The "illumination" is not something that occurs as an effect of our agency as a form of causality, but of our agency as a form of receptivity:

> I do not make it; I arrive there, and behold what was there already.[30]
>
> All I know is reception; I am and I have: but I do not get, and when I have fancied that I have gotten anything, I found I did not.[31]
>
> But I have not found that much was gained by manipular attempts to realize the world of thought.[32]

---

[29] "Do but observe the mode of our illumination. When I converse with a profound mind, or if at any time being alone I have good thoughts, I do not at once arrive at satisfactions, as when, being thirsty, I drink water, or go to the fire, being cold: no! but I am at first apprised of my vicinity to a new and excellent region of life. By persisting to read or to think, this region gives further sign of itself, as it were in flashes of light, in sudden discoveries of its profound beauty and repose, as if the clouds that covered it parted at intervals, and showed the approaching traveller the inland mountains, with the tranquil eternal meadows spread at their base, whereon flocks graze, and shepherds pipe and dance. But every insight from this realm of thought is felt as initial, and promises a sequel. I do not make it; I arrive there, and behold what was there already." Ralph Waldo Emerson, "Experience," in *Emerson. Essays: First and Second Series* (New York: Vintage, 1990) pp. 254–5.

[30] Emerson, "Experience," in *Emerson. Essays: First and Second Series*, p. 255.

[31] Ibid., p. 261.

[32] Ibid., p. 262.

> I take this evanescence and lubricity of all objects, which lets them slip through our fingers then when we clutch hardest, to be the most unhandsome part of our condition.[33]

In these remarkable observations—inversions of our inherited philosophical conceptions of epistemic and practical agency, not reversions to mindless empiricism—Emerson reconceives mindedness as requiring exposure to human vulnerability—the vulnerability of a being that can be "marked," "struck," "impressed" by experience, by what it encounters in the world."[34] In *Beyond Good and Evil* 295 there is an echo of this Emersonian intuition when Nietzsche writes of "the genius of the heart who teaches the doltish and rash hand to hesitate and reach out more delicately; [....] the genius of the heart from whose touch everyone walks away richer, not having received grace and surprised, not as blessed and oppressed by alien goods, but richer in himself, newer to himself than before, broken open and sounded out by a thawing wind; more uncertain, perhaps; tenderer, more fragile, more broken, but full of hopes that as yet have no name." Orlie cites this passage from Nietzsche to point political theorists to a side of Nietzsche's thought that is much too unseen, a Nietzsche "beckoning receptivity into the still unlovely human mind."

In her contribution to the volume, "'Writing a Name in the Sky:' Rancière, Cavell, and the possibility of egalitarian inscription," Aletta Norval shows how the Cavellian, Emersonian, and indeed, Nietzschean concern with a politics of receptivity and responsiveness can and, indeed, must, complement Rancière's emphasis on a politics of disruptive staging and *dissensus*.[35] As she points out, "at stake for Rancière and Cavell... is the possibility of speaking and being heard." They differ, however, in how they think about the processes that either block or enable speaking and being heard. But both are interested in "the relationship between speech and that which exceeds speech, insofar as it involves an emphasis on seeing and staging." Whereas Rancière is inclined to focus on the rupture and interruptions to normal politics—the "police order"—Cavell "focuses overtly on questions of responsiveness," through which focus it is possible to make better sense of the tension between founding moments and processes of institutionalization, between extraordinary politics and quotidian politics.

---

[33] Ibid., p. 243.

[34] For commentary on these passages from Emerson that lays out Emerson's account of receptivity as an inversion of Kant's idea of agency, see Stanley Cavell, *This New Yet Unapproachable America* (Albuquerque: Living Batch Press, 1989) pp. 108–14, and Nikolas Kompridis, *Critique and Disclosure*, pp. 203–10.

[35] For a rich set of reflections on the possibilities of a "politics of receptivity," see the special issue on this theme with contributions by Aletta Norval, Jennifer Nedelsky, Romand Coles, and Nikolas Kompridis, in *Ethics and Global Politics*, 2011, Vol. 4, No. 4, Nikolas Kompridis, guest editor.

Norval argues that Rancière fails adequately to address "the processes through which democratic challenges find a foothold in existing orders." Rather than simply identifying this shortcoming in Rancière, which is a consequence of Rancière's lack of emphasis on responsiveness and receptivity,[36] she finds resources within Rancière's body of work that she can conjoin with Cavell's emphasis on responsiveness. Aiming to answer the question of how the "energies, freedom, and imagination that are associated with acts of founding" might be retained in the quotidian forms of everyday politics, she focuses on texts of Rancière's in which the conceptualization of the police order does not set up an insuperable dichotomy between an undifferentiated, homogeneous police order on the one hand, or as an ensemble of ruptural, disruptive democratic interventions on the other. The focus of those texts is on forms of *world disclosure*[37] that Norval argues "would do the work of disruption and distancing that Rancière has in mind, but that would also... be capable of inscribing and distancing into a way of being, an ethos, yet in a manner that would not by definition fall prey to the order of the police." By connecting Rancièrian practices of disruption and distancing to Cavellian practices of responsiveness Norval sets in motion a promising constructive dialogue between Rancière and Cavell. That it can be set in motion at all is a function of the view of politics that they hold in common, according to which the matter of what is seeable and hearable, what can appear at all, is an inescapably *political* matter. Now if there is anything with which the aesthetic turn in political thought can be most clearly and saliently identified it is this, and this above all which makes politics aesthetic in principle.

In "Blankets, screens, and projections: Or, the claim of film," Davide Panagia draws on Cavell, especially his work on the ontology of film, *The World Viewed*, to outline a "politics of appearances." Things appear or they fail to appear; and when they appear, their appearance as the something they are supposes and at the same time calls forth the "capacity for regarding things... in the sense of caring... caring enough to turn one's attention and look." This receptive, attentive regard for things is one that Cavell connects to the "human capacity for seeing or for treating something *as* something," the subject of the early Heidegger's phenomenological and the later Wittgenstein's conceptual investigations. But just what that something is to appear *as*, its very intelligibility as *something*, can be an urgent or perplexing question for us. In line with the contributions by Kompridis and Orlie, Panagia suggests that a provisional but not final

[36] I have offered a similar critique of Rancière's lack of a notion of receptivity or responsiveness in his account of politics. See Kompridis, "Receptivity, Possibility, and Democratic Politics," pp. 260–2.

[37] On the multiple aspects and critical possibilities of the idea of world disclosure, see Nikolas Kompridis, *Critique and Disclosure*.

answer to this question can be given when we let ourselves be touched by something, say, "an aspect of humanness," and thereby resist our own refusal or "non-acceptance of what other human somethings offer up to view as potentially human, as an unfinished (or perhaps even new) aspect of humanness."

Since Cavell claims that human beings projected on a screen appear as "a human something... unlike anything else we know" (WV 26) and since, as Panagia rightly points out, the issue of how we respond to "the projection of the human somethingness of an other is, for Cavell, ethically, aesthetically and ontologically the same issue," the disregard of the claim of film is in a sense a disregard of that "human somethingness projected in film." Cavell's quarrel with professional Anglo-American philosophy's long-standing disregard of the significance of film, part of its general disregard of the significance of culture, compelled him to grapple with the question, "Why film?" Cavell's answer to that question involved a justification of the claim of film "in the appearance on screen of a human something... unlike anything else we know." To the extent that professional philosophy has disregarded or has been indifferent to the claim of film, it has missed some human something "unlike anything else we know," and by missing that human something its sense of the human has gone amiss.

The same point can be made at another level of generality when it is not just the question of "Why film?" but of "Why aesthetics?" In their disregard of the significance of the aesthetic dimension of politics, political philosophy and political theory have missed some "human somethings" that appear—and can only appear—through aesthetic modes of inquiry and experience. To speak of an aesthetic turn in political thought in this context then, is to speak of how something that had not come into appearance before can come into appearance through a change not only in how we make sense of things, but also through a change in the very senses through which things make sense. To reiterate, how things appear or whether they appear at all is a profoundly political question. On this note then, the volume closes fittingly with Jacques Rancière's contribution, "The aesthetic dimension: Aesthetics, politics, knowledge," in which Rancière outlines "an aesthetic practice of philosophy" that "can also be called a method of equality." Taking Kant's account of aesthetic judgment as a starting point, Rancière discusses three ways in which making sense of something can happen, for example, in the case of a palace. The palace can be approached as an object of knowledge, it can be approached as an object of desire, and it can be approached "neither as an object of knowledge nor as an object of desire." This third way "escapes the hierarchical relationship between a high faculty [of knowledge] and a low faculty [of desire], that is, escapes in the form of a *positive* neither/nor." Such a rejection of the hierarchical relation "between the faculties that make sense involves a certain neutralization of the social hierarchy," through which is prefigured an aesthetic practice of philosophy as a method of equality.

Of course this is not the typical picture of aesthetics as a kind of politics, and part of Rancière's critical strategy is to contrast this picture with the different, widely held view offered by Bourdieu, according to which aesthetic judgments are translations of the social hierarchies they ideologically mask and simultaneously uphold. To amplify the differences between these two pictures, Rancière draws on a series of articles from a workers' newspaper published during the 1848 revolution in France. Rancière reads this diary-like series about the working days of a joiner as a "personalized paraphrase" of the *Critique of Judgment*, in particular, of Kant's account of disinterested judgment—judgment in the positive form of "neither/nor," giving social or epistemic priority neither to the faculty of knowledge nor to the faculty of desire. The joiner narrates his day laying the floor at a sumptuous home, and does so in a way that could conform to what Bourdieu describes as an aesthetic illusion. Since the joiner's free imagination is disconnected from the labor performed by his hands, it seems to create only an illusion of freedom, while at the same time reinscribing very real social hierarchies and existing relations of property and power. But Rancière proposes another reading of the joiner's experience:

> Ignoring to whom the palace actually belongs, the vanity of the nobles, and the sweat of the people incorporated in the palace are the conditions of aesthetic judgment. This ignorance is by no means the illusion that concedes the reality of possession. Rather, it is the means for building a new sensible world, which is a world of equality with the world of possession and inequality. This... dismantling of the worker's body of experience is the condition for a worker's political voice... The aesthetic judgment acts as if the palace were not an object of possession and domination... This as if is no illusion. It is a redistribution of the sensible, a redistribution of the parts supposedly played by the higher and the lower faculties, the higher and the lower classes...
>
> Everything revolves around the status of the as if... Aesthetics means that the eyes of the worker can be disconnected from his hands, that his belief can be disconnected from his condition.

Everything revolves around the status of the "as if" for Rancière, in just the same way that for Adrienne Rich everything revolves around the "*What if?* – the possible... the questions dying forces don't know how to ask."[38] What if our relation to things political, to the "object" of politics, was not based on grasping and possessing, a relation through which the political

[38] Adrienne Rich, *What is Found There*, cited by Haro and Coles in this volume.

"object" was unmade as an object of knowledge or of desire and remade as the object of a practice of equality in Rancière's sense, of freedom in Arendt's, of acknowledgment in Cavell's, of receptivity in Emerson's, and of affirmation in Nietzsche's? What would it mean, what would it require (of us), to initiate and sustain such a politics, a revivified democratic politics that does not stop asking the question of "What if?", that does not stop judging and acting "as if" things could be otherwise, and not as they are already given to sense? Does this sound too utopian, too aesthetic to our skeptical ears? Haro and Coles anticipate this response:

> Doesn't all this talk... take us so far beyond the limits and possibilities of living realities that we risk falling off the map of actual political life and action? After all, what does the "news of poetry" have to do with power, governance, negotiation, matters of life and death, and the everyday mechanical drudgery of political change? Cultivating aesthetic sensibilities in politics can easily seem like a worthless or even damaging distraction in our contemporary political culture, saturated as it is by technocratic, administrative logic... While we do acknowledge the incredible challenges inherent in an apoetic milieu such as our own, we argue that, far from useless romanticism, aesthetic energy with poetic commitment and sensibility is precisely what we urgently need to address those challenges in genuinely transformative ways. When all else has failed to create enduring change, it may be time to tap dance towards a new model of political engagement. After all, anyone familiar with the radical countercultural history of tap dancing in African-American tradition knows that it is infused black counter-public spaces in ways that animated and informed a long history of creative struggle.

This candid and hope-infused answer may intensify rather than allay the sceptic's doubts about an aesthetic politics. But then it is hard to see how there could even be a politics without its aesthetic dimension, when the only possible politics is "normal politics," the politics of "dead power" or of death-dealing power. Can we imagine a *democratic* politics in which the possibility of seeing and hearing differently, of seeing and hearing what could not be seen or heard before, was no longer a political possibility? Can we imagine a politics in which the question of what can appear and what cannot appear in the space of everyday appearances is not a *political* question? Can we imagine a politics in which, "You are different, what you recognize as problems are different, your world is different," is merely useless romanticism?[39] Of course, any empirical test of these questions

[39]For a very different view of romanticism and its contemporary possibilities, see Nikolas Kompridis, "Romanticism," in *The Oxford Handbook of Philosophy and Literature*, edited by Richard Eldridge (Oxford: Oxford University Press, 2008) pp. 247–70.

would have to presuppose what is to be tested; namely, that the aesthetic is a condition of the possibility of politics as such. But whatever form it takes, a politics of the "as if" and the "what if?" is sustainable only to the extent that the aesthetic in all of its multi-dimensionality is given expressive political form. As Lewis R. Gordon points out in connection with another African-American art form, revolutionaries, too, "must sing the blues... because their goal is the understanding and transformation of life."

PART ONE

Aesthetic politics, judgment, and worldly things

CHAPTER ONE

"Delightful Horror": Edmund Burke and the aesthetics of democratic revolution

Jason Frank
Cornell University

Acknowledgments: This essay has benefitted from the questions of political theory workshop audiences at Trinity College (Hartford, Connecticut), Northwestern University, University of Pennsylvania, New School for Social Research, and the University of California, Los Angeles. I would like to thank Lida Maxwell, Bonnie Honig, André Munro, Ella Myers, Anne Norton, Banu Bargu and Rebekah Sterling for their insightful comments on earlier drafts. Kyong-Min Son provided valuable research and editing assistance, and I owe an enormous debt to my colleague Isaac Kramnick for many conversations on these and related topics.

Abstract: This essay examines Burke's aesthetics in order to grasp a central but slippery category of his political thought: his concept of authority. Burke's theory of the sublime identifies an instinctive "delight" that human beings take in their own subordination. It is an affective device for naturalizing order and rank in human society and the psychological foundation of such distinctive Burkean formulations as "proud submission," "dignified obedience," and "ennobled freedom." The French Revolution however, and its enthusiastic reception by British radicals, occasioned a dramatic revision of Burke's political aesthetics, whereby the sublime was no longer associated with astonishment, novelty and ennobling disorientation but with the gravity of an historical inheritance transmitted across time by the ancient constitution. Burke's anti-revolutionary writings mark a transition in his thinking from a political aesthetics of sublime transcendence to one of immanence. Burke's critical account of the aesthetics of democratic revolution provides useful orientation for contemporary theorists engaging the aesthetic dimensions of democratic authority.

> *Out of the tomb of murdered monarchy in France has arisen a vast tremendous unformed specter, in a far more terrific guise than any which ever yet has overpowered the imagination and subdued the fortitude of man.*
>
> —EDMUND BURKE, *LETTERS ON A REGICIDE PEACE*

Edmund Burke lives in the popular imagination as the prophet of modern political conservatism. He stands for conservatism in the same way that John Locke stands for liberalism, or Karl Marx for communism: a foundational thinker who established the basic parameters of discourse defining a political ideology (Kramnick 1977). For much of the history of Burke scholarship however, this was not how he was received. He has been celebrated as a utilitarian reformer, a romantic critic of the Enlightenment, a Christian philosopher of Natural Law and, most recently, as a sophisticated critic of British imperialism and a theorist of cultural difference (Morley 1993; Stanlis 1958; Mehta 1999). All of these frameworks illuminate distinct patterns of thinking in the rich tapestry of Burke's writing, but do not give the reader a confident sense of interpretive finality. There is something in Burke that prevents us from fitting him into one of the ready-made paradigms that often frame scholarship in the history of political thought.

One central element of Burke's political thinking that previous approaches have often neglected is his aesthetics. Burke's readers have often recognized what one scholar, Neal Wood, calls the "aesthetic strain in Burke's responses to political events and theories," and there is a growing awareness that Burke's aesthetics might offer a robust theoretical framework for tracing continuities across the diversity of his more explicitly political works (Furniss 1993; Wood 1964; White 1994; Hindson 1988; Eagleton 1989; O'Neill 2011; Gibbons 2003). While C. B. Macpherson once easily dismissed Burke's aesthetics as "of little theoretical interest," some Burke scholars argue that his aesthetics provide "a unifying element of Burke's social and political outlook," giving "a degree of coherence and system to the welter of words which he bequeathed to mankind" (Macpherson 1980, 19; Wood 1964, 42).

The turn to Burke's political aesthetics has history on its side, because it was the aesthetic dimensions of Burke's political thinking that some of his most insightful and influential contemporaries—both admirers and critics—emphasized in their encounters with his work, particularly his anti-revolutionary writings. Two of Burke's radical critics, Mary Wollstonecraft and Thomas Paine, wrote books condemning Burke's aestheticization of political life and defending the French Revolution. Those books have become canonical works of political theory in their own right. Like such readers, I see aesthetics as central to Burke's political thinking, but this essay departs from their accounts to explore how Burke's aesthetic theory illuminates a central but notoriously slippery category in his political thought: his concept of authority. The internal relationship that I will identify between Burke's aesthetics and his account of authority is first presented in his *Philosophical Enquiry into the Sublime and the Beautiful* (1756) (the *Enquiry*), but can also be traced across many of Burke's subsequent political works, including his parliamentary speeches from the 1770s urging conciliation with the colonies in America, and his later rousing condemnations of imperial corruption in India. The relationship between Burke's aesthetics and his account of authority is most fully articulated however in his famous attacks on the French Revolution, not only in his *Reflections on the Revolution in France* (1790) (the *Reflections*), but also in such important texts as his *Appeal from the New to the Old Whigs* (1790) (the *Appeal*), *Letter to a Noble Lord* (1796), and *Letters on a Regicide Peace* (1795–6), the last work Burke published before his death in 1797.

The essay proceeds in two parts. In the first part I outline Burke's aesthetics as presented in the *Enquiry*, emphasizing the centrality of the sublime to his account, and showing how Burke's innovative conceptualization of the sublime enabled him to identify a natural and instinctive "delight" human beings take in their subordination, inscribing this passion into the very structure of human experience and subjectivity.[1] Burke's early theory of the sublime is an affective device for the naturalization of order and rank in human society. This account of the sublime is essential for an understanding of how Burke conceptualizes the complementary rather than antagonistic relationship between individual freedom and authority that he places at the very center of his political thinking. It is the psychological foundation of Burke's understanding of such important concepts as "proud submission," "dignified obedience" and "ennobled freedom." A more textured and broadly experiential account of authority emerges from these

[1]Dan O'Neill insightfully writes "Burke's subject matter in the *Enquiry* is precisely individual subject formation understood as an effect of power." O'Neill 2011, p. 2.

reflections than the juridical emphasis that political theorists usually place on the role of prescription in Burke's work.

In the second part I turn to Burke's writing on the astonishing spectacle of the French Revolution. In his anti-revolutionary writings Burke identified a worrisome aesthetic pleasure animating and uniting the various classes of revolutionaries and their radical admirers across the Channel. In this emerging ethos "the mere pleasure of the beginner" became "the sole guide" of political action, with devastating consequences for authority and the "orderly and social freedom" Burke affirms (*A* 184, 71). Burke's concern with the radical democratic sublime enacted by the Revolution bears a discomforting similarity to central elements of his own earlier aesthetics, which were themselves revolutionary in the central emphasis Burke placed on the overriding aesthetic value of the unexpected and unrecognizable. The pressure of political events surrounding the French Revolution occasions a shift in Burke's aesthetics, whereby the sublime is no longer primarily associated with the characteristics of astonishment, novelty, and productive or ennobling disorientation, but with the gravity of an immanent historical inheritance transmitted across time by the ancient constitution. Burke's *Reflections* marks a development in his thinking from an aesthetics of sublime transcendence to one of immanence, although one that contrasts with the dangerously willful immanence exemplified for Burke by the Age of Democratic Revolutions.

Aesthetics and authority

In the opening pages of the *Enquiry* Burke announces he will provide nothing less than "an exact theory of our passions, [and] a knowledge of their general sources" (1998, 51). Signaling his engagement with the broad eighteenth-century understanding of aesthetics as a discourse on experience, sensation and judgment, Burke writes that the *Enquiry* will examine how the properties of objects in the world: their color, size, smell, sound etc., work through uniform laws of nature to affect the body, and through the body to incite particular passions in the subjects that experience them. Burke thus offers an inductive and empirical survey of the scale of human passions along with detailed discussions of the specific properties of the objects that produce them. He attempts to establish a solid foundation for the legislation of taste by appealing beyond the relatively weak capacities of human understanding and reason to the reliable uniformity of visceral responses to the surrounding world. All objects are, in this sense, aesthetic for Burke, which leads Terry Eagleton to describe the *Enquiry* as a "subtle phenomenology of the senses" (Eagleton 1989, 54).

For political theorists, two things may stand out immediately in this summary description of Burke's *Enquiry*. The first is his attempt to establish universal but highly particular criteria for aesthetic judgments, universal because shared across cultures and classes, particular because grounded in the evaluation of individual sensory experience. The second is Burke's radical diminishment of reason's role in producing these judgments. As he makes clear in the introductory chapter, "On Taste" (added to the second edition of the *Enquiry* in response to David Hume's essay of the same title), Burke seeks to avoid the pitfalls of subjectivism—placing beauty merely in the eye of the beholder and relegating aesthetics to the realm of unreliable whims and fancies—by anchoring aesthetic evaluation in a uniform and corporeal response to physical sensation. Agreements in sensation are surely stronger than tenuous agreements in ideas or opinions, and Burke grounds the authority of these judgments in the natural responses of the human body to its environment. Like many subsequent conservative political thinkers, Burke urges his readers to go with their gut reactions and trust their God-given senses and "untaught feelings." Burke seeks to establish the natural grounds of a passionate social consensus. If aesthetic judgments were unstable, then so too would be the social sympathies founded upon them, and with them the whole fabric of social and political life. What David Bromwich calls the "physiologism" of Burke's aesthetics is rooted not in custom or tradition but in the shared sensory apparatus of human beings (Bromwich 1989; see also Ryan 2001). "We do and we must suppose," Burke writes, that "since the physical organs have the same conformation the same sensation must be common to all men" (1998, 65).

In basing aesthetic evaluation in physical response Burke frees aesthetics from the uncertain dictates of human reason. Burke's diminishment of rational faculties is frequently reiterated in his later political writings, but the *Enquiry* gives this theme powerful theoretical articulation. "The cause of feelings arises from the mechanical structure of our bodies," Burke writes, "from the natural frame and constitution of our minds," not from the uncertain dictates of our "reasoning faculty" (1998, 91). Burke has sometimes been described as a "philosopher of unreason in the age of reason," as the "gravedigger of the Enlightenment," but these familiar descriptions rest on a caricatured, highly rationalist view of the Enlightenment itself, one Burke's own later writing did much to promote (Cobban 1960). The diminishment of reason's role in making aesthetic and moral judgments was actually extremely widespread in eighteenth-century Anglophone thought, especially in the moral sentimentalism of the Scottish thinkers who so deeply influenced Burke; Francis Hutchinson, David Hume and Adam Smith. Instinctive passionate response was for Burke a more reliable guide to judgment in aesthetics as well as politics.

Burke believed the visceral responses to the surrounding world were at once natural and infused with divine purpose. In trusting our uncorrupted senses we follow a providentially ordained authority and align ourselves with the harmonious order of the universe where everything—and everyone—is assigned its proper place. "Whenever the wisdom of our Creator intended that we should be affected with any thing, he did not confide the execution of his design to the languid and precarious operation of our reason," Burke writes, "but he endowed it with powers and properties that...captivate the soul before the understanding is ready either to join with them or to oppose them" (1998,142). These affectations were animated by and sustained the divine order of the world. While very much a man of the Enlightenment, Burke was also committed to a theistic "great chain of being" that was such an essential part of an older Elizabethan worldview: a "great primeval contract of eternal society...which holds all physical and all moral natures, each in their appointed place" (1987, 85). As Don Herzog writes, for Burke this meant that "politics extends far past King, parliament, and the like. Instead, relations of rule and authority pervade all the orderly regularities of the universe" (Herzog 1991, 340). Burke relied on this hierarchical metaphysics to ground his critique of emerging conceptions of moral autonomy, in which the *Enquiry* played an important role (see Schneewind 1998). Moral subjectivity required that human beings be "brought into subjection," Burke writes, "and this can only be done by a power outside of themselves." Instinctive aesthetic response "seizing upon the senses and imagination" before the "understanding" or "even the will" could assess and evaluate, was the Creator's way of captivating the human heart—Burke also uses the term "enchain"—in the "execution of his design."

Burke's distinctive theory of the beautiful and the sublime, categories which he argued had been hopelessly confused in most previous accounts, is based on these visceral responses to the physical world, and interwoven into this hierarchical metaphysics, beginning with a hedonistic calculus of pleasures and pains. Burke associates pleasures with the urge of procreation and the desire to enjoy the society of others, grouping sympathy and various forms of love with these (relatively weak) longings, and in turn associating them with beauty. The sublime is linked to pain—by far the more powerful motivator for Burke—and thus with self-preservation, solitude and fear. "I call beauty a social quality," Burke writes, in that it inspires "sentiments of tenderness and affection" which lead us "to draw willingly into a kind of relation with the objects that incite this passion" (1998, 89). Beauty is for Burke "that quality...in bodies, by which they cause love, or some passion similar." Burke envisions beauty as a crucial component of sociality, immanent to human history and sustaining the social relations that make up that history over time; it draws on the allure of peaceful coexistence and the pleasant, if notably unheroic, recreation of civilizing social norms. The "beautiful" works by way of sympathy and imitation, where "men yield to each other, ... which is extremely flattering to all" (1998, 95). Beauty prompts "mutual compliance" rather than authority. It is always haunted however, by the enervating possibility of a "languid inactive state" of an overly "relaxed state of the body" (1998, 164). Beauty by itself bears an indexical relation in Burke's work to decadence, cultural exhaustion and the etiolation of social and political life.

Although the title of Burke's *Enquiry* promises an examination of the sublime and the beautiful, his real focus is on the sublime, a preoccupation Burke shared with many British contemporaries in the wake of the 1739 English translation and publication of Longinus's *On the Sublime*, a classical Greek investigation into the "transportive" power of language, its ability to "take us out of ourselves" (Longinus [1957] 1991). The eighteenth-century discourse on the sublime, as Andrew Ashfield and Peter De Bolla write, typically "celebrated the energetic, the obscure, the disruptive, the unlimited, the powerful and the terrible as a new set of positive aesthetic terms" (Ashfield and de Bolla 1996). While for Burke "terror is the ruling principle of the sublime," he emphasized that the sublime was not simply *equivalent* to terror. If something terrifying immediately threatens us we take away no aesthetic assessment from it at all; terror simply overwhelms our capacity for judgment. Such objects and instances, Burke writes, "are incapable of giving any delight whatsoever, and are simply terrible." However, "at certain distances, and with certain modifications, they may be, and they are delightful" (1998, 86). The key phrase for understanding Burke's theory of the sublime is, therefore, "delightful horror," which Burke describes as "the most genuine effect and truest test of the sublime" (1998, 24). It is an evocative phrase, but one with a technical meaning in Burke's aesthetics. He conceptually distinguishes "delight" from "pleasure," arguing that delight "expresses the sensation which accompanies the *removal* of pain or danger" (1998, 84; my emphasis). Delight, unlike pleasure, is a passion of "solid, strong, and severe nature." Whereas pleasure is indolent and voluptuous, delight enlivens in the subject a sense of fortitude and "exertion." It is not merely relief. That we take delight in terror—that we are naturally fit to experience the sublime—is evidence for Burke that we live in an enchanted world commanded by an awful power that will remain forever incomprehensible to us. The sublime is intrinsically connected to epistemic blindness, the obscure and the mysterious, that which exceeds human enquiry and legibility. There is a critical engagement with deism in the *Enquiry* where Burke explicitly associates the sublime with an idea of powerful divinity defined by its inaccessibility to human reason. When we draw our attention to this "almighty power," Burke writes, "we shrink into the minuteness of our own nature, and are, in a manner annihilated before him...If we rejoice, we rejoice with trembling" (1998, 111). This "salutary fear" is, Burke writes, the essence of all "true religion," and is also the hallmark of the Burkean sublime (*E* 112). Job's terrible confrontation with the whirlwind is a paradigmatic literary instance of Burke's sublime, as is Milton's Satan and his dreadful fall from grace.

The passion that Burke identifies with the sublime is first and foremost "astonishment," by which he means a shocking or disruptive incapacitation of reason. Its secondary effects are "admiration, reverence, and respect" (1998, 101). This ordering: astonishment then reverence, is important and I will return to it in my discussion of Burke's aesthetic response to the French Revolution. The longest chapter of the *Enquiry* is on "Power," which Burke describes as a "capital source of the sublime" (1998, 107) because of its identification with whatever escapes human use and mastery and exceeds the calculations of instrumental reason. Stephen White has recently enlisted Burke in a "mortal humanist" project that contrasts with the willful or capacious humanism of political liberalism.[2] Burke's emphasis in the *Enquiry* however, is on the experience of terror in the face of some greater power in which we nonetheless take delight, not simply a positive evaluation of the basic experience of human limitation. If Kant's later theory of the sublime enabled individuals to intuit their own capacity to reason, and thereby affectively enhanced the individual's sense of efficacy, capaciousness and power, Burke's sublime explains our natural and deeply affective attachments to our own subordination (Kant 2000). Burke's sublime lodges a politics of hierarchy in the very center of human subjectivity. His sublime is at the experiential heart of his far-reaching account of the ordering and vitalizing role of authority in human life. It grounds his theory of authority in natural dispositions and affective orientations.

Both the beautiful and the sublime deal with issues of authority insofar as they achieve what Burke calls the "compliance" of the affected subject. In the realm of beauty however, subjects are flattered or tenderly enchanted into compliance by an object that is ultimately under their control. The beautiful object, Burke writes, produces in us a "melting" acquiescence whereby we risk losing ourselves in the pleasant sympathies of domestic communion. Some contemporary Burke scholars have associated the social acquiescence of beauty with the habitual authority of custom (Ferguson 1985). Mary Wollstonecraft uses this element of Burke's aesthetics as the basis of her critique of his "feminine" submission to the authority of tradition in his *Reflections* (Wollstonecraft 1995). Even in the case of the beautiful however, Burke emphasizes that aesthetic response is keyed primarily to human curiosity and the value of the unexpected and the new. The opening chapter of the *Enquiry* is titled "Novelty" and Burke writes that "some degree of novelty must be one of the materials of every instrument which works upon the mind; and curiosity blends itself more or less with all our passions" (1998, 80). In the *Enquiry,* "habit and custom are constantly presented as eroding the liveliness of the sensations we had in the morning of our days...when the whole man was awake in every part,

[2]In addition to White 1994 see White 2009. I take the useful phrase "mortal humanism" from Honig 2010.

and the gloss of novelty fresh upon all the objects that surrounded us" (Eagleton 1989).

Burke's sublime takes this general evaluation of novelty to its apotheosis. The sublime is that which jolts us out of "mediocrity and indifference" (1998, 138). The sublime disrupts the habitual, defies coherence and marks an abrupt transition in experience. Doing so, the sublime object stimulates the imagination to envision a terrain beyond the empirically existent. It "entertains the imagination with the promise of something more" (1998, 118). The sublime of the *Enquiry* is a transcendent ordering authority without which the pleasurable sympathies and "mutual compliance" of social life would degenerate into an entropic state of vapid imitation and repetition. A world that is merely beautiful is, for Burke, a dangerously disenchanted world subject to human plan, use, and the calculations of instrumental reason. Burke's sublime therefore prefigures familiar critiques of the instrumental rationality of the Enlightenment like those forwarded later by members of the Frankfurt School (Horkheimer 1974). Burke does not argue for the social utility of the sublime, its function to endow the state with an aura of majesty crucial for securing the submission of its subjects. His point is precisely not to reduce the sublime to social utility, which would undermine its commanding authority. Burke writes that "whenever strength is only useful, and employed for our benefit or our pleasure, then it is never sublime, for nothing can act agreeably to us that does not act in conformity to our will; but to act agreeably to our will, it must be subject to us; and can therefore never be the cause of a grand and commanding conception" (1998, 109). We must never confuse the domesticated horse with the one "*whose neck is cloathed with thunder, and … who swalloweth the ground with fierceness and rage*" (1998, 108). Burke's sublime authority is defined by dangerous excess, a terrible surplus that escapes human control.

This aspect of Burke's sublime has been missed by most political theorists who have written on Burke's understanding of authority and who typically focus on the role of prescription in his work, meaning a "natural and dutiful reverence to any institution that has existed through the ages and persists to the present day" (Kramnick 1977). David Hume famously articulated prescriptive authority when he wrote: "Time and custom give authority to all forms of government, and all successions of princes; and that power which at first was founded only on injustice and violence, becomes in time legal and obligatory" (Hume 1973). Burke echoes this view in a 1782 speech to the House of Commons: "Our constitution is a prescriptive constitution; it is a constitution whose sole authority is that it has existed time out of mind" (*W* 7, 94). Burke embeds this idea of prescriptive authority in a normative account of historical development: because constitutional orders (prior to the French Revolution) emerged slowly, as the result of countless small, prudential judgments, they embodied an acquired wisdom superior to any rational plan conceived by the design of one, or even the design of a single generation.

Readers who approach Burke's account of authority primarily through the lens of prescription focus on the legal authority of the state, and neglect the extent to which authority in one sphere of life resonates and interacts with its operation in myriad others. Paine insightfully recognized this dimension of Burke's account of authority in his *Rights of Man*, when he wrote that Burke envisioned society as "a wilderness of turnpike gates" (Paine 1989b, 86). While the focus on prescription allows scholars to efficiently contrast Burke's theory of authority to other dominant eighteenth-century approaches, especially those associated with the social contract tradition, on the one hand, and utilitarianism on the other, it obscures Burke's vision of authority as a complex tapestry of social relations, sustained by aesthetic response. The political community, as Burke writes, is not based in "tumultuary and giddy choice; it is a deliberation of the ages and of generations; it is a constitution made by what is ten thousand times better than choice, it is made by the peculiar circumstances, occasions, tempers, dispositions, and moral, civil, and social habitudes of the people" (*W* 7, 95). For Burke, authority is not only dispersed vertically across generations, but also horizontally across the richly textured practices of social interaction. Authority is not abstractly lodged in the state's formal legal institutions, but interwoven in the subjective experiences of daily life that produce and sustain those institutions.

Burke's emphasis on the complex social assemblage of hierarchical relations is essential not only to his account of authority, but also to his related account of freedom. Burke refused to isolate freedom or liberty as conceptual abstractions "stripped of every relation." Instead he circumstantially embedded freedom in lived experience. "Social and civil freedom like all other things in common life, are variously mixed and modified... and shaped into an infinite diversity of forms, according to the temper and circumstances of every community" (1998, 429). This meant embedding freedom within the dense and "infinitely complex" network of authoritative relations that pattern and define social life. In his *Appeal from the New to the Old Whigs* Burke claimed that he consistently proclaimed and acted upon a single principle in his many years in public life, which he described as a commitment to an "orderly and social freedom" (*A* 71). This core idea is given different articulations across his work in such evocative and seemingly paradoxical phrases as "proud submission," "dignified obedience," "spirit of exalted freedom" in the face of "servitude" and even "free bondage." In his English history Burke calls it "voluntary inequality and dependence" (*W* 7, 295). All of these formulations share the idea of freedom that is not only constrained by authority or rank, but also enhanced, even enobled by that constraint. Burke never provided a systematic theoretical articulation of this principle—it is not a question of "abstract speculation"—but he most closely approaches such an articulation in his idea of the sublime, which allowed him to identify an instinctive and ennobling delight that human beings—freely—take in their own subordination. "We fear God," Burke writes, "we look up with awe at kings, and with respect at nobility. Why? Because when such ideas are brought before our minds, it is *natural* to be so affected; because all other feelings are false and spurious, and tend to corrupt our minds... and to render us unfit for rational liberty" (1987, 76). The structure of sublime experience corresponds to and anchors this ennobling subordination that Burke affirmed in relations throughout social and political life.

Burke offers a host of concrete examples of this idea's operation. Examples—"the school of mankind"—are Burke's primary mode of theorizing politics (*SL* 260). In the *Reflections*, famously, Burke contrasts the ennobled freedom practiced under the inherited authority of the ancient constitution with the shameless libertinage he associates with "French Liberty." Because the British have always viewed their liberties from an outside and higher perspective—"in the light of an inheritance"—the spirit of freedom is enhanced and vivified rather than diminished.

> Always acting as if in the presence of canonized forefathers, the spirit of freedom, leading in itself to misrule and excess, is tempered with an awful gravity... By this means our liberty becomes a noble freedom. It carries an imposing and majestic aspect. It has a pedigree and illustrious ancestors. It has its bearings and its ensigns armorial. It has its gallery of portraits, its monumental inscriptions, its records, evidences, and titles... All your sophisters cannot produce anything better adapted to preserve a rational and manly freedom than the course we have pursued. (*R* 30)

This aestheticized passage echoes those in the *Enquiry* dealing with the sublime where "without danger we are conversant with terrible objects" that, although more powerful, nonetheless produce a "sort of *swelling* and triumph that is extremely grateful to the human mind" (1998, 96). Burke effectively ennobles freedom by embedding it within the temporizing spectacle of sublime inheritance. This is not only about the authority of the past but the authority of the aesthetic markers through which the past lives in experience, and which lend it its "majestic and imposing aspect." The superior power of the sublime raises the quality of the freedom, endowing it with "a habitual native dignity." The experience of the sublime productively sustains without resolving the animating tension in Burke's work between freedom and authority, doing so by lodging it in the dispositional orientation of subjectivity itself. The sublime is the key to understanding Burke's emphasis on hierarchy that does not diminish but enlivens and enriches the freedom of the individual. It is an essential part of his challenge to the natural egalitarianism of the age, although the theory of the sublime was itself challenged by what he called the "most astonishing spectacle" of that age: the Revolution that aimed to enact its defining equality.

The revolutionary spectacle

The French Revolution "provoked the biggest public debate on political principles in Britain since the Civil War" of the 1640s (Hampshire-Monk 2005). During the 1790s the Revolution Controversy engaged with the most fundamental questions of politics: what is the basis of political legitimacy? What are the basic rights and duties of citizenship? What is the proper end of government and the appropriate sphere of governmental authority? Who is qualified to speak and act politically? At stake were the very meaning and extent of political modernity, and more than any other single text it was Burke's *Reflections on the Revolution in France* that ignited the public debate in Britain. No work more definitively framed the controversy's central preoccupations; over seventy books and pamphlets were written in response to Burke's attack on the National Assembly and its radical British admirers. Alongside this cluster of important issues raised by Burke's text however, was another that has received less attention from political theorists. As John Barrell writes, aesthetic categories like the imagination "occur with surprising frequency in the political writing and oratory of the late eighteenth century," becoming "objects of political conflict every bit as intense as those being fought over such large political words as sovereignty, liberty, or the constitution" (Barrell 2000, 4). Among the central questions Burke asked was whether there was an appropriate place for political aesthetics in the Age of Democratic Revolutions.

Readers today are often surprised by how little space Burke devotes to the underlying causes of the Revolution in his text and, conversely, how much he devotes to dissecting details of the revolutionary spectacle and analysing the feelings this spectacle incited—or failed to incite—in its public. In the *Reflections*, as Linda M. G. Zerilli writes, "persuasion is primarily a matter of inducing the reader to share the author's feelings" (Zerilli 1994, 75). This is most obviously true with Burke's infamously theatrical description of Marie Antoinette's violation by the unruly mob at Versailles, a scene which drew "natural" tears of outrage from Burke, and raillery and ridicule from his critics. For Burke, the Queen's "high rank," "great splendor of descent," "personal elegance" and "outward accomplishments" were important criteria in condemning the "atrocious spectacle" that unfolded on 6 October 1789. Burke's critics rejected his assertion of his "melancholy" as "pure foppery" or worse. He "pities the plumage," Paine would memorably write, "but forgets the dying bird" (Paine 1989b). However infamous this single episode, Burke elaborates on theatrical spectacle and aesthetic response throughout his anti-revolutionary writings. Burke's public in these texts is usually construed as a theatrical audience (Melvin 1975), and they clearly exemplify Burke's "dramatic theory of politics" (Hindson 1988).

That aesthetic considerations would frame Burke's assessment of the Revolution was indicated in his first written response to the events of 1789. In a letter to Lord Charlemond on 9 August Burke wrote, "our thoughts of everything at home are suspended, by our astonishment at the wonderful spectacle which is exhibited in a Neighboring and rival Country—what spectators, and what actors! England gazing with astonishment at a French struggle for liberty and not knowing whether to blame or applaud!" (*SL*) While Burke quickly overcame his initial ambivalence, his astonishment never waned. Burke compares the Revolution to an "insolent bloody theater," to be judged as one would judge a drama or as, Burke believed, a grotesque "tragic-comic scene." This initial response of thought-suspending astonishment and wonder, so resonant with his earlier account of the sublime, transforms across his anti-revolutionary writings, in a shift prefigured in his earlier work. Where in the *Enquiry* the sublime was an experience of ineffable transcendence that prevented social life from degenerating into narrow instrumental rationality, in the anti-revolutionary writings it becomes an experience of embedded historicity best exemplified by the *Reflections*' invocation of freedom ennobled by the inheritance of the ancient constitution. If Burke's earlier account of the sublime prioritized rapturous astonishment, the anti-revolutionary writings emphasize what had been the secondary characteristics of veneration and reverence. The sublime remains essential to Burke's account of authority, but the transcendent sublime is displaced by the immanent sublime of historicity and tradition.[3] Some of Burke's critics, most notably Mary Wollstonecraft, recognized this shift in his thinking, and criticized him for it, invoking, in effect, the earlier Burke's aesthetics to criticize the later Burke's political analysis (see Blakemore 1997). This shift in Burke's aesthetics was occasioned by the wholly new and unexpected political situation that he faced after 1789.

Burke wrote the *Reflections* most immediately in response to Richard Price's *Discourse on the Love of Our Country*. Price was an influential dissenting minister, active in the political reform movements of the time, and his sermon set out to "explain the duty we owe our country, and the nature, foundations, and proper expression of that love to it which we ought to cultivate" (Price 1991, 177). He recognized that love of country emerged partly from shared historical memory. Price delivered his address before London's Revolution Society on the hundred and first anniversary of the Glorious Revolution of 1688. Price's sermon, however, ultimately

---

[3]This may be another way of approaching the tension in Burke's work between appeals to transcendent "Nature" and historicist "Artifice." (See Strauss 1953, pp. 294–323)

pronounces illegitimate all forms of political obligation that emerge merely from customs or what he called "wretched, partial affections [which] blind the understanding" (Price 1991). For Price, allegiance to the constitutional settlement of 1688, in particular its mutually implicated ideals of truth, virtue and liberty, exemplified rational attachment to enlightened principle rather than irrational prejudices arising from commitment to land and soil or particular national traditions. Price's address envisioned an enlightened patriotism that set out "to correct and purify" the love of country and make it a "just and rational principle of action" (Price 1991). In the vocabulary of contemporary democratic theory, Price lays out an early case for "constitutional patriotism," where political attachments are engendered by reasonable commitments to the universalistic norms, principles and values enshrined, however imperfectly, in constitutional law rather than to affective attachments to a particular cultural identity (see Müller 2007).

Burke dedicates large sections of the *Reflections* to contesting Price's radical Lockean interpretation of the constitutional settlement of 1688 (Pocock 1987, xi), arguing that 1688 was an extension of the principles animating the ancient constitution, not a mark of its abrupt popular rupture. Burke's critique of Price however, also engaged with the more fundamental question of how human attachments and political communities are engendered. Before you enter an argument about whether the authority of the government is ultimately based in the willing consent of the people, and whether this authority has been enshrined in legal precedent, you had better have a response to the logically prior question of who constitutes that people in the first place and what defines the attachments that bind them (Frank 2010). Price and other radicals largely assumed the coherence of a pre-political collective identity called "the people." Burke did not.

Burke's clearest elaboration of the dilemmas involved with identifying with precision the legal authorizing fiction of the people comes in the *Appeal*, where he writes in answer to his radical critics that "in a state of rude nature there is no such thing as a people. A number of men in themselves have no collective capacity. The idea of a people is the idea of a corporation. It is wholly artificial, and made like all other legal fictions by common agreement" (*A* 169). Burke does not envision this "common agreement" as an original moment of majoritarian consent. He rightly points out that the authority of majority rule is itself premised on a primary unanimity around that decision procedure itself, which only reopens the dilemma around the identity of the very collective which must unanimously consent (Honig 2007). Rather than ending in a moment of paradox however, Burke posits a conception of peoplehood that places it not as the basis of authority, but as an *effect* of authority. The people is created through "long habits of obedience," Burke writes, "by a sort of discipline" (*A* 171). They are given shape through molecular authoritative relations that are themselves importantly aesthetic.

Burke was not persuaded by the efforts of Price and other radicals to filter political attachments through the clarifying medium of reason. The radicals, Burke wrote, sought to "divest men of all love for their country," not to set it on firmer principles. For Burke, the radicals' attempt to base political authority on individual reasoned consent only prepared "the minds of the people for treason and rebellion," replaced duties with doubts and "poisoned the minds of the lower orders" (Herzog 1998). However, behind Burke's anti-democratic rhetoric here is an account of the aesthetic dimensions of political belonging that is not as easily dismissed as many of his radical critics seemed to believe. Burke's insights here are related to his familiar emphasis on the centrality of tradition, prejudice and custom, and on the failure of rationally organized systems and plans to engender such attachments. "Men are not tied to one another by paper and seals," Burke writes, "they are led to associate by resemblances, by conformities, by sympathies" (*L* 317). Taken alone however, the familiar portrait of Burke the conservative traditionalist is incomplete, as it neglects the importance of aesthetic mechanisms in securing and sustaining these vital resemblances, conformities and sympathies. It neglects, for example, how important the unifying imagination is for Burke in engendering this sense of collective attachment and authority.

Consider how Burke envisions the relationship between public life and familial attachment and domestic authority. We are invested and affected by our country "from old prejudices" and "unreasoned habits," Burke writes, and these first take root in the "little platoon" of the family (*R* 173). Local habitual connections, especially the warm attachments of domestic life, provide what Burke calls "a sort of elemental training" for larger public affections and love of country. "We have given to the frame of polity the image of a relation in blood, binding up the constitution of our country with our dearest domestic ties; adopting our fundamental laws into the bosom of our family affections..., keeping inseparable and cherishing with the warmth of all their combined and mutually reflected charities our state, our hearths, our sepulchers, and our altars" (*R* 30). It is the beneficial "image" of a "relation in blood" that has been given to the "frame of polity" and that sutures the experience of political belonging and domestic attachment, unifying in perception what might otherwise be experienced as the isolated spheres of state, hearth, sepulcher and altar. It is a unifying *image* that establishes inseparable connections among these domains and engenders warm attachments to their "mutually reflected charities." This is not an isolated instance of Burke's emphasis on the formative power of the appealing image in public life. When Burke invokes the "little platoon" of the family for example, he writes that such local "inns and resting places" are "so many little images of the great country in which the heart found something which it could fill" (*R* 173). Burke's appeal to the politically productive and unifying image must be read in light of his account of aesthetic response and its importance for securing sympathy (in the case of beauty), and reverential awe and subordination to governing authority (in the case of the sublime). For Burke, peoplehood is sustained through the senses; "the people" is first and foremost a community of sense. He insists not only upon the familiar authority of a given tradition but on its less noted or theorized sensory manifestations in "ensigns armorial," "its gallery of portraits, its monumental inscriptions," to cohere the community, and provide markers for its sensuous attachments.

Burke also frames an aesthetic response to Price's de-aestheticized account of political attachment in his affirmations of the importance of "pleasing illusions" and elegant manners, and the vital role they play in making "power gentle" and "obedience liberal," submitting sovereign power to "the soft collar of social esteem," and capable of harmonizing "the different shades of life." In the resounding summary passages after Burke's dramatic account of the queen's violation, he worries that stripping power of all "pleasing illusions" and "decent drapery" would denude civil life of the enchantments that ennoble and sustain it, "raising our civic selves to dignity in our own estimation," and reducing politics to brutal materialism, substituting reverential authority with brute force. Just as the image of collectivity coheres a people through attracting their collective gaze, so do the sensuous markers of authority work to at once subordinate the people while placing limits on the powerful. They are what Burke calls "legitimate presumptions." Without them, "laws are to be supported only by their own terrors." "At the end of every vista," the revolutionaries and their admirers, "see nothing but the gallows" (*R* 68).

Because Burke identifies the Revolution with a brutal disenchantment of authority, a politics stripped of adornment and reduced to cold utility and instrumental reason, his text provokes important questions about the role of political aesthetics in the Age of Democratic Revolutions. The rule of law requires "pleasing illusions," Burke suggests, because these sensuous markers sustain the authority of law itself. "These public affections, combined with manners, are required as supplements, sometimes as correctives, always as aids to law. The precept given by a wise man, as well as a great critic, for the construction of poems is equally true to states: *Non satis est pulchra esse poemata, dulcio sunto*. There ought to be a system of manners in every nation which a well-informed mind would be disposed to relish... To make us love our country, our country ought to be lovely" (*R* 68). It is precisely such loveliness that Burke believed Price had neglected in his attempt to detach public authority from the dense web of social relations in which it is embedded. Burke's "body politick" was a civic expression of that providential chain of authorities linking man to man, citizens to government, government to church and church to God. The great chain of being animates Burke's anti-revolutionary writing like a unifying metaphor that coheres his disparate examples and proliferating images, giving a rhetorical and perhaps poetic force to the whole (Walzer 1967). He relies on the "philosophical analogy" between divine, natural, constitutional and familial orders of being. "The awful author of our being," Burke writes, "is the author of our place in existence," and our duties, he argues, are strictly correlated to our proper place within this order.

If the *Enquiry* portrays aesthetic response as essential to this "disposition" and "marshaling," Burke's anti-revolutionary writings depict a world in which these celestial harmonies have been unnaturally *dis*ordered. As a result, aesthetic responses, particularly the overwhelming passion of the sublime, are no longer reliable indicators of divine and natural disposition. "Everything seems out of nature," Burke writes, "in this strange chaos of levity and ferocity" (*R* 9). Burke's arguments concerning the Revolution's perversion of natural "orders, ranks, and distinctions" are given sensuous and imagistic form in his account of the violation of Marie Antoinette's bedchamber, and his notorious figuration of political revolution there in terms of unnatural sexual violation.[4] This scene stands as a kind of synecdoche for the *Reflections*' portrayal of the Revolution as a whole, embodying Burke's labyrinth of anti-revolutionary arguments in one memorable example. Just as the Revolution comes to signify a rejection of those habituated into "playing the part which belongs to the place assigned," so it provoked what he describes as a disorder and incoherence of the natural sensation in the beholder of the revolutionary spectacle: "contempt mixes with indignation; alternate laughter and tears, scorn and horror."

Burke's emphasis on the interrelated disorganization of social roles and aesthetic response can be found in the *Reflections*, the *Appeal*, and the *Thoughts on French Affairs*, but it is given its fullest articulation six years later, after the Jacobin Terror, in the *Letters on a Regicide Peace*. For Burke, in the wake of Revolution, aesthetic response, particularly to the sublime, no longer works to dispose subjects toward submission to the interlocking authorities of the Old Regime, but rather enlists subjects in the subversion that threatens natural rank and hierarchy. For Burke, the French Revolution was about much more than the replacement of one political authority, monarchy, with another, republic. Burke believed this focus on mere "nomenclature" was both superficial and misleading.[5] Rather than approach the French Revolution as a contemporary instance of the familiar and age-old revolution in government, Burke understood it as the assertion of "a system which is by its essence inimical to all other governments" (*L* 250). By "government" here, Burke means not only the institutions of the

---

[4]Linda M. G. Zerilli notes "Burke's gendered coding of social crisis." (Zerilli 1994, p. 60) See also Hertz 1985.

[5]The nation, Burke writes, "is a moral essence, not a geographical arrangement, or a denomination of the nomenclature" (*L* 326).

state, but the manifold ways in which human conduct submits to "the discipline of social life." The "body politick" was made up of an assemblage of "particular moleculae" united in their organization of social authority. In France these "moleculae" were found, for example, in "the dignity of its nobility, in the honor of its gentry, in the sanctity of its clergy, [and] in the reverence of its majesty" (*L* 326). The disorder of the Revolution resonated throughout this entire assemblage of interlinking authorities ordering social life, threatening property, the family, the workplace and the school. Its consequences were felt "throughout all the relations of life," (*L* 315) Burke wrote, not just between governors and governed, aristocrats and commons, priest and parishioner, but between employer and employee, husbands and wives, parents and children. It threatened nothing less than the "destruction and decomposition of the whole society" (*L* 325). It "inverted the natural order in all things, setting up high in the air what is required to be low on the ground."

Underwriting this democratic inversion of order was not only "a new power of an old kind," Burke writes, "but a new power of a new species" (*L* 360). The unprecedented quality of this emergent power challenges scholars who situate Burke's interpretation of the Revolution within the inherited Scottish Enlightenment framework of savagery and civilization (see O'Neill 2007). More persuasive is Stephen White's emphasis on Burke's preoccupation with a distinctively modern conflagration of human willfulness, the troubling assertion of unbounded human agency across social life. White describes this as the "humanization of the sublime," in that "the object of sublime experience is increasingly associated with feats of human subjectivity... Human beings themselves now produce a sort of human infinite that displaces what had before stood for the infinite, God, or fate" (White 1994, 75). No one better personified this tendency for Burke than his onetime acquaintance then bitter enemy Thomas Paine, who declared in *Common Sense* that, "we have it in our power to begin the world over again" (Paine 1989a). Paine—a self-made man and, by the 1790s, the most influential proponent of a radical theory of popular sovereignty—represented both the individual and collective dimensions of this unbridled willfulness.

This pervasive, threatening sense of insolent agency and willful innovation animates Burke's anti-revolutionary writings. Willful assertion and self-making unite the groups Burke believed to be chiefly responsible for the French Revolution. Financial speculators, philosophical men of letters and the ambitious politicians of the Third Estate had a variety of competing interests and motives, but were unified by their shared "dreadful energy" coursing through modern life, unencumbered will freed from historical circumstance and contextual limitation. All these groups were engaged in political action "taken on grounds which liberate the intellect and permit it to engage in a total criticism and a total reconstruction of the social order."

The Revolution was the evident and astonishing sign of the historical emergence of this autonomy of will; the revolution in French politics had been long prepared by a revolution in its "sentiments, manners, and moral opinions." The Revolution revealed to Burke that "the world of contingency and political combination is much larger than we are apt to imagine" (*T* 51); indeed, much larger than he himself seems to have imagined in earlier works like the *Enquiry*. The Revolution challenged Burke's faith that Nature can consensually command a universal legislation of taste.

The Revolution's inversion of natural order troubled the core assurances of Burke's earlier aesthetic theory, as he came to see that the conflagration of willfulness was accompanied and sustained by a new and dangerous aesthetic sensibility: the radical democratic sublime. While Burke continued to rely on aesthetic categories for assessing and evaluating the Revolution and its progress, his aesthetic theory changed under the pressure of new political circumstances. His understanding of the sublime, in particular, shifts during his later work, with his pervasive concern at once emerging from and responding to his earlier aesthetic theory. The change's principal characteristics are most clearly articulated in his *Appeal*, where Burke writes that more than any coherent ideology or social or economic interest, what unites and animates the revolutionaries and their radical admirers in Britain is "the mere pleasure of the beginner" (*A* 184). This pleasure taken in the power of beginning something anew is an aesthetic sensibility that helps Burke explain the widespread appreciation that a broader European public was taking in the unfolding spectacle of Revolution before the Terror of 1794. By means of this aesthetic sensibility, "arbitrary will... step by step, poisons the heart of every citizen." "It wants nothing but a disposition to trouble the established order, to give title to the enterprise" (*A* 185). The danger posed by the Revolutionaries was not simply the subversive content of their doctrines, but the contagious sensibility of beginning anew that the spectacle of Revolution engendered. "All love to our country, all pious veneration and attachment to its laws and customs, are obliterated from our minds; and nothing can result from this opinion... but a series of conspiracies and seditions, sometimes ruinous to their authors, always noxious to the state" (*A* 184).

This pleasure in beginning anew appears throughout many of Burke's anti-revolutionary writings. It is found, for example, in the *Reflections* when he writes that for the revolutionaries, "cheap bloodless reformation, a guiltless liberty appear flat and vapid to their taste. There must instead be a great change of scene; there must be magnificent stage effect; there must be grand spectacle to rouse the imagination grown torpid with... lazy enjoyment" (*R* 57). In the *Letters* it is found in the "delight" that the revolutionaries have in "defacing, degrading, torturing and tearing to pieces [the image of God] in man" (*L* 163); a delight Burke elsewhere describes as a "complexional disposition... to pull everything to pieces." It is found also in the giddy *jouissance* that Burke associates with philosophical enthusiasm and abstract speculation in politics and morals, and in "the exclusive confidence in ourselves" and the "restless disposition" that emerges from what he calls "desperate enterprises of [political] innovation" (*A* 266). The radical democratic sublime and the pleasure it takes in beginning anew is for Burke associated with the drama of the clean slate, the "spirited and daring" but also "shameless" enterprise of democracy itself.

There is a discomforting similarity between the aesthetic appreciation of the French Revolution and its pleasure of beginning and Burke's earlier aesthetics of the sublime. In the *Appeal* Burke seems to invoke the view of the *Enquiry* when he writes that "our complexion is such that we are so palled with enjoyment and stimulated with hope; that we become less sensible to a long-possessed benefit, from the very circumstance that it becomes habitual. Specious, untried, ambiguous prospects of new advantage, recommend themselves to the spirit of adventure which more or less prevails in every mind" (*A* 76). According to Tom Furniss, Burke worried that his writings on the sublime were being used by radicals such as Price to enlist enthusiasm for the Revolution. Burke worried that his own aesthetics became "the model through which radicalism came to represent the Revolution" (Furniss, 1993). He was openly concerned with the "exultation and rapture" that greeted the Revolution, instead of "contempt and indignation" (*R* 9). This worry perhaps contributed to the development of what Frances Ferguson has called the growing "unnaturalness of [Burke's] account of nature" (1985). The anti-revolutionary writings seem more clearly preoccupied with the difficulty of appeals to nature for the uncontroversial command of judgment and assent. If the Revolution upends Burke's faith in a stable natural order of aesthetic judgment, it also provokes what we now recognize as the distinctly "Burkean" argument that custom, prejudice, habit—in short, art—*is* human nature (*A* 218).[6] Burke responds to this by shifting his account of the sublime from the commands of a transcendent nature to those of an immanent human history. Burke's anti-revolutionary writings endow these traditions themselves with sublime gravity, opposing them not to torpid repetition but to the convulsive suddenness of revolutionary politics. In these changing oppositions Burke's sublime takes on a different character. The earlier primacy of astonishment is replaced by the primacy of reverence and awe. We can most clearly see this refiguring of the sublime in the already-cited passage on the "imposing and majestic aspect" of Britain's ancestral inheritance, but it is not only found there. Unlike radicals like Paine, who sought to expose the violence of historical origin by exposing it to the light of critical reason, Burke invoked origins forever hidden in the mist of the past and inaccessible to

---

[6]Bromwich (1989) discusses the originality of this claim.

human inquiry. Burke presents human history as an ineffable mystery, commanding a reverential awe unappreciated by insolent revolutionaries intent on destroying the *ancien regime*'s authority by attacking the images and symbols that had helped to sustain it (see Gamboni 1997). Over the course of the anti-revolutionary writings an aesthetics of immanence subtly replaces Burke's earlier aesthetics of transcendence, and the sublime is, along with the beautiful, accommodated to the world of human making.

Conclusion

For Burke's most insightful and influential radical critics—Mary Wollstonecraft and Thomas Paine, respectively—Burke's efforts to restore the "decent drapery" of authority followed from his affirmation of the aesthetic dimensions of social and political life. Their arguments against Burke's anti-revolutionary efforts at re-enchantment are tied to corresponding arguments about the place of political aesthetics in the Age of Democratic Revolutions. Burke's critics in the 1790s speak with surprising unanimity against the central role aesthetics play in Burke's account of political life. Many agree that Burke called for a return to discredited and irrational authority based in the captivation and enchantment of the public by way of the "splendor of dazzling images." He has wrapped "tyrannic principles" in "gorgeous drapery," Wollstonecraft writes, and distracted the imaginations of his reading public with the "fascinating pomp of ceremonial grandeur" (Wollstonecraft 1995, 52).

In his *Rights of Man,* which at the time of its publication sold more copies than any book printed in English other than the bible, Paine established an influential precedent for much liberal democratic theory to come. Rather than engaging with Burke's political aesthetics, as Wollstonecraft had done with great subtlety, Paine contemptuously dismissed aesthetics almost entirely as irrelevant to politics, including Burke's privileged category of the sublime. "When authors and critics talk about the sublime," Paine writes, "they see not how nearly it borders on the ridiculous. The sublime of the critics, like some parts of Edmund Burke's sublime and beautiful is like a windmill just visible in a fog, which imagination might distort into a flying mountain, or an archangel, or a flying flock of geese" (Paine 1989b, 45). Paine aspired to free politics of such rhapsodies of imagination. Paine's windmills cast Burke as an anachronism longing nostalgically for a "Quixotic age of chivalrous nonsense." Paine ridicules Burke's "well-wrought veil" of political authority, based on "legitimate presumptions" never fully articulated, as nothing more than a means of domination by way of enchantment; all part of the "puppet show of state and aristocracy." Paine thought monarchy was itself intrinsically connected to rule through sensuous enchantment, authority through aesthetics, and when Paine sought to destroy the monarchy he set out simultaneously to destroy the illegitimate basis of its authority. For Paine, monarchy came to stand for an original political alienation, a form of political idolatry where the authority engendered by the people themselves assumes monstrous sensual form, taking on a life of its own and ruling over the people that created it. It was captivation by metaphor (Paine 1989b, 135). In England, Paine wrote, sovereignty resides in a mere "metaphor, shown at the tower for sixpence ...; and it would be a step nearer to reason to say [sovereignty] resided in them, for any inanimate metaphor is no more than a hat or a cap. We can all see the absurdity of worshipping Aaron's molten calf... but why do men continue to practice on themselves the absurdities they despise in others?" (Paine 1989b, 94). Paine's democratic iconoclasm is supremely confident in the ability to articulate democratic authority free from such mystifying "devices" and "gewgaws." He contrasts the rule of metaphor in England with the self-evident rule of "the nation" and France. But if the "crown," or the "monarchy," is not necessary to the nation, and if noble titles are like so many "circles drawn by the magician's wand to contract the sphere of man's felicity" (Paine 1989b, 97), is it equally true that a democratic people can so easily emancipate itself from the rule of metaphor, or be disenthralled from the "Bastille of a word?" Is the democracy that Paine envisions, and the people he celebrates, so easily emancipated from political aesthetics as his work demands?

Common Sense shares with the *Rights of Man* an uncompromising attack on monarchy, and it does so from multiple angles: social contract theory, moral sentimentalism, even biblical history. In America, as Paine famously writes, "THE LAW IS KING" (Paine 1989a, 28). Rather than being in thrall to the personal character of a monarch, the American people abide by the authority of simple republican principles dictated by Nature and embodied in law. But it is not often remembered that Paine's famous phrase is invoked in the context of an elaborate ceremony of state that he recommends to provide "earthly honors" to a utilitarian government directed to achieving "the greatest sum of individual happiness, with the least national expense."

> Let a day be solemnly set apart for proclaiming the charter [of the newly proclaimed government]; let it be brought forth placed on the divine law, the Word of God; let a crown be placed thereon, by which the world may know, that so far as we approve of monarchy, that in America THE LAW IS KING. ...But lest any ill use should afterwards arise, let the crown at the conclusion of the ceremony be demolished, and scattered among the people whose right it is (Paine 1989a, 28).

What are we to make of this? Does the destruction of the metaphor of sovereign power disenthrall a pre-existing people from its authority, or does the de-coronation ceremony of destruction and ritual distribution itself give shape to that people and the democratic authority they proclaim? Does the ceremony actuate the entity it sets out to commemorate?

"The social sciences," John Adams wrote near the end of the Revolutionary War, "will never be much improved, until the people unanimously know and consider themselves as the fountains of power... Reformation must begin with the body of the people... They must be taught to reverence themselves, instead of adoring their servants, their generals, admirals, bishops, and statesmen" (Adams 1854, 540). Adams considered this spectacle of reverential self-regard as essential to engendering an enduring sense of the people's political capacities, although, like Burke, he came to fear their unbridled democratic insolence in the 1780s. Conservatives such as Burke and Adams perhaps saw more clearly than radicals such as Paine and Price that the Revolutionary spectacle was intimately related to the democratic agency it enacted. They understood there was something captivating and sublime in popular rule, that emerging democracy too relied upon and elicited the popular imagination in ways that its most ardent advocates disavowed. Of course both Burke and Adams also believed that "the gross mass of people" only cohered as a people through their collective reverential appreciation of the great, who were gazed upon as their natural leaders and "an essential ingredient part of any large body rightly constituted." "When you disturb this harmony," Burke would write, "when you break up this beautiful order... when you separate the common sort of men from their proper chieftains so as to form them into an adversary army, I no longer know that venerable object called the people in such a race of deserters and vagabonds" (*A* 176).

The Revolution had, among other things, irrevocably changed the direction of this popular gaze. It had "inverted order in all things," and placed "the gallery... in the place of the house" (R 60). For Burke, the self-regarding spectacle of a people—at once actors and spectators—beholding their own democratic capacities for willful innovation and being further enlivened by the sight, was the threatening essence of the radical democratic sublime. But its effect was for him the opposite of edifying. It did not inspire true greatness and moral exertion, but was "the most shameless thing in the world" (*R* 82) in the sense that it offered no higher perspective from which to view and judge its own actions. The democratic people in revolt was the specter that haunted the European political imagination in the Age of Revolutions. The self-regarding and egalitarian spectacle of democracy in the making and of a people disenthralled from their "proper chieftans" was, for Burke, a terrible prophecy of a Godless world without limits.

Tocqueville wrote *Democracy in America* "under the pressure of a kind of religious terror" provoked "by the sight of this irresistible revolution which has progressed over so many centuries" (Tocqueville 2003, 15). In a democracy, he writes, "the people reign over the political world as God rules over the universe. It is the cause and the end of all things; everything rises out of it and is absorbed back into it" (Tocqueville 2003, 60). That the people's authority—terrible yet undefined, absolute but forever receding—might rely upon a pervasive sense of its own sublimity was something that most of its advocates—then and now—would disavow, but that some of its most insightful critics clearly understood. Burke does not openly make this argument, of course, but his political aesthetics allow us to discern the outlines of a sublime democratic authority engendered by what Claude Lefort describes as, "the experience of an ungraspable, uncontrollable society in which the people will be said to be sovereign, of course, but whose identity will constantly be open to question" (Lefort 1986, 303–4). Burke glimpsed dilemmas of democratic authority that democratic theorists like Paine simply neglected or shunted aside, and that remain with us still. In recalling us to these dilemmas, and suggesting that aesthetics might provide a language for engaging with them, the anti-democratic founder of modern conservatism may have more to teach contemporary democratic theorists than does the prophet of democratic revolution.

References

Adams, J. (1854), "Letter to John Jebb, 10 September 1785," in *Works of John Adams, vol. 9*, Boston: Little, Brown and Company, pp. 538–43.

Ashfield, A. and De Bolla, P. eds (1996), *The Sublime: A Reader in British Eighteenth-Century Aesthetic Theory*. Cambridge: Cambridge University Press.

Barrell, J. (2000), *Imagining the King's Death: Figurative Treason, Fantasies of Regicide, 1793–1796*. Oxford: Oxford University Press.

Blakemore, S. (1997), "Hic mulier, Haec vir: The Feminization of Burke in The Rights of Men," in *Intertextual War: Edmund Burke and the French Revolution in the Writings of Mary Wollstonecraft, Thomas Paine, and James MacKintosh*. London: Associated University Presses, pp. 26–39.

Bromwich, D. (1989), *A Choice of Inheritance: Self and Community from Edmund Burke to Robert Frost*. Cambridge, MA: Harvard University Press.

——(1995), "Wollstonecraft as a Critic of Burke," *Political Theory* 23 (4) pp. 617–34.

Burke, E. (1869), *The Works of the Right Honorable Edmund Burke* (third edn) 12 vols. Boston: Little, Brown.

——(1984), *Selected Letters of Edmund Burke*, Harvey C. Mansfield ed., Chicago: University of Chicago Press.

——(1987), *Reflections on the Revolution in France*, J. G. A. Pocock ed., Indianapolis, IN: Hackett.

——(1998), *A Philosophical Enquiry into the Origins of the Sublime and Beautiful: And Other Pre-Revolutionary Writings*. New York: Penguin Classics.

Cobban, A. (1960), *Edmund Burke and the Revolt Against the Eighteenth Century: A Study of the Political and Social Thinking of Burke, Wordsworth, Coleridge and Southey*. London: Allen & Unwin.

de Tocqueville, A. (2003), *Democracy in America and Two Essays on America*, G. E. Bevan trans., I. Kramnick intro. London: Penguin.

Eagleton, T. (1989), "Aesthetics and Politics in Edmund Burke," in *History Workshop* 28, pp. 53–62.

Ferguson, F. (1985), "Legislating the Sublime," in *Studies in Eighteenth-Century British Art and Aesthetics*, R. Cohen ed. Berkeley, CA: University of California Press, pp. 128–47.

Frank, J. (2010), *Constituent Moments: Enacting the People in Postrevolutionary America*. Durham: Duke University Press.

Furniss, T. (1993), *Edmund Burke's Aesthetic Ideology: Language, Gender, and Political Economy in Revolution*. Cambridge: Cambridge University Press.

Gamboni, D. (1997), *The Destruction of Art: Iconoclasm and Vandalism since the French Revolution*. London: Reaktion Books.

Gibbons, L. (2003), *Edmund Burke and Ireland: Aesthetics, Politics and the Colonial Sublime*. Cambridge: Cambridge University Press.

Hampshire-Monk, I. ed. (2005), *Impact of the French Revolution: Texts from Britain in the 1790s*. Cambridge: Cambridge University Press.

Hertz, N. (1985), "Medusa's Head: Male Hysteria under Political Pressure," in *The End of the Line: Essays on Psychoanalysis and the Sublime*. New York: Columbia University Press, pp. 199–250.

Herzog, D. (1991), "Puzzling Through Burke," in *Political Theory* 19 (3), pp. 336–63.

——(1998), *Poisoning the Minds of the Lower Orders*. Princeton, NJ: Princeton University Press.

Hindson, P. (1988), *Burke's Dramatic Theory of Politics*. Aldershot: Avebury.

Honig, B. (2007), "Between Deliberation and Decision: Political Paradox in Democratic Theory," in *American Political Science Review* 101 (1), pp. 1–17.

——(2010), "Antigone's Two Laws: Greek Tragedy and the Politics of Humanism," in *New Literary History* 41, pp. 1–34.

Horkheimer, M. (1974), *Critique of Instrumental Reason*. New York: Seabury Press.

Hume, D. (1973), *A Treatise of Human Nature*, L. A. Selby-Bigge ed. Oxford: Clarendon.

Kaiser, D. A. (1999), *Romanticism, Aesthetics, and Nationalism*. Cambridge: Cambridge University Press.

Kant, I. (2000), *Critique of the Power of Judgment*, P. Guyer ed. Cambridge: Cambridge University Press.

Kramnick, I. (1977), *The Rage of Edmund Burke: A Portrait of an Ambivalent Conservative*. New York: Basic Books.

——ed. (1999), *The Portable Edmund Burke*. New York: Penguin.

Lefort, C. (1986), *The Political Forms of Modern Society: Bureaucracy, Democracy, Totalitarianism*. Cambridge, MA: MIT Press.

Longinus. [1957] 1991. *On Great Writing (On the Sublime)*, G. M. A. Grube trans. Indianapolis: IN: Hackett.

Lovejoy, A. O. (1936), *The Great Chain of Being: A Study of the History of an Idea*. Cambridge, MA: Harvard University Press.
Macpherson, C. B. (1980), *Burke*. New York: Hill and Wang.
Mehta, U. (1999), *Liberalism and Empire: Study in Nineteenth-Century British Liberal Thought*. Chicago: University of Chicago Press.
Melvin, P. H. (1975), "Burke on Theatricality and Revolution," in *Journal of the History of Ideas* 36 (3). 447–68.
Morley, J. (1993), *Edmund Burke*. Belfast: Athol Books.
Müller, J.-W. (2007), *Constitutional Patriotism*. Princeton, NJ: Princeton University Press.
O'Brian, C. C. (1992), *The Great Melody: A Thematic Biography and Commented Anthology of Edmund Burke*. Chicago: University of Chicago.
O'Neill, D. (2007), *The Burke-Wollstonecraft Debate: Savagery, Civilization, and Democracy*. University Park, PA: Pennsylvania State University Press.
——(2011), "The Sublime, the Beautiful, and the Political in Burke's Work," in *The Science of Sensibility: Reading Burke's Philosophical Enquiry*, K. Vermeir and M. Funk Deckard eds. Springer.
Paine, T. (1989a), "Common Sense," in *Thomas Paine: Political Writings*, B. Kuklick ed. Cambridge: Cambridge University Press, pp. 1–45.
——(1989b), "Rights of Man," in *Thomas Paine: Political Writings*, B. Kuklick ed. Cambridge: Cambridge University Press, pp. 57–264.
Paulson, R. (1983), *Representations of Revolution, 1789–1820*. New Haven, CT: Yale University Press.
Pocock, J. G. A. (1987), "Introduction," in *Reflections on the Revolution in France*, J. G. A. Pocock ed. Indianapolis, IN: Hackett, pp. vii–lvi.
Price, R. (1991), "A Discourse on the Love of our Country," in *Political Writings*, D. O. Thomas ed. Cambridge: Cambridge University Press, pp. 176–96.
Ryan, V. L. (2001), "The Physiological Sublime: Burke's Critique of Reason," in *Journal of the History of Ideas* 62 (2), 265–79.
Schneewind, J. B. (1998), *The Invention of Autonomy: A History of Modern Moral Philosophy*. Cambridge: Cambridge University Press.
Stanlis, P. J. (1958), *Edmund Burke and the Natural Law*. Ann Arbor: University of Michigan Press.
Strauss, L. (1953), *Natural Right and History*. Chicago: University of Chicago Press.
Walzer, M. (June 1967), "On the Role of Symbolism in Political Thought," in Political Science Quarterly 82 (2), pp. 191–204.
White, S. K. (1994), *Edmund Burke: Modernity, Politics, and Aesthetics*. Thousand Oaks, CA: Sage.
——(2009), *The Ethos of a Late-Modern Citizen*. Cambridge, MA: Harvard University Press.
Wollstonecraft, M. (1995), *A Vindication of the Rights of Men and A Vindication of the Rights of Woman*, Sylvana Tomaselli ed. Cambridge: Cambridge University Press.
Wood, N. (1964), "The Aesthetic Dimension of Burke's Political Thought," in *Journal of British Studies* 4 (1), pp. 41–64.
Zerilli, L. M. G. (1994), "The 'Furies of Hell': Women in Burke's 'French Revolution,'" in *Signifying Woman: Culture and Chaos in Rousseau, Burke, and Mill*. Ithaca, NY: Cornell University Press, pp. 60–94.

CHAPTER TWO

"We Feel Our Freedom": Imagination and judgment in the thought of Hannah Arendt

Linda M. G. Zerilli
University of Chicago

Critics of Hannah Arendt's Lectures on Kant's Political Philosophy *argue that Arendt fails to address the most important problem of political judgment, namely, validity. This essay shows that Arendt does indeed have an answer to the problem that preoccupies her critics, with one important caveat: she does not think that validity is the all-important problem of political judgment—the affirmation of human freedom is.*

Keywords: political judgment; political freedom; Hannah Arendt; Critique of Judgment*; rhetoric*

AUTHOR'S NOTE: *Thanks to Mary Dietz, Christine Froula, Gregor Gnaedig, Michael Hanchard, Peter Meyers, Mika La Vaque-Manty, George Shulman, and, especially, Bonnie Honig for their help with this essay. Edits to this original essay have been made by Linda M. G. Zerilli.*
POLITICAL THEORY, Vol. 33 No. 2, April 2005 158–188
DOI: 10.1177/0090591704272958

At the end of reasons comes persuasion.

—WITTGENSTEIN

There never has been any 'aestheticization' of politics in the modem age because politics is aesthetic in principle.

—JACQUES RANCIÈRE

A central question raised by Hannah Arendt's *Lectures on Kant's Political Philosophy* is the relationship between aesthetic judgment and political judgment.[1] In this otherwise elusive, posthumous text, Arendt tenaciously held that Kant's account of aesthetic judgment in the third *Critique* provides a model for political judgment: both forms of judgment concern appearances *qua* appearances and make an appeal to universality while eschewing truth criteria and the subsumption under rules that characterize cognitive and logical judgments (e.g., the syllogism: All men are mortal. Socrates is a man. Socrates is mortal).

In Arendt's account, political claims, like aesthetic claims, are examples of what Kant calls "reflective judgment," in which, by contrast with a "determinate judgment," the rule is not given. "If you say, 'What a beautiful rose!' you do not arrive at this judgment by first saying, 'All roses are beautiful, this flower is a rose, hence this rose is beautiful'" (*LKPP*, pp. 13–14), writes Arendt.[2] What confronts you in a reflective judgment, then, is not the general category "rose" but the particular, *this* rose. That *this* rose is beautiful is not given in the universal nature of roses. There is nothing necessary about the beauty of *this* rose. The claim about beauty is not grounded in a property of the object, which could be objectively ascertained (as is the case with cognitive judgments). Such a claim belongs to the structure of feeling rather than concepts. "[B]eauty is not a property of the flower itself" (*CJ*, §32, p. 145), writes Kant, but only an expression of the pleasure felt by the judging subject in the reflective mode of apprehending it.

---

[1]For accounts of politics as an aesthetic practice, see Kennan Ferguson, *The Politics of Judgment: Aesthetics, Identity, and Political Theory* (Lanham, MD: Lexington Books, 1999); and F. R. Ankersmit, *Aesthetic Politics: Political Philosophy beyond Fact and Value* (Stanford, CA: Stanford University Press, 1996).

[2]The same point applies in reverse:

For example, I may look at a rose and make a judgment of taste declaring it to be beautiful. But if I compare many singular roses and so arrive at the judgment, Roses in general are beautiful, then my judgment is not longer merely aesthetic but is a logical judgment based on an aesthetic one. (Immanuel Kant, *Critique of Judgment*, trans. Werner S. Pluhar [Indianapolis, IN: Hackett, 1987], §8, 59. Hereafter cited in the text as *CJ* with section and page numbers.)

Arendt's insistence that political judgments cannot be truth claims has puzzled her otherwise sympathetic readers. Most famous among them is Jürgen Habermas, who more or less accuses Arendt of aestheticizing politics, that is, of identifying this realm with opinions that cannot be subjected to rational processes of validation any more than we can validate judgments of taste. Arendt's turn to Kant's account of aesthetic judgment in the third *Critique,* Habermas maintains, is symptomatic of her refusal to provide a "cognitive foundation" for politics and public debate. This leaves "a yawning abyss between knowledge and opinion that cannot be closed with arguments."[3] Taking up Habermas's critique, Ronald Beiner, editor of Arendt's Kant lectures, also emphasizes the problems associated with "the all-important contrast between persuasive judgment and compelling truth" in Arendt's thought and wonders why she failed to recognize that "all human judgments, including aesthetic (and certainly political) judgments, incorporate a necessary cognitive dimension." (You will be a better judge of art if you know something about the art you are judging.) A Kantian approach, which excludes knowledge from political judgment, says Beiner, "renders one incapable of speaking of 'uninformed' judgment and of distinguishing differential capacities for knowledge so that some persons may be recognized as more qualified, and some as less qualified, to judge."[4]

Does Arendt sever the link between argument and judgment? In my view, the critical charge entirely misses the mark. Her point is not to exclude arguments from the practice of aesthetic or political judgment—as if something or someone could stop us from making arguments in public contexts—but to press us to think about what we are doing when we reduce the practice of politics to the contest of better arguments. Arendt disputes not the idea of argument as such but rather the assumption that agreement in procedures for making arguments ought to produce agreement in conclusions, hence agreement in the political realm can be reached in the manner of giving proofs. Arendt is struggling with a difficult problem to which her critics, focused as they are on the rational adjudication of political claims, are blind: our deep sense of necessity in human affairs. If Arendt brackets the legitimation problematic that dominates the thought of Habermas, it is because she sees in our practices of justification a strong tendency toward compulsion, which, in turn, destroys the particular *qua* particular and the

[3]Jürgen Habermas, "Hannah Arendt's Communications Concept of Power," *Hannah Arendt, Critical Essays,* ed. by Lewis Hinchman and Sandra Hinchman (Albany: State University of New York Press, 1994), 225. For a similar argument, see Albrecht Wellmer, "Hannah Arendt on Judgment: The Unwritten Doctrine of Reason," *Judgment, Imagination, and Politics: Themes from Kant and Arendt,* ed. by Ronald Beiner and Jennifer Nedlesky (Boston: Rowman & Littlefield, 2001), 165–81; quotation is from p. 169.

[4]Ronald Beiner, "Interpretive Essay: Hannah Arendt on Judging," in Hannah Arendt, *Lectures on Kant's Political Philosophy,* ed. by Ronald Beiner (Chicago: University of Chicago Press, 1982), 36.

very space in which political speech (including arguments) can appear.[5] She sees how we tend to run the space of reasons into the space of causes: logical reasoning is transformed from a dialogic tool of thought, with which we aim at agreement, into a monologic tool of thought, with which we compel it. What Habermas calls "the rationality claim immanent in speech" risks becoming what Wittgenstein calls "the hardness of the logical *must*."[6]

Thinking through the blind spots that attend critiques of Arendt's unfinished project to develop an account of judgment, we should ask, why did Arendt think she needed an account of the judging faculty? To what problem was judgment to be an answer? According to Beiner, it was this: "How to affirm freedom?" Present throughout her writings and explicitly posed in the final paragraph of *Willing,* the second volume of the *Life of the Mind,* Arendt saw in the judging faculty something that "allows us to experience a sense of positive pleasure in the contingency of the particular." Beiner continues,

> Arendt's thought here is that human beings have commonly felt the "awesome responsibility" of freedom to be an insupportable weight, which they have sought to evade by various doctrines, such as fatalism or the idea of historical process, and that the only way in which human freedom can be affirmed is by eliciting pleasure from the free acts of men by reflecting upon and judging them.[7]

Having astutely identified the importance of affect and the central problem of freedom in Arendt's work on judgment, Beiner goes on—quite inexplicably in my view—to endorse the aforementioned Habermasian critique, which ignores the theme of freedom as Arendt understood it (i.e., how to affirm the human capacity to begin anew) and casts the problem of judgment strictly as one of ascertaining intersubjective validity. Seyla Benhabib, working within the Habermasian framework, captures this decisive interpretive gesture when, likewise trying to comprehend Arendt's turn to the third *Critique,* she writes, "What Arendt saw in Kant's doctrine of aesthetic judgment was [...] a procedure for ascertaining intersubjective agreement in the public realm."[8] This "procedure" is the process of imagi-

---

[5]See Dana Villa, *Arendt and Heidegger: The Fate of the Political* (Princeton, NJ: Princeton University Press, 1996), 72. For another defense of Arendt contra Habermas, see Lisa Jane Disch, *Hannah Arendt and the Limits of Philosophy* (Ithaca, NY: Cornell University Press, 1994).

[6]Ludwig Wittgenstein, *Remarks on the Foundations of Mathematics,* ed. by G. H. Wright, R. Rhees, and G. E. M. Anscombe (Cambridge, MA: MIT Press, 1996), I, 121.Hereafter cited as *RFM*.

[7]Beiner, "Interpretive Essay," 13.

[8]Seyla Benhabib, *The Reluctant Modernism of Hannah Arendt* (Thousand Oaks, CA: Sage, 1996), 188–9. Benhabib finds a "normative lacuna in Arendt's thought" and the turn to the

natively thinking from standpoints not one's own and forming what Kant called an "enlarged mentality." Once this interpretive move is in place, Benhabib, too, finds the turn to Kant not only curious but also deeply mistaken.

And perhaps it is. If your primary concern is intersubjective validity in the political realm, why not turn to a more empirical and practical form of rationality like the Aristotelean notion of *phronesis?*[9] Why turn to a highly philosophical text that offers at best a highly formalized account of validity that posits the agreement of others, but has no need of their actual consent? Worse still, why endorse a form of validity that is not objective but subjective, for it makes reference to nothing more than the subject's own feeling of pleasure and merely anticipates the assent of all? Before deciding who is "right," Arendt or her critics, let us first try to understand what this judging faculty is and why it might be relevant to democratic politics.

Judgment and the problem of the new

In the widest sense of the term, judgment is the faculty that allows us to order or make sense of our experience. Be it the particulars of objects that need to be related to concepts for the purposes of cognition or the particulars of events that need to be organized into narratives for the purposes of political life, judgment gives coherence and meaning to human experience. Whether what I see over there is a "tree," what I hear on the radio is a commentary on "the latest famine in Africa," or what I read in the paper is an editorial on the "war between the sexes," I am at once engaged in and a witness to the practice of judgment. The ubiquity of the judging faculty in all human activities, however, makes it almost invisible to us *as* judgment, as something *we* do. This is especially true in the case of cognitive judgments, where we seem only to report a fact that stands there quite independently from how we judge (for example, I see that tree over there because there really is a tree over there, I see two sexes because there really are two sexes, and so on).

Kant—and later Wittgenstein—called into question the idea that cognition turns on the mere physiological fact of something like perception and emphasized the crucial role of judgment in anything that has meaning for human beings. For judgment generally speaking is the ability to think the particular as contained under the universal or, writes Kant, "the faculty

third, rather than the second, *Critique* to be one more "disturbing" example of Arendt's refusal or failure to provide the "normative dimension of the political" (Benhabib, *The Reluctant Modernism*, 193, 194).

[9]See Wellmer, "Hannah Arendt on Judgment," 166; and Beiner, "Interpretative Essay," 134.

of subsuming under rules; that is, of determining whether something stands under a given rule [...] or not."[10] Without the faculty of judgment we could have no knowledge, for in the absence of concepts that function as rules for subsuming particulars, we would have only "this" and "this," but not anything that we could call an object of experience (for example, this "woman" or this "man"). Every "object" comes into being as such through recognition in a concept, Kant holds.

According to the logic of recognition at work in what Kant calls a "determinate judgment" (that is, logical and cognitive), it is hard to see—as the philosopher himself recognized—how there could be a new object or event, that is, something that cannot be explained as the continuation of a preceding series and in terms of what is already known. What Arendt called "the problem of the new," however, is more than an epistemological question about how we have knowledge of particulars; and it is more than a moral question about how to save the freedom of the subject in a phenomenal world that can only be cognized through the law of causality.[11] The problem of the new is a political question about how we, members of democratic communities, can affirm human freedom as a political reality in a world of objects and events whose causes and effects we can neither control nor predict with certainty. Arendt vividly captures the difficulty we have in so affirming:

> Whenever we are confronted with something frighteningly new, our first impulse is to recognize it in a blind and uncontrolled reaction strong enough to coin a new word; our second impulse seems to be to regain control by denying that we saw anything new at all, by pretending that something similar is already known to us; only a third impulse can lead us back to what we saw and knew in the beginning. It is here that true [political] understanding begins.[12]

At stake in the kind of judgment that is relevant to politics is not knowledge but understanding, or rather the understanding, as Arendt says, that "makes knowledge meaningful." At stake is trying to be at home in a

---

[10]Immanuel Kant, *Critique of Pure Reason,* trans. and ed. by Paul Guyer and Alan W. Wood (Cambridge, MA: Cambridge University Press, 1977), B 171.

[11]Hannah Arendt, *The Life of the Mind. Two: Willing* (New York: Harcourt Brace Jovanovich, Inc. 1978), 28–34.

[12]Hannah Arendt, "Understanding and Politics," *Essays in Understanding, 1930–1954,* ed. by Jerome Kohn (New York: Harcourt Brace, 1994), 307–27; quotation is from p. 325, n7. "The loss of [inherited] standards," Arendt observes, "is only a catastrophe for the moral [and political] world when one assumes that individuals are not capable of judging things in themselves [...] one cannot expect of them anything more than the application of known rules." Hannah Arendt, *Was ist Politik ?* ed. by Ursula Ludz (Munich: Piper Verlag, 1993), 22. Hereafter, this is cited in the text as *WIP.* All translations are my own.

world composed of relations and events not of our own choosing, without succumbing to various forms of fatalism or determinism—whose other face is the idea of freedom as sovereignty.[13]

Our ability to come to terms with what is given (that is, the past that can be neither forgotten nor changed) in a way that affirms a nonsovereign human freedom (that is, freedom that begins in political community, not outside it) can only be achieved through a critical practice of judgment. Such a practice cannot be based on the "autonomy principle" that Hume disrobed as a philosophical conceit (i.e., the idea that reason judges critically by emancipating itself completely from the customs or prejudices that compose our preliminary understanding).[14] There is no place outside this understanding from which we can judge. When not seen as something to be leapt over in our reach for the external standpoint, this groundless ground of our judging practices is too often treated as if it determines what we can encounter in the world or it were somehow immune to revision. In that case, our precognitive understanding of meaning is transformed from an enabling condition of democratic politics and our critical orientation in an ever-changing world into what Arendt called a "worldview" that works to "protect us against experience [and the new] insofar as everything real is already given in [it]" (*WIP*, p. 21).

A freedom-centered practice of judgment, then, cannot be modeled on the rule-following that characterizes what Kant called a determinate judgment. To obtain critical purchase on our social arrangements and the ungrounded ground of our form of life, but without yielding to the temptation of the external standpoint, we need to develop a practice of judgment that is not rule-governed. Judging without the mediation of a concept is a quotidian skill we do well to learn and practice.[15] It always carries the risk that we will fall back on known concepts or rules for making sense of political reality out of our own sense of frustration or inadequacy. And yet if we want to come to terms with new objects and events, including those that have no

---

[13]In Arendt's view, totalitarianism is the paradigmatic event that strains our faculty of judgment, for "the death factories erected in the heart of Europe" confront us with an unprecedented sense of meaninglessness. How are we to judge an event that reveals the ruin of "our categories of thought and standards of judgment?" (Arendt, "Understanding and Politics," 313). If we stubbornly cling to rules that no longer speak to our experience, she argues, it is because what we have gotten used to is not so much the substance of any particular rule, but the fact of having rules with which to judge. Hannah Arendt, "Thinking and Moral Considerations," *Social Research: Fiftieth Anniversary Issue* 38, no. 3 (Autumn 1971): 416–46; see especially p. 436.

[14]On the relationship of judgments (*Urteile*) to prejudices (*Vorurteile*), see *W/P*, 17–23.

[15]This point is emphasized in Samuel Fleischacker, *A Third Concept of Liberty: Judgment and Freedom in Kant and Adam Smith* (Princeton, NJ: Princeton University Press, 1999). Fleischaker, too, sees freedom as deeply connected to the development of the judging faculty. In contrast to Arendt, however, he develops a theory of judgment from within the liberal tradition.

place within our system of reference save as curious anomalies to the rule that merely preserve the rule, we need to develop the faculty of judgment. And developing this faculty involves more than the affirmation of contingency that postfoundationalist political thinkers have stressed. Or, better, it involves the creation of coherence and meaning that does not efface contingency and thus freedom.[16]

Arendt holds that precisely whatever is not an object of knowledge is an occasion for developing the critical aspects of the faculty of judgment itself. It is in cases where what Kant called determinate judgment strains or fails that true judgment begins. In cases where a judgment can produce no knowledge (as a concept is not already given), the common sense or harmony of the faculties that obtains in a judgment is no longer under the legislation of the understanding (that is, the faculty of concepts), but attains a free accord. In the "free play of the faculties," as we shall see, imagination in particular is no longer bound to the logic of recognition, which requires that it reproduce absent objects in accordance with the concept-governed linear temporality of the understanding. Imagination, when it is considered in its freedom—nothing compels us to consider it as such—is not bound to the law of causality, but is productive and spontaneous, not merely reproductive of what is already known, but generative of new forms and figures.

Foregrounding the productive role of the imagination in the faculty of judgment, I at once take up and depart from Arendt's own unfinished project to develop a theory of political judgment. Despite her heavy reliance on Kant's third *Critique,* she never really considered the imagination in its freedom, for she never thought of it as anything more than reproductive. Arendt's limited view of imagination is all the more curious when we recognize that the reproductive imagination is bound to the faculty of the understanding and thus to concepts in a way that is difficult to square with her own vigorous refusal of cognition as the task of political judgment. Such neglect of the free play of imagination in a practice of judging without a concept is one reason that Arendt's scattered reflections on the topic have lent themselves to both the appropriation and criticism of thinkers such as

[16]For Arendt, the development of a freedom-affirming faculty of judgment requires more than an acknowledgment of contingency. Although she fiercely defends contingency against the Western philosophical tradition's equally fierce defense of necessity, she is adamant that we need to be able to judge new political objects and events. We need to be able to judge them in their freedom, that is, produce a sense of coherence that is neither given in our pre-understanding nor exhausted by the application of known concepts. Merely affirming the contingency of objects and events does not address the quest for meaning that is at the heart of the judging faculty. And it does not take seriously the ever-present temptation, when confronted with "the haphazard character of the particular," to assume a stance devoid of care for the world, as if "any order, any necessity, any meaning you wish to impose will do" (Arendt, "The Concept of History," 89).

Habermas, for whom validity looms as the single unanswered question that threatens to render her entire account incoherent.

Presupposed in such a charge is a conception of politics as the adjudication of an otherwise "impenetrable pluralism" (Habermas) of opinions.[17] In order to adjudicate competing claims, we need a way to establish their correctness. Thus political opinions, Habermas insists, must have a cognitive foundation and be subjected to rational procedures of validation. Although Arendt's critics distance themselves from philosophical objectivism or any metaphysical notion of truth, they never consider the possibility that there could be a form of validity specific to democratic politics that would not be based on the application of rules to particulars. They thus never see, really, that Arendt does have an answer of sorts to the question of validity that preoccupies them, with one crucial caveat: she does not think that validity in itself is the all-important problem or task for political judgment—the affirmation of human freedom is.

The rhetorical basis of rational speech

> Wherever people judge the things of the world that are common to them, there is more implied in their judgments than these things. By his manner of judging, the person discloses to an extent also himself, what kind of person he is, and this disclosure, which is involuntary, gains in validity to the degree that it has liberated itself from individual idiosyncracies.[18]

Arendt introduces here two crucial ideas: (1) the act of judging creates significant relations among judging persons, relations that disclose "who one is," a public rather than private persona; and (2) this disclosure of oneself as a judging person obtains validity (that is, solicits the agreement

---

[17] "The limits of a decisionistic treatment of practical questions are overcome as soon as argumentation is expected to test the generalizability of interests, instead of being resigned to an impenetrable pluralism of apparently ultimate value orientations," writes Habermas. "It is not the fact of this pluralism that is here disputed, but the assertion that it is impossible to separate by argumentation generalizable interests from those that remain particular." Citing this passage, Richard Bernstein finds a parallel in Arendt's claim that "judgment must liberate itself from 'subjective private conditions'." Richard Bernstein, *Between Objectivism and Relativism: Science Hermeneutics and Praxis* (Philadelphia: University of Pennsylvania Press, 1983), 220. But Arendt's approach to the plurality of opinions is different from that of Habermas. For her, this plurality is something to preserve, not overcome, in the exercise of judgment. I examine this difference in Linda M. G. Zerilli, *Feminism and the Abyss of Freedom* (Chicago: Chicago University Press, 2005), chap. 4.

[18] Hannah Arendt, "The Crisis in Culture," *Between Past and Future: Eight Exercises in Political Thought* (New York: Penguin, 1993), 221. Hereafter cited in the text as CC.

of others) to the extent that it attains impartiality (that is, takes those others into account).[19]

What one discovers in the act of judging, says Arendt, is both one's differences with some judging persons and one's commonalities with others:

> We all know very well how quickly people recognize each other, and how unequivocally they can feel that they belong [or do not belong] to each other, when they discover [or fail to discover] a kinship in questions of what pleases and displeases. (*CC*, p. 223)

Based in the activity of taste ("the it-pleases-or-displeases-me"), judging allows differences and commonalities to emerge that are by no means given in advance of the act itself. Judging may well call into question my sense of community with some persons and reveal a new sense of community with others. This discovery of community is not guaranteed by the rule-following associated with a determinate judgment. Such rule-following, says Arendt, compels everyone who has the power of reason and could be done in solitude.

Deeply critical of the subjectivism of modernity, Arendt's turn to aesthetic judgment is based on what she calls the fundamental, if mostly denied, reality of the human condition, namely, plurality. Arendt refuses to ground intersubjectivity in shared human nature (for example, rationality) or in shared experience (for example, class, ethnic, or national belonging). What she understands by plurality, however, is more than an ontological condition, the fact that "men, not Man, inhabit the earth." Understood as a *political* concept, plurality is something of which we need to take account when we decide what will count as part of our shared or common world. Judging is the activity that enables us to take account of plurality in this distinctly political sense. Following Kant's account of judgments of taste, Arendt argues that the kind of validity at stake in political judgments requires not simply that one "be in agreement with one's own self [logic's principle of noncontradiction], but [...] consist[s] of being able to 'think in the place of everybody else'" (*CC*, p. 220). Such judgments are by nature intersubjective and reflect the plurality of ways in which the world can be seen and understood.

The worldly relations that judging creates turn crucially on the ability to see the same thing from multiple points of view, an ability that, in Arendt's telling, is identical with what it means to see politically ("die Sachen wirklich von verschiedenen Seiten zu *sehen,* und das heißt politisch" [*WIP*,

---

[19]Who someone is, by contrast with what she is (e.g., a white middle-class American woman, qualities she necessarily shares with others like her), is the unique disclosure of human action that emerges in the stories and other human artifacts that speak of it. Hannah Arendt, *The Human Condition* (Chicago: Chicago University Press, 1989), 181, 182.

p. 96]). The origins of this way of seeing lie in "Homeric objectivity" (i.e., the ability to see the same thing from *opposite* points of view: to see the Trojan War from the standpoint of both Achilles and Hector).[20] What transforms this Homeric way of seeing into the ability to see from multiple points of view is the daily practice of public speech, "citizens talking with one another." [Arendt continues,]

> In this incessant talk the Greeks discovered that the world we have in common is usually regarded from an infinite number of different standpoints, to which correspond the most diverse points of view. In a sheer inexhaustible flow of arguments, as the Sophists presented them to the citizenry of Athens, the Greek learned to exchange his own viewpoint, his own "opinion"—the way the world appeared and opened up to him [...] with those of his fellow citizens. Greeks learned to *understand*—not to understand one another as individual persons, but to look upon the same world from one another's standpoint, to see the same in very different and frequently opposing aspects. (*CH*, p. 51)

It would be easy to mistake what Arendt means by the "exchange of opinions" and the "inexhaustible flow of arguments, as the Sophists presented them," for a conception of speech as rhetorical, where rhetoric is understood as the mere form (composed of tropes and figures) that makes a certain content (composed of rational premises and ultimate principles [*archai*]) more persuasive to one's interlocutor. "Incessant talk" would be an expression of the various guises rhetoric takes in its attempt to bring an interlocutor to see something that, if human reason operated as most Western philosophers think it should, she would grasp by following logical rules. To be human is to be condemned to politics understood as incessant rhetorical talk.

What distinguishes Arendt's account of political speech from the idea of rhetoric as a technique of persuasion is her stubborn insistence that this speech is composed not of truths dressed up in rhetorical form but of opinions: "it appears to me" (*CH*, p. 51)—nothing more. In contrast to this political speech, she writes, is "the philosophical form of speaking [... which is] concerned with knowledge and the finding of truth and therefore demands a process of compelling proof" (*CC*, p. 223). This process entails

[20]This Homeric impartiality is still the highest type of objectivity we know. Not only does it leave behind the common interest in one's side and one's own people which, up to our own days, characterizes almost all national historiography, but it also discards the alternative of victory or defeat, which moderns have felt expresses the "objective" judgment of history itself. (Hannah Arendt, "The Concept of History," *Between Past and Future: Eight Exercises in Political Thought* [New York: Penguin, 1993), 41–90; quotation is from p. 51. Hereafter cited in the text as *CH*.)

the rule-following of logical reasoning: the deduction from premises that we hold to be apodictic.

By making plurality the condition of, rather than the problem for, intersubjective validity, Arendt shifts the question of opinion formation and political judgment from the epistemological realm, where it concerns the application of concepts to particulars and the rational adjudication of knowledge/truth claims, to the political realm, where it concerns opinion formation and practices of freedom. Politics involves the exchange of arguments in the sense of opening up the world that has been disclosed to us through language, our criteria or concepts. However one understands the attempt to give reasons, it takes for granted a prior "opening up of [the] world where argument can be received and have an impact," as Jacques Rancière reminds us.[21] This opening up is nothing other than the poetic, rhetorical, and world-creating capacity of language that Habermas sets fully at odds with what he holds to be the proper communicative use of language that makes possible the "intersubjective recognition of criticizable validity claims."[22] By contrast with Habermas, Rancière, like Arendt, holds rhetorical language to be the condition of anything we might count as validation by proofs. Proofs work on the basis of deduction from accepted premises. Opening up creates the context in which a change in perspective may happen and things we may have known all along get counted differently.

We can grasp the problems associated with Habermas's attempt to keep separate the rhetorical and the rational aspects of language by turning to Ernesto Grassi. A contemporary of Arendt's and student of Heidegger's, Grassi critically examines the nature of rational discourse and its status in the philosophical tradition. According to that tradition, "to resort to images and metaphors, to the full set of implements proper to rhetoric," writes Grassi, "merely serves to make it 'easier' to absorb rational truth."[23] Turning the tables, he questions the view that rhetorical speech is not only inferior to rational or philosophical speech but also distinct from it.

> To prove [*apo-deiknumi*] means to *show* something to be something, on the basis of something. [...] Apodictic, demonstrative speech is the kind

---

[21]Jacques Rancière, *Dis-agreement: Politics and Philosophy*, trans. Julie Rose (Minneapolis: University of Minnesota Press, 1999), 56.

[22]Jürgen Habermas, *Between Facts and Norms: Contributions to a Discourse Theory of Law and Democracy*, trans. William Rehg (Cambridge, MA: MIT Press, 1996), 20; and Jürgen Habermas, *The Philosophical Discourse of Modernity: Twelve Lectures* (Cambridge, MA: MIT Press, 1987), 204. Habermas accuses Derrida, among other "postmodern" thinkers, of foregrounding the rhetorical capacity of language over its problem-solving capacity.

[23]Ernesto Grassi, *Rhetoric as Philosophy: The Humanist Tradition* (Carbondale: Southern Illinois University Press, 1980), 26. Hereafter cited in the text as *RP*.

> of speech which establishes the definition of phenomenon by tracing it back to ultimate principles, or *archai*. It is clear that the first *archai* of any proof and hence of knowledge cannot be proved themselves because they cannot be the object of apodictic, demonstrative, logical speech; otherwise they would not be the first assertions. [...] But if the original assertions are not demonstrable, what is the character of the speech in which we express them? Obviously this type of speech cannot have a rational-theoretical character. (*RP*, p. 19)

Grassi's answer is simple but significant: he shows that the "indicative or allusive [*semeinein*] speech that grounds philosophical or rational speech provides the very framework within which the proof can come into existence at all." This indicative speech

> is immediately a 'showing'—and for this reason 'figurative' or 'imaginative', and thus in the original sense 'theoretical' [*theroein*—i.e., to see]. It is metaphorical: it shows something that has a sense and this means that to the figure, to that which is shown, the speech transfers [*metapherein*] a signification. Such speech 'leads before the eyes' [*phainesthai*] a significance.

The basis of rational speech, writes Grassi, "is and must be in its structure an imaginative language" (*RP*, p. 20). This conclusion radically alters the relationship of rational speech and rhetorical speech: "The term 'rhetoric' assumes a fundamentally new significance; 'rhetoric' is not [...] the technique of an exterior persuasion; it is rather the speech which is the basis of rational thought" (*RP*, p. 20).

What distinguishes rational speech from rhetorical speech, then, is not that the former proceeds from premises that are, in Arendt's vivid description of logical reasoning, like iron "laws" that "are ultimately rooted in the structure of the human brain ... [and which] possess ... the same force of compulsion as the driving necessity which regulates the function of our bodies."[24] Grassi would question not the sense of necessity Arendt describes but its source: necessity lies not in the ultimate principles from which logical reasoning proceeds, let alone in the universal structure of the human brain, but in the images and figures that generate belief. What gives us the sense of necessity, what "holds us captive," is, as Wittgenstein would say, "a picture."[25] I hasten to add that this picture is not, as the *archai* of rational speech pretend to be, necessary and universally valid

---

[24] Arendt, *The Human Condition*, 171.

[25] "'The picture forces itself on us. [...]' It is very interesting that pictures do force themselves on us. And if that were not so, how could such a sentence as 'What's done cannot be undone' mean anything to us?" (*RFM*, I §14). Wittgenstein gives a close reading of the picture of "the

apart from time and place. The picture has meaning and necessity only as part of a praxis; thus it can change with the times. The fact that rhetoric is a praxis (i.e., concrete individuals talking to each other in specific contexts) is why the philosophical tradition, in the quest for a timeless Truth, rejected it.[26] For Arendt, it is a central task of judgment to loosen our sense of such truth and necessity in human affairs. And such loosening requires different images and practices, new ways of producing meaning.

Learning to see politically

We have seen that Arendt formulates the faculty of political judgment in terms of the ability to see the same object from multiple perspectives. Arendt sets this ability against what she calls the "tricks of the Sophists," namely, the strategy of turning arguments around so as to conclude, as the ancient skeptics held, that no judgment is possible (*WIP*, p. 96). However vital the Sophists were for attenuating dogmatism and teaching the skill of public speaking, writes Arendt, at a certain point what becomes "important is not that one can turn arguments around and assertions on their head, but that one developed the ability really to see things from multiple perspectives, and that means politically" (*WIP*, p. 96). Arendt recognizes the value of argument in the public realm, but her account of judgment turns on the difference between, on the one side, being compelled by the better argument or doubting that any compelling argument can be made (skepticism) and, on the other side, learning to see what the world looks like to all who share it. This difference of emphasis pulls her account in the direction of both Grassi's recovery of the humanist tradition's conception of rhetoric and Wittgenstein's notion of the pictures that ground our language-games. She emphasizes what it means to see differently, to form a different picture.

I said earlier that aesthetic judgment has subjective not objective validity. To conclude that such judgments are not rational, however, would be to concede (with Arendt's critics) a rather narrow understanding of what rationality is, namely, a form of thinking based on giving proofs. This includes not only the scientific rationality Habermas accuses Arendt of uncritically inheriting from Kant's first *Critique* but also the practical rationality associated with the central role of arguments in a discourse ethics. Following Stanley Cavell's reading of the third *Critique,* we might question the idea that rationality is a matter of reaching agreement in conclusions on the basis of agreement in procedures. Kant's whole

machine as symbol," which lies at the origin of the language game of logical necessity, our sense of the "logical must" (ibid., I, §§121–122).

[26] Ernesto Grassi, *Die unerhörte Metapher* (Frankfurt am Main: Anton Hain, 1992), 29, 27.

point, after all, was to respond to critics like Hume who claimed that the notorious lack of agreement in aesthetic judgments shows they lack rationality. Although Kant refuted the idea that aesthetics could ever be a science or that such judgments could be proved, he insisted that, when we judge aesthetically, our claim is not merely subjective. The claim "this painting is beautiful" is different from the claim "I like canary wine," says Kant. It would be ridiculous to say, this painting "is beautiful *for me*" (*CJ*, §7, p. 55); a judgment of beauty posits the agreement of others. Lacking concepts, such a judgment exhibits a necessity that "can only be called *exemplary*, i.e., a necessity of the assent of *everyone* to a judgment that is regarded as an example of a rule that we are unable to state" (*CJ*, §18, p. 85).[27]

Whether others do so agree is another matter. In any case, the validity of my judgment does not depend on their empirical assent, Kant holds. But if the validity of my judgment does not depend on such assent and cannot compel it on the basis of proofs, why bother exchanging views at all? "For if it is granted that we can quarrel about something, then there must be some hope for us to arrive at agreement about it," as Kant puts it (*CJ*, §56, p. 211). This hope indicates that such judgments are not merely subjective, but also, as Cavell emphasizes, that the debate lives on *despite* the lack of guarantee of reaching agreement. The possibility of such agreement is not excluded, but the validity of an aesthetic judgment in no way depends on it. We expect people to support their judgments, but even if we agree with their arguments we need not agree with their conclusion. For example, I can accept your argument about why a certain painting is beautiful (such as its unique place in the history of art, the artist's vivid use of color, or the representation of perspective) and still disagree with your judgment of beauty. That refusal may make my sense of taste deficient in your eyes, but not in the sense of being mistaken.

This suggests that the rationality of such judgments is of a different kind. Cavell takes up the Kantian notion of the subjective validity of aesthetic judgments to call our attention to the notion of "pattern and support," rather than agreement in conclusions, as the crucial element in rational argument. Stephen Mulhall parses Cavell's view thus:

> Cavell is not suggesting that logic or rationality is a matter of the existence of patterns (of support, objection, response) *rather than* of agreement (in

[27]Kant writes: This necessity is of a special kind. It is not a theoretical objective necessity, allowing us to cognize a priori that everyone will feel this liking for the object I call beautiful. Nor is it a practical objective necessity, where, through concepts of a pure rational will that serves freely acting beings as a rule, this liking is the necessary consequence of an objective law and means nothing other than that one absolutely (without any further aim) ought to act in a certain way. (Kant, *CJ*, §18, p. 85)

> conclusions); he is suggesting that logic or rationality might be more fruitfully thought of as a matter of agreement in *patterns* rather than agreement in *conclusions*. Whether the particular patterns or procedures are such that those competent in following them are guaranteed to reach an agreed conclusion is part of what distinguishes one type or aspect of rationality from another; but what distinguishes rationality from irrationality in any domain is agreement in—a commitment to—patterns or procedures of speaking and acting.[28]

The issue, then, cannot be that aesthetic judgments lack rationality. In the third *Critique,* Kant no more ruled out giving reasons for our aesthetic judgments than does Arendt in her reading of him.[29] Someone who is unable to support her judgments is not engaging in aesthetic (Kant) or political (Arendt) judgment at all, but merely stating a subjective preference. What Kant ruled out, rather, was the idea that reasons could compel others to agree with an aesthetic judgment. Criteria are to be considered when choosing between competing judgments, but these criteria can never function as proof that a judgment is correct. Consequently, there is no single argument that can or should persuade everyone capable of reason, regardless of standpoint or context, of a particular aesthetic or political judgment. That is why rhetoric, which takes account of such things, is an enabling mode of speech in the interlocution proper to such judgments.

Aesthetic and political judgments are arguable, in other words, but in a particular way. They belong to the interlocution Kant calls *streiten* (to quarrel or contend) rather than *disputieren* (to dispute), that is, the kind of interlocution that, if it generates agreement, does so on the basis of persuasion rather than irrefutable proofs (*CJ,* §56). Whereas *disputieren* assumes that agreement can be reached through an exchange of arguments constrained by the rules set out by conceptual logic and objective knowledge (as with determinate judgments), *streiten* occurs when concepts are lacking and agreement cannot be reached through the giving of proofs (as with reflective judgments). And yet, despite the absence of the objective necessity of an agreement reached by proofs, the debate lives on, for each judging subject makes an aesthetic claim that posits the agreement of others and attempts to persuade them of her or his view.

To attempt to persuade with argument in the political realm, says Arendt, is "to give an account—not to prove, but to be able to say how one came to an opinion, and for what reasons one formed it" (*LKPP,*

---

[28] Stephen Mulhall, *Stanley Cavell: Philosophy's Recounting of the Ordinary* (Oxford: Oxford University Press, 1998), 26.

[29] See Kant, *CJ,* §34, p. 149. See also Stanley Cavell, *Must We Mean What We Say?* (Cambridge: Cambridge University Press, 1976), 88.

p. 41). She does not dispute the idea (precious to Habermas's notion of the practical rationality in communication "oriented toward mutual understanding") that speakers should—he would say must—be able, if asked, to justify their own speech acts. What she disputes is the idea that agreement follows necessarily from our acceptance of certain arguments and principles of argumentation. Arendt takes up Kant's insight that we can well follow and even accept the arguments brought to defend a judgment without having to accept the conclusion. Disagreement—even deep disagreement—is possible, although neither side is making a mistake or failing to grasp that a particular judgment is well supported. This sounds strange because we are so accustomed to thinking that agreement in conclusions follows from agreement in premises and procedures, follows in such a way that anyone who accepted the premises and procedures but not the conclusion is either making a mistake or is mentally deficient. And in the case of judgments in which we apply concepts, this is more or less the case.

But the poet who judges his poem beautiful, contrary to the judgments of his audience, may accept their criticisms based on the conventions (for example, rhyme, meter, and so on) of poetry—yet stubbornly hold to his view (*CJ*, §32, p. 145). The signers of the 1848 *Declaration of Sentiments,* who judge men and women to be created equal, contrary to the judgments of the American Founding Fathers and most nineteenth-century Americans, may well accept the criticism that men and women are different by nature—yet stubbornly hold to their view. What we hold to in the face of the apparent contradiction between these moments of agreement is neither illogical nor irrational, but rather values that have not yet found expression in the sense of a determinate concept. To anticipate the argument that follows, what we hold to in aesthetic judgments and political judgments alike (as the claim to gender *equality* suggests) is not necessarily something that is irreducibly nonconceptual (as Jean François Lyotard, in his preference for the Kantian sublime, argues).[30] Rather, we hold to an imaginative extension of a concept beyond its ordinary use in cognitive judgments and affirm freedom. Whether we eventually abandon a judgment on the basis of sharpening our own power of reflective judgment (as Kant's poet does) or hold to it in the face of a world that declared us scandalous (as the signers of the *Declaration* did), we must judge for ourselves and try to persuade others of our views. This involves an imagi-

[30]Jean-François Lyotard, *Lessons on the Analytic of the Sublime (Kant's "Critique of Judgment," §§23–29),* trans. Elizabeth Rottenberg (Stanford, CA: Stanford University Press, 1994). Lyotard finds in Kantian judgments of taste a resistance to reaching consensus through the giving of proofs. Although this is correct, Lyotard tends to exclude the possibility of coming to any agreement whatsoever. He thus turns to the aesthetic of the sublime, in which the faculties of imagination and reason are caught in a *Wiederstreit,* a quarrel with no possible resolution.

native "exhibition of the concept [for example, of equality]," to speak with Kant, that "expands the concept itself in an unlimited way" (*CJ*, §49, p. 183).

This ability to persuade others of one's views does not depend on facility in logic. One may well have the so-called force of the better argument and fail to convince one's interlocutors (and not because they lack competence, that is, fail to understand what a good argument is). The ability to persuade depends upon the capacity to elicit criteria that speak to the particular case at hand and in relation to particular interlocutors. It is a rhetorical ability, fundamentally creative and imaginative, to project a word like *beautiful* or a phrase like *created equal* into a new context in ways that others can accept, not because they (necessarily) already agree with the projection (or would have to agree if they are thinking properly), but because they are brought to see something new, a different way of framing their responses to certain objects and events. Arguments are put forward like the *examples* that Kant holds to be the irreducible "go-carts" of an aesthetic judgment: they *exhibit* connections that cannot be rationally deduced from given premises. If an argument has "force," it is more as the vehicle of an imaginative "seeing" (to stay with Arendt's language) than an irrefutable logic. And its force is never separable from the person making the judgment and the context into which she speaks. There can no more be *the* final or conclusive argument for the equality of the sexes than there can be *the* final or conclusive argument for the beautiful. Every political or aesthetic argument must be articulated in relation to a set of particulars that vary according to time and place and appeal to what we have in common.

Sensus communis

Citing Kant, Arendt emphasizes that judgments of taste, far from being merely subjective (*de gustibus non disputandum est*), have "subjective validity," which entails "an anticipated communication with others with whom I know I must finally come to some agreement" (*CC*, pp. 220–221; *CJ*, §18–22). This anticipated agreement relies on common sense or *sensus communis*, "the very opposite of 'private feelings'" (*CC*, p. 222). "Common sense," she writes,

> discloses to us the nature of the world insofar as it is a common world; we owe to it the fact that our strictly private and 'subjective' five senses and their sensory data can adjust themselves to a non-subjective and 'objective' world which we have in common and share with others. (*CC*, p. 221)

Appeal to the *sensus communis* is not striving for agreement with a community's norms. Like Kant, Arendt recognizes that empirical communities can be deeply flawed in their judgments.[31] Furthermore, to judge according to the common understanding of a given community is, says Kant, "to judge not by feeling but always by concepts, even though these concepts are usually only principles conceived obscurely" (*CJ*, §20, p. 87). For Kant, however, what makes concepts obscure is itself connected to feeling: it is none other than rhetoric, which, in *Critique of Judgment,* he accuses of being a perfect cheat and of "merit[ing] no respect whatsoever." Rhetoric stands accused of being "the art of transacting a serious business of the understanding as if it were a free play of the imagination." As Robert Dostal observes, "it is just this play of imagination that Arendt wishes to affirm." In contrast to Kant, for whom the *ars oratoria,* "insofar as this is taken to mean the art of persuasion," deceives us by means of a "beautiful illusion" and makes our "judgments unfree," writes Dostal, Arendt affirms that "the rhetorical arguments of our fellow spectators free us."[32] Rhetoric understood as a quotidian practice of public speech is, for Arendt, the condition of our freedom; it opens up the world to us in new ways. That opening up is dependent on the faculty of imagination, a faculty that Arendt's critics generally want to keep under the control of reason and the understanding, lest imagination lead us astray with the rhetoricians who disguise opinions as truths.

To appreciate the imaginative character of rhetoric we need to recognize that, when we appeal to the *sensus communis,* we are not appealing to a fixed set of opinions but to what is communicable. Far from guaranteeing agreement in advance, *sensus communis* allows differences of perspective to emerge and become visible. *Sensus communis* is not a static concept

---

[31]Kant excludes community standards as the basis for judgment.

[W]henever a subject offers a judgment as proof of his taste [concerning some object], we demand that he judge for himself; he should not have to grope about among other people's judgments. [...] [T]o make other people's judgments the basis determining one's own would be heteronomy. (Kant, *CJ*, §32, pp. 145–6)

This is the basis for Hans-George Gadamer's controversial claim that the Kantian *sensus communis* marks an unfortunate departure from the tradition of Cicero, Vico, and Shaftesbury, for whom common sense is a way of knowing based in the moral and civic community. Hans-George Gadamer, *Truth and Method,* trans. Joel Weinsheimer and Donald G. Marshall (New York: Continuum, 1989), pt. 1, chap. 2. See also Ernesto Grassi, "The Priority of Common Sense and Imagination: Vico's Philosophical Relevance Today," *Social Research* 43 (1976): 553–80; quotation is from p. 560. For a critique of the Gadamerian view, see Lyotard, *Lessons.* Arendt's compressed discussion in *LKPP* (pp. 70–72) understands common sense neither as an a priori principle (Kant) nor as a communal mode of knowledge (Gadamer), but simply as a way of marking what is public and communicable rather than private.

[32]Kant quoted in Robert J. Dostal, "Judging Human Action," *Judgment, Imagination, and Politics: Themes from Kant and Arendt,* ed. by Ronald Beiner and Jennifer Nedlesky (Boston: Rowman & Littlefield, 200I), 139–64; quotation is from p. 154. Dostal accuses Arendt of losing sight of the importance of rationality in Kant's thought.

grounded in eternal truths but a creative force that generates our sense of reality. It is based in the figurative power of language, hence subject to change. *Sensus communis,* as Grassi (following Vico and Cicero) writes, "lies outside the rational process, within the sphere of ingenuity, so that it assumes an inventive character";[33] it is based on "the activity of *ingenium* [which] consists in catching sight of relationships or *similitudines* among things" (*RP,* p. 8). These relationships are external to their terms: they are not given in the things themselves, but are a creation. They are

> never eternally valid, never absolutely 'true', because they always emerge within limited situations bound in space and time; i.e., they are probable and seem to be true [*verisimile*], true only within the confines of 'here' and 'now', in which the needs and problems that confront human beings are met. (*RP,* p. 10)

Through this ingenious activity, writes Grassi, "we surpass what lies before us in sensory awareness" (*RP,* p. 8). By contrast with the deductive activity of logical reasoning, which "must restrict itself to finding what already is contained in the premises" (*RP,* p. 97), ingenium is the art of invention. The creative discovery of relationships among appearances that have no logical connection, it is an exercise of radical imagination.

The imagination at work in judging without a concept is much more than the faculty of re-presentation, making present what is absent, which is "the reproductive imagination" in Kant. In the third *Critique,* Kant emphasizes not the reproductive power of imagination but its productive or generative power:

> [I]n a judgment of taste the imagination must be considered in its freedom. This implies, first of all, that this power is here not taken as reproductive, where it is subject to the laws of association, but as productive and spontaneous (as the originator of chosen forms of intuition). (*CJ,* "General Comment on the First Division of the Analytic," p. 91)

Arendt's account of judgment does not explore Kant's account of imagination as a generative force (which she associates strictly with genius and the creation of new aesthetic objects of judgment). Nevertheless, she clearly sees that imagination is crucial for breaking the boundaries of identity-based experience: taking account of plurality and affirming freedom. Accordingly, Arendt declares imagination (rather than reason or understanding) the political faculty par excellence—once again, much to the dismay of her critics—but she never explains why foregrounding imagination is crucial

---

[33]Grassi, "The Priority of Common Sense and Imagination,' 565.

to her own account of political judgment as a non-rule-governed practice. If imagination were only reproductive, it would fall under the law of the understanding, as it does in cognitive judgments, rather than be in free play, as it is in aesthetic judgments. This failure to specify the productive character of imagination in aesthetic and political judgments has consequences for how we understand Arendt's famous account of "representative thinking."

Political imagination (or "being and thinking in my own identity where actually I am not")

We have seen that Arendt refigures the validity that is appropriate to democratic politics as unthinkable apart from plurality. For her critics, validity obtains when impartiality is achieved through the discursive adjudication of rationality claims, that is, the separation of particular from general interests. Consequently, impartiality obtains when opinions and judgments are purified of interests that are strictly private—but what remains is a form of interest nonetheless, only now this interest is said to be rational and universal in a nontranscendental sense. Although Arendt, too, holds impartiality to be the condition of a properly political opinion or judgment, what she understands by impartiality is akin to what Kant means when he says that concepts cannot play any role in an aesthetic judgment because they refer to objects and introduce interest, that is, the pleasure or liking "we connect with the presentation of an object's existence." This interest is related to the object's purpose, its ability to serve an end: "interest here refers to usefulness," observes Arendt (*LKPP*, p. 94). Concepts are to be excluded, according to Kant, because they entangle aesthetic—Arendt would say political—judgments in an economy of use and the causal nexus.[34] The "inability to think and judge a thing apart from its function or utility," writes Arendt, indicates a "utilitarian mentality" and "philistinism." She continues,

> And the Greeks rightly suspected that this philistinism threatens [...] the political realm [...] because it will judge action by the same standards of utility which are valid for fabrication, demand that action obtain a

[34]The task of aesthetic and teleological judgment, as Kant explains, is to judge without a concept and thus the notion of a "purpose" (end [*Zweck*]). But judgment is only possible if we assume that nature has an order that we can discern and could potentially cognize, hence a purposiveness (finality [*Zweckmässigkeit*]). Thus aesthetic judgments have "finality without an end" or "purposiveness without a purpose" (*Zweckmässigkeit ohne Zweck*).

> pre-determined end and that it be permitted to seize on all means likely to further this end. (*CC*, p. 216)

For Arendt, who held means-ends thinking to be a denial of the freedom exhibited in action and speech, the introduction of interests, be they private or general, introduces the instrumentalist attitude. If her critics cannot think the idea of disinterestedness in terms other than objective validity, it is because they are not centrally concerned, as she is, with the problem of freedom, and thus never see any need to relinquish the object as ground zero of every judgment. The relation among subjects is, for them, mediated through objects and thus through the exercise of reason and the faculty of the understanding and its application of concepts.

As no concept determines the formation of opinion according to Arendt, such formation cannot entail—not in the first place—the subject's relation to the object, which defines cognitive judgments. Rather, the relation to the object is mediated through the subject's relation to the standpoints of other subjects or, more precisely, by taking the viewpoints of others on the same object into account. Arendt describes this intersubjective relation as "representative thinking":

> I form an opinion by considering a given issue from different viewpoints, by making present to my mind the standpoints of those who are absent; that is, I represent them. This process of representation does not blindly adopt the actual views of those who stand somewhere else, and hence look upon the world from a different perspective; this is a question neither of empathy, as though I tried to be or to feel like somebody else, nor of counting noses and joining a majority but of being and thinking in my own identity where actually I am not. The more people's standpoints I have present in my mind while I am pondering a given issue, and the better I can imagine how I would feel and think if I were in their place, the stronger will be my capacity for representative thinking and the more valid my final conclusions, my opinion.[35]

The Kantian name for representative thinking, says Arendt, is "enlarged mentality" (*CC*, p. 220) or, more exactly, an enlarged manner of thinking (*eine erweiterte Denkungsart*) whose condition of possibility is not the faculty of understanding, but imagination.[36] This faculty, at work in

---

[35] Hannah Arendt, "Truth and Politics," *Between Past and Future: Eight Exercises in Political Thought* (New York: Penguin, 1993), 227–64; quotation is from p. 241.

[36] This process is the "enlargement of the mind," in which "we compare our judgment not so much with the actual as rather with the merely possible judgments of others, and [thus] put ourselves in the position of everyone else" (Kant, *CJ*, §40, p. 160). Like Kant, Arendt does not exclude the role that the actual judgments of other people might play in our own. But

seeing from the standpoints of other people, keeps enlarged thought from becoming either an enlarged empathy or the majority opinion. Imagination is a means, writes Arendt,

> to see things in their proper perspective, to be strong enough to put that which is too close at a certain distance so that we can see and understand it without bias and prejudice, to be generous enough to bridge abysses of remoteness until we can see and understand everything that is too far away from us as though it were our own affair.[37]

Imagination mediates: it moves neither above perspectives, as if they were something to transcend in the name of pure objectivity, nor at the same level as those perspectives, as if they were identities in need of our recognition. Rather, imagination enables "being and thinking in my own identity where actually I am not."

To unpack this curious formulation of enlarged thinking let us consider the special art upon which it is based, what Arendt calls "training the imagination to go visiting" (*LKPP*, p. 43). Commenting on this art of imaginatively occupying the standpoints of other people, Iris Marion Young argues that it assumes a reversibility in social positions that denies structured relations of power and ultimately difference. "Dialogue participants are able to take account of the perspective of others because they have heard those perspectives expressed," writes Young, not because "the person judging imagines what the world looks like from other perspectives."[38] Likewise, Lisa Disch is critical of the notion that

> a single person can imaginatively anticipate each one of the different perspectives that are relevant to a situation. It is this presupposition that reproduces an aspect of [the very] empathy [Arendt otherwise rejects in her account of representative thinking]; it effects an erasure of difference.[39]

Both Young and Disch agree, then, that the idea of enlarged thought must be based in *actual* dialogue, not *imaginative* dialogue. This "*actual* dialogue between *real* (rather than hypothetical) interlocutors," as Beiner writes, sets the parameters for the kind of validity or universality that is proper

---

neither does she dispute his claim that enlarged thought is not based on re-presenting to oneself opinions one has heard or of transposing oneself into the place of another person. *See LKPP*, 43.

[37]Arendt, "Understanding and Politics," 323.

[38]Iris Marion Young, "Asymmetrical Reciprocity: On Moral Respect, Wonder, and Enlarged Thought," *Judgment, Imagination, and Politics,* ed. by Ronald Beiner and Jennifer Nedelsky (New York: Rowman & Littlefield, 2001), 205–28; quotation is from p. 225.

[39]Disch, *Hannah Arendt and the Limits of Philosophy,* 168.

to political judgment and whose condition is common sense.[40] We could qualify this critique and say that imagination is no substitute for hearing other perspectives but nonetheless necessary because, empirically speaking, we cannot possibly hear all relevant perspectives. To do so, however, would be to accept the conception of imagination implicit in the critique, namely, that this faculty is at best a stand-in for real objects, including the actual opinions of other people, and at worst a distortion of those objects, in accordance with the interests of the subject exercising imagination.[41]

In contrast with the emphasis on actual dialogue and an "interpersonal relationship" (centered on mutual understanding or recognition) in a "discourse ethics," Arendt's invokes imagination to develop reference to a third perspective from which one observes and attempts to see from other standpoints, but at a distance. Arendt does not discount the importance of actual dialogue anymore than did Kant, but, again like Kant, she emphasizes the unique position of *outsideness* from which we judge. It is this third perspective that Arendt had in mind when she said that imaginative visiting involves not the mutual understanding of "one another as individual persons" but the understanding that involves coming to "see the same world from one another's standpoint, to see the same in very different and frequently opposing aspects." At stake is the difference between understanding another *person* and understanding the *world*, the world not as an object we cognize but "the space in which things become public," as Arendt says.[42]

For Arendt, the kind of understanding made possible by exercising imagination concerns our ability to see objects and events outside the

---

[40]Ronald Beiner, "Rereading Hannah Arendt's Kant Lectures," *Judgment, Imagination, and Politics: Themes from Kant and Arendt*, ed. by Ronald Beiner and Jennifer Nedlesky (Boston: Rowman & Littlefield, 2001), 91–102; quotation is from p. 97. Beiner, Young, and Disch share the view that Arendt was mistaken to turn to Kant, for she is really interested in empirical sociability as the basis for judgment and he is not. I find it misleading to ascribe to Arendt an empirical conception of *sensus communis*, as if the universal voice were the result of a vote, and it is conversely misleading to assert that, for Kant's transcendental conception of *sensus communis*, nothing empirical matters. Kant makes numerous gestures toward the actual social practices of judgment, not to dismiss these as totally irrelevant to what an aesthetic judgment is, but to discern the existence of our mutual attunement.

[41]This limited view of imagination as empirical and reproductive is tied to certain suppositions about the status of normative political claims and the kind of rationality that is proper to politics, both of which are central to Habermas's discourse ethics: (1) that political claims are cognitive and can be treated like claims to truth; and (2) that the justification of claims requires that speakers engage in an actual practice of argumentative justification. Even defenders of Arendt's noncognitive account of political judgment against Habermas's charge of incoherence (e.g., Lisa Disch) take for granted (2) because they never really find a way to counter (1), beholden as they are to the validity problematic that defines our understanding of politics.

[42]Hannah Arendt, "What Remains? The Language Remains," *Essays in Understanding, 1930–1954*, ed. by Jerome Kohn (New York: Harcourt Brace, 1994), 1–23; quotation is from p. 20.

economy of use and the causal nexus. "Being and thinking in my own identity where actually I am not" is the position achieved not when, understanding another person (as in a discourse ethics), I yield my private to the general interest, but when I look at the world from multiple standpoints (not identity positions) to which I am always something of an outsider and also something of an outsider to my self as an acting being.[43] This is the position of the spectator that Arendt describes in her Kant lectures. The spectator is the one who, through the use of imagination, can reflect on the whole in a disinterested manner, that is, a manner free not simply from private interest but also from interest *tout court,* which is to say from any standard of utility whatsoever. Were the imagination merely reproductive and concept-governed, however (as Arendt herself seems to assume or at least never questions), it might be possible to attain the kind of impartiality that Arendt's readers associate with the position of the spectator, namely, the impartiality of the general interest. But would one be poised to apprehend objects and events outside the economy of use and the causal nexus—to apprehend them in their freedom?

Being so poised Kant could express enthusiasm about the world-historical event of the French Revolution, though from the standpoint of a moral acting being, Kant said, he would have to condemn it. From the standpoint of the spectator, however, he could find in this event "signs" of progress. These "signs of history" are not facts to be presented by the reproductive imagination in accordance with the understanding and judged according to a rule of cognition. Rather, David Carroll observes, such signs "have as their referent the future which they in some sense anticipate but can in no way be considered to determine."[44] The French Revolution does not provide cognitive confirmation for the spectator that mankind is progressing; it inspires "hope," as Arendt writes, by "opening up new horizons for the future" (*LKPP,* p. 56). A world-historical event, the Revolution indicated what cannot be known, but must be exhibited, presented: human freedom.

The freedom-affirming position of the spectator "does not tell one how *to act,*" writes Arendt of Kant's enthusiasm (*LKPP,* p. 44). What one sees from this impartial standpoint, then, is not the general interest or anything that could be considered a guide to political action or further judgment. The judgment of the spectator is in no way connected with an end. Indeed, "even if the end viewed in connection with this event [the French Revolution] should not now be attained, even if the revolution or reform of a national constitution should finally miscarry," says Arendt

[43]For Habermas, the perspective of the third installs the objectification typical of the philosophy of consciousness. Habermas, *The Philosophical Discourse of Modernity,* 297.

[44]David Carroll, "Rephrasing the Political with Kant and Lyotard: From Aesthetic to Political Judgments," *Diacritics* 14, no. 3 (Autumn 1984): 73–88; quotation is from p. 82.

citing Kant, nothing can destroy the hope that the event inspired (*LKPP*, p. 46). For a new event, from the perspective of the spectator poised to apprehend it in its freedom, is not a means toward an empirical end of any kind, and thus the validity of the judgment in no way turns on the realization of an end. Validity is rather tied to an affirmation of freedom that expands the very peculiar kind of objectivity that Arendt associates with the political sphere, namely, the objectivity or sense of reality that turns on seeing an object or event from as many sides as possible. Like "the highest form of objectivity" that arose when Homer, setting aside the judgment of History, sang the praise of both the Greeks and the Trojans, so does Kant's judgment of the French Revolution expand our sense of the real, for it refuses to judge on the basis of victory and defeat, of any interest or end whatsoever.

The judgment that at once expands our sense of reality and affirms freedom is possible only once the faculties are "in free play," as Kant puts it. Only where the imagination is not restrained by a concept (given by the understanding) or the moral law (given by reason) can such a judgment come to pass. And the French Revolution was for Kant a world-historical event for which we have no rule of cognition. In free play, the imagination is no longer in the service of the application of concepts. But the application of a concept was not the task Kant had in mind when he expressed enthusiasm for the French Revolution, which provided no concepts and no maxim for acting whatsoever. To judge objects and events in their freedom expands our sense of community, not because it tells us what is morally or politically justified and thus what we should do, but because it expands our sense of what is real or communicable.

Judging creates political space

Judging is a way of constructing and discovering community and its limits, but this does not mean that it would or ought to translate into a blueprint for political action. That judgment need not provide a guide for action and, in fact, may even be at radical odds with any maxim for action—as it was in Kant's enthusiasm for the French Revolution—is crucial to Arendt's claim that the spectator position is one from which we are able to see the whole without the mediation of a concept based on the presence of an interest. Contra what critics like Beiner claim, Arendt in no way turns her back on the *vita active* or denies the importance of judging for politics. Rather, she refuses to define this activity in terms of the production of a normative basis for political action.[45] Spectators do not produce judgments

[45]Beiner, "Interpretive Essay," 92–3. Beiner argues that Arendt's earliest writings on judgment

that ought then serve as *principles* for action or for other judgments; they create the *space* in which the objects of political judgment, the actors and actions themselves, can appear, and thus alter our sense of what belongs in the common world.

If the world is the space in which things become public, then judging is a practice that alters what we will count as such. In this space, created by judging, the objects of judgment appear. She writes,

> [T]he judgment of the spectator creates the space without which no such objects could appear at all. The public realm is constituted by the critics and the spectators, not the actors and the makers. And this critic and spectator sits in every actor. (*LKPP,* p. 63)

"Spectator" is not another person, but simply a different mode of relating to, or being in, the common world. This shift in emphasis amounts to a Copernican turn in the relationship of action to judgment: without the judging spectators and the artifacts of judgment (for example, narratives and stories), action would have no meaning, it would vanish without a trace—it would not be a world-building activity. Arendt attributes this turn to Kant, but it is Hannah Arendt herself who discovers, in her idiosyncratic reading of Kant, that it is the judging activity of the spectators, not the object they judge or its maker, that creates the public space.

Calling our attention to the activity of judging as formative of the public realm, Arendt emphasizes what aesthetic theory calls practices of reception. But she seems to discount the potentially transformative and generative contribution of the object of judgment itself, as well as the creative activity of the artist, actor, or maker. By contrast with Arendt, Kant emphasizes not only the spectators but also the role of the artist and the formative power of creative imagination, the ability to present objects in new, unfamiliar ways—what he calls "genius." In his discussion of "aesthetic ideas" Kant describes the imagination as "very mighty when it creates, as it were, another nature out of the material that actual nature gives it" (*CJ,* §49, p. 182). Indeed, "we may even restructure experience" and

> [i]n this process *we feel our freedom* from the law of association (which attaches to the empirical [i.e., reproductive]) use of the imagination; for although it is under that law that nature lends us material, yet we can process that material into something quite different, namely, into something that surpasses nature. (Ibid., emphasis added)

(e.g., "The Crisis in Culture" and "Truth and Politics") reflect her concern with the actual dialogic activity of judging citizens. In her later work, Arendt describes a solitary judging subject, who "weighs the possible judgments of an imagined Other, not the actual judgments of real interlocutors" (ibid., 92).

This faculty of presentation is that which "prompts so much thought, but to which no determinate thought whatsoever, i.e., no [determinate] *concept*, can be adequate, so that no language can express it completely and allow us to grasp it" (ibid.). Such aesthetic presentations "strive toward something that lies beyond the bounds of experience" (hence they are called "aesthetic ideas" and are the counterpart of "rational ideas"), but they are presentations nonetheless. The faculty of presentation at work in the exhibition of aesthetic ideas, Kant writes, "expands the concept itself in an unlimited way" (*CJ*, §49). The imagination can work on or order material in such a way that we are able to create out of it noncausal associations and even a new nature. If concepts themselves are not so much excluded as expanded in an indefinite way, this has important consequences for how we think about our own political (Arendt) or aesthetic (Kant) activity.

We might ask whether this concept-transforming activity of the imagination is confined to the activity of genius. Although Kant inclines to cast taste as the faculty that "clips its [genius'] wings," bringing it in line with what is communicable (what others can follow and assent to), he also argues that the spectator, too (including the spectator that exists in every actor or artist), is called upon to exert imagination in trying to comprehend a work. In this way, then, our sense of what is communicable is not static but dynamic. The imagination is, after all, "in free play" when we judge reflectivity, not only when we create new objects of judgment. If Arendt associates the faculty of productive imagination exclusively with genius, applauding Kant's subordination of genius to taste, that may be because she was determined to emphasize the importance of plurality in judging. In contrast with the solitary genius, "spectators exist only in the plural" (*LKPP*, p. 63), as she claimed, and the need to take account of plurality, of other views, is what distinguishes a political or aesthetic judgment from a logical or cognitive one. Arendt was concerned with the creation of the public, the space in which objects of judgment appear.

But of course a text like the 1848 *Declaration of Sentiments* puts forward at once a collective judgment, which has been reached individually by each of its signers, and an imaginative "object," which not only serves as the occasion for future judgments, but also stimulates the imagination of judging spectators and expands their sense of what is communicable, what they will count as part of the common world. Like a work of art, such a document is potentially defamiliarizing: working with what is communicable (for example, the idea, put forward in the *Declaration of Independence*, that all men are created equal), it expands our sense of what we can communicate. Positing the agreement of all ("We hold these truths to be self-evident"), such a document creatively (re)presents the concept of equality in a way that, to cite Kant on productive imagination again, "quickens the mind by opening up for it a view" (*CJ*, §49), which is excluded by every logical presentation of the concept of equality.

We miss this creative expansion of the concept whenever we talk about the logical extension of something like equality or rights. The original concept of political equality, after all, is a determinate concept, historically constituted in relation to white, propertied male citizens. The *Declaration of Sentiments* did not simply apply this concept like a rule to a new particular (women). Rather, it exhibited the idea of equality much like an aesthetic idea: "a presentation of the imagination which prompts much thought, but to which ... no [determinate] *concept,* can be adequate," to cite Kant again. Thus the "thought" that such a presentation "prompts" always exceeds the terms of the concept; "it expands the concept itself in an unlimited way." This expansion is not logical—the concept of equality does not contain within itself the mechanism for its own extension to disenfranchised groups—but imaginative: we create new relations between things that have none (for example, between the concept of equality and the relations between the sexes, or between the rights of man and the sexual division of labor). Every extension of a political concept always involves an imaginative opening up of the world that allows us to see and articulate relations between things that have none (in any necessary, logical sense), to create relations that are external to their terms. Political relations are always external to their terms: they involve not so much the ability to subsume particulars under concepts, but an imaginative element, the ability to see or to forge new connections.

Calling attention to this creative expansion of our concepts, I want to suggest an alternative not only to Habermas's cognitivist dismissal of the third *Critique* as relevant to political community but also to Lyotard's celebration of the Kantian sublime as a critical response to Habermas: the affirmation of a *differend* or *Wiederstreit,* that is, a conflict that permits no resolution whatsoever. It is important to stress the impossibility of achieving permanent resolution of any conflict we would call political; but Lyotard's reading tends to foreclose any possibility of a politically mediated agreement about community whatsoever. Lyotard excludes more than the *disputieren* that Habermas endorses in a politics oriented toward mutual understanding (i.e., the exchange of proofs). He excludes as well the kind of agreement peculiar to democratic politics, namely, the *übereinkommen* that can be reached through *streiten* as persuading speech. Indeed, what for Arendt is the contingent achievement of this interlocution (i.e., the constitution of community through shared judgments) is for Lyotard just one more dangerous illusion of "empirical realism."[46]

Lyotard sees something crucially important that Arendt's other critics miss: the imagination, considered in its freedom, opens a *question* of

[46]Lyotard, *Lessons,* 18. For a similar critique, see David Carroll, "Community after Devastation: Culture, Politics, and the 'Public Space'," *Politics, Theory, and Contemporary Culture,* ed. by Mark Poster (New York: Columbia University Press, 1993), 159–196.

community that cannot be settled by a practice of politics centered on the exchange of proofs, for such a practice tends to conceal how we misunderstand precisely at those moments when we understand and also occlude from view the source of the misunderstanding. But Lyotard offers little in the way of an alternative conception of community, other than saying that it is always in process, always anticipated but never reached. This is a familiar idea taken up by many political theorists after identity politics. Although we should remain critically vigilant about the exclusions that constitute community, the question remains as to how a more democratic community based in practices of freedom might be formed. On what basis are we in community with others and what role is played by judgments that affirm freedom in the creation of community?

Conclusion

I began this essay with Habermas's claim that Arendt excludes the role of argument in the political realm. Grassi showed us that rational speech rests on rhetorical, ungrounded premises, and Cavell showed us that aesthetic judgments are arguable in certain ways—what Kant called *streiten*. Emphasizing *streiten* over *disputieren* as the interlocution appropriate to politics, I agreed with Lyotard when he questioned the idea that is central to communicative theories of the political such as liberalism: all conflicts are in principle resolvable so long as they put forward rational arguments that obey the rules of conceptual logic and the giving of proofs. The idea that one can dispute different points of view in this way occludes the question of what could possibly count as proof of an empirical concept. Proofs fail in the absence of the shared premises from which they are deduced.

Rejecting a consensus won by proofs, Arendt neither denies the place of argument in the political realm (as Habermas contended) nor excludes the possibility of reaching agreement (as Lyotard would have us do). Her point is not that political judgments must eschew all cognitive claims. It is rather, to paraphrase Cavell, to remind us that our relation to others and to the world is based on something other than knowing. "Knowledge is based on acknowledgment," observes Wittgenstein, that is, on a mode of counting something as something, which is the condition of knowledge, but also doing something in relation to what one knows (for example, taking account of plurality). To say, for example, that a political issue like gay marriage calls for our judgment is not to foreclose cognitive questions. It is rather to say that a cognitive judgment of a thing's existence (i.e., its function or purpose or ability to satisfy an end or a use) is not what we are being called upon to make, any more than a botanist, as Kant says, is called upon to explain the flower as a reproductive organ of a plant when he declares the flower beautiful (*CJ* §16, p. 76). One can well know such things about plants, just as one can well know certain things about nonheterosexual practices. To judge aesthetically or politically, however, requires that we count what we know differently, count the flower as beautiful quite apart from its use, count nonheteronormative sexual practices as part of the common world, quite apart from whatever social function they might serve. Contrary to her critics' charge, Arendt's critique of cognitive claims in the political realm was not: never make a cognitive judgment when you judge politically; it was: do not confuse a cognitive judgment for judging politically. Something else is required, for a political judgment reveals not some property of the object but something of political significance about the one who makes it—"*who* one is."

We can judge without a concept, exactly as Arendt held, because we are not limited to *disputieren* (i.e., agreement on the basis of proofs from established premises); we can create new forms or figures with which to make sense of objects and events. And we can argue about the meaning of those objects and events without declaring a *Wiederstreit*. In this process of judging reflectively we refuse to limit ourselves to proofs based on concepts and instead alter our sense of what is common or shared: we alter the world, the space in which things become public. With time, the forms and figures given by the reflective judgment, too, become ossified as rules that, in turn, too, demand the response of imagination to break up the closure of rule-governed practices. Like Kant, Arendt emphasizes judging as an activity, not judgments as the result of an activity, judgments that, being valid for all, could be extended beyond the activity of judging subjects and applied in rule-like fashion by other subjects.

What we affirm in a political judgment is experienced not as a cognitive commitment to a set of rationally agreed upon precepts (as they are encoded in, say, a constitution—though it *can* be experienced as that too) but as pleasure, as shared sensibility. "We feel our freedom," as Kant put it, when we judge aesthetically or, as Arendt shows, politically. If the pleasure that obtains in a judgment arises not out of the immediate apprehension of an object but out of reflection (that is, it arises in relation to nothing other than the judgment itself), then we are thrown back on ourselves and our own practice: we take pleasure in what we hold (e.g., that these truths are self-evident). *What gives us pleasure is how we judge, that is to say, that we judge objects and events in their freedom.* We don't have to hold these truths to be self-evident any more than we have to hold men and women equal or the rose beautiful; nothing compels us. There is nothing necessary in what we hold. That we do so hold is an expression of our freedom. In the judgment, we affirm our freedom and discover the nature and limits of what we hold in common. This is the simple but crucial lesson to be learned from Arendt's account of political judgment.

Linda M. G. Zerilli is professor of political science at the University of Chicago. She is the author of Signifying Woman: Culture and Chaos in Rousseau, Burke and Mill *(Cornell University Press, 1994) and* Feminism and the Abyss of Freedom *(University of Chicago Press, 2005)*; and Toward a Democratic Theory and Judgment *(University of Chicago Press, forthcoming 2014).*

CHAPTER THREE

Arendt, aesthetics, and "The Crisis in Culture"

Patchen Markell
University of Chicago

Hannah Arendt made many aesthetic turns, but it is tempting to say all of them were variations on a single thought: that by appealing to the autonomy of aesthetic experience, she could explain and defend the analogous purity of the political. In *The Human Condition*, for instance, Arendt characterized action, the "political activity *par excellence*,"[1] in the language of dramatic performance, and she insisted that genuine action must be unconstrained by extra-political considerations, including—and especially—moral rules. This was a stance whose echo of scandalous *fin-de-siècle* aestheticism Martin Jay has captured in the slogan "*la politique pour la politique*."[2] Yet if some readers found *The Human Condition*'s political aestheticism dangerous in its disregard for action's consequences,[3] others pointed out that this was not her last word. After 1958, the story goes, as Arendt shifted her attention from action to spectatorship, she rethought

---

[1]Arendt, H. (1958), *The Human Condition*. Chicago: University of Chicago Press, p. 9. (Hereafter *HC*)

[2]Jay, M. (2005), *Songs of Experience: Modern American and European Variations on a Universal Theme*. Berkeley: University of California Press, 176. See also Jay, M. (Spring 1992), "'The Aesthetic Ideology' as Ideology; or, What Does It Mean to Aestheticize Politics," *Cultural Critique* 21, pp. 41–61.

[3]On Arendt's subordination of morality to aesthetics see Kateb, G. (1983), *Hannah Arendt: Politics, Conscience, Evil*. Totowa, NJ: Rowman and Allanheld, and (2006), *Patriotism and Other Mistakes*. New Haven: Yale University Press, chs. 6–7.

the relation between aesthetics and politics with the help of the sober, respectable Immanuel Kant, whose study of aesthetic judgment in the third *Critique* taught a more widely applicable lesson about how people make judgments "reflectively," when particular cases must be adjudicated without the aid of general rules given in advance. But while Kant may have helped Arendt "tame" *The Human Condition*'s aestheticized conception of action without subordinating politics to morality,[4] her use of Kant has also provoked a different worry about her commitment to the autonomy of the political; namely, that it is as problematically austere—and as ideological—as the doctrine of aesthetic autonomy it parallels, falsely universalizing a specific mode of politics predicated on the exclusion of bodily need and material interest in the same way that Kant himself, in elevating "taste" above mere agreeableness, gave philosophical backing to a specific European high-cultural regime of disinterested sensory perception.[5]

This chapter tells a very different story about Arendt and aesthetics, and particularly about the essay that is usually thought to mark her turn from the supposedly wanton aestheticism of *The Human Condition* to the all-too-refined Kantianism of her later work: "The Crisis in Culture," initially published in 1961 as the concluding chapter to *Between Past and Future*.[6] At first glance, "The Crisis in Culture" looks precisely like a deployment of Kant's aesthetics as part of a staunch defense of high-cultural standards. Its first half intervenes into what was, by the late fifties, a crowded field of controversy over the fate of culture in mass society, and includes a memorable attack on the reduction of culture to entertainment, while its second half contains an extended discussion of the third *Critique*. But this impression is misleading. "The Crisis in Culture" does not represent a turn away from Arendt's earlier work. Instead, it is an extension of her effort—already under way, and already undertaken with reference to Kant, in *The Human Condition*—to articulate a conception of action's autonomy that would nevertheless be capacious and contentful, and that wouldn't

[4]Villa, D. (May 1992), "Beyond Good and Evil: Arendt, Nietzsche, and the Aestheticization of Political Action," *Political Theory* 20, no. 2., p. 292, and Jay, "'Aesthetic Ideology'," p. 56.
[5]For elements of this critique of Arendt's Kantianism see Connolly, W. E. (June 1999), "A Critique of Pure Politics," *Why I Am Not A Secularist*. Minneapolis: University of Minnesota Press, and Klausen, J. C. (June 2010), "Hannah Arendt's Antiprimitivism," *Political Theory* 38, no. 3, esp. pp. 411–16. On the broader concern about Kantian aesthetics see Eagleton, T. (1990), *The Ideology of the Aesthetic*. Oxford: Blackwell, and Bourdieu, P. (1984), *Distinction: A Social Critique of the Judgment of Taste*. Cambridge, MA: Harvard University Press. For an argument that Kant himself aimed to detach aesthetic judgment from social hierarchy (and a treatment of Arendt) see Storey, I. (2012), *The Taste of Politics: Kant's Aesthetics, Judgment, and Belonging in the World*. Ph.D. diss., University of Chicago, 2012, ch. 1.
[6]Arendt, H. (1961), "The Crisis in Culture: Its Social and Its Political Significance," *Between Past and Future: Six Exercises in Political Thought*. New York: Vintage. Hereafter CC. Citations from this essay will include page numbers for the original edition (given first) and the repaginated 2006 Penguin edition.

entail confining the constituent activities of the *vita activa* (labor, work and action) within separate, heavily fortified domains.[7] To this end, rather than invoke Kant to help defend aesthetic purity against the incursions of mass culture, "The Crisis in Culture" joins an idiosyncratic reading of Kant to a pointed *critique* of the impulse toward purification in cultural life and aesthetics; an impulse that, Arendt thought, stifles the beautiful appearances it is meant to protect, and corrodes the power of judgment it is meant to manifest, by converting them into currencies of social status and markers of aesthetic and political righteousness.

In what follows, I make this argument by reconstructing three important contexts for "The Crisis in Culture." The first context is set by Arendt's own earlier writing, and especially by her treatment in *The Human Condition* of the ideas of work and of the work of art. The second context is set by Kant's *Critique of Judgment*, and particularly by a systematic ambiguity in Kant's efforts to spell out the ground of judgments of beauty and to specify their relation to morality. The third and widest context is set by the ongoing disputes about mass culture into which Arendt's essay intervened, especially including the contributions made to those disputes, sometimes with reference to Kant, by two of Arendt's acquaintances in the New York intellectual world, Clement Greenberg and Harold Rosenberg. Read in these contexts, "The Crisis in Culture" shows us how Arendt—originally as suspicious of Kant's aesthetics as she was of his moral philosophy—found a way to mobilize certain aspects of the third *Critique* against the problematic effects that appeals to taste could generate, including the reinforcement of hierarchical distinctions between "high" and "low" culture, the austere separation of beauty from use, the conversion of aesthetic judgment into the province of experts, and the deployment of settled bodies of aesthetic opinion as weapons in ideological battles.

1

We usually think of Arendt's interest in Kant's aesthetics as a development that postdates her work on *The Human Condition*. As Ronald Beiner observes, her earliest extended discussions of Kant's third *Critique* appear in the essays "Freedom and Politics" and "The Crisis in Culture," both published in English in 1961, three years after the appearance of *The Human Condition*.[8] Yet the gap is not quite as wide as it first appears. The

---

[7] I develop this reading of *HC* in Markell, P. (Winter 2011), "Arendt's Work: On the Architecture of *The Human Condition*," *College Literature* 38, no. 1, pp. 15–44.

[8] Beiner, R. ed. (1982), "Interpretive Essay," in Hannah Arendt, *Lectures on Kant's Political Philosophy*. Chicago: University of Chicago Press, pp. 101, 166 note 30.

earliest versions of these essays were presented as lectures in Europe in the spring and summer of 1958, as *The Human Condition* was rolling off the presses.[9] Moreover, Arendt's correspondence and notebooks indicate that her engagement with Kant in these essays grew out of her reading of Karl Jaspers's *Die Großen Philosophen,* and Kant's third *Critique*—which she apparently already thought of as an old favorite—in August of 1957, just after she delivered the final manuscript of *The Human Condition* to the University of Chicago Press.[10] The remarkable proximity of Arendt's Kantian turn to her completion of *The Human Condition* makes it hard to think of her interest in Kant as representing a dramatic reassessment of that book's stance; and while Arendt may well have picked up Jaspers and Kant with relief at being able to pursue fresh subjects, she was in any case drawn by her reading back into the problematics of *The Human Condition,* as though following up a loose end in the manuscript she had just finished. (Philip Rahv, at *Partisan Review*, wrote to Arendt that an early version of "The Crisis in Culture" struck him as "perhaps a part of your book that somehow didn't fit in." He was technically wrong, but he was on to something.[11]) The best way to grasp these continuities between the concerns of *The Human Condition* and those of "The Crisis in Culture" is to attend to the small yet crucial role that Kant, and the *Critique of Judgment*, had already played in *The Human Condition* itself.

[9]Arendt, H. (1958), "Freiheit und Politik: Ein Vortrag," *Die Neue Rundschau* 69, no. 4, pp. 670–94 (lecture given in Zürich, May 1958); Arendt, H. (December 1958), "Kultur und Politik," *Merkur* 12, no. 12, pp. 1122–45 (from a conference in Munich, June–July 1958). *CC* is a hybrid of this essay and Arendt's remarks from a summer 1959 conference on mass culture in the Poconos ([Spring 1960], "Society and Culture," *Daedalus* 89, no. 2, pp. 278–87). The former served mostly as Arendt's source for the first half, while the latter served mostly as her source for the second half, though she revised extensively and added several pages' worth of new material throughout. For a new translation of "Kultur und Politik" with editorial annotations see "Culture and Politics," in Arendt, H. (2007), *Reflections on Literature and Culture*, Susannah Young-Ah Gottlieb ed., Stanford: Stanford University Press, pp. 179–202 and pp. 331–3. For bibliographic information see Arendt, H. (1996), *Ich will verstehen: Selbstauskünfte zu Leben und Werk*, Ursula Ludz ed., Munich: Piper.

[10]Arendt sent the manuscript of *HC* to the University of Chicago Press on 5 August 1957 (Hannah Arendt to Alexander Morin, 2 August 1957, University of Chicago Press Records, Special Collections Research Center, The University of Chicago Library, box 39, folder 1). She read *Die Großen Philosophen* almost immediately after this and began the reading of the *Critique of Judgement* that would inform *CC* either contemporaneously with or immediately after Jaspers's book (Hannah Arendt to Karl Jaspers, 29 August 1957, in Arendt, H. and Jaspers, K. (1992), *Correspondence, 1926–1969*, Lotte Köhler and Hans Saner ed., Robert and Rita Kimber trans., New York: Harcourt Brace Jovanovich, pp. 316–19; Arendt, H. (2002), *Denktagebuch, 1950–1973*, Ursula Ludz ed., 2 vols. Munich: Piper, 569 ff. For more on the history of Arendt's reading of Kant, see Marshall, D. (April 2010), "The Origin and Character of Hannah Arendt's Theory of Judgement," *Political Theory* 38, no. 3, pp. 367–93.

[11]Philip Rahv to Hannah Arendt, 7 November 1958, in "Partisan Review, 1944–64," Hannah Arendt Papers, Manuscript Division, Library of Congress, Washington, D.C.

Kant's third *Critique* makes its brief appearance in chapter four of *The Human Condition*, which is devoted to "work," one of the three human activities that together make up what Arendt calls the *vita activa*. Arendt's book has often been read as an effort to clarify the differences among these activities, so that each one can be confined to its own domain and prevented from encroaching on the territory of the others. Elsewhere, I have argued that this "territorial" reading of *The Human Condition* is an oversimplification,[12] but it is true that one of the book's central purposes is to recover what Arendt calls an "unusual" distinction between labor and work; so central in fact, that when Arendt agreed to give the Walgreen Lectures at the University of Chicago, on which *The Human Condition* was based, she initially proposed calling them "The Labor of Our Body and the Work of our Hands."[13] Labor, in Arendt's vocabulary, is the circular process through which human beings meet their physical needs, whereas work involves the production of durable objects that will outlast the activity by which they were fabricated. This durability makes work into the purest expression of the principle of instrumentality – that is, of the categories of means and end—for only in work does the "end" of the activity in the sense of its stopping point coincide with its "end" in the sense of its purpose, and only in work do means and end remain distinct. The products of labor, unlike those of work, are no sooner produced than they "become means again, means of subsistence and reproduction of labor power" (*HC* 143).

In the middle of the chapter however, Arendt introduces a problem: the distinction between means and ends is not as secure in the case of work as it had appeared to be and neither, as a consequence, is the larger distinction between work and labor.[14] The product of work, Arendt now explains, may well be "an end with respect to the means by which it is produced," and it may be "the end of the fabrication process," but "it never becomes, so to speak, an end in itself, at least not as long as it remains an object for use" (*HC* 153). Instead, just as labor's products "become means again" in being consumed, the products of work *also* become means to further ends, whether by being used or by being exchanged for other useful objects. "The trouble with the utility standard inherent in the very activity of fabrication," Arendt concludes, "is that the relationship between means and end on which it relies is very much like a chain whose every end can serve again as a means in some other context. In other words, in a strictly utilitarian

[12]Markell, "Arendt's Work."

[13]Arendt, *HC*, p. 79; Hannah Arendt to Jerome Kerwin, 22 May 1955, Walgreen Foundation Papers, Special Collections Research Center, University of Chicago Library, box 2, folder 17. This phrase, taken from Locke, survived as the title of the first section of the chapter on labor.

[14]This paragraph and the next draw on Markell, "Arendt's Work," 28ff, which deals with the same problem but without regard to the third *Critique*.

world, all ends are bound to be of short duration and to be transformed into means for some further ends." This "unending chain of means and ends" erodes the supposedly firm boundary between labor and work that Arendt had tried to establish, infusing work with a vicious circularity that mimics the natural circularity of biological life (*HC* 153–4).

This problem brings Arendt to Kant, who at first seems to offer a solution to the difficulty. The way to "end the chain of means and ends," Arendt says, is "to declare that one thing or another is an 'end in itself'," as Kant does in one statement of the categorical imperative (*HC* 154).[15] Arendt, however, rejects this strategy, which she regards not as the opposite but rather as the consummation of instrumentalism, insofar as it segregates humanity as an inviolable end from everything around it, which is thereby made available *to* humanity as a means. What is most striking is that Arendt extends this criticism not only to Kant's moral philosophy, but also to his aesthetics. She writes:

> Kant did not mean to formulate or conceptualize the tenets of the utilitarianism of his time, but on the contrary wanted first of all to relegate the means-end category to its proper place and prevent its use in the field of political action. His formula, however, can no more deny its origin in utilitarian thinking than his other famous and also inherently paradoxical interpretation of man's attitude toward the only objects that are not "for use," namely works of art, in which he said we take "pleasure without any interest." For the same operation which establishes man as the "supreme end" permits him "if he can [to] subject the whole of nature to it," that is, to degrade nature and the world into mere means, robbing both of their independent dignity (*HC* 156, square brackets Arendt's).

The references here to art, aesthetic judgment and the third *Critique* are made almost in passing; but not quite, for they anticipate a dramatic shift at the end of the chapter, where Arendt switches rather abruptly from the consideration of use-objects to the consideration of works of art. In that section, Arendt most fully confronts the implications of her own critique of instrumentalism, and of her rejection of the Kantian strategy for limiting instrumentalism. On the one hand, that critique has revealed the instability of Arendt's effort to separate labor from work, at least as long as work is conceived in terms of the production of useful objects. On the other hand, the same critique has also revealed to Arendt that she can't respond to this

---

[15] See Kant, I. (1996), "Groundwork of the Metaphysics of Morals," in *Practical Philosophy*, Mary J. Gregor ed. and trans. Cambridge: Cambridge University Press, pp. 78–80 (Akademie 4: pp. 428–9). All citations to Kant will include the Akademie pagination in parentheses or square brackets following the pages of the English translation.

problem by identifying some third domain of human activity that can be regarded as an end in itself, separate from and superior to labor and work, for that would be a version of the Kantian move she has just ruled out. Arendt's response to this problem is to turn at least partly away from a "territorial" understanding of the operation of her own conceptual distinctions. Within the chapter on work, this move is exemplified by a single, literally pivotal sentence in which Arendt first reiterates but then rejects the idea of a sharp distinction between objects fit to be judged only in terms of use, and works of art suitable for aesthetic judgment: "To be sure, an ordinary use object is not and should not be intended to be beautiful; yet whatever has a shape at all and is seen cannot help being either beautiful, ugly, or something in-between" (*HC* 172–3). As *The Human Condition* proceeds, the same move is manifest in the textual and conceptual intertwining of work and action, in which—for instance—the "physical, worldly in-between" is not segregated from the intangible "in-between" generated by speech and action, but "overlaid" and "overgrown" by the words and deeds that, in its appearance, the physical in-between occasions and enables (*HC* 182–3, 173). After *The Human Condition*, Arendt would give a name to this zone of interrelation between work and action, and to the kind of attention and care required to sustain it: she would call it "culture" (*CC* 225 [222], 218 [215]).

What changes in the vanishingly brief interval between *The Human Condition* and "The Crisis in Culture," then, is not Arendt's larger theoretical agenda, but her assessment of Kant and in particular her understanding of the relation between Kant's moral philosophy and his aesthetics. In *The Human Condition*, she presents these domains of Kant's thought as parallel, on the grounds that each manifests a problematic kind of purism; about "humanity" and "disinterested pleasure," respectively. By contrast, after her 1957 re-reading of the third *Critique* Arendt's appropriations of Kant are always founded on the idea of a fundamental discontinuity between Kant's moral philosophy and his aesthetics. The former involves the subordination of particular human actions to the universal law expressed in the categorical imperative, while the latter involves the judgment of particulars in the absence of a universal rule given in advance. But this does not necessarily mean that before 1957, Arendt had simply failed to grasp the distinctiveness of the third *Critique*; for as we will now see, Arendt's shifting estimate of the relation between Kant's moral philosophy and his aesthetics reflects a real problem in the *Critique of Judgment* itself, a problem that, as Arendt sensed, was related to an ambiguity in Kant's account of the purely formal nature of aesthetic judgments. Arendt's Kantian turn thus involved more than just getting Kant right: it involved a series of interpretive decisions through which she constructed a specific, idiosyncratic brand of Kantianism, one she thought could advance the non-purifying, anti-territorial agenda of *The Human*

Condition, and in so doing, resist the collapse of aesthetic judgment back into rule-governed morality.

2

Kant's third *Critique* was not only a founding document of modern aesthetic theory, it was also an ambitious effort on Kant's part to resolve fundamental questions about his philosophical system that the cumulative force of the first two *Critiques* had rendered especially acute.[16] The critiques of pure theoretical and practical reason had sought to render the claims of these faculties more secure by distinguishing clearly between their object-domains, and by keeping each from "ventur[ing] out beyond its proper limits."[17] The consequence of these exercises in territorial delimitation, however, had been to leave these two domains, "the domain of the concept of nature" and the "domain of the concept of freedom," separated by an "incalculable gulf" (*CJ* 63 [5: 175–6]). In particular, they left unclear how human beings might acquire confidence that the natural world—the world in which we are, after all, bound to exercise our freedom—is hospitable to our purposes. The third *Critique* responds to this problem through an analysis of the power of judgment, through which Kant thinks human beings express their sensitivity to "purposiveness," particularly though not exclusively in nature. Although the exercise of judgment doesn't provide anything like scientific knowledge of nature's purposes, it at least reassures us there may be more to the natural world than an indifferent multitude of causal laws. Judgment thus serves as what Kant calls an "intermediary" between the domains of the concepts of nature and freedom. It is "the means for combining the two parts of philosophy into one whole" (*CJ* 64 [5: 176–7]).[18] This, however, means that Kant faces a unique challenge in the third *Critique*, for he now has to turn the same critical techniques he had deployed in his earlier work to new ends, bounding and differentiating the power of judgment precisely in order to allow it to restore connections between the faculties his first two critiques had divorced.[19] In the

[16] See Paul Guyer's account of the place of the third *Critique* in the Kantian system in his (2000) "Introduction" to Immanuel Kant, *Critique of the Power of Judgement*, Guyer, P. ed., Guyer, P. and Matthews, E. trans. Cambridge: Cambridge University Press, esp. pp. xiii–xxiii. Hereafter *CJ*.

[17] Smith, N. K. trans. (1965), Kant, *Critique of Pure Reason*. New York: St. Martin's, 26 (B xxiv).

[18] On "purposiveness" as the central thread linking the two parts of *CJ* see Zuckert, R. (2007), *Kant on Beauty and Biology: An Interpretation of the Critique of Judgment*. Cambridge: Cambridge University Press. Zuckert also discusses the mediating role of *CJ* at pp. 368–82.

[19] The difficulty of this task can be seen in Kant's uncertain handling of his political metaphors. Even as he insists that judgment is an "intermediary" between reason and the understanding

space defined by this problem, an ambiguity arises in Kant's account of the ground of aesthetic judgments and of the relationship between aesthetics and morality.[20]

In the early sections of the *Critique of Judgment*, this relationship seems clear enough. The "Analytic of the Beautiful" begins by distinguishing the sort of satisfaction that beautiful objects occasion from the satisfaction involved in the immediate experience of "agreeable" sensations (*CJ* 91–2 [5: 205–6]), and the pleasure involved in finding something "good," whether good for some instrumental reason or good "in itself," which is to say: "morally good" (*CJ* 92–4 [5: 207–9]). Both of these other kinds of satisfaction, Kant contends, necessarily involve an interest, whether sensual, utilitarian or ethical, in the existence of their objects, whereas judgments of taste are disinterested in that they respond to the "the *mere representation* of the object" (*CJ* 90–1 [5: 205], emphasis added). Moreover, unlike judgments of goodness, including moral goodness, judgments of taste do not depend on the availability of a concept under which the object of judgment can be subsumed. "In order to find something good," Kant says, "I must always know what sort of thing the object is supposed to be; i.e., I must have a concept of it." To judge a tool to be useful, I must have a determinate idea of the end to which it is to be put; to judge an action to be morally good, I must apply to it the concept of a will that is good in itself; but "I do not need that in order to find beauty in something" (*CJ* 93 [5: 207]). Thus Kant declares that "The judgment of taste is not a cognitive judgment (neither a theoretical nor a practical one), and hence it is neither **grounded** on concepts nor **aimed** at them" (*CJ* 95 [5: 209], emphases in original). This is why there can be "no rule in accordance with which someone could be compelled to acknowledge something as beautiful"—one of the features of Kant's aesthetics that Arendt found most appealing (*CJ* 101 [5: 215]).

How, then, *do* judgments of taste work, and what distinguishes them from judgments of mere agreeableness, which are also non-cognitive? In judging an object to be beautiful, Kant suggests, what we're really saying is that when we represent this object to ourselves, our cognitive powers—the imagination and the understanding—are brought into a certain state that he variously calls "animation," "free play" and "harmony," and that we take pleasure in our reflective awareness of this subjective condition (*CJ* 102 [5:

---

and *not* a third faculty with a distinct field of objects as its "domain," he adds that judgment must have, "if not exactly its own legislation, then still a proper principle of its own for seeking laws," and that it "can nevertheless have some territory and a certain constitution" (*CJ* 64 [5: 177]).

[20]Because this section deals exclusively with judgments of taste or beauty, I use these terms, as well as "aesthetic judgment," interchangeably, though for Kant, "aesthetic" is a wider category, and also only half of the concern of *CJ*, whose second half addresses "teleological" judgments of the purposiveness of natural organisms and of nature as a whole.

217], 104 [5: 219], 168 [5: 287]). What's pleasing in this state of free play is simply that it expresses a kind of fit, not between the representation of the object and some determinate concept, but between the representation of the object and our powers of cognition "in general" (*CJ* 102–3 [5: 217–218]); a fatefully unclear expression but one that allows Kant to situate judgments of taste midway between the non-conceptual pleasures of sensory gratification and the full-blown use of the understanding to subsume particular objects under determinate concepts or, in the analogous case of action, the use of reason to determine the will according to a concept. This idea of an indeterminate fittedness between the representation of an object and our powers of cognition in general—you could call it "conceptualizability without a concept"—is further elaborated in Kant's claim that judgments of taste ultimately turn on whether the representation of an object and the subjective state it provokes exhibit purposiveness "without a purpose," or the "mere form of purposiveness" (*CJ* 105–6 [5: 220–1]).[21]

Crucially however, Kant invites us to understand this state of general, indeterminate fittedness, and the closely connected idea of purposiveness without a purpose, in at least two different ways. On the one hand, Kant's use of the language of "free play" and "animation" may suggest that the indeterminacy involved here is a matter of *time*, a matter of the purely aesthetic pleasure a subject can take in the extended, unconsummated activity of conceptualization—that is, in seeing that this representation *might* be thought in these terms, or from this angle, or in still another way, but without yet (or perhaps ever) finally settling on a particular concept. Kant seems to encourage this reading when he describes the way in which we "linger over the consideration of the beautiful," finding pleasure in the "occupation of the cognitive powers without a further aim" (*CJ* 107 [5: 222]). On the other hand, Kant's references to the "mere form" of purposiveness may suggest that the indeterminacy involved here is a matter of *abstraction*, that is: that judgments of taste respond—in a flash, as it were—to the presence or absence of some structural feature common to *all* representations of objects. Kant seems to encourage this reading when, reiterating the point that a judgment of taste does not rest on a concept of "what the thing is supposed to be," he suggests that aesthetic judgment instead involves "abstraction" from such particular ends so that "nothing remains" but the merely formal "subjective purposiveness of representations in the mind of the beholder" (*CJ* 112 [5: 227]).

Much hangs on this difference, for this second understanding of purposiveness without a purpose is tied in Kant to a narrowing of the range of phenomena that might occasion pure judgments of beauty. "Free natural

---

[21]In the phrase "without a purpose" (*ohne Zweck*) I've changed the translation of *Zweck* from "end" to "purpose" to capture the analogy between *Zweckmäßigkeit ohne Zweck* and *Gesetzmäßigkeit ohne Gesetz* (lawfulness without a law).

beauties," like flowers, as well as human creations whose design does not "signify" or "represent anything," are straightforward candidates for pure judgments of taste (*CJ* 114 [5: 229]), but just as the admixture of charming colors or decorations can actually "do damage to the judgment of taste if they attract attention to themselves as grounds for the judging of beauty" (*CJ* 109–10 [5: 225]), corrupting taste with mere agreeableness, things that have determinate ends (Kant mentions buildings, horses, and human beings) also "damage" the purity of judgments of taste by inviting us to judge them according to some standard of perfection, which is why, in contemplating such things, we must rigorously "abstract" from their particular ends and the concepts they invite us to employ (*CJ* 114–15 [5: 230–1]).[22] This aesthetic formalism extends even to the production of art. While Kant does not go so far as to demand that art purge itself of content, he does suggest that the imaginatively generated material of fine art must be kept decisively subordinated to formal discipline if an object is to be judged beautiful. For an artist, Kant says, "to be rich and original in ideas is not as necessary as is the suitability of the imagination in its freedom to the lawfulness of the understanding. For all the richness of the former produces, in its lawless freedom, nothing but nonsense; the power of judgement, however, is the faculty for bringing it in line with the understanding." Only by "clipping the wings" of imaginative genius through the introduction of "clarity and order into the abundance of thoughts," Kant continues, can the artist produce an object "capable of an enduring and universal approval, of enjoying a posterity among others and in an ever progressing culture" (*CJ* 197 [5: 319]); and that, it seems, is because such an object will be best suited to bring a spectator's faculties—the "imagination in its freedom" and the "understanding with its lawfulness"—into the same relation (*CJ* 167 [5: 287]). Notice that in both of these characterizations, Kant has shifted from ascribing freedom to the ongoing relationship *between* the faculties—a picture that would be consonant with the first view of purposiveness without a purpose—to a more static picture in which the imagination has become the bearer of lawless freedom, the understanding has become the source of lawfulness, and the relation between them has become settled and hierarchical. Purposiveness without a purpose, understood as mere form, becomes something like the mere form of discipline, an arrangement that expresses a "principle of subsumption, not of intuitions under **concepts**,

[22]Kant does allow that there can be impure judgments of taste that respond not to "free" but to "adherent" beauty, in which we judge that the aesthetic satisfaction we take from an object is appropriate to the *kind* of object it is and therefore fits with our intellectual satisfaction in its conformity to a concept. Judgment of this kind, however, can have "rules prescribed to it"—rules "for the unification...of the beautiful with the good" (*CJ* 114–15 [5: 229–31]). On the importance of this distinction for a full understanding of Kant's theory of fine art, see Costello, D. (Spring 2007), "Greenberg's Kant and the Fate of Aesthetics in Contemporary Art Theory," *Journal of Aesthetics and Art Criticism* 65, no. 2, pp. 217–28.

but of the **faculty** of intuitions or presentations (i.e. of the imagination) under the **faculty** of concepts (i.e. the understanding)" (*CJ* 167–8 [5: 287], emphases in original).

The irony, however, is that in specifying the idea of purposiveness without a purpose in this way, Kant actually begins to erode the difference between judgments of taste and judgments of goodness, particularly of moral goodness, that this notion had originally been intended to secure. The elaboration of purposiveness without a purpose in terms of the "mere form" of purposiveness, combined with Kant's suggestion that the mere form of purposiveness is expressed in the subsumption of the freedom of the imagination under the lawfulness of the understanding (though not under any particular law it might issue) ought to remind us precisely of Kant's explanation of the operation of the moral law. "What kind of law can that be," Kant asks in the *Groundwork*, "the representation of which must determine the will, even without regard for the effect expected from it, in order for the will to be called good absolutely and without limitation?" It can't be a particular law, since particular laws have purposes and are obeyed out of an inclination to achieve their ends. The moral law must therefore consist in "mere lawfulness [*bloße Gesetzmäßigkeit*] as such, without having as its basis some law [*Gesetz*] determined for certain actions...if duty is not to be everywhere an empty delusion and a chimerical concept."[23] This law, Kant elaborates, is concerned not with the "matter" of the action but with its "form";[24] and can itself be characterized both as the "mere form of lawfulness" (*bloße Form der Gesetzmäßigkeit*) and as "mere lawgiving form" (*bloße gesetzgebende Form*).[25] But if this is right and if, as Kant insisted in trying to express the distinctiveness of aesthetic judgment, judgments of moral goodness are always conceptual, then the determination of the faculty of judgment by the "mere form of purposiveness" of a representation, understood in terms of the subsumption of the faculty of imagination in its freedom under the faculty of the understanding in its lawfulness, can be no more and no less conceptual than the determination of the will by the categorical imperative.

This result should not be surprising because, in keeping with the larger aims of the third *Critique*, Kant increasingly moves to join together what he has sundered as the book proceeds. Most famously, the "Dialectic" of aesthetic judgment brings the first half of the book to a close by identifying the beautiful as a "symbol" of morality (*CJ* 225–8 [5: 351–4]). At the same time, however, those larger aims also seem to have driven Kant to overshoot

[23]Kant, "Groundwork," pp. 56–7 (4: 402), translation modified.

[24]Ibid., 69 (4: 416).

[25]Kant, I. (1997), "Kant on the Metaphysics of Morals," in *Lectures on Ethics*, Heath, P. and Schneewind, J. ed. Cambridge: Cambridge University Press, p. 267 (27: 501); "Critique of Practical Reason," *Practical Philosophy*, p. 162 (5: 29).

his target. In order to be able to make the beautiful into a symbol of the moral, Kant has to adopt an interpretation of "purposiveness without a purpose" that casts the faculties involved in aesthetic judgment in terms analogous to those found in the analysis of morality. The accord between the freedom of the imagination and the lawfulness of the understanding, Kant says, is analogous to the accord of the free will with the universal laws of reason (*CJ* 228 [5: 334]), but that, I have suggested, not only bridges aesthetics and morality but collapses the difference between them on which Kant had originally insisted. Thus Arendt's early suggestion of a deep parallel between the Kantian notion of disinterested beauty and the Kantian idea of the moral law, rooted in the idea of humanity as an end in itself, can't be lightly dismissed as the result of a superficial misreading of Kant, for it captures something important about the third *Critique*. At the same time, the existence within the third *Critique* of a different conception of purposiveness without a purpose, one that isn't ultimately subordinated to the systematic task of establishing a parallel between aesthetics and morality, will help us understand the potential that Arendt found in the *Critique of Judgment* when she returned to the text in 1957, and the interpretive work she had to perform to employ Kant's ideas for her own purposes, which were different both from Kant's, and from those of some other Kantians among her contemporaries.

3

The meaning and prospects of culture in mass society have been topics of debate in American intellectual life since the end of the nineteenth century, among disputants ranging from moralizing ministers to settlement-house progressives to mix-tape enthusiasts; but the particular conversation into which Hannah Arendt intervened in the first half of "The Crisis in Culture" had a shorter history and a narrower cast of characters. Its center of gravity was in the world of the so-called "New York intellectuals," that loose constellation of writers—mostly Jewish; many of them veterans of the efflorescence of American Marxism and the wilting of its radical aspirations in the thirties and forties; some turned militantly anti-communist during and after the war—whose institutional centers and favored venues for publication, over the years, included the magazines *Partisan Review, Commentary*, *politics*, and *Dissent*.[26] These journals presented a steady

[26]On this milieu see Wald, A. (1987), *The New York Intellectuals: The Rise and Decline of the Anti-Stalinist Left from the 1930s to the 1980s*. Chapel Hill: University of North Carolina Press; Jumonville, N. (1991), *Critical Crossings: The New York Intellectuals in Postwar America*. Berkeley: University of California Press; and Wilford, H. (1995), *The New York Intellectuals: From Vanguard to Institution*. Manchester: Manchester University Press.

stream of writing on the prospects of avant-garde art and literature and their relationship to social and political life; on the relations among "high," "popular," "mass" and "middlebrow" culture; and on the consequences for human freedom of technological innovation, the growth of leisure, the democratization of higher education, and consumerism fed by postwar prosperity.[27] This writing could sound hyperbolically pessimistic, none more so than that of Arendt's friend Dwight Macdonald, who revised his four-page 1944 essay "A Theory of Popular Culture" twice, converting it into a screed against the "spreading ooze of Mass Culture" that, by 1960, had itself grown to seventy-four pages and had to be published across two separate issues of *Partisan Review*.[28]

Still, this body of criticism wasn't simply a conservative defense of traditional cultural standards against all modern developments. From the beginning, for example, one of the distinguishing features of *Partisan Review* had been its editors' deep commitment to literary and artistic modernism, which was partly responsible—along with the disclosure of the Moscow trials—for the magazine's break from the Communist Party.[29] Even during the magazine's early days, the editors worried that the reductive literary criticism of official Party organs arose from an underlying misunderstanding of Marxism as a "mechanical materialism," which "assumes a direct determination of the whole superstructure by the economic foundation,"[30] and in the first issue of the newly independent magazine, they declared that while they were "aware of [the magazine's] responsibility to the revolutionary movement in general," they "disclaim[ed] obligation to any of its organized political expressions" and identified this distinction between "the

---

[27]For a survey of the theme of mass culture in the writings of the New York intellectuals see Jumonville, *Critical Crossings*, ch. 4.

[28]Macdonald, D. (February 1944), "A Theory of Popular Culture," *politics*, pp. 20–3; (Summer 1953), "A Theory of Mass Culture," *Diogenes* no. 3, pp. 1–17; (Spring 1960), "Masscult and Midcult," *Partisan Review* 27, no. 2, pp. 203–33 and (Fall 1960), no. 4, pp. 589–631. The phrase "spreading ooze of Mass Culture" concludes the second version of the article (17); the other passages are drawn from the final version (627). Macdonald may have been one of the most hyperbolic mass culture critics, but he was also the funniest: observing the tendency of "homogenized" magazines like *Life* to present, say, "nine color pages of Renoir paintings followed by a picture of a roller-skating horse." He writes: "Defenders of our Masscult society like Professor Edward Shils of the University of Chicago—he is, of course, a sociologist—see phenomena like *Life* as inspiriting attempts at popular education—just think, nine pages of Renoirs! But that roller-skating horse comes along, and the final impression is that both Renoir and the horse were talented" ("Masscult and Midcult," p. 213). The horse was not Macdonald's invention. See "Merrily He Rolls Along," *Life* (19 May 1952), p. 168.

[29]See Wald, *New York Intellectuals*, pp. 75–97. The "editors" were several but the key figures were William Phillips and Philip Rahv.

[30]Phelps, W. P. and Rahv, P. (June–July 1934), "Problems and Perspectives in Revolutionary Literature," *Partisan Review* 1, no. 3, p. 6. On the break and its background see Cooney, T. A. (1986), *The Rise of the New York Intellectuals: Partisan Review and its Circle, 1934–1945*. Madison: University of Wisconsin Press.

interests of literature" and "those of factional politics" as their debt to literary "aestheticism."[31] Indeed, the early *Partisan Review*'s fraught effort to pursue a broadly revolutionary social and political agenda through an enforcement of the separateness of the literary resonates with the strategy Kant adopted in the third *Critique*. If for Kant aesthetic judgment, properly delimited, promised to mediate between human freedom and nature, for *Partisan Review*, aesthetic modernism, precisely by establishing boundaries between the literary and the political, promised to mediate in the same way between freedom and the force of history.

This shape of thought is exemplified by what proved to be one of the most important contributions of any of the New York intellectuals to the critique of mass culture: Clement Greenberg's "Avant-Garde and Kitsch," published in *Partisan Review* in the fall of 1939, and widely republished over the following decades.[32] Greenberg, who would later become, for a while, the preeminent critic and interpreter of modern painting and sculpture in the United States, was at that point a thirty-year-old aspiring writer, sympathetic to Trotskyism, who had been easing his way into Greenwich Village literary and political circles since 1936. In early 1939 Greenberg sent a letter to the editors of *Partisan Review* taking issue with Dwight Macdonald's recent reviews of Soviet cinema, which Greenberg thought overestimated the extent to which Russian peasants' apparent taste for kitsch could be blamed on conditioning at the hands of the Soviet state apparatus. Macdonald urged him to expand the letter into an essay. The results were stunning.[33] "One and the same civilization produces simultaneously two such different things," Greenberg begins, "as a poem by T. S. Eliot and a Tin Pan Alley song, or a painting by Braque and a *Saturday Evening Post* cover" (*CEC* 1: 5–6). The latter partner in each of these pairs is an example of kitsch, "a product of the industrial revolution which urbanized the masses of Western Europe and America and established what is called universal literacy" (*CEC* 1: 11). These new urban masses, alienated from the folk culture that had traditionally been theirs, "set up pressure on society to provide them with a kind of culture fit for their own consumption," that is, fit for people "insensitive to the values of genuine culture." The result was a highly profitable industry devoted to the production of kitsch, that

---

[31] "Editorial Statement" (December 1937), *Partisan Review* 4, no. 1, p. 3.

[32] Greenberg, C. (1986), "Avant-Garde and Kitsch" in *The Collected Essays and Criticism*, John O'Brian ed., vol. 1, *Perceptions and Judgements: 1939–1944*. Chicago: University of Chicago Press, pp. 5–22. All citations of Greenberg's published work will be from this four-volume edition (hereafter *CEC* 1, *CEC* 2, etc.), which reprints his original texts, not the often heavily revised versions collected in *Art and Culture* (1961).

[33]. See John O'Brian's "Introduction" to *CEC* 1; Rubenfeld, F. (1997), *Clement Greenberg: A Life*. New York: Scribner; and Goldfarb Marquis, A., (2006), *Art Czar: The Rise and Fall of Clement Greenberg*. Boston: MFA.

is: of mechanical, formulaic, predigested, watered-down imitations of "genuine" culture, which offers "vicarious experience and faked sensations" and is thus "the epitome of all that is spurious in the life of our times" (*CEC* 1: 12).

In contrast and opposition to the power of kitsch stand the literary and artistic avant-gardes, whose rejection of bourgeois values has been nurtured since the mid-nineteenth century by the existence of an atmosphere of revolutionary ideas but who have, in the end, "repudiate[d] revolutionary as well as bourgeois politics" in favor of "art for art's sake" and "pure poetry"—terms that, for Greenberg, refer not to scandalous sensualism but to the highly disciplined, wholly reflexive engagement with the "medium of [the artist's or poet's] own craft" (*CEC* 1: 7–9). It is unclear what kind of political force Greenberg thought such avant-garde art and literature could have. On the one hand his account of the "rapidly shrinking" base of financial support for avant-garde art within the very ruling class it spurned (*CEC* 1: 10–11) could be read as forecasting, or perhaps as a last-ditch effort to foment, a sense of cultural crisis that might reinvigorate socialist movements, as Greenberg seems to intimate in the final paragraph of the essay (*CEC* 1: 22). On the other hand, the very weakness of this intimation can also be read as a confession of the impotence of the revolutionary aspirations of the thirties and, however unintentionally, as preparation for the Cold War re-articulation of the social significance of avant-garde art as one expression of Western and especially American freedom, a re-articulation in which Greenberg would participate vigorously.[34] (Indeed, the tension between *that* element of the emerging American strategy on the cultural front of the Cold War and the massive extension of economic assistance, meant to undermine communism and neutralism abroad by acquainting Europeans with the benefits of "American-style consumerism," would help re-energize some of the New York intellectuals' anxieties about mass culture in the forties and fifties.[35]) Yet the precise character of Greenberg's politics in 1939 is less important than the ways in which he distinguishes genuine, avant-garde culture from its spurious other. The pleasures of kitsch, he argues, are troublesome not simply because they're easy, but because they're *immediate*. The Russian peasant who gets pleasure from Ilya Repin's

[34]See, for example, the reading of "Avant-Garde and Kitsch" in Guilbaut, S. (1983), *How New York Stole the Idea of Modern Art: Abstract Expressionism, Freedom, and the Cold War*, Goldhammer, A. trans., Chicago: University of Chicago Press, 33ff. On the limits of Guilbaut's larger narrative about New York School art and artists: Craven, D. (1999), *Abstract Expressionism as Cultural Critique*. Cambridge: Cambridge University Press, pp. 40–50, and Sandler, I. (2009), *Abstract Expressionism and the American Experience: A Reevaluation*. Lenox, MA: Hard Press Editions, ch. 5.

[35]Scott-Smith, G. (2002), *The Politics of Apolitical Culture: The Congress for Cultural Freedom, the CIA and post-war American hegemony*. London: Routledge, p. 56.

dramatic battle scenes does so because Repin has, in some sense, included the pleasurable effect *in* the picture, in the story it represents; while the "cultivated spectator" who contemplates a Picasso takes his pleasure only "at a second remove, as a result of reflection upon the immediate impression" left by the painting (*CEC* 1: 16). This means that the Repin painting involves "no discontinuity between art and life," no appreciation of "the distinction between those values only to be found in art and the values which can be found elsewhere," a distinction that avant-garde art takes as its touchstone (*CEC* 1: 15–16). Whether Greenberg hoped for avant-garde art to mediate between freedom and the historical laws expressed in Marxism, or merely between freedom and the laws physically embodied in various artistic media, even in this early essay his conception of genuine aesthetic pleasure—and of the sorts of objects that can provoke it—is recognizably if broadly Kantian.[36]

Over the next decade Greenberg would develop this early conception of the defining features of the avant-garde into the principle of an influential corpus of art criticism, focused especially on contemporary American abstract art and its immediate European antecedents. By arguing that the best art of the moment consisted, as avant-garde art always had, in an increasingly self-referential exploration and testing of the limits imposed by each art's own specific medium—for example, in painting, of the limits imposed by the fundamental fact of the flatness of the picture plane[37]—Greenberg positioned himself both as an interpreter of and advocate for artistic modernism in general, and as a judge of its most advanced, and most retrograde, tendencies and practitioners. And in this critical practice, Greenberg was caught in a bind similar to the one that

---

[36]Greenberg's first unequivocal reference to the *Critique of Judgment* in his published writing is in 1943 (*CEC* 1, p. 161), though he read Kant (it is unclear which text) as early as 1931 (Greenberg, C. [2000], *The Harold Letters: The Making of an American Intellectual.* Van Horne, J. ed. Washington, D.C.: Counterpoint, p. 43). Kant is mentioned off and on in Greenberg's writings of the 1940s and 1950s, and Greenberg taught a seminar on Kant's *Critique of Judgment* at Black Mountain College in 1950, but it isn't until "Modernist Painting," his 1960 Voice of America address and essay, that Greenberg first gives an explicit account of the relationship of his conception of artistic modernism to Kantian philosophy (*CEC* 4, pp. 85–106; see also John O'Brian's "Introduction," *CEC* 3, p. xxii); and the only really extended interpretation of Kant's aesthetics in his work doesn't come until his Bennington College seminars of the 1970s: Greenberg, C. (1999), *Homemade Esthetics: Observations on Art and Taste.* New York: Oxford University Press. For important discussions of Greenberg's appropriation of Kant see de Duve, T. (1996), *Kant After Duchamp.* Cambridge, MA: MIT Press, esp. ch. 4; Gaiger, J. (October 1999), "Constraints and Conventions: Kant and Greenberg on Aesthetic Judgement," *British Journal of Aesthetics* 39, no. 4, pp. 376–91; Cheetham, M. A. (2001), *Kant, Art, and Art History.* Cambridge: Cambridge University Press, pp. 87–99.

[37]Some important statements of this and related ideas in Greenberg's earlier work include "Towards a Newer Laocoon," *CEC* 1, pp. 23–38; "Abstract Art," *CEC* 1, pp. 199–204 and "The Crisis of the Easel Picture," *CEC* 2, pp. 221–5.

emerged in Kant's third *Critique*. Echoing Kant's claim that aesthetic judgments don't involve the application of a concept given in advance to a particular case, and that they therefore aren't demonstrable in the way scientific or moral claims might be, Greenberg insisted—sometimes citing Kant—that aesthetic judgments can't be rendered compulsory "by the rules of evidence or logic" (*CEC* 3: 216). He declared, when accused of dogmatism, that he "does not prescribe to art" but responds only to his own enjoyment (*CEC* 2: 205) and indeed he presented himself as allergic to "any sort of dogmatic prescription in art," since "historical tendenc[ies]" and existing "hierarchies of style" are "powerless to govern the future" (*CEC* 2: 19). Yet the charges of prescriptive dogmatism that followed Greenberg throughout his career were hardly without warrant, not because he expressed strong judgments about particular works, but because he repeatedly made claims that an aesthetic response to a particular work couldn't possibly redeem: for instance, that a particular artist "has absorbed enough cubism, in spite of himself, never to lose sight of the direction in which the pictorial art of our times must go in order to be great" (*CEC* 1: 99); that "abstract art today is the only stream that flows toward an ocean" (*CEC* 1: 171); that Baziotes will become "emphatically good" when he forces himself to take months to finish his pictures; that Motherwell's *Jeune Fille* points "the direction he must go to realize his talent" (*CEC* 1: 240), and so on.

What makes such pronouncements more than hypocrisy on Greenberg's part—though it does not render them consistent with his professed anti-prescriptivism—is precisely his understanding of what Kant would have called the ground of aesthetic judgment, or in Greenberg's terms, of what it means for an avant-garde work to be preoccupied with its own medium. Only a year after "Avant-Garde and Kitsch," in his next piece for *Partisan Review*, "Towards a Newer Laocoon," Greenberg spelled out the idea at length. There, importantly, he distinguished more clearly than he had before between the operation of "pure poetry" and "pure painting," to revealing effect. Poetry, he argued, can never be made *quite* as pure as painting. An avant-garde poem "still offers possibilities of meaning—but only possibilities. Should any of them be too precisely realized, the poem would lose the greatest part of its efficacy, which is to agitate the consciousness with infinite possibilities by approaching the brink of meaning and yet never falling over it" (*CEC* 1: 33). But because it is "easier to isolate the medium in the case of the plastic arts," Greenberg continued, "avant-garde painting and sculpture can be said to have attained a much more radical purity than avant-garde poetry," a purity in which "the purely plastic or abstract qualities of the work are the only ones that count." In short, "pure poetry strives for infinite suggestion, pure plastic art for the minimum" (*CEC* 1: 34). Faced with a close analogy to Kant's two ways of understanding purposiveness without a purpose in other words, Greenberg inclined in the same direction as—in the end—did Kant.[38] With analogous consequences: when the conceptual indeterminacy of aesthetic judgment is taken to grow out of the abstractedness of its object, emptied of everything inessential to its confrontation with its bare, physical support, then the critic, and the artist too, can have standards after all—not the timeless standards of practical reason but the historical standards made into an "imperative" by "history," by "the particular moment reached in a particular tradition of art" (*CEC* 1: 37). And for analogous reasons: in a period of unprecedented prosperity, in which the emergence of vast new markets for art, or of art-like products, appeared to Greenberg to present artists with irresistible temptations to indulge the uneducated lowbrow or middlebrow preferences of the masses, perhaps only aesthetic judgments spoken in the imperative voice seemed able to carry forward the hope that the industrial world might somehow be, or become, hospitable to the ongoing tradition of high culture.[39]

4

When we turn to "The Crisis in Culture" itself against the background of these three contexts—the trajectory of *The Human Condition*, the ambiguity of Kant's third *Critique* and the character of the discourse about mass culture in the New York intellectual world—some important but neglected features of that essay come into sharp relief. The first part of Arendt's essay, for example, does contain a forceful argument about the dangers posed by mass society to the phenomenon of culture, an argument that is often taken to be her central point. But that argument, it turns out, is crucially different from many of the most influential critiques of mass culture that circulated in her milieu in the forties and fifties. Of course there are important points of overlap. The notion of a consumers' society as a sort of transgressive creature, possessed of "gargantuan appetites" that "eat...up" and "destroy" cultural objects (*CC* 207 [203–4]) is reminiscent of Macdonald, though Arendt's rhetoric is relatively tame and her treatment of this issue remarkably brief by comparison. Likewise, in rejecting the notion that a consumers' society "will become more 'cultured' as time goes on and education has done its work" (*CC* 211 [208]), Arendt seems to align herself with Greenberg and Macdonald against the more

---

[38]See also Greenberg's later insistence on the importance of grasping the unity of a painting "in an indivisible instant of time," which is easier in abstract painting because it offers less "inducement for the eye to do such wandering [in space and time]," "The Case for Abstract Art," *CEC* 4, p. 80.

[39]For Greenberg's ongoing struggle with this problem see, for example, "The Present Prospects of American Painting and Sculpture," *CEC* 2, pp. 160–70; "A Symposium: The State of American Art," *CEC* 2, pp. 287–9; and "The Plight of Our Culture," *CEC* 3, pp. 122–52.

sanguine Edward Shils, who diagnosed these critics' "aggrieved preoccupation with mass culture" as, in part, a reaction to the "frustration of [their] socialist expectations."[40] Yet Arendt's reasons for refusing such optimism are characteristically idiosyncratic. Arendt makes no mention of the unavoidable leveling effects of democratization, or the loss or dilution of standards. The distinction between "high" and "low" culture is not an important part of her theoretical vocabulary. She makes no indignant references, as Greenberg does, to "ignorant Russian peasants" (*CEC* 1: 15) or to masses who prefer easy enjoyments to difficult pleasures and who are no longer "so ashamed as they used to be of bad taste" (*CEC* 1: 288). Indeed, she specifies that the "relatively new trouble with mass society" arises "not because of the masses themselves," but because of a structural tendency in the entertainment industry to convert even durable cultural objects into disposable consumer goods, and thereby to draw attention away from the status of those objects as part of the "space of worldly appearances" (*CC* 211 [208]).

Even more importantly, Arendt's unconventional line of argument about culture and mass society comes only in the last few pages of the first part of her essay. Most of its first part is devoted to the exposition of a very different idea: that the original and more serious threat to culture comes not from mass society but from what Arendt variously calls "good" or "educated" society (*CC* 204 [201]). The trouble, she explains, is not that good society is philistine in the conventional sense, lacking an "interest in art" (*CC* 201 [198]). The trouble lies instead in good society's instrumentalization of culture as a marker of social status and a means of social advancement, a tendency Arendt refers to as "cultured" or "educated" philistinism (*CC* 202 [199]). This attitude, no less than the attitude embodied in a consumers' society, corrodes the power of judgment, because it deprives cultural objects of their "most important and elemental quality," which, Arendt says, is the durable power to "grasp and move the reader or the spectator," or to "arres[t] our attention and mov[e] us" (*CC* 203–4 [199, 201]). "The trouble with the educated philistine," she concludes, "was not that he read the classics but that he did so prompted by the ulterior motive of self-perfection, remaining quite unaware of the fact that Shakespeare or Plato might have to tell him more important things than how to educate himself; the trouble was that he fled into a region of 'pure poetry' in order to keep reality out of his life" (*CC* 203 [200]).[41] Here Arendt does not simply distance herself from appeals to aesthetic purity. She worries that

[40] Shils, E. (1972), "Daydreams and Nightmares: Reflections on the Criticism of Mass Culture," *The Intellectuals and the Powers and other Essays*. Chicago: University of Chicago Press, pp. 248–64 (originally published 1957).

[41] The sentence continues: "—for instance, such 'prosaic' things as a potato famine—or to look at it through a veil of 'sweetness and light'."

such appeals, insofar as they function as signifiers of social status, actually smother the aesthetic response to art they purport to enable. And in this, she departs sharply from mass-culture critics like Greenberg, who tended to treat aesthetic and social distinction as inseparable: inseparable historically, in the sense that on Greenberg's account, "high culture" has in the past always been sustained by "sharp class distinctions," and inseparable prospectively, in the sense that the only viable future for high art that Greenberg could imagine in the late forties and early fifties appeared to him to rest on the aspiration of the newly prosperous "American 'common man'" to achieve "social position" through "self-cultivation" (*CEC* 2: 163).

Indeed, "The Crisis in Culture" sometimes reads like an indictment of a tendency toward 'cultured philistinism' expressed precisely in dominant modes of mass cultural criticism like Greenberg's. Consider, for instance, how Arendt begins the essay: not with the phenomenon of mass culture as such, but with a retrospective observation about the remarkable growth of interest in mass culture among *intellectuals*, who have devoted "innumerable studies and research projects" to the topic. She adds that their "chief effect, as Harold Rosenberg pointed out, is 'to add to kitsch an intellectual dimension'" (*CC* 197 [194]).[42] Arendt's reference to her friend Rosenberg, whose competing interpretation of postwar American abstraction through the notion of "action painting" had made him into Greenberg's art-critical *bête noire* during the fifties, is important not least because some of her contemporary readers would surely have been struck by her invocation of *him* as an authority on a theme—kitsch—that was so closely associated with Greenberg, just as the two critics' rivalry was nearing its peak.[43] More deeply, the reference points to the strong affinities between Arendt's critique of the reduction of culture to an instrument of social positioning and Rosenberg's own unconventional angle of attack on the problem of mass culture. As early as 1948, in an essay for *Commentary* called "The Herd of Independent Minds" (tellingly subtitled "Has the Avant-Garde its Own Mass Culture?"), Rosenberg had mischievously proposed that the defining feature of "mass" culture was not the wide scope or low social altitude of its audience, but the fact that its power came

[42]Arendt's reference is to what she calls Rosenberg's "brilliantly witty" essay "Pop Culture: Kitsch Criticism," included in (1959) *The Tradition of the New*. New York: Horizon, and initially published in (Winter 1958), *Dissent* 5, no. 1, pp. 14–19.

[43]Its peak might be said to have come in 1962 with the publication of Greenberg, C. (March 1962), "How Art Writing Earns its Bad Name," *The Second Coming Magazine* 1, no. 3. A longer version published in *Encounter* in December of that year is reprinted in *CEC* 4, pp. 135–44, and Rosenberg, H. (December 1962), "Action Painting: A Decade of Distortion," *Art News* 61, no. 8, pp. 42–4 and pp. 62–3, reprinted in (1982), *The Anxious Object*. Chicago: University of Chicago Press. Their rivalry received renewed attention as the frame for a sweeping exhibition of postwar American art: see Kleeblatt, N. L. ed. (2008), *Action/Abstraction: Pollock, de Kooning, and American Art*. New York: The Jewish Museum.

from its appeal to "common experiences" (which belong to the register of third-personally describable facts about the states of mind one may or may not share with others) rather than from its ability to disclose "common situations" (which are intrinsically first-personal, a matter of where one stands in relation to meaningful facts, events, and possibilities).[44] From this point of view, Rosenberg argues, even small, self-consciously exclusive groups, such as the "intellectual captains" of an "anti-mass-culture organ like *Partisan Review*," can participate in the dynamics of "mass" culture on a smaller scale, insofar as they treat cultural objects as occasions for the reproduction of group solidarity via a common, if rarefied, experience. "The peak of the mass-culture pyramid and its base," he concludes, "are made of the same material."[45]

Arendt is not as explicit about her polemical targets as Rosenberg, but "The Crisis in Culture" echoes his reflexive critique of the enterprise of mass-culture criticism, and not just in her citation of his work. Early in the essay, when Arendt first intimates that the "more fundamental problem" of culture concerns its relationship to society in general, including not only "mass" but also "good" society, she also suggests that this more fundamental issue is difficult for Americans to notice because the United

---

[44]Rosenberg, H. (1973), "The Herd of Independent Minds," *Discovering the Present*. Chicago: University of Chicago Press, pp. 24–8. Rosenberg developed this distinction between experiences and situations in the course of an attack on Robert Warshow's claim that the "Communist experience" of the 1930s was formative for most contemporary American intellectuals, a claim that Rosenberg says treats communism as a "mass event," a way of suturing together a contemporary group through a reference to a historical phenomenon, but only at the cost of eliding the different ways in which that event may have been "significant" or "pertinent" for various individuals. This concern about the conversion of communism into an event with only a "mass-culture meaning" (25) would take on new significance for Rosenberg, and also for Arendt, during and after the McCarthy era. In "Couch Liberalism and the Guilty Past," an essay that grew out of Rosenberg's reactions to a 1953 essay on the other, recently executed Rosenbergs published in the first issue of the British magazine *Encounter* (sponsored by the Congress for Cultural Freedom), Rosenberg attacked the constitution of a new mass of anti-Communist liberal intellectuals out of a practice of "confession" to having once been radical (Rosenberg [1959], "Couch Liberalism and the Guilty Past," *The Tradition of the New*. New York: Horizon Press [written in 1955]); and in doing so he echoed Arendt's own 1953 critique of the moralizing politics of confessed ex-Communists (Arendt, H. (1994), "The Ex-Communists," in *Essays in Understanding, 1930–1954*, Kohn, J. ed. New York: Harcourt, Brace and Company. See also Arendt, H. to Jaspers, K., 13 May 1953, in Arendt and Jaspers, *Correspondence 1926–1969*, pp. 209–17. I explore the significance of the politics of the early Cold War in this context and in Arendt's work more broadly in more detail in *The Architecture of* The Human Condition (work in progress).

[45]Rosenberg, "Herd," pp. 20–21. Rosenberg doesn't name particular *Partisan Review* authors, but he does refer to a series of essays published in 1947 and 1948 that can be identified as the work of James Burnham, Leslie Fiedler, William Barrett and perhaps Philip Rahv. This central line of argument in "Herd" is overlooked in Kleeblatt's discussion of the essay in *Action/Abstraction*, which treats the essay simply as an expression of Rosenberg's opposition to the "oppressive nature of mass culture" (7).

States, "though only too well acquainted with the barbarian philistinism of the nouveaux-riches, has only a nodding acquaintance with the equally annoying cultural and educated philistinism of European society, where culture has acquired snob-value." This, she says, is why "the facile yearning of so many critics of mass culture for a Golden Age of good and genteel society" is "much more widespread today in America than it is in Europe" (*CC* 198 [195]). It is not immediately obvious whom Arendt has in mind here, but an earlier text on which the first half of "Crisis" was based makes it clearer. "It would be unfortunate indeed," she had written there, "if out of the dilemmas and contradictions of mass culture and mass society there should arise an altogether unwarranted and idle yearning for a state of affairs which is not better but only a bit more old-fashioned. *And the eager and uncritical acceptance of such obviously snobbish and philistine terms as highbrow, middlebrow, and lowbrow is a rather ominous sign.*"[46] Perhaps it shouldn't be surprising that when Rosenberg reviewed *Between Past and Future* in glowing terms for the *New York Times*, he singled out "The Crisis in Culture," and in particular its line about the "facile yearning" of the mass-culture critics, for special praise.[47]

5

Arendt's concern with the phenomenon of cultured philistinism in the first half of "The Crisis in Culture" leaves its mark on the second half of the essay as well, and in particular on her appropriation of Kant's third *Critique*, for in turning to Kant in order to explicate a conception of aesthetic judgment that resists being converted into a tool of social advancement or a marker of social status, Arendt not only insists upon the difference between aesthetics and morality (*CC* 219–20 [216]), she does so more consistently than did Kant himself, abandoning the specific understanding of "purposiveness without a purpose" that had, in the end, allowed Kant to cast the beautiful as a symbol of the moral—which was also the specific version of Kantianism that had proved useful for Greenberg's critical project. Arendt's resistance to the dominant tendency of Kant's thought can be seen most clearly in her treatment of the scope and nature of the validity of aesthetic judgments, a topic she engages by exploring Kant's claim, in the "Deduction of Pure Aesthetic Judgments," that judgment involves the cultivation of an "enlarged mentality," through which the judging subject thinks "in the place of everyone else" (*CC* 220 [217]).[48] Her most obvious departure

---

[46] Arendt, "Society and Culture," p. 280 (emphasis added).
[47] Rosenberg, H. (30 July 1961), "Concepts We Live By," *The New York Times*, BR6.
[48] These are Arendt's renderings of phrases in *CJ*, pp. 174–5 (5, pp. 294–5).

from Kant, as other readers have noted, is that by her account, judgment is "never universally valid," but claims validity only among "those others in whose place the judging person has put himself for his considerations" (*CC* 221 [217]). (In the English edition of the *Critique of Judgment* in Arendt's personal library, held at Bard College, Arendt has repeatedly struck through the translator's rendering of the term *Allgemeinheit* as "universality" and replaced it with "generality."[49]) Yet underlying this difference is an even more important divergence between Kant and Arendt on the question of the ground of judgments of taste.

By the time Kant takes up the theme of the enlarged mentality in the "Deduction," he seems to have settled on an understanding of purposiveness without a purpose in terms of the "mere form" of purposiveness, understood as the product of an operation of abstraction, for he says that in judgments of taste we put ourselves "in the position of everyone else" by "abstracting" from the contingent matter of our representations (since this is where our representations will tend to be contaminated by charm and emotion) and "attending solely to the formal particularities" of our own representational states (*CJ* 174 [5: 294]). Doing this entitles us to claim the assent of "all human beings" by virtue of the fact that the formal relations among the faculties that are brought into play in an act of judgment are identical across the species (*CJ* 170 [5: 290]). For Arendt, by contrast, the operation of the "enlarged mentality" occurs not via an act of abstraction away from the matter and towards the form of our representations, but by the use of the imagination, and the "position" into which we imaginatively put ourselves is neither the subjectivity of a particular other, nor the subjective position of a human being in general, but the worldly standpoint or location of the other: "the place where they stand, the worldly conditions they are subject to," as Arendt will later put it in her Kant lectures.[50] In "The Crisis in Culture," in other words, Arendt takes up and develops the first of the two Kantian conceptions of purposiveness without a purpose we considered earlier, locating the ground of judgments of taste in the temporally extended, unconsummated activity of free play, which she understands not simply as a relation between one subject's faculties of imagination and understanding, or even as a relation between one subject's faculties and an object, but as a way of being in and toward a world inhabited by others.

It is important to emphasize that the difference between Kant and Arendt on this point is not merely the quantitative difference between taking the position of *all* others (Kant) and taking the position of *some* others (Arendt). For Kant, the operation of abstraction involved in the enlarged mentality

---

[49]This is J. H. Bernard's translation (New York: Hafner, 1951, repr. 1964).

[50]Arendt, *Lectures on Kant's Political Philosophy*, p. 43. In "The Crisis in Culture" Arendt does not yet use of the idea of the imagination to explicate the notion of the enlarged mentality, but she does repeatedly refer to the "place" and "perspective" of others.

authorizes us to presuppose an identity between certain aspects of our own subjective states, and the subjective states of anyone else who happens to observe the same object. It grounds the expectation of what Rosenberg would have called a "common experience." For Arendt, by contrast, the play of the imagination involved in the enlarged mentality constitutes what Rosenberg would have called a "common situation," in which what people share with others is not a mental state but an orientation, a condition in which the same worldly object comes to be "pertinent" or relevant to them.[51] And this difference has crucial implications for the capacity of taste to resist moralism and cultured philistinism. To be sure, Kant insists that judgments of taste can't be proved or disproved, which might seem to be an antidote against smugness or self-righteousness (*CJ* 166 [5: 285]), but the impossibility of aesthetic proofs means only that there is no point in trying to argue someone into a feeling. It gives us no reason not to conclude—among ourselves, as it were—that someone who fails to see the beauty of this flower or this artifact has simply been corrupted by more immediate forms of sensory gratification. Indeed, Kant reminds us that the operation of the enlarged mentality involves "holding [one's] judgment up not so much to the actual as to the merely possible judgments of others," since the actual judgments of others may be contaminated by the human susceptibility to charm and emotion, corrupted by inadequate cultivation and so on, whereas the merely possible judgments of others are judgments which others *could* arrive at if they judged well. They represent a kind of horizon at which the aesthetic responses of different subjects, suitably purified, would converge in their expression of "human reason" in the singular (*CJ* 173 [5: 293]). Arendt will cite this same distinction between the possible and actual judgments of others in her Kant lectures. For her, however, the point of the distinction is not to keep the enlarged mentality tethered to an ideal from which actual judgments, in their impurity, threaten to fall away, but simply to remind us that in enlarging our mentality we need not imagine "what actually goes on in [others'] mind[s]" at all, that our responsibility is to take account of others' worldly circumstances, not their mental states.[52] Since worldly circumstances do not *determine* the actual judgments of those who inhabit them—two people in the same circumstances might well judge the same object differently—the judgment that I imagine I would make if I were in someone else's place cannot be anything more than the *possible* judgment of that other. In Arendt's usage, therefore,

[51]Rosenberg uses the word "pertinent" to talk about the difference between experiences and situations in "Herd," p. 24, cf. Arendt's use of "relevant" at (e.g.) *HC*, p. 51 and p. 179. I owe particular thanks to Lena Zuckerwise for conversations on the meaning of "relevance" in *HC*.

[52]On the difference between the enlarged mentality and the operation of empathy in Arendt's reading of Kant, see Zerilli, L. (Winter 2009), "Toward a Feminist Theory of Judgement," *Signs* 34, no. 2, pp. 313–14.

the gap between the possible and the actual is not a sign of corruption but a marker of the irreducible fact of human plurality, a way of defusing the expectation that common situations will issue in common experiences, and a check against the condescension and moralism that can result when this expectation is frustrated.

None of this is to say that aesthetic judgment, for Arendt, is purely and simply dissensual. She acknowledges that people do "recognize each other" and "feel that they belong to each other" when they "discover a kinship in questions of what pleases and displeases" (*CC* 223 [220]). Yet Arendt specifically denies that taste should be understood as an "essentially aristocratic principle of organization." What draws her to aesthetic judgment, it seems, is that it can be the occasion for the discovery of *surprising* affinities among people, and between people and objects—affinities that cut against the grain of existing bodies of determinate judgment. Hence one of her paradigmatic instances of the exercise of the faculty of taste is the "outrageously bold" and dissensual Ciceronian pronouncement: "I prefer before heaven to go astray with Plato rather than hold true views with his opponents" (*CC* 224–5 [221]), which she explicitly contrasts both with the convergent judgments of a body of scientists, and with the authoritative judgments of experts in beauty who, "have trained their senses as much as most of us have trained our minds," and therefore find beauty "no less compelling" (that is, compulsory) "than truth" (*CC* 225 [222]).[53] Indeed, it is tempting to read "The Crisis in Culture" as a pointed expression of just such a dissensual affiliation, especially in light of three elements that Arendt appears to have added to the essay during the same revision: the surprising citation in the opening paragraph to Rosenberg's observations about kitsch; the last three words of her gloss on Cicero, "in what concerns my association with men and things, I refuse to be coerced even by truth, *even by beauty*" (*CC* 225 [222]), and the essay's final sentence: "At any rate, we may remember what the Romans—the first people that took culture seriously the way we do—thought a cultivated person ought to be: one who knows how to choose his company among men, among things, among thoughts, in the present as well as in the past" [*CC* 226 (222)].

Finally, just as Arendt's turn to Kantian aesthetics is meant not to underwrite but to undermine the deployment of the category of taste to establish or secure social hierarchies among judging subjects, it has similar consequences when it comes to the objects of judgment. Early in this chapter, I noted that Arendt's account of the idea of the work of art in *The Human Condition* serves as a point of connection between the ideas of work and of action, and that the transition between these takes place

[53] On Arendt's use of taste as a bridge between the objective qualities of the arti-factual world and the self-disclosure that takes place in action, see Markell, "Arendt's Work" and Storey, *The Taste of Politics*, ch. 3.

through a remarkable pivot in Arendt's writing, in which she moves from the idea of the work of art as naming a specific subset of durable objects to the idea that judgments of beauty are appropriate to "whatever has a shape at all and is seen," including ordinary use objects as well as what we conventionally think of as artworks (*HC* 172–3). In "The Crisis in Culture" Arendt reproduces both sides of this thought, repeatedly distinguishing between artworks and use-objects *and* insisting that, "if we wanted to judge objects, even ordinary use-objects, by their use-value alone and not also by their appearance—that is, by whether they are beautiful or ugly or something in between—we would have to pluck out our eyes" (*CC* 210 [207]). In one statement of the distinction between artworks and other objects, Arendt proposes that the key difference is that works of art are "deliberately *removed* from the processes of consumption and usage," and that this removal, which "can be achieved in a great variety of ways," is what gives rise to "culture, in the specific sense" (*CC* 209 [206], emphasis added). What's crucial about the idea of "removal" however, is that while Arendt first introduces it as a way of making sense of the distinctiveness of a certain subset of artifacts, nothing in the idea tells us anything about the properties of those artifacts themselves. To say that something is "without a purpose" because it has been removed from an immediately utilitarian context is not at all to say, for instance, that it belongs to a special category of objects that provoke the experience of aesthetic pleasure because they display the "mere form of purposiveness," or because they are purified of all reference to anything except the formal properties of their physical medium. Rather than tie purposiveness without a purpose in this way to some feature of the object itself, Arendt locates it in the way in which an object—potentially *any* object—is treated. Whenever we insulate an artifact from the immediate demands of use in order to encounter it differently, to linger—as Kant says—over the shape that it cannot help but display, to let the question of what the object is good for to open out into the larger question of "how [the world] is to look, what kind of things are to appear in it" (*CC* 223 [219–20]), we're establishing the conditions for an aesthetic experience or—better yet—for an experience that is at once aesthetic and political.[54] In the act of removal, what has changed is not the object but the object's context and surroundings: its situation, our situation in relation to it, and, through it, our situation in relation to each other. To speak of

[54]If Kant's strategy is to make the beautiful into a symbol of the good, one might say that Arendt's strategy is, instead, to show the dependence of goodness on beauty or, more broadly, on appearance—a strategy that she expresses in the suggestion that something's *usefulness* and its *look* are interrelated (*HC*, p. 173), and which resonates with her idiosyncratic reading of Plato's theory of ideas, in which she proposes that Plato only subordinated the beautiful to the good when he needed to represent the ideas as "standards, measurements and rules of behavior" through which the notoriously unreliable world of human affairs might be subjected to a more stable order (*HC*, pp. 225–6).

a "crisis in culture" is to speak of a crisis in our situation in relation to worldly objects, an unresponsiveness or inattentiveness to their appearances. And neither the insistent dissemination of standards of aesthetic quality, nor the effort to render advanced art independent of the depredations of the vulgar masses, nor the defense of purity—of the aesthetic or of the political—constitute solutions to this crisis. Rather, they are among its symptoms and its sources.

Earlier versions of this chapter were presented at the Western Political Science Association meetings and at UCLA, Notre Dame, Toronto, Cornell, and DePaul. My thanks to all the audiences and to the participants in my Chicago seminars on Arendt and on aesthetics. I owe special thanks to Joshua Dienstag, Kennan Ferguson, Andrea Frank, Nick Kompridis, James Martel, Keally McBride, Kirstie McClure, Davide Panagia, Tracy Strong, Linda M. G. Zerilli, Lena Zuckerwise, and most of all Ian Storey for comments and conversations. The research and writing of this chapter was supported by grants from the American Council of Learned Societies and the Social Sciences Division of the University of Chicago.

PART TWO

Poetics, theory, and utopian politics

CHAPTER FOUR

Fanon's decolonial aesthetic

Lewis R. Gordon
University of Connecticut

Man cannot live in a valueless world.
ALAIN LOCKE

I arrived in the world anxious to make sense of things, my spirit filled with desire to be at the origin of the world, and here I discovered myself an object amongst other objects.
FRANTZ FANON

Fanon, his readers often surmise, was a poet. It wasn't that he intentionally wrote poetry but that his work was poetic. To some extent this aspect of his writing emerged from the influence of Aimé Césaire, the famed Martinican poet who also coined the term *Négritude* (hereafter "Negritude"), the name for the initially surrealist and then Pan-African movement organized by African and Afro-Caribbean students in France in the 1930s.[1] On the other,

[1]See Césaire, A. (1995), *Notebook of a Return to My Native Land (Cahier d'un retour au pays natal)*. Rosello, M. with Pritchard, A. trans., Rosello, M. intro., Newcastle upon Tyne, UK: Bloodaxe Books. For an insightful critical study of this movement, see Abiola Irele, F. (2011), *The Negritude Movement: Explorations in Francophone African and Caribbean Literature and Thought*. Trenton, NJ: Africa World Press; cf. also Jones, D. (2010), *The Racial*

it was also out of his philosophical proclivities, which dated back to his childhood engagements with the work of Henri Bergson, the famed French Jewish philosopher who was also a winner of the Nobel Prize for literature, and life-long interest in the thought of Jean-Paul Sartre, the French gentile philosopher who rejected the same prize even though he preferred to be remembered as a writer than anything else.[2] The meeting of these worlds in Fanon's thought, however, was more than convergence because beyond Negritude, European *Lebensphilosophie* and existentialism, there were the challenges posed by black thought and those imposed upon it. The black thinker was supposedly antinomious to thought, which made the resources for her or his appearance wrought with irony, paradox and resistance to the cynical and the futile.

Commentary on Fanon's style abounds. David Macey and—building on his formulation—Reiland Rabaka, refer to his writings as *bricolage*.[3] This conception appears as such, however, if one takes Fanon out of the problematics raised by black intellectual traditions, where the challenges posed by articulating the humanity of black people led to reflection on the means by which such thought was attempted. Reading Anna Julia Cooper's *A Voice from the South* and W. E. B. Du Bois's *Souls of Black Folk*, for instance, one finds stark similarities in form and structure.[4] In one sense, the work is a collection of essays. In another sense, each chapter is not exactly essay, partially poetry, somewhat musical, spiritually riveting, and always critical. And still earlier, there are writings of protest such as David Walker's *Appeal to All Colored Citizens of the World* on one hand and meditations on the human sciences as found in Anténor Firmin's *The Equality of the Races* on the other.[5] In all these works, including Fanon's, there is the paradox faced by the black writer. If he or she writes exclusively to black readers, there is an immediate audience but a strange affirmation of seclusion and presuppositions of non-appearance. To write exclusively to

Discourses of Life Philosophy: Négritude, Vitalism and Modernity (NY: . Columbia University Press).

[2]For biographical commentary see, for example, Cherki, A. (2006), *Frantz Fanon: A Portrait.* Ithaca, NY: Cornell University Press, and recollections from childhood friends in Cheikh Djemai's documentary film *Frantz Fanon: His Life, His Struggle, His Work* (ArtMattan Productions, 2001).

[3]Macey, D. (2002), *Frantz Fanon: A Biography.* New York: Picador and Rabaka, R. (2011), *Forms of Fanonism: Fanon's Critical Theory and the Dialectics of Decolonization.* Lanham, MD: Lexington Books.

[4]Cooper, A. J. (1892), *A Voice from the South.* Xenia, OH: The Adline Printing House, and Du Bois, W. E. B. (1903), *The Souls of Black Folk.* Chicago: A. C. McClurg & Co.

[5]Walker, D. and Highland Garnet, H. (2007), *Walker's Appeal, With a Brief Sketch of His Life, and Also Garnet's Address to the Slaves of the United States of America.* New South Wales, Australia: Dodo Press (original, 1829) and Firmin, A. (1999), *The Equality of the Human Races: A Nineteenth Century Haitian Scholar's Response to European Racialism*, Charles, A. trans. New York: Garland (original 1885).

the white reader is to erase the self and the world of blackness since what is demanded from the white world is often a narcissistic reflection or affirmation of reality as that world prefers it to be. The task, then, is to break down the schism, the segregation of thought, through which ideas could be articulated beyond the racial structure by which blacks are locked, subjugated and located beneath everyone else.

There is much irony in Fanon's style. Although he had written plays and articles while a student of medicine at Lyons, the work by which he was introduced to the world was *Black Skin, White Masks*, which he had originally posed as his doctoral thesis.[6] It was rejected as inappropriate by the committee, so he quickly produced, reputedly in two weeks, a study meeting the expectations of the positivist-oriented committee: "Troubles mentaux et syndromes psychiatriques dans l'Hérédo-Dégéneration-Spino-Cérébelleuse. Un cas de maladie de Friedrich avec délire de possession" ("Mental Illness and Psychiatric Syndromes in Hereditary Cereberal Spinal Degeneration: A Case Study of Friedrich's Illness with Possession Delirium"), which he defended in 1951. Although it could be surmised that it was the topic of the originally proposed thesis that was problematic to the committee, one could also infer that it was written in a way that the committee could not actually see what he was doing. Researchers and scholars of scientific literature today know very well that mediocre work often comes to print more by virtue of format and ordered familiarity than anything else. This is not to say that Fanon's all-white jury of professors would not have rejected the work if they saw its significance. After all, the history of Africana thought is replete with great works suppressed or discarded for the sake of preserving the racial order.[7] Assuming racism was not involved, which unfortunately is unlikely, the original rejected thesis turned out to be a classic work of twentieth-century thought whose reach is already felt in the twenty-first. This is because the twenty-six-year-old medical student had offered more than his proposed program for the disalienation of the black. Understanding how black alienation was linked to that of the human being – for at the end of the day the black is, after all, of that world – Fanon outlined a more radical project as the leitmotif of the work, namely, the disalienation of the human being from the disaster of crushed relationships between one set of human beings and all others. Such a task, he argued, demanded radical intervention not only at the level of thought and deed

[6]Fanon, F. (1967), *Black Skin, White Masks*, Markmann, C. L. trans. New York: Grove Press. My references will be to this version with my revisions to the translation from the original French. (1952), *Peau noire, masques blancs* (Paris: Éditions du Seuil).

[7]For example, Leonard Harris's anthology *Philosophy Born of Struggle* (Dubuque, Iowa: Kendall/Hunt, 1981) was rejected by every philosophy acquisition editor on the grounds that there was no white audience for it. The presumption of there being no black audience for a work on Afro-American philosophy being put to the side, it took nearly a decade, as he recounted to me, for Harris to find a non-philosophy press interested in branching out.

but also about the conditions and ways by which such could be effected. The failure occasioned by his style, then, marked its success, and in similar kind its initial success would have marked its failure precisely because it would have contained it within the confines of the containable. Its rejection enabled it to reach beyond the decadent realm of fetishized methods and disciplinarily closed corridors of positivist science.

Fanon proposed the liberation of the human being at the level of *how* she or he thinks. This meant addressing the problem of the colonization of knowledge at its methodological levels. We could call this the task of decolonizing knowledge, but such a task, Fanon saw, required more than simply setting thought free. It also required recognizing the extent to which the colonization of thought required derailing it from the relationships by which it could be made meaningful. This assault, which he regarded as a correlate of the colonized human being's condition of being forced out of the relationships by which life itself could be meaningful, demanded intervention beyond the normative expectations of rhetorical strategies the consequence of which is systemic affirmation. What Fanon had to *say*, in other words, needed to be said differently.

It is no accident that Fanon's *voice* is so present in *Black Skin, White Masks*. He had in fact dictated the text to his wife, Josie Fanon, who typed it. The result is the feel of the young doctor, pacing back and forth, stopping for reflection, raising his hands to illustrate a point here and there, looking over at the ashtray as he discussed reaching for a cigarette at one moment, grimacing, abruptly standing up, slowly sitting down as he recomposed himself, as he went through, almost as the patient to the therapist, who, as his other half, listens, types, and returns those ideas to him as the text to which he also relates as a critic, and hence a metatext. Reading *Black Skin, White Masks* requires understanding the multiple voices and positions it manifests from its avowed author, for the book has that rare quality of simultaneously being textual and metatextual, with the author standing in opposition to both: the internal subject, the voice reaching for recognition in the work, stands as the naïve black modern subject; the critic, the metatheoretical voice of the work, sees the invested subject as nothing short of a lamb for slaughter. The two opposing positions, meeting in the body from which the narrative was dictated, find themselves in a face-off in a war premised on failure, where the success of each is marked by the failure of the other. The metacritic demands changing the social structure, so his proof comes from the assimilating subject's failure to realize his goal of working within the system. The naïve subject *needs*, in other words, the failure of the metacritic.

This observation of critic and critique brings to the fore the existential dimension underlying this classic foray into what could be called *decolonial reflection*. Both terms have origins, after all, in the Greek word *krinein* (to decide), which, when made into a noun, refers to a decider or judge (*kritēs*). It is not remiss, then, in being critical, to evoke its other meaning, as when things are critical, when decisions have to be made. To make such decisions requires *criteria*: standards and rules by which something is judged or decided upon. The existential heart of this reflection, then, is the realization that choices have to be made, including those of presentation, and how these choices are made will bring to the fore the investments we make in those choices, including the standards we maintain in such practice. A familiar existential theme is at work here, namely, the question of seriousness, where the presumed materiality of values could lead to the erasure or forgetting of human responsibility for them. Fanon's mode of presentation thus brings to the fore the age-old consideration of practical reason as that which could be otherwise. The reader, in other words, is compelled to ask what is Fanon doing, which leads to a reflection on not only what is to be done but also, so to speak, what *could be done*.

The question of possibility raises the problem of failure that, for Fanon, points to a diagnosis, or, more properly, a *sociodiagnosis*, since he argues that the normative situation is a social phenomenon that lends itself to psychoanalysis: "If there can be no discussion on a philosophical level—that is, the plane of the basic needs of human reality—I am willing to work on the psychoanalytical level—in other words, the level of the 'failures' in the sense in which one speaks of engine failures."[8] His course of action is to take a path through a minefield of failures. From the outset, he announced the failures of species-oriented and individualized analyses and offered the path of a sociogenic analysis, which calls for admitting the generative richness of culture in the production of meaning. That path calls for a reminder, however, of the role of human agency: "[For] society, unlike biochmencial processes, cannot escape human influences. Man is what brings society into being" (p. 11). The black, here also marked as the "black soul," since its separation has already been rejected by the limits of inner-outer failures, demands demystification through an analysis of its source: "what is called the black soul is a white construction" (p. 14, trans. revised). This construction, a failure of human understanding, asserts itself through a variety of, if we will, idolatrous offerings: language, bad-faith love and law-like constitutional theories of psychic life, among others. In each, the force of deviation and imitation reveals failure. To speak (and to write), not as a speaker or writer, but as a white, makes black speech and writing an imitation and hence not actual speech, not agency speech. Even as an effect of a wider structure, the problem is that the black effect is treated as a shadow of white normality. Such an effort, in other words, is *like* a white's:

[8]Fanon, *Black Skin, White Masks*, p. 23. For discussion, see Gordon, L. R. (Summer 2005), "Through the Zone of Nonbeing: A Reading of *Black Skin, White Masks* in Celebration of Fanon's Eightieth Birthday," *The C.L.R. James Journal* 11, no. 1, 1–43.

> Nothing is more astonishing than to hear a black express himself properly, for then in truth he is putting on the white world. I have had occasion to talk with students of foreign origin. They speak French badly: Little Crusoe, alias Prospero, is at ease then. He explains, informs, interprets, helps them with their studies (p. 36).

With love, the ordered expectations, in at least Lacanian semiology, of a normative order in which gender difference is ontologically basic falls under the weight of colonial imposition: whether black woman or black man, the normative center is *white man*, not even white woman. And at the constitutional level, the symbolic expectations fall sway to the factual correlates of analogical and reductive interpretation: a gun, in the dream life of the colonized, *is a gun*. These series of failures are revisited through an autobiography of the author that, since his individuality was already marked out of the schema, is not an autobiography. Put differently, the metastructure of self-reference means that Fanon, referring to Fanon, fails at the individuated narrative, since he collapses into *the black* through whom the meaning of autobiography as inner-life, as mythic self-report, functions on a plane that is different from that of *ordinary autobiography*. Fanon, in other words, in the autobiographical moment is asserting the upsurge of that whose possibility was already denied as possible. Such a performance is nothing short of magical.

Fanon's magical, autobiographical, poetic philosophical reflection announces itself immediately from the body pacing back and forth in those unfolding reflections brought to print. In the fifth chapter, "The Lived-Experience of the Black" (trans. revised), this motion is interrupted through recounting ensnared embodiment brought to realization by a frightened little white boy:

"'Dirty *nègre!*' or simply, 'Look, a *nègre!*'"[9]

The chapter's thematic of lived-experience, of being willing to work on the plane of lived-experience of a structural imposition, raises the question of the subject through whom language speaks and by whom it is written. The language, embodied in the little white boy who made the exclamation when he saw Fanon walking in Lyon, left him momentarily frozen, perhaps reminiscent of the center of the *Inferno* as portrayed by Dante—a center of icy hatred and revenge—facing a struggle against a consequent cold exteriority where he stood "outside," devoid of an inside; of, in other words, an intentional point of view. For Fanon, who had achieved a level of naivety that enabled him to walk through the world as belonging to the language, the culture, the social world as a relationship of possibility, the effect was of what could be called *a fallen fall*:

---

[9]Given the ambiguity of the word *nègre*, meaning *Negro* and *nigger*, I'll refer to the French term from this point onward.

> I arrived in the world anxious to make sense of things, my spirit filled with desire to be at the origin of the world, and here I discovered myself an object amongst other objects.
>
> Imprisoned in this overwhelming objectivity, I implored others. Their liberating look, running over my body, which suddenly became smooth, returns to me a lightness that I believed lost, and, absenting me from the world, returns me to the world. But there, just at the opposite slope, I stumble, and the other, by gestures, attitudes, looks, fixed me, in the sense that one fixes a chemical preparation with a dye. I was furious. I demanded an explanation.... Nothing happened. I exploded. Now, the tiny pieces are collected by another self (p. 109, trans. revised).

The recollection of the self of which Fanon writes is his body offered back to him, a body that appears in mirrors, albeit looked at before, now seen in a different way. The mirror, after all, becomes a perspective from which he had presumed himself a participant in a shared attitude toward a particular object—the *nègre*—to which he was not identical. In seeing himself through the perspective of how he is seen by whites (and anti-black people of color), his perspective shifted from an anti-*nègre* one to that of the *nègre* self. That self, which he never associated with himself, fell from the fallen into his perceptual field. The result was two movements of double consciousness. The first, seeing himself through the eyes of the hostile Other, is the alienated reality from which Fanon's text is an effort to liberate the black reader. The second, *potentiated double consciousness*, is the realization of the first as a constructed reality.[10] That involves demonstration of the contradictions of the imposed self (the fall after the fall) on the lived-reality of the self in mundane life, which offers itself as a dialectical demonstration of conflicting cultural logics where once-universals become particularized. For Fanon, this demonstration had already begun with the appeal to social diagnostics and continued through the analysis of failures. It went further through the radicality of the analysis, which challenged even its methodological assumptions: "There is a point at which methods devour themselves" (*Black Skin*, p. 12). That even method must be subject to critique meant that the radicality of object formation called for its normative assumptions being parenthesized, marked or suspended. The move is patently phenomenological, but since it cannot even presume phenomenology as valid, it is,

---

[10]For the classic treatment of this form of double consciousness, see Du Bois, W. E. B. (Summer 2005), *The Souls of Black Folk*. For discussion, see Henry, P. (Summer 2005) "Africana Phenomenology: Its Philosophical Implications," *The C.L.R. James Journal* 11, no. 1), 79–112; Gordon, J. A. (2007), "The Gift of Double Consciousness: Some Obstacles to Grasping the Contributions of the Colonized," in *Postcolonialism and Political Theory*, Persram, N. ed. Lanham, MD: Lexington Books, pp. 143–61; and Gordon, L. R. (2008), *An Introduction to Africana Philosophy*. Cambridge, UK: Cambridge University Press, pp. 73–80, 174–7.

as Nelson Maldonado-Torres recently argued, *decolonial*.[11] This decolonial movement brings phenomena to the fore in an act of potentiated double consciousness.

That the subject here is the human being raises, in addition, the question of the scope of any disciplinary, methodological and stylistic stratagem. That it is the human being Fanon wanted to liberate raises as well the problem of the human being as a subject or object of study. In stream with a long line of African Diasporic critics, Fanon understood that the incompleteness of the human being challenged the extent to which any methodological or rhetorical approach could encapsulate the human subject. To make the human being contained by any singular discipline or method would require an isomorphic relationship between that epistemic model and the human being. But that would collapse the human being into an identity relation with that model, which would, in effect, make the human being epistemically closed. Human reality would, then, in the language of old, become a substance. If, however, substance is defined as that which could be without relations to other things, the notion of non-relational human reality would emerge. This model fails, however, the moment the human being faces the negation of such closure through the question of possibility. In the human world, that amounts to the sociality of human existence. The human being, in other words, is not a thing but a *relationship*. The scope of this relationship challenges the extent to which a single discipline could say all that needs to be said. In effect, it demands not only coverage of a wide range of dimensions of human reality but also establishing the *relationships* between those approaches, the consequence of which is a communicative transcending of disciplinary and rhetorical reductionism. This is indicative of an important aspect of human reality: its transformation from signification to symbolization. The sign, pertaining to signification, which human beings share with many other animals, points beyond itself, but the symbol—in Greek the conjunction of the words *syn* (together) and *ballein* (thrown)—brings together an array of signs decipherable through the relationships meaningful to human beings. That human beings share what phenomenologists call an *intersubjective* relationship to these modes of meaning enables not only the production of the human world but also, within that world, that of new forms of meaning and, consequently, life.

Understanding the human being as relational and consequently produced by relationships raises challenges regarding the limits of the production of everyday value. Aesthetics here goes beyond modernist expectations of art to the question of lived reality, to what it means for human beings to organize a world in which they could actually live. The preceding discussion

---

[11] Maldonado-Torres, N. (2007), *Against War: Views from the Underside of Modernity*. Durham, NC: Duke University Press.

argues that human beings should think about what it means to live in a human world. Colonialism and its correlative epistemic order, Fanon argues, regard the human being as fundamentally problematic, no doubt because of the precariousness and contingency of human existence. In a world where the project is control and predictability, the human being is annoyingly unstable and, even worse, *metastable*. The former at least could be governed by a principle of fluidity. But where there is *meta*stability, there is a transcending of stability through acts of locating stability. In other words, instead of contradiction, metastability raises problems of paradox, where self-reference also becomes self-displacing.

The approach to writing about these matters, then, is conditioned by the problem of a misbehaving subject. The kind of writing called for in the study of such elusiveness is one that is reflectively and admittedly human at its core. Thus, to say what it *is* in terms of a singular, isomorphic disciplinary model would misrepresent it. Additionally, to assert it in terms of an *interdisciplinary* approach would also be a mistake, for that could be as closed, intersecting lines wrapped in a two-dimensional logic of, say, Euclidian geometry. To move to the *human* world requires acts of production and disclosure on multiple dimensional levels. The communicative multidimensionality of the human being, then, brings the many manifestations from poetry to science, music and dance to sacred reflection, and grammatical levels from the adverbial to the interrogative. It requires, in other words, a form of writing that is not subjugated or *disciplinarily decadent*.

Disciplinary decadence is a form of fetishism wherein the practitioner turns away from reality through over investment in a discipline or its method. The result is a form of solipsism, where the discipline or its practices and methodology become *the world*. From a disciplinarily decadent perspective, the task is not one of articulating or understanding reality; it is to bend reality to the dictates of disciplinary expectations since, from such a perspective, that is all reality could be, what would supposedly make reality meaningful. It is decadent because it presumes its own completeness where, as isomorphic with reality, it no longer needs the latter and thus has nowhere to grow or go. A living discipline is unfolding and growing through realization of the scope of reality always exceeding the disciplinary reach. This is because, as expressions of human reality, disciplines have an intentional structure. They reach out, and in that process produce knowledge. As expressions of living human reality, they also go through fatigue and decay, which leads to disciplinary introspection to a point of ignoring the animus of disciplinary formation. Eventually, the communicability of disciplinary knowledge also loses sway to the decaying process. Eventually, the only way out is to transcend the discipline. It demands the paradoxical act of a discipline going beyond itself—discipline beyond discipline, so to speak. Using Kierkegaard as inspiration, let us call this a *teleological suspension of disciplinarity*. It is where a discipline transcends itself for the sake of re-establishing its relationship with reality.[12]

Fanon addressed all these concerns in his writings, although most especially so in his inaugural work. As art and writing go, it offers a form of art beyond art (by virtue of not explicitly being offered as a work of art but nevertheless is such) and writing beyond writing, or more properly, a teleological suspension of writing through Fanon's making writing always more than itself for the sake of the reality that beckons it.

Should Revolutionaries Sing the Blues?

Fanon, preferring the medium of poetry, did not care much for the blues. He concluded:

> Thus the blues—"the black slave lament"—was offered up for the admiration of the oppressors. This modicum of stylized oppression is the exploiter's and the racist's rightful due. Without oppression and without racism you have no blues. The end of racism would sound the knell of great Negro music... As the all-too-famous Toynbee might say, the blues are the slave's response to the challenge of oppression.
>
> Still today, for many men, even colored, Armstrong's music has a real meaning only in this perspective.
>
> Racism bloats and disfigures the face of the culture that practices it. Literature, the plastic arts, songs for shopgirls, proverbs, habits, patterns, whether they set out to attack it or to vulgarize it, restore racism.[13]

The radical change of building new concepts and setting the material infrastructure for a new humanity, which he eventually announced at the end of *The Wretched of the Earth*, entails, for Fanon, as we see in the quoted passage from "Racism and Culture," a clarion call for the death of the blues.[14] Yet, we must wonder, what would modern struggles for social transformation and freedom be without the blues? Also, must the blues be characterized as so symbiotically linked to racial oppression and resistance that the path of a negative moment in a historical dialectical battle for freedom, as Sartre exposed in his discussion of Negritude, be its only epithet?[15]

---

[12]For more on these concepts, see Gordon, L. R. (2006), *Disciplinary Decadence: Living Thought in Trying Times*, Boulder, CO: Paradigm Publishers.

[13]Fanon, F. (1967), "Racism and Culture," in Fanon, J. ed., *Toward the African Revolution*, Haakon Chevalier, H. trans. New York: Grove Press.

[14]See Fanon, F. (1963), *The Wretched of the Earth*, Farrington, C. trans. New York: Grove Press.

[15]"Black Orpheus" trans. John MacCombie, in Steven Ungar (ed.), "*What Is Literature?" and Other Essays* (Cambridge, MA: Harvard University Press, 1988), pp. 289–330.

Fanon's aim is, as he consistently made it known, revolution. Yet, to talk about revolutionaries in the contemporary climate often carries a tinge of nostalgia, if not, for some, shame and embarrassment, which is awfully ironic since the whole point of a revolutionary consciousness is to look forward. The nostalgia of revolution in neo-conservative and neo-liberal times exemplifies a spirit caught in the winds of an enveloping mood, where even moving forward seems to be understood in backward terms.[16] The human condition, bullied against building public arenas for political activities beyond the proceduralism of hegemonic liberal democracies, finds itself punctuated, increasingly, by resources of force and a retreat from reality instead of an exploration of its possibilities. The question of revolution is, after all, one of radical social change, but making the social world change carries with it the two horns of consequence on what we are and what we ought to become. Such is the strange dualism of an epoch marked by suffering and expectations of material redemption.[17]

The path of material redemption has received its classic formulation in the thought of Max Weber.[18] The process of modernization carries with it, however, multiple teleological promises, as also observed by Weber as "polytheistic," among which is the claim of secularization. Such a path promises a move from religious-ethical demands on lived reality to a near imperial ascent of the reach of law.[19] Yet, the hopes of legalization as the manifestation of modern conquest of the social world brings with it accompanying limits.[20] The gravity that underlies the concept of law in the physical world haunts such avowed sedimentation of the social world; created by human actions, it faces its demise through such agency. The social world is not, however, one simply of rationalization and control. It is also premised upon directed activities whose exhaustion is beyond morality and law and stand, instead, in upward and downward poles of faith and lived-experience of beauty and ugliness—the world, that is, of value.[21]

---

[16]See the literature on conservatism and neoconservatism:, e.g., Brown, W. (2006), "American Nightmare: Neoliberalism, Neoconservatism, and De-democratization," *Political Theory* 34, no. 6, 690–714.

[17]Cf., for example, Barber, B. R. (2008), *Consumed: How Markets Corrupt Children, Infantilize Adults, and Swallow Citizens Whole*. New York: W. W. Norton.

[18]See Baehr, P. and Wells, G. C. ed., trans. and intro. (2000), *The Protestant Work Ethic and the Spirit of Capitalism in The Protestant Ethic and the "Spirit" of Capitalism and Other Writings*. New York: Penguin Books.

[19]See Weber, M. (1978), *Economy and Society: An Outline of Interpretive Sociology*, Roth, G. and Wittich, C. ed. 2 volumes. Berkeley: University of California Press, and Heller, A. (1999), *A Theory of Modernity*. Malden, MA: Blackwell Publishers, "*Values*," pp. 200–20.

[20]See, for example, Jean Comaroff and John Comaroff, eds., (2006), *Law and Disorder in the Postcolony*. Chicago: University of Chicago Press.

[21]See Alain Locke's "Values and Imperatives" in Harris, L. ed. (1989), *The Philosophy of Alain Locke: Harlem Renaissance and Beyond*. Philadelphia: Temple University Press and Søren Kierkegaard, *Either/Or*, Hong, H. V. and Hong, E. H. trans. (1987). Princeton, N.J.: Princeton University Press.

The problem of value, particularly in its aesthetic form, in the modern world is that it resists the completeness of rational colonization. That values are also practices of *assessment* requires, in a paradoxically "logical" way, that even the source of valuing logic must be beyond logic itself. One *brings value* to one's practices, even, as Nietzsche has shown, *to one's values*.[22] This transcending capacity of values has occasioned many great expectations for their role in processes of social transformation. For colonization practices to continue, the assertion of systemic control must include a value that is an anti-value, one that attacks the conditions by which values could emerge in the first place. The source of such a value is most explicit in early modern thought, although its roots are ancient.[23] It reverberates into the present with the familiar phrase, "G-d's will." In a world governed by the will of an omniscient, omnipotent and all-just god, we find ourselves constantly in the face of human limits. What we see as unjust could be a function of our own finitude. An infinite being could see the ultimate justice in what at first appears to be unjust. This rationalization is known as *theodicy*, from *theo* (god) and *dikē* (justice), to mean *god's justice*. If the god's work is perfect and inherently just, then there are at least two accounts of evil available to us: (1) there is ultimately no evil in the world, only its appearance, and (2) evil emerges in the world as a consequence of human freedom, which makes the god's complete goodness compatible with the reality of evil. On both accounts, the notion of evil is extraneous to the god. What, however, should we conclude about a world that is both devoid of gods and is unjust? How should we account for injustice and suffering in the modern world? Here, too, we have a variety of accounts, of which we could consider two: (1) there is ultimately no injustice in the world (although there is suffering) because justice is a value and values are not, in the end, "real" or "objective" or (2) well-organized systems of knowledge and social regulations should not be blamed for the proclivities of bad people. We find, in these accounts, a secularized version of the theocentric model in the form of a system-centric model.

The system-centric model occasions reflection on the enduring grammar of idolatry and the ascription of that which is evil, unjust and ugly to things unassimilable. Theodicy, in other words, could ironically continue through modern aspirations to the secular in the form of secular*ism*. This move leads to new forms of rationalizations while maintaining very old

---

[22]See, for example, Nietzsche, F., Kaufmann, W. and Hollingdale, R. J. trans., Kaufmann, W. ed. with commentary (1967), *On the Genealogy of Morals*. Hollingdale, New York: Vintage. And cf. his *The Will to Power*, trans. Walter Kaufmann and R. J. Hollingdale, edited, with commentary, by Walter Kaufmann, with facsimiles of the original manuscript (1967), New York: Random House.

[23]For discussion, see Hicks, J. (1978), *Evil and the God of Love*, revised edn, New York: Harper & Row.

legitimating forms. The god is replaced by new systemic markers, and we find "science" and "political system" to be two instances of such rationalizations. With science, the aim is epistemic. It becomes the ultimate source of rigor in systematic productions of knowledge. With a political system, the result is, as W. E. B. Du Bois has shown in *The Souls of Black Folk*, the production of "problem people." Both are consequences of systems lived as complete and closed. Their contradictions must be "outside."

It is no accident, then, that politically engaged, revolutionary thinkers such as Du Bois and Fanon faced a peculiar theodicean battle. They had to unveil the contradictions of the system (epistemological and political) as *internal*, which led to the revelation of the need for *alternatives*. The result was, then, a doubled-relation to the normative practices of the societies in which they lived. They both had to see their society as it saw itself and—literally—see the way it really was, see its contradictions. For revolutionaries, their society has a narcissistic feature of seeking self-deceiving reflections. The revolutionary critic's job—at least that of revolutionary intellectuals (who include artists)—is to eliminate such narcissism and enable society to respond to its contradictions, to, in effect, become what that society has lived up to such a point as a misguided notion of such an event marking the end of the world.

This language of doubling and double envisioning brings to the fore another insight from W. E. B. Du Bois. Implicit in his observation of double consciousness is the accusation of hidden contradictions of many modern societies that are lived each day by their pariah. How could justice be reconciled as separate but purportedly equal?

The resources available for the unveiling of societal contradictions are manifold. Although the world of prose offers theoretical reflection, such an effort also requires the force of sight and feeling. For the group of writers in Addison Gayle's classic anthology *The Black Aesthetic* (1971), for instance, art could not be defended for its own sake to people who so desperately demanded social change, especially in the form of Black Power.[24] For them, there was an artistic dimension to Marx's famous eleventh thesis on Feuerbach: the point is to change the world. Although the political dimensions of black artistic production are well known (often under the rubric of "protest"), and although the classic interpretive techniques of modernism versus avant garde, and formalism and surrealism, have been utilized in the interpretation and assessment of such production, an aspect that is not often discussed, but is crucial for addressing Fanon's seemingly archaeological challenge, is the existential dimension of producing work in black. This is the case not only because of Fanon's own philosophical predilections, but also because of the peculiar set of existential problematics

[24]Gayle, A. ed. (1971), *The Black Aesthetic*. Garden City, NY: Doubleday Publishers.

posed by the weight of European modernity on black souls, including the forms of alienation that mark modern life in both its masked and unveiled contradictions.

A feature of modern European life has been the suppression of many of its subjects to the point of their suffering near (although with an aim for complete) social invisibility. To exist, a word whose etymological root is in the Latin expression *ex* (out) *sistere* (to stand), means to stand out, to become—among other things—visible. For black people, there is paradox here, for, as is well known, blacks face problems of hypervisibility. The paradox is that hypervisibility is a form of invisibility. For to be hypervisible is to be seen, but to be seen in a way that crushes the self under the weight of a projected, alien self ("Look, a *nègre*!"). Let us call this phenomenon *epistemic closure*.[25] It means to be seen in a way that closes off the process of inquiry and understanding, to be seen without being seen, to be encountered without the modalities of interrogatives, to be "known" as "nothing more to know." Because existence entails emergence, such a perspective on the human condition entails a thesis of openness. The human being, in other words, is always a possibility beyond his or her immediate sedimentations or claims of permanence and fixedness. Moreover, the human being, because of such fundamental incompleteness, creates frameworks of collective activities that eventually meet in the form of a social world. Such a world is the framework of meaning that transcends, often, the intentions of individual human beings who live such structures. In effect, human beings encounter their reflections as projections (the effect side of projects), and these projections take many forms, aesthetic productions being a set of them.

To read aesthetic productions with an eye for their existential dimensions means, then, to examine the ways in which forms of humanity appear as symbol and meaning. Why symbol and meaning? Because although a consequence of human activity (what Hannah Arendt calls *work*, that is, world-creating activity), the creation points in a variety of directions that transcend itself.[26] It "points" to having a creator, and thus works as a constructed and artefactual reality, and then "points" to its own realms of significations, as do most signs. Think of the etymology of "symbol," in the Greek words *syn* (together) and *ballein* (thrown). An existential analysis poses the problem of emergence, further, as a distancing of self from self. In other words, the posing of existential questions inward leads to a displacement of self that leads to the elusiveness of self. Meaning, thus, shifts from its ordinary law-like structure as we find in lexicographical

---

[25] For more on this concept, see *Fanon and the Crisis of European Man*, ch. 3, and Gordon, L. R. (2000), *Existentia Africana: Understanding Africana Existential Thought*. New York: Routledge, ch. 4.

[26] See Arendt, H. (1958), *The Human Condition*. Chicago: University of Chicago Press.

definitions (that has its roots in Greek words that refer, ironically, to speech and words, for example: *lexis* and subsequently in Latin *lex* for what we now know as *law*) to a new, lived reality of making life meaningful. To have a meaning and to be meaningful is a distinction that brings to the fore the "given" in the former and agency in the latter. It is this link between meaningfulness and agency that stimulated another existential distinction, one between liberty (unencumbered movement) and freedom (living one's humanity). Freedom requires the ability to raise the question of the absence of meaningful liberty and reveals the importance of the imagination in the human condition. What would life be were human beings incapable of imagination? Is not even happiness haunted by the possibility of living a dream and unhappiness the hope of only living a nightmare from which, one day, to arise through an imagined alternative? This is not to say that existence and freedom call for delusion. The whole point is that in our struggles with reality, we simultaneously, as Freud observed, "daydream."[27] And just as implicit in children's daydreaming is the desire to be adults, in adult daydreaming there is, too, an ironic maturation process of transcending too much *seriousness*. There needs, in other words, to be possibility for life to live.

Such themes are taken to more explicit aesthetic reflection in Toni Morrison's *The Bluest Eye*.[28] As Gary Schwartz pointed out in his insightful essay, "Toni Morrison at the Movies," one of the consequences of chaining black emergence is the motif of imitation.[29] To be an imitation is to be without a standard of one's own. The original, the prototype, becomes the generator of value, and thus an analytic of inferiority is always implicit. Morrison's exploration of imitation at the heart of racialized questions of beauty, with the imitation always having an analytic of less-than on a slippery slope to the ugly, with the mixed (racial, cultural or otherwise) suffering the displacement of incoherence (look at the ugliness of generational incestuous mixture in the form of adults' and children's language at the beginning of the text), brings to the fore the limits of dialectics of recognition. To be as another's standard of value is to be submerged and, consequently, not to appear except as alien, even to one's self. Of course, part of the lie of blackness as imitation is that original black productions are imitated by whites all across the globe to being, in truth, creolizations of black, white—and, for that matter, brown, yellow, and red.[30] We see here

---

[27]Freud, S. (1963), "The Relation of the Poet to Day-Dreaming," *Character and Culture*, Rieff, P. intro. New York: Collier Books, especially p. 36.

[28]Morrison, T. (1972), *The Bluest Eye*. New York: Washington Square Press.

[29]Schwartz, G. (1997), "Toni Morrison at the Movies: Theorizing Race Through Imitation of Life (for Barbara Siegel)," *Existence in Black: An Anthology of Black Existential Philosophy*, Gordon, L. R. ed. and intro. New York: Routledge, pp. 111–28.

[30]See, for example, Trouillot, M.-R. (2003), *Global Transformations: Anthropology and the Modern World*. New York: Palgrave Macmillan. Also, Monahan, M. (2011), *The Creolizing*

a return of Du Bois's theme of double consciousness, for the originality of black aesthetic production is lived as the contradiction of white normativity but is imitated by the white mainstream as a denied originality.

The existential and the meaningful raise the question of what we shall call semiotic resistance. Implicit in signs and symbols is their displacement, their always pointing beyond themselves. Meditations on freedom often take symbolic form precisely because of the always beyond yet reclaiming status of existence and values. Although Morrison's *The Bluest Eye* appeared after the emergence of the Black Arts Movement of the 1960s, it was the culmination of a set of existential reflections that lay bare the folly of the dialectics of white recognition. Just as the afro and the black fist signaled *only violence* for the world that feared black equality, just as "Say it loud: 'I'm Black and I'm Proud!'" meant for some, "I'm Black and I am Dangerous," the bloated and disfigured face of which Fanon wrote found itself needing to look inward, not for the sake of escape, but for the reclamation of agency through which to construct different epistemic and aesthetic conditions for that much-needed new humanity. The problem, however, is that this move manifested itself politically—that is, *outwardly*—which means that however inward one's search for self-love and struggle against self-loathing might be, it goes nowhere if it makes one cease to be actional. The needed form of writing, then, is one that expresses this outwardly-moving call paradoxically in relation to its inwardness or subjectivity.

Writing to make one actional

There is for Fanon no point in talking about the political without addressing what it means to be actional. He argued that this was needed because of the impact of overly structural (phylogenetic) and individualist (ontogenetic) accounts of the limits on black existence. Between both, as we saw, are things created by a social world (the sociogenetic) that, we should also be reminded, unlike biochemical processes require human beings for its continued existence. Fanon, in effect, called for revolution because he also called for changing the social world.

Fanon was not, however, naive. He realized that the kind of changes he was calling for were tantamount to calling for a second death of G-d. For the contemporary world has its own idols on whose shoulders stand the value system of racial oppression and colonialism. The transformations he

Subject: Race, Reason, and the Politics of Purity. New York: Fordham University Press; and Gordon, J. A. (2014), *Creolizing Political Theory: Reading Rousseau through Fanon*. New York: Fordham University Press.

was calling for require, as well, then, the critical unmasking of theodicean dynamics. The familiar Du Boisian motif of "problem people," of contradictions of a system that avows its own completeness, returned. Fanon revealed this through unmasking the folly of the dialectics of recognition in the delusions of linguistic mastery, white love as a source of legitimation, and, more germane to this chapter, the poetics of Negritude. For Fanon, as for many of the artists of the later black intellectual and arts movements, Negritude offered a form of poetic salvation. It offered a way to love blackness and, thus, love himself. But, as he learned from Jean-Paul Sartre's "Black Orpheus," such a retreat required an absolute conviction in order not to collapse into the relativism of a negative moment that re-centered Europeans as what it means to be human. Loving blackness *against* whiteness has the reactionary effect of reinforcing whiteness. In Fanon's words, "I needed not to know." Later on, in *A Dying Colonialism*, Fanon takes heed in the positive dimension of Negritude as that which was created by blacks, as an exemplar of black agency.[31] But at the end of being robbed of his "last chance" in the fifth chapter of *Black Skin, White Masks*, Fanon began to weep and wash away the narcissistic impediments to his confrontation with white social reality. It is then that he is able to explore the psychopathological dimensions of anti-black racism, and it is there that he sees clearly that the world created by European modernity lacks the concept of a normal black adult. This is because whether in the direction of the black outcast, the criminal or in the direction of the "assimilated black subject," both have blackness and normality in opposition. The former is an accepted intersection (black *and* criminal have been conjoined as into "black equals criminal" into "black/criminal") and the latter is elimination (black does not equal normal/white; thus, assimilation equals white/normal, which means "the assimilated black" is "the black who is not black," which makes contradictory the mode of being for such a figure). How could blacks be liberated by developing a healthy self-identity if black identity is locked in the category of abnormality?

In "Racism and Culture" and his books *A Dying Colonialism* and *The Wretched of the Earth*, Fanon explored the question of cultural resistance and social transformation that brings to the fore the role of aesthetics as broadly understood. In all these texts, the leitmotif of tragic drama is set in classic fashion of competing notions of rights. There is the colonizer's "right" over all that has been colonized, and there is the colonized's "right" to fight against colonization and reclaim his or her humanity. The problem is exacerbated by the agents of struggle not often having been those at the original moment of constructing the colonial state. They are, in other words, born into the colonial condition. Such a reciprocal face-off of

[31] Fanon, F. (1967), *A Dying Colonialism*, Chevalier, H. trans., Gilly, A. intro. New York: Grove Press.

relative claims suspends ethical dictates without prior political resolutions. And in a world in which ethics has been suspended, what could one expect but violence to be the consequence?

That these texts are brilliant instances of a symbiosis of the poetic and the historical, as Paget Henry has shown in *Caliban's Reason*, reveals their message to the politicization of art as exemplified by, for example, the Black Arts Movement.[32] Particularly prescient, but often overlooked, is Fanon's argument in *The Wretched of the Earth*, that national consciousness must supervene over nationalism. National consciousness is the realization that a nation must be built. Nationalism is the attachment to identities that carry dangers of collapsing into ethnocentrism, tribalism and racism. The former is an inclusive "we" that includes even responsibility of building a world for subsequent generations. The latter is always an "us versus them": "the consciousness of self is not the closing of a door to communication. Philosophic thought teaches us, on the contrary, that it is its guarantee. National consciousness, which is not nationalism, is the only thing that will give us an international dimension" (*Wretched of the Earth*, p. 247).

The existential dimension of Fanon's thought comes to the fore here in his discussion of the role of cultural production in relation to social transformation. He argued, in effect, that existence precedes essence by insisting that art should come out of struggles instead of being created as conditions for struggle: "If man is known by his acts, then we will say that the most urgent thing today for the intellectual [also read as artist] is to build up his nation. If this building up is true, that is to say if it interprets the manifest will of the people and reveals the eager African peoples, then the building of a nation is of necessity accompanied by the discovery and encouragement of universalizing values" (ibid.). At this point, Fanon would appear in opposition to any artistic project of social transformation premised on nationalism instead of the question of national consciousness. That conclusion would, however, be incorrect. Observe: "A frequent mistake, and one which is moreover hardly justifiable, is to try to find cultural expressions for and to give new values to native culture within the framework of colonial domination. This is why we arrive at a proposition which at first sight seems paradoxical: the fact that in a colonized country the most elementary, most savage, and the most undifferentiated nationalism is the most fervent and efficient means of defending national cultures" (*Wretched*, p. 244). Fanon's argument suggests that sometimes nationalist art is necessary for the formation of normative infrastructures through which struggles could emerge for the decolonizing practices that will raise the question of *national consciousness* versus nationalism.[33] The

[32]Henry, P. (2000), *Caliban's Reason: Introducing Afro-Caribbean Philosophy*. New York: Routledge.

[33]For elaboration of this distinction, see Gordon, J. A. (2011), "Revolutionary in

people, in other words, must be in a position to build their nation for such a problematic to be meaningful. The question of decolonization as a condition for this post-colonial move is vital. And we see here a more positive reassertion of the dialectical elements that led to his earlier resolve to weep, and we ironically see him endorsing a version of the argument Sartre used in support of Negritude as a form of "anti-racist racism."

In these discussions, Fanon offered some insights on what could be called the semiotic moment of art in the formation of national consciousness. For without the development of new modes of expressing nationhood, old forms of identities will reign as the foundations of national identity. Although Fanon mentions a variety of artistic practices, poetry is, without question, the most privileged activity for him and many whose black revolutionary imagination was first stimulated by Negritude. This would explain why, although he is critical of Negritude, Fanon is at first especially critical of the blues. For he sees the blues as more linked to the underlying condition of white oppression, which stimulates the worst of the reflection of white desire. The indictment from "Racism and Culture" returns in more generalized form: "To believe it is possible to create black culture is to forget that *nègres* are disappearing just as those people who brought them into being are seeing the break-up of their economic and cultural supremacy" (*Wretched*, p. 234). History has not borne out this observation, given the emergence of neo-liberal globalism, but the argument still holds so long as we lay claim to a necessary linkage to the continued creation of "*nègres*" by New World orders of racist exploitation. The argument itself rests on functionalist foundations, where aesthetic productions have well defined roles to play, and these roles are not assessable in aesthetic but political terms. From this point of view, the defense of centering poetry is its link to writing and speech and hence to intellectuals who are not artists. In ways, it is affirmation of the value of the word over the moan and the kinetic revolt of dance.

Is this assessment of the blues, and by extension black aesthetics, sustainable?

Blues thinking, blues writing

Fanon's reflections on racism and colonialism and his observation of the absence of normality in the study of black psychopathology lead to the question of the meaning of health. For in the absence of ethical foundations,

---

Counter-Revolutionary Times: Elaborating Fanonian National Consciousness into the Twenty-First Century," *Journal of French and Francophone Philosophy (Revue de la philosophie française et de langue française)*, vol. 19, no. 1, 37–47.

what he calls in *Wretched* the "Graeco-Latin pedestal," justice, too, has to fall sway to the reorganization of social forces for its possibility. Thus, in the absence of even the possibility of justice is left the reflection on what it means to be healthy.

Here, I should like to enlist Nietzsche's theory of social health that underlies, in his early work, his theory of ancient Greek tragedy. For Nietzsche, health should not be interpreted as an absence of disease or adversity. It should be understood as an organism's or agent's or community's ability to deal with such travails through an affirmation of life. In *The Birth of Tragedy from the Spirit of Music*, he argued that the ancient Greeks responded to life's misfortunes through the creation of tragic drama. This response first took form in music and the chorus and eventually gave way to more dialogue and the emergence of the hero. The hero, however, was afforded no respite through pleas of innocence, because in tragedy it is the reconciliation of opposing forces—one, Dionysian (god of music, fluids, intoxication, women and drama) and the other, Apollonian (god of plastic arts, order, harmony, form, masculine beauty)—with different periods of emphasis but in each instance an understanding that life offers suffering, however good our souls may be. Nietzsche adds to this view of tragedy a theory of decadence, where as life decays so too do its values, which often take nihilistic forms. During periods of growth, however, there is the vibrant affirmation of life.

Nietzsche could very well be describing the plight of black people in the modern world and the aesthetic response, the blues, that has emerged from such suffering. But in stream with Nietzsche's reflections on the ancient Greeks, we should question the wisdom of reducing black suffering *only* to racism and colonialism. Black people do not, after all, live only through such terms. There are times when the situatedness of life itself intervenes, and it is often those aspects of life that are sung about in blues music, lamented on in blues poetry, and underlie the blues aspects of the performing and visual arts. The blues is thus not only an aesthetic of racism but also the leitmotif of everyday life under modernity. As Ralph Ellison reflects in his poignant essay, "Richard Wright's Blues":

> The blues is an impulse to keep the painful details and episodes of a brutal experience alive in one's aching consciousness, to finger its jagged grain, and to transcend it, not by the consolation of philosophy but by squeezing from it a near-tragic, near-comic lyricism. As a form, the blues is an autobiographical chronicle of personal catastrophe expressed lyrically.[34]

[34]In Ellison, R. (1964), *Shadow and Act*. New York: Vintage, pp. 78–9.

That the blues should not be reduced only to racism suggests a broader role for the blues. The blues is about dealing with life's suffering of any kind. Because of this, it has become the leitmotif of modernity itself. We need only think through the many musical manifestations of the blues that have permeated the twentieth century and continue into the twenty first: swing, jazz, rhythm and blues, soul, rock 'n' roll, salsa, samba, rock steady, calypso, samba and now hip hop. Fanon, interestingly enough, applauded bebop, which he saw as bereft of the pathologies of white recognition and ressentiment:

> It is the colonialists who become defenders of the native style. We remember perfectly...the white jazz specialists when after the Second World War new styles such as the bebop took definite shape. The fact is that in their eyes jazz should only be the despairing, broken-down nostalgia of an old *nègre* who is trapped between five glasses of whiskey, the curse of his race, and the racial hatred of the white men. As soon as the *nègre* comes to an understanding of himself, and understands the rest of the world differently, when he give birth to hope and forces back the racist universe, it is clear that his trumpet sounds more clearly and his voice less hoarsely (*Wretched*, pp. 242–3).

While true about bebop, Fanon's remarks could also apply to the blues and many of its other forms. There are aspects of the blues that exemplify its own aesthetic sensibility. Blues music is full of irony. Its sadness exemplifies an adult understanding of life that is both sober and, ironically, happy. It is a non-delusional happiness; the kind of happiness that is a realization instead of a diversion. It is the beauty of moonlight versus sunshine, although the blues dimensions of a sunny day could be understood through our realization of how much can be hidden in plain sight. Think of the numbness one seeks from alcohol and the realization offered by the blues; that numbness gets us nowhere. All blues productions remind us that life is not something to escape but something to confront. And it does so in its very form. The classical blues structure is full of repetitions, for instance, that reveal new layers of meaning about the cyclicality of life. And in this structure, although a story is retold, it is understood at different levels the effect of which is cathartic and after which is a renewed understanding of the point of origin.

The irony here is that Fanon's *Black Skin, White Masks* fits the structural description of the blues at the end of the previous paragraph. In that work, Fanon tells a story that is retold in mounting layers of revelation. At the moment of catharsis—the weeping—the sobriety offers confrontation with a reality that was too much to bear at the outset, reality without hope of normative approval, a reality in which the dialectics of recognition must be abandoned.

Consider this

Fanon, in effect, was calling on his readers to join him in the task of constructing a liveable world, by which he also meant a genuinely mature one. The assessment of the successes and failures of the artist should be considered in terms of the limitations of art itself as a medium of social change. After all, it may be the case that to demand that art change the world may be to demand too much of art. For how much could art remain art when it ceases to affect us at the level of how we feel, and how politically transformative could the stimulation of affect be by itself? This is not to say that the aesthetic realm isn't important. My argument throughout has been that it is a viable dimension of transforming inhabited spaces into livable places. It is, in other words, part of how human beings *live*.

This question of liveability comes back to the writer, however, in terms of the teleological suspensions involved in engaging reality. The humanness of Fanon's writing, so to speak, brings art to bear on thought, since the methodological resources brought to bear on decolonizing theoretical expression demand delinking bonds even at the level of genre. To speak to human beings, then, requires understanding, as well, that the future listener may already have a transformed ear through having established relationships with a different world connected by the at times thin but strong thread of human communicability.

Revolutionaries must, then, sing the blues because their goal is the understanding and transformation of life. Fanon, I am suggesting, did so in spite of himself.

So let us close where we began, with our epigraph from Alain Locke now as a very short epilogue: "Man cannot live in a valueless world."[35]

---

[35]Locke, A. "Values and Imperatives," in *The Philosophy of Alain Locke*, *op. cit.*, p. 34.

CHAPTER FIVE

Journeys to farther shores: Intersecting movements of poetics, politics, and theory beyond Utopia

Lia Haro, Duke University, and Romand Coles, Northern Arizona University

> *Dead power is everywhere among us—in the forest chopping down the songs; at night in the industrial landscape, wasting and stiffening the new life; in the streets of the city, throwing away the day. We wanted something different for our people: not to find ourselves an old, reactionary republic, full of ghost-fears, the fears of death and the fears of birth.* ***We want something else****.*
>
> MURIEL RUKEYSER (OUR EMPHASIS)

The life of poetry[1]

We live in a present characterized by previously unimaginable accelerations of inequality, planetary destruction and perpetual crises and catastrophes,

[1]Rukeyser, Muriel. *The Life of Poetry* (Williamsburg, Mass.: Paris Press, 1996), p. 86.

accompanied by daily liturgies and media storms that proclaim and insinuate the fate-like character of the current order of things. These daily conditions of material life so often devitalize the senses and sensibilities that would enable us to imagine pathways that would not loop back into this quagmire. In a time saturated with dead power, what practices might solicit and animate that "something else?" How might we thaw sensibilities and creative powers frozen by "ghost-fears" that endlessly reiterate what Adrienne Rich calls "the avant-garde that always remains the same?"

We find possible responses to these questions in what Rich elaborates as "a poetics searching for transformative meaning on the shoreline of what can now be thought or said."[2] In literature, politics and theory the search has often happened in the realm of utopian discourses and practices. In its best sense, the utopian impulse in aesthetics, theory and politics has always called us to movements of perception and being, toward possibilities with and beyond the damaging textures of the given. However, responses to events of the past two decades have declared the death of Utopia in discrepant ways that would seem to suggest we are somehow *beyond* Utopia. If we are truly beyond Utopia, how do we now imagine and actualize radical alternatives to what can be said and thought? And how should we think about the relationships between aesthetics, theory, and politics in relationship to this question?

In 1989, with the fall of the former Soviet Union, a triumphant narrative of capitalism declared the "end of history" as a condition beyond the delusions of Utopia. This account, while not without a certain melancholic relationship to the "last man," was almost exclusively euphoric in its political as well as its theoretical forms concerning the death of utopian vision. Proponents of this view held that the gap between utopian aspirations and real world possibilities was responsible for totalitarian terror in communist regimes as well as legitimation crises that overloaded and undermined capitalist regimes. Freed of its Other, a victorious global neo-liberal order unleashed dynamic growth and resounding proclamations that augured worldwide prosperity for all. It was as if the end of communist utopia was the condition for the maximal realist approximation of the good. However, little more than a decade later, an explosion from the "outside" shook the end-of-history euphoria to its foundations with 9/11 and the ensuing wars in Afghanistan and Iraq. The financial crises, beginning in 2008, matched that explosion with an ongoing set of implosions across the global economic order.

The death of the euphoria over the death of Utopia has led to numerous melancholic political formations—each of which harbors a certain utopian nostalgia. On the far right in the United States, this takes the carnivalesque form of Tea Party utopian calls for unregulated capitalism, a

---

[2]Rich, Adrienne. *A Human Eye: Essays on Art in Society, 1997–2008*, 1st ed. (New York: W. W. Norton & Co., 2009), p. 3.

night-watchman state, and (paradoxically) an increasingly constantinian Christianity. In a variety of centrist formations (which have absorbed many former progressives) the regulatory technocratic state, which properly penalizes corruption and provides some infrastructural support for market society, becomes a beacon. From the politically impotent academic far left, a "new Leninism" reappears with bravado crying out for a revolutionary vanguard. What constitutes the utopian nostalgia of each of these forms is not an explicitly utopian rhetoric, but rather a sense that the entire system will function in an ideal and enduring—rather than contradictory self-erosive and malignant—manner when properly articulated and embodied.

In some ways then, we appear to inhabit a time that—far from being "beyond Utopia"— revivifies Utopias we already know quite well. Indeed, one could argue that the striking character of our time consists precisely of strident and unapologetic re-articulations of utopian thematics lacking even whispers of the need to move "beyond" that which has already been expressed and exhausted. On the other hand, the nostalgic utopianism of such formations, ironically, places them *beyond Utopia* insofar as they foreclose the dynamic movement of "searching for transformative meaning on the shorelines": critical examinations of the past and present that could respond creatively to suffering and open toward more promising alternatives. Dead power, indeed.

We wager that interweaving a searching poetics (and aesthetics, more broadly) with similarly searching politics and theory is an indispensable task for cultivating political sensibilities and angles of vision sufficiently receptive and imaginative to orient democratic work and action toward shorelines of the possible, beyond the deadening registers of the present. The separation of aesthetics, theory and politics impoverishes our powers to move beyond merely carrying out the pre-ordained business of the day. Power is deeply invested in this division because it stifles the radical potential of imagination, which Rich sharply defines as "the capacity to feel, see what we aren't supposed to feel and see, find expressive forms where we're supposed to shut up."[3] Bringing this aesthetic sensibility together with politics and theory would intensify the energies needed to make journeys to farther shores. Keeping them apart, on the other hand, degrades poetry to innocuous play, confines politics to what Hannah Arendt called "administration," and reduces theory to re-arranging the furniture of the established order. Rich writes, "We might hope to find the three activities—poetry, science (theory), politics—triangulated, with extraordinary electrical exchanges moving from each to each and through our lives."[4] But how are we to imagine these exchanges?

[3]Ibid. p. 92.
[4]Rich, Adrienne *What is found there: notebooks on poetry and politics* (New York: W. W. Norton, 2003), p. 6.

The relationship between aesthetics, theory and politics is never a simple and immediate one. Rich illuminates the agonistic yet intimate relationship in a meditation on Jacob Epstein's sculptural rendition of the biblical struggle between Jacob and the angel: "Each bears weight on one foot, with the opposite knee pressing into the body of the other."[5] Rich reads the angel's tablet-like wings to be representative of "barricades" of lived reality. Poetry (and aesthetic practice, more broadly) must grapple with the political—"the messenger from the barricades" of lived reality, bestower of suffering and dreams under siege—in order not to atrophy and become trite. Politics needs the knee of poetry in its gut in order not to become spellbound by the limits of the present. Aesthetic energy must imbue the constitutive fibers of daily democratic action and the political theories that would inform and be informed by it. Such aesthetics must be attentive to the quotidian possibilities left unexplored by dominant regimes and sensibilities—in order to change them. Finally, theory must cultivate an intimate witness of their struggle in order not to replicate the world picture that would reign undisturbed in its absence. Nevertheless, the fact that each bears weight on a distinct foot evokes a certain relational autonomy without which everything would collapse.

In what follows, we explore what we take to be the indelible features of aesthetics, politics and theory in this intertwinement. We will move around the entanglement of Jacob and the angel, poetry and politics, in an effort to discern the distinctions and debts of each in relation to the other. For several decades, the American poets Adrienne Rich and Muriel Rukeyser have been among the most reflective writers working the intersections of poetry, theory and politics. We find Rich's essays in *What Is Found There* and *The Human Eye* alongside Rukeyser's *Life of Poetry* to be rich sources for thinking about what it might mean to reinvigorate aesthetic utopian impulses in the search for "something else" beyond the dead and deadening configurations of the present. Following our discussion of poetics as such, we shift the accent of our inquiry to investigate a poetics of quotidian politics and political natality. We bring their reflections together with the political theory of peace-builder John Paul Lederach, the deep democratic practices described and theorized by anthropologist Arjun Appadurai, and insights we have gleaned from many years of creative political organizing in places as diverse as Northern Arizona and Western Kenya. Insofar as we write toward reciprocal infusions of quotidian action and aesthetic sensibilities, we might refer to our project as a utopian pragmatics, a concept we hope to have fleshed out by the end. Finally, we reflect on how the theoretical imagination may be renewed and revitalized in the practice of intimate witness in relation to political poetics and poetic politics. We end

---

[5]Ibid., p. xiii.

by pulling these three strands together in an overlapping domain constitutive of a utopian pragmatics, which we take to be a most hopeful promise of political spring.

****

The title of Rich's book of essays, *What is Found There: Notebooks on Poetry and Politics,* comes from a short poem by William Carlos Williams:

It is difficult
to get the news from poems
yet men die miserably every day
for lack
of what is found there[6]

What kind of "news" might we get from poetry and what kind of poetry conveys such news? Why would it be so difficult to receive "the news from poems?" What could it mean to "die miserably every day" from a "lack" of such "news?" Unlike the news we get from mainstream media outlets, the news in poetry "will not tell you who or when to kill, what or when to burn or even how to theorize."[7] It will not give you the latest updates on what everyone is talking about, nor data on the "state of the world" for passive consumption. Rather, poetic language, as Rich understands it, "engage[s] with states that themselves would deprive us of language and reduce us to passive sufferers."[8] (Of course, we acknowledge that many poetries exist in the world. Many poems speak in numbing clichés, keep us dumb, obfuscate reality, serve as tools of oppression. We do not wish to romanticize poetry broadly. We do find this interpretation of the politically active and transformative *capacity* of poetry to be compelling and worth exploration. Hence, when we refer to the poetic here, we mean it in the political, radical sense that Rich explores.)

Rich argues that poetry releases the power of imagination, the power, recalling the definition quoted above, "to feel, see what we aren't supposed to feel and see, find expressive forms where we're supposed to shut up."[9] Such imagination emerges in perceptions, thoughts, sensations and desires that are silenced not only in public life but in our most intimate inner awareness as well: "You are drawn in not because this is a description of your world, but because you begin to be reminded of your own desire and need... You listen, if you do, not simply to the

---

[6]Ibid., Epigraph.
[7]Ibid., p. 241.
[8]Ibid., p. 10.
[9]Rich, *A Human Eye,* p. 92.

poem, but to a part of you reawakened by the poem, momentarily made aware."[10] Poetry enables a seeing that goes deep into our personal and political reality in a way that awakens and enlivens desire. "It reminds you (for you have known, somehow, all along, maybe lost track) where and when and how you are living and might live—it is a wick of desire."[11] Political poetry, then, must dwell reflectively and creatively on the painful edges between the "is" to creatively reach the shores of desire where desire ignites into flames of new possibilities. In other words, this kind of poetry can "alchemize" the apparent horrendous limits of the present into questions of possibility:

> Truly revolutionary art is an *alchemy* through which waste, greed, brutality, frozen indifference, blind sorrow and anger are transmuted into some drenching recognition of the *What if?*—the possible... the question dying forces don't know how to ask... Edges between ruin and celebration. Naming and mourning damage, keeping pain vocal so that it cannot become normalized and acceptable. Yet through that burning gauze in a poem which flickers over words and images, through the energy of desire, summoning a different reality.[12]

In other words, politically transformative (alchemical) poetry *dives deep into the wreck.*[13] The news poetry brings is difficult, in large part, because it is does not turn away from the catastrophes, violence, decaying life worlds and destructive material conditions of the present world: "Imagining... a different reality requires telling and retelling the terrible true story: a poetry that narrates and witnesses" (247). In that process of witnessing, "what is represented as intolerable—as crushing—becomes the figure of its own transformation, through the beauty of the medium."[14]

That radical alchemy of such poetic transformation must struggle mightily with another, more widespread and antithetical alchemy that deploys metaphors and language in the service of a very different kind of transformation. Using James Baldwin's term for the wilful ignorance of injustice, we might call this an alchemy of "innocence," a psychological energy that produces some of the most deleterious pressures that bend our angles of vision. In Baldwin's view, the alchemy of innocence seeks to whitewash flaws and outrun critique:

---

[10]Rich, *What Is Found There*, p. 12.
[11]Ibid., p. 241.
[12]Ibid., p. 42.
[13]Rich, Adrienne. *Diving Into The Wreck: Poems 1971–1972* (New York: W. W. Norton, 1994).
[14]Rich, *What Is Found There*, p. 247.

> Americans, unhappily have the most remarkable ability to alchemize all bitter truths into an innocuous but piquant confection and to transform their moral contradictions or public discussion of such contradictions, into a proud decoration such as are given for heroism on the field of battle.[15]

This alchemization of "bitter truths" into "piquant confection" is engendered by our tendency under conditions of arbitrary hierarchy (and particularly when we find ourselves on the top of such hierarchies) to deeply invest ourselves in what Baldwin calls "innocence"—the wilful refusal to acknowledge the ways in which one is profoundly implicated in suffering, violence and tragic blindness. Baldwin's notion of innocence is elaborated in his "Lockridge: 'The American Myth'":

> The gulf between our dream and the realities that we live with is something that we do not understand and do not wish to admit. It is almost as though we were asking that others look at what we want and turn their eyes, as we do, away from what we are.[16]

Baldwin argues that "this rigid refusal to look at ourselves may well destroy us,"[17] which returns us to the question of what William Carlos Williams meant when he wrote that "men die miserably every day/for lack/of what is found there."[18] There are a number of ways to think about dying miserably every day. Avoiding Baldwin's "unsparing mirror," we spin blindly with "numbed senses" in spirals of oblivious and forgetful violence that take untold human lives whether from prejudice, war, poverty, incarceration, toxic waste, etc. We also die daily by foregoing countless relationships and opportunities due to our "particular shallowness of mind."[19] However, perhaps our most miserable dying each day lies in our repeated refusal to be born—our "fear of birth," to echo the Rukeyser passage above. As Bob Dylan once sang: "He not busy being born is busy dying."[20]

If we are not to perpetuate the daily business of dying, how might we become busy being born? As we have suggested with Rich, poetic "news" produces a counter-current that reaches across the gulfs of our innocence by refusing to invisibilize "what we are" (bitter truths) in order to privilege a

---

[15]Baldwin, James, "Many Thousands Gone" quoted in Rich, *A Human Eye*, p. 53. For the best discussion of Baldwin and Innocence see Shulman, George, *American Prophecy: Race and Redemption in American Political Culture* (Minneaolis: University of Minnesota Press).
[16]Rich, *A Human Eye*, p. 52.
[17]Ibid.
[18]Rich, *What Is Found There*, Epigraph.
[19]Rich, *A Human Eye*, p. 52.
[20]Dylan, Bob, "It's Alright Ma (I'm Only Bleeding)" in *Bob Dylan Lyrics: 1962–2001* (New York: Simon and Schuster, 2004), pp. 156–7.

degraded version of "what we want" (our mythic portrayals of ourselves). In the kiln of expressed suffering and reawakened desire, revolutionary poetry, as Rich imagines it, would further express and foster conditions for natality, understood as that which would break the fateful sequence of events perpetuated by "dead power" and alchemies of innocence. With Marx, she speaks of this process of poetry as one that gives birth to "new passions and new forces": "the process of poetry itself temporarily releases me into that realm of human power which Marx said is its own end... the power to engender, to create, to bring forth fuller life."[21] This process is one that works not only upon individual creators but, rather, one which works at the cellular level and proceeds through complex assemblages of poetic communities. This poetic activity is a condition for "revolution in permanence," which "does not turn in on itself... [and] repeatedly arise[s] as the creative currents of each and all f[i]nd voice."[22]

Rich's poetics thirst for the natality born amidst these creative currents. She describes poetry itself as an "exchange of electrical currents through language": "Someone is writing a poem. Words are being set down in a force field. It's as if the words themselves have magnetic charges."[23] Words vibrate with the histories of their utterances—their taste in struggles across centuries, their muffled tones in dark corners, their pitch when shouted in the streets, their histories of opening and closing possibilities, their softness in intimate whispers, their repetitions, modulations and translations. Words also vibrate with the feelings and desires they evoke.

Most often, these charges circulate in inter-corporeal force fields created by alchemies of innocence. Poetry, as Rich imagines it is an "art reaching into us for what's still passionate, still unintimidated, still unquenched" (*HE* 137). It does so by performing itself as a charged body capable of such reaching. Rich describes this poetic activity as a relational formation by reading Rukeyser's "Poem Out of Childhood":

> Organize the full results of that rich past
> open the windows: potent catalyst[24]

Poetry here draws together the full results of the past, the words laden with history and lives, to simultaneously open windows in the present and catalyze change. In Rich's reading, "the word 'organize' is significant here, in its activist connotation but even more in its sense of dynamic relational system."[25] Poetry as the act of organizing "the full results of that rich

---

[21] Rich, *What Is Found There*, pp. 46, 50.
[22] Ibid., p. 46.
[23] Ibid., pp. 83, 87
[24] Rich, *A Human Eye*, p. 37.
[25] Ibid.

past," traces of relationships between disparate echoes and voices across vast discrepancies of time and circumstance, a movement that utilizes what she calls "the great muscle of metaphor, drawing strength from resemblance in difference... The great muscle of the unconstricted throat."[26] The result, at its best, is a language charged with such "metaphoric density" that we are enabled to work our way through the contradictions and concealments of an oppressive world and fuel transformative journeys to farther shores within the present. Denise Levertov, in Rich's reading of her personal letters, renders that powerful, dynamic relational system of engaged poems as "solid bodies in movement, instead of (what so many modern poems are) fluid substances (in movement or at worst stagnant)."[27] Overly fluid poetry does not organize the "full results" in a meaningful dynamism and thus lack the potency to catalyze deep connections that respond to the specific urgencies of our lives. Levertov adds: "They lack 'sharpness of necessity.'"[28] They are devoid of the muscular power needed to open better futures, or as Levertov puts it, "they lack moral backbone."[29]

The unique moving energy of such poetic flesh produces a vibrating resonance of resemblance in difference—our "private vision[s] suddenly connect... with a life greater than [our] own, an existence not merely personal."[30] Rich gives us a wonderful illustration of how such energy gives birth to community in her description of a poetry reading in the Nuyorican Poet's Café in New York's Lower East Side. Rich describes how an array of people from very different backgrounds and political, social and aesthetic differences are brought together by poetry. What is interesting here is that poetry or the energy created by the poetry reading is agentive and creative beyond and between any individual subject-listener insofar as poetry in that moment "*lived,* pulling us toward each other."[31]

This gravitational power, which is continually gathering together new collective bodies and assemblages, is precisely how Edouard Glissant defines poetics—"a kind of expressive consciousness, embedded in language, a movement toward coexistence and connection."[32] Rich adds that Glissant characterizes this kind of relationality as "turbulence, exposure, an identity not of roots but of meeting places; not a lingua franca but a multiplicity of languages, articulations, messages... We fear it means chaos. But, it is a transformational mode of apprehending."[33]

---

[26]Ibid., p. 142.
[27]Ibid., p. 75.
[28]Ibid.
[29]Ibid.
[30]Ibid., p. 25.
[31]Ibid., p. 39.
[32]Ibid., p. 257.
[33]Ibid., p. 258.

In other words, the poetic language Rich affirms creates commonalities not by leveling personal experience but by resonating with and among different apprehensions of a complex world. A poem "depends on a delicate, vibrating range of difference, that an 'I' can become a 'we' without extinguishing others, that a partly common language exists to which strangers can bring their own heartbeat."[34] Most fundamentally, this "vibrating range of differences" enables proximities of a polymorphous "seeing-together," or what Rich calls an "impulse to enter, with other humans, through language, into the order and disorder of the world."[35] Poetic resonance permeates our isolation and resistances, slackens fear and intensifies hospitality in ways that exceed the specific contexts and subjects. A public space emerges.

Rich perceives a U.S. teeming with an underground alchemy that is continually giving birth to and reborn in small poetic public spaces. She writes, "On most evenings around the U.S., there must be several thousand poetry readings."[36] We read a double voicing in the word "must" here to be both disclosive and *imperative* for any polity with energy for radical change. Opening hospitable spaces of polymorphous resonance through and for the poetic—beyond and even *upon* the walls that would resist them—can enable the rough and tumble of human dialogue to become fruitful.

Consider, for example, the wall outside Pablo Neruda's former home in Chile, which Rich discusses. The Chilean military regime erected a wall as a barrier to isolate the dead poet from those who might be inspired and ignited by his poetry. Yet the resonance of Neruda's poetry with the Chilean people transformed the wall into what Rich calls "a dialogue reaching beyond death... a collective page greater than the poet's books, a page made possible because of the poet's books, because of the hand that had once crawled line after line, writing the poems": "All kinds of people came surreptitiously to write or scratch graffiti on the boards of the fence, messages to the poet, words of resistance, brief phrases, names."[37] Perhaps more than any other, this image evokes the alchemy of radical political poetry, which seizes spaces of isolation and innocence and transforms—rebirths—them into places of public relationship.

Rich's own poetic politics is rooted the most dynamic "collective page" of the United States in the 1960s:

> A spirit of the times... That I absorbed through teaching and activism in an institution where the question of white Western supremacism was already being talked about, where students were occupying buildings and

[34]Ibid., p. 85.
[35]Ibid., p. 6.
[36]Ibid., p. 37.
[37]Rich, *What Is Found There*, pp. 35, 36.

> teaching "liberation" classes; in a city where parents were demanding community control of the schools; through a certain kind of openness and searching for transformed relationships in the New Left, which soon led to thousands of women asking "the Woman Question" in women's voices; and from reading Malcolm X, Chekhov's Sakhalin Journals, Barbara Deming's Prison Notes, Frantz Fanon, James Baldwin, and the writing of my students. I could feel around me—in the city, in the country at large—the "spontaneity of the masses" (later I would find the words in Rosa Luxemburg), and this was powerfully akin to the experience of writing poetry. Politics as expression of the impulse to create, an expanded sense of what's "humanly possible" – this in the late 1960s and the early women's movement, was what we tasted, not just the necessities of reactive organizing and fighting back. I have never forgotten that taste.[38]

Beyond the narrow confines of identity, technique and ideology of any given political frame, Rich illuminates an inter-animative creative energy at the core of both poetry and politics. Poetic energy is not simply awake in the dramatic moments and voices of the era. Instead, Rich finds it in her students' papers, in campus conversations, and in the spontaneous creativity involved in everyday political work at its best.

****

The sceptic will probably be asking: doesn't all this talk of utopian poetics, aesthetics of resonance across differences and alchemical transmutations of communities take us so far beyond the limits and possibilities of living realities that we risk falling off the map of actual political life and action? After all, what does the "news of poetry" have to do with power, governance, negotiation, matters of life and death and the everyday mechanical drudgery of political change? Cultivating aesthetic sensibilities in politics can easily seem like a worthless or even damaging distraction in our contemporary political culture, saturated as it is by technocratic, administrative logic. We live in a world that is decidedly not the one that Rich powerfully evokes in comparing the relationship between politics and poetics (and aesthetic expression more generally) to the intimate entanglement of Jacob and the Angel. Rather, as a recent commentator in the Utne Reader so clearly expressed it, "poetry occupies a cultural [and political] space in contemporary American society somewhere between tap dancing and ventriloquism."[39] In that case, one could easily argue that only romantics detached from the "fierce urgencies"

---

[38] Ibid., p. 25.

[39] Behrle, Jim, "How to Write a Love Poem," *Utne Reader* (Jan–Feb 2012), www.utne.com/arts/how-to-write-a-love-poem (Accessed 2 December 2013).

of our contemporary political and social crises can afford to waste time with aesthetic "tap dancing" while the planet burns, endless wars perpetuate and democracy withers on the desiccated vine.

While we do acknowledge the incredible challenges inherent in an apoetic milieu such as our own, we argue that, far from useless romanticism, aesthetic energy with poetic commitment and sensibility is precisely what we urgently need to address those challenges in genuinely transformative ways. When all else has failed to create enduring change, it may be time to tap dance toward a new mode of political engagement. After all, anyone familiar with the radical counter-cultural history of tap dancing in the African American tradition knows that it infused black counter-public spaces in ways that animated and informed a long history of creative struggle. In an analogous vein, Cornel West has noted the centrality of dance and music through centuries of unrelenting white supremacy. He reminds us that the singing of slave spirituals in hush arbours, as well as jazz riffs and blues melodies, have played an indispensable role in enabling black communities to endure and manifest dark shimmers of transformative energy—"a hope not hopeless but unhopeful."[40]

Like West, Rich calls us to re-inhabit mundane, everyday politics with imaginative aesthetic energies so absent in both political slumbers and myopic activism. She writes:

> Working with others to plan a demonstration, draft and distribute a flier, write a collective pamphlet, set up a conference, is a different mode of creation, and... a different mode of language. Yet the same thirst lies underneath, and the need for a taproot into the imagination. Politics is imagination or it is a treadmill—disintegrative, stifling, finally brutalizing—or ineffectual.[41]

Allowing the poetic, creative impulse to remain fallow in our actual political practices leaves us weakened, reactive and too often resentful. Thinking of the analogy above between poetry and tapdance, we might say that poetic tapdancing enables indispensable connections to myriad taproots and rhizomatic crabgrass with powers to crack the concrete we so often take as the immutable limit of political life. Yet this is the movement that we've marginalized. Muriel Rukeyser perceptively laments this particular loss and political need:

> It seems to me that we have cut ourselves off, that we impoverish ourselves just here. I think we are ruling out one source of power, the

---

[40] West, Cornel. "Black strivings in a twighlight civilization," in *The Cornel West Reader* (New York: Basic Civitas Books), p. 118.

[41] Rich, *What Is Found There*, p. 49.

> one that is precisely what we need. Now, when it is hard to hold for a moment the giant clusters of event and meaning that every day appear, it is time to remember this other kind of knowledge and love, which has forever been a way of reaching complexes of emotion and relationship.... the attitude of poetry.[42]

Because Rich and Rukeyser focus their creative energy on poetry, they do not provide us with a sense of the micro-textures of the poetic attitude in political life. Peace Studies scholar and activist John Paul Lederach helps fill the gaps in *The Moral Imagination* by drawing on his thirty years of mediating entrenched conflict in war-torn zones including Colombia, Ghana, the Kenya-Somalia border and elsewhere around the world. His many efforts to shape pathways toward peace in such contexts have led him to move away from an earlier position advocating a more technical engineering of social change toward a much more aesthetic peacemaking process: "my feeling is that we have over-emphasized the technical aspects and political content to the detriment of the art of giving birth to and keeping a process creatively alive. In so doing we have missed the core of what creates and sustains constructive social change."[43]

Cultivating the art of giving birth to (natality) and keeping the peace-building processes alive involves a strategic poetics in Lederach's view. The "discipline of poetry" in the context of politics involves a specific orientation to the world and artful crafting of resonant images and/or events that alter how people perceive and imagine each other and their worlds. Crucial here is "a discipline [that] holds complexity and simplicity together. The art is to capture both in an ah-hah image."[44] For Lederach, the Japanese poetics of *haiku* serve particularly well in the incredibly difficult situations in which he finds himself.

A *haiku*, which is constrained to the length of a breath, must capture in clear, brief images the organic complexity of a multidimensional situation: "this kind of imagination captures the depth of the challenge and at the same time casts light on the way forward."[45] Lederach calls this the "*haiku* attitude"—"the discipline of preparation, a predisposition for touching and being touched by the aesthetic ... a readiness for such perception."[46] Lederach explains that he carries that discipline into conflict zones. "There is a poetry to conflict embedded in everyday conversation... I watch spoken images. In common parlance these might be referred to as metaphors... I

---

[42]Rukeyser, *Life of Poetry*, p. 7.

[43]John Paul Lederach, *The Moral Imagination: The Art and Soul of Building Peace* (Oxford: Oxford University Press, 2005), p. 70.

[44]Ibid., p. 71.

[45]Ibid.

[46]Ibid., p. 68.

have come to treat metaphor as if it were a canvas. Metaphor is a creative act.... Metaphors are like a living museum of conflict resources. They usually lead me toward an aesthetic appreciation of the context, the process and the challenges of change."[47] A deeply sensitive mode of listening for and seeing powerful organizing images and metaphors in the discourses and actions of those involved taps into a political tendency that has long been present in effective social change although not intentionally developed as such. He explains: "time and again, social change that sticks and makes a difference has behind it the artist's intuition: the complexity of human experience captured in a simple image and in a way that moves individuals and whole societies."[48] Therefore, for Lederach, as for the poet Audre Lorde, *poetics is not a luxury*. It becomes an orienting framework for the action and attention of actual practitioners and communities involved in reconciliation of deep social wounds.

While the *haiku* attitude in politics means actively listening for organizing images and tropes in the stories of those involved and developing a "deep intuition" from the connections between them and the broader situation, the "*haiku* moment ... happens with the appearance of resonance. Something resonates deeply. It connects."[49] The *haiku* moment picks up and brings forth pregnancies in the background of our perceptual field—what Lederach calls the intimations of things. These, in turn, intensify, make explicit and proliferate new connections that reconfigure our sense of the world—and indeed the shapes of the world itself—and echo with continuous solicitations to political innovation, work and activity.

Lederach illustrates such a moment by recounting a story from within the midst of inter-ethnic war in Ghana. The conflict between the Dogomba and Konkomba tribes is at least as old as colonialism. Lederach describes a crucial transformative moment when the two groups convene for their first meeting after several bloody altercations for a mediated reconciliation process. The Dogomba paramount chief opens the meeting in a most derisive manner with an attitude of intense superiority. Barely acknowledging the young man representing the Konkombas, he addresses himself to the mediators: "look at them... Who are they even that I should be in this room with them? They do not even have a chief... They are just boys born yesterday".[50] In so doing, the chief seeks in that moment to establish the scene as one ordered by multiple hierarchies—his great status over the young man who had little, the superiority of chiefly tribes over non-chiefly tribes, and the age-old weighty asymmetry of a history that had repeatedly conferred such advantages in a nearly fate-like manner. Precisely at this

---

[47]Ibid., p. 72.
[48]Ibid., p. 73.
[49]Ibid., p. 68.
[50]Ibid., p. 9.

moment when the chances of weaving webs of reciprocity seemed to be diminishingly slim, the young man acts to seize possibilities lurking in the claustrophobic background in a manner that re-articulated the space and temporality of relationships. Slipping beyond the grip of the derisive and distancing imaginary, the young man unwontedly moves into intimate proximity with the chief by addressing him as father with unimaginable gentleness and politeness. "You are perfectly right, father," the boy said. "The reason our people go on rampages... resulting in all these killings and destruction arises from this fact. We do not have what you have... I beg you, listen to my words, father. I am calling you father because we do not wish to disrespect you. You are a great chief. But what is left to us?" [51] The chief is silent for a while, then shifts his attitude 180 degrees to beg for forgiveness, and respond with a will to reciprocity.

The young man generates a *haiku* moment of great resonance to which the chief responds in kind. Exemplifying the *haiku* attitude, the young man manifests a radical receptivity in relation to the possibilities of reciprocity in the chief's assertion of hierarchy. "The young Konkomba man... in a moment of great tension, in a short phrase with the use of the image 'father' captured the sense of historical conflict but in such a way that it created whole new meaning."[52]

The youth's performative utterance of the metaphor "father" enables the young man's voice to resonate within the chief in a manner that Rich ascribes to the poetic—it "reawakens" him by "remind[ing] him of his own desire and need."[53] This resonance animates a metaphoric muscle that enables each party to extend himself more hospitably toward the other in a manner that weaves a thread of connection across tortuous social space and transfigures the conflictive geography. The metaphor as performance and image changes the existing order of resemblances and differences. It enables the chief to hear the constative aspect of the utterance, in which hierarchies are posited as a *lack,* soliciting compassionate connection instead of providing positive grounds for humiliation. The efficacy of that *haiku* moment manifests itself not only in the changed behavior of the chief but in the response of all who were present: "the room was electrified, charged with high feeling and emotion."[54] While problems and disagreements continued, of course, the moment transfigured social space in an enduring manner such that "what happened in that moment created an impact on everything that followed"—an echo that has continued for many years to animate searching, non-violent responsiveness. We can see here the operation of a poetic alchemy that proliferates relationships of receptive

---

[51]Ibid.

[52]Ibid., 10.

[53]Rich, *What Is Found There,* p. 12.

[54]Ibid., p. 10.

reciprocity wherein new subjects, new communities and new possibilities can be born.

Lederach himself conceives the work of building peaceful and just communities through the central image of spiders weaving webs. Spiders typically start their webs by identifying "strategic anchor points" between which they attach strong threads of connection. They then weave a vast network of intersections with substantial resilience. Lederach takes this to be illuminative of the art of building political relationships in situations of violence and subjugation in which an artful web-weaver can discern unexpected potential actors and unanticipated potentials *in* actors, draw them into relationships of enhanced reciprocity, and construct pathways for collaborative action. With and beyond spiders, the web-weaving of poetic politics often transforms the very space in which it intervenes. Like all living things, spiders must build their webs in spaces that are dynamic in ways that render them highly vulnerable. Rather than rigid, finished abodes, they must fashion living spaces that enable them to become "smart flexible."

> *Smart flexible* is the ability to adapt to, respond to and take advantage of emerging and context-based challenges. Scientists call spiders 'actors of continuous movement.' Peace building can learn from spiders that 'web making is the art of creating platforms to generate responses more than creating the solution itself. A platform represents the *ongoing capacity* to generate processes, ideas and solutions.'[55]

Lederach's discussion of generative platforms and *haiku* aesthetics enables us to begin to grasp political textures of the exercise, what Rich called the "great muscle of metaphor" in response to emerging and context-based challenges.

The anthropologist Arjun Appadurai provides two clear illustrations of what such poetic attitude and moment can look like (and already does look like) in politics and how metaphoric resources can be wielded powerfully by those who would otherwise have few resources to mobilize. In his essays "Deep Democracy" and "The Capacity to Aspire," Appadurai discusses the urban activism of Mumbai slum dwellers who have formed a partnership (the Alliance) between various groups differently committed to making visible and redressing the basic injustices of slums. While 40 per cent of Mumbai's population of over 20 million inhabitants live in slums, they occupy only eight per cent of the already cramped land area. Appadurai calls them "citizens without a city."[56] Slum dwellers are severely disenfran-

---

[55] Ibid., p. 85. Our emphasis.

[56] Arjun Appadurai, "The Capacity to Aspire," in *Culture and Public Action*, ed. Vijayendra Rao and Michael Walton (Stanford, Calif.: Stanford University Press: Stanford Social Sciences, 2004), p. 72.

chised due to their lack of permanent housing and adequate sanitation. Appadurai explains the context in "The Capacity to Aspire":

> Their lack of sanitary facilities increases their need for doctors to whom they have poor access. And their inability to document their claims to housing may snowball into general invisibility in urban life, making it impossible for them to claim any rights to such things as rationed foods, municipal health and education facilities, police protection and voting rights.[57]

Although Appadurai does not theorize them as such, the examples of slum dweller action in response to the catastrophe of housing and sanitation can be read, within the framework we have outlined here, as innovative examples of a poetic politics with transformative, web-building resonances at local and global levels.

Alliance members have developed a politics of what they call "precedent setting," a politics of "show and tell" in which the effective, often "illegal," mechanisms of survival that the poor have developed in response to their crises are performed, shared and celebrated in exhibitions and festivals. The philosophy behind the strategy, as Appadurai describes it, is "that the poor need to claim, capture, refine and define certain ways of doing things in spaces they already control and then use these to show donors, city officials and other activists that these 'precedents' are good ones and encourage other actors to invest in them further."[58] As pragmatic as this sounds, the power of these "precedents" lies in the aesthetics of their performance.

The two "precedent setting" initiatives discussed by Appadurai are housing exhibitions and toilet festivals by and for the poor. In both cases, the central image (housing or toilets) serves to create platforms for ongoing, smart flexible transformation at multiple levels of society by changing the established terms and modes of recognition prevalent in development (expert-subject, slum dweller-object), and changing what is considered possible and legitimate in the context. Appadurai explains that the linguistic strategies and representational tactics involved in the performance of alternatives "provide the nervous system of a whole body of broader technical, institutional and representational practices" by "lending vision and horizon to immediate strategies and choices, lending immediacy and materiality to abstract wishes and desires, and struggling to reconcile the demands of the moment against the disciplines of patience."[59]

The housing exhibitions take place in the middle of the destitution of the slums and are surrounded by inadequate shacks. The durable model

---

[57]Ibid., p. 72.
[58]Ibid., p. 75.
[59]Ibid., p. 76.

house, constructed by and for the poor by improvising from "the flimsiest of resources and in the most insecure of circumstances," functions as a powerful metaphor for the strength and creative possibilities of slum dwellers themselves. The dramatically charged community exhibitions with these metaphorically-muscled houses at their center become dialogical platforms for the ongoing—"smart flexible"— transformation of the subjectivities and horizons of slum dwellers, housing experts and state authorities. In other words, like the most powerful political poetry described by Rich, in the housing exhibition "what is represented as intolerable—as crushing—becomes the figure of its own transformation."[60] The "gravitational pull" (Rich) of the metaphorical "platform" (Lederach) of the housing exhibition facilitates the weaving together a denser web of relationships among the poor themselves. Appadurai notes that "poor families and activists travel from different cities to attend housing exhibitions... [and are] enabled to see that they had always been architects and engineers and could continue to play that role in the building of more secure housing."[61] For the poor individuals and families who gather around it, then, the model house (like the revolutionary poem for Rich) becomes a "wick of desire" that can then be shared, discussed and legitimized with representatives of the dominant order in ways that bring the latter into solidarity with the aspirations of the poor. Professional housing experts are brought into discussion and debate about design with the poor in ways that reverse the standard flow of expertise by foregrounding slum dwellers' "own ideas of the good life, of adequate space and of realistic costs."[62] As invited state officials cut ceremonial ribbons, they are drawn into the new aesthetic image created by the poor (in a manner analogous to how the Dogomba elder is drawn into the image provided by the Konkomba youth) and give speeches that must respond to all that the image of their model house represents with its metaphoric implications and to the capacity of the poor to creatively implement solutions to the undeniable housing crisis surrounding them. Appadurai explains: "As politicians and bureaucrats join these events, in which much speech making is substantially spontaneous, they also find themselves drawn into the lexicon of plans, commitments, hopes and trust... poor communities draw politicians into public commitments to expand the resources and recognitions available to the poor."[63] A new disclosure of the world begins to emerge and generate transformative relationships and political effects.

In the second example discussed by Appadurai, "Toilet Festivals" bring the unsparing mirror to bear on the most intimate and personal of injustices

[60]Rich, *What Is Found There: Notebooks on Poetry and Politics*, p. 249.
[61]Appadurai, "The Capacity to Aspire," p. 79.
[62]Ibid., p. 77.
[63]Ibid., p. 78.

in the slums—the "politics of shit." The virtual absence of human waste management (facilities, running water, private spaces, sewage systems) in the slums means that people of all ages endure the deep humiliation of "shitting in broad daylight in public view" in addition to the daily "ecology of fecal odors, piles and channels, where cooking water, washing water and shit-bearing water are not carefully insulated from one another."[64] The Toilet Festival powerfully occupies the transformative, poetic "edge between ruin and celebration" that Rich described by placing real public toilets, which have been made by and are for actual use among the poor, at the center of carnivalesque festivals that paradoxically refuse the privatization of shit. The toilets that have been denied to slum dwellers are powerful metaphors for class injustice on the one hand, and for self-generated alternatives on the other: "In India, where distance from your own shit is the virtual marker of class distinction… the politics of shit is turned on its head, and humiliation and victimization are turned into exercises in technical initiative and self-dignification."[65] In other words, like the truly revolutionary poem for Rich, "what is represented as intolerable—as crushing—becomes the figure of its own transformation."[66] The Toilet Festival obliterates the mythic distance of the powerful from the human grit of shit when the toilets become spaces into which dignitaries are invited and engaged: "When a World Bank official has to examine the virtues of a public toilet and to discuss the merits of this form of shit management with the shitters themselves, the materiality of poverty turns from abjectivity to subjectivity." Appadurai discusses a particularly powerful moment of such poetic alchemy in 2001 when the Alliance and global partners brought a model house and toilet into the lobby of the main United Nations building (against much official resistance):

> [Secretary General Kofi] Annan was surrounded by poor women from India and South Africa, singing and dancing, as he walked through the model house and the model toilet, in the heart of his own bureaucratic empire. It was a magical moment full of possibilities for the Alliance and for the secretary-general, as they engaged jointly with the global politics of poverty.[67]

The image of the most powerful person in the UN occupying the slum dweller toilet surrounded by singing and swaying slum dwellers is full of metaphoric muscle that reorganizes, if briefly, the established hierarchy of global power while serving as a generative platform through which new

---

[64]Ibid., p. 79.
[65]Ibid.
[66]Rich, *What Is Found There: Notebooks on Poetry and Politics*, p. 249.
[67]Appadurai, "The Capacity to Aspire," p. 80.

webs can be formed in new ways. As an effective "*haiku* moment," the images of house and toilet opened "magically" onto the broader politics of poverty in a way that "left an indelible impression of material empowerment on the world of UN bureaucrats and NGO officials present."[68] Far beyond the exchange of reasons accented in most versions of deliberative democracy, these examples operate by means of aesthetic interventions that dramatically alter the Arendtian democratic "tables" around which political dialogue and action occurs.

****

In our own grassroots organizing efforts, we have sought collaboratively to actualize the counter-alchemies of this kind of poetic politics. Our two contexts seem absolutely dissimilar at first glance and, in terms of geography, culture, historic specificity, economic realities and concrete challenges, they are. On the one hand, we have been organizing within the institutional framework of Northern Arizona University and the region of Northern Arizona to enliven democratic enthusiasm and proliferate civic engagement across generations (from elementary students to elders) and across a wide spectrum of issues, interests and backgrounds. On the other hand, we have been deeply engaged in a rural Luo village in Kenya, which has been torn apart socially by intense development interventions in the past decade. In 2008 and 2009, various concerns and obligations led each of us, separately, to move to new places (Northern Arizona/Western Kenya) and become intimately aware of the specific challenges facing each. We did not begin with any sense of commonality between these two distant places. As we each deepened our relationships with the communities though, we found ourselves and our communities facing strikingly similar institutional and cultural resonance machines of neoliberal capitalism with the power to direct social hope and democratic energy into soul-twisting channels of global consumerism, technocratic knowledge production and the "opportunities" of capitalist individualism. In both contexts, questions of possibility and shared futurity were frozen in a dead, anti-poetic language of hegemonic administrative rhetoric of "best practices," "professional and consistent messaging," "deliverables," "evidence-based assessments," "measurable outcomes," "targets," "benchmarks," etc. What became obvious at different times and in different ways was the need to enliven powers of imagination and affect in ways that could carry us beyond the limits of this landscape. While we understand why many well-intentioned efforts in this climate give in to the temptation to secure legitimacy in the technocratic discourses that singularly frame the business of our day, the move inevitably severs the

[68] Ibid.

"taproots of the imagination" and deprives us of poetic resources in ways that are, as Rich so poignantly observed above, "disintegrative, stifling, finally brutalizing—or ineffectual."[69] In our own efforts, we have sought to invigorate the poetic attitude in the capillary textures of receptive political relationships in daily organizing and to amplify metaphoric resonances through the cultivation of broader narratives and shared images.

As we have seen, the "attitude of poetry" implies a receptive, careful relationship to the world, events and other people in ways that do not turn away from complexity but draw powerful knowledge by opening reflectively to the truths in the unsparing mirror. That poetic attitude, Rukeyser reminds us, "might equip our imagination to deal with our lives [and to] hold for a moment the giant clusters of event and meaning that every day appear."[70] However, such a radically democratic poetic attitude cannot be assumed to be a natural inclination of most people, especially given the anti-democratic main currents of our global moment. Like many attitudes and tastes, then, it must be learned, nurtured and given space to grow.

In our collaborations in Arizona and Kenya, we have found that a powerful, practical way to do that is through the art of "public narrative," an engaged/engaging mode of storytelling developed by long-time activist and Harvard scholar Marshall Ganz. Public narrative asks each person getting involved in a political process to begin by stepping back to reflect deeply and craft a succinct narrative for public conversation, which is "woven from three elements, a story of why I have been called, story of self; why we have been called, story of us; and a story of the urgent challenge on which we are called to act, story of now."[71] The public narrative format asks each of us to consider key sources and relationships that inform our ethical and political vision, important events and choices we have made which have shaped our lives, and our sense of this historic moment and how we wish to act in relation to it, etc. The ethos of articulating and sharing public narratives is one in which the distinct and evolving interests, passions, visions and voices of each person are—and are storied as—integral to the evolution of the work of action teams, communities in which they are involved and to the broader movement of democratization. Hence, each seeks to develop a profoundly receptive relation both to their own lives *and* to those of the others involved as well, which happens in numerous one-on-one meetings and small group gatherings in which individuals share and refine their public narratives with one another. Such receptivity—the myriad intense perspectives and affects it affords—is an indispensable condition of fresh political relationships, vision and natality. Through careful attentiveness

---

[69]Rich, *What Is Found There*, p. 49.

[70]Rukeyser, *The Life of Poetry*, p. 7.

[71]Marshall Ganz, "What is Public Narrative?" Self-published at: http://grassrootsfund.org/docs/whatispublicnarrative08.pdf

to our selves, each other, and our contexts, we nurture a receptive culture that is more generative of—as well as hospitable and creative in response to—the question: "What if?" This practice provides indispensable elements for a democratic alchemy engendering richly attentive senses capable of resisting the dense network of distractive technologies and kindling complex and differentiated powers of flourishing commonwealths

While the poetic moments of public narrative may not have the same dramatic quality of the housing exhibitions or the toilet festivals, they can and do have similar effects of fostering deeper awareness of the "is" and "what we can do" in ways that draw people together in connection with new (or at least renewed) collective horizons of "what if?" and "what might become?" Public narrative proliferates those "ah-ha" moments in micrological encounters and relationships that accumulate in ways that can radically change the general fabric of affect and imagination.

In the Kenyan context, for example, the art of crafting and sharing public narratives has repeatedly opened onto new understandings of problems and possibilities that go far beyond the hegemonic terms of outside development experts. Sauri, the community in which we have done most of our work in Kenya, has hosted a motley parade of Non-Governmental Organizations (NGOs) since the 1990s.[72] Material traces of the good intentions and philanthropic fads of the Western world lie around the village—a rusted plow from Africa Now, a cow from Heiffer International, a solar oven from Sweden, a tree planted by Jeffrey Sachs, mosquito nets meant to eradicate malaria functioning as chicken coop netting, and so on. Given the frequent, often unexpected arrival of aid organizations and their action-plans, a supplicant ethos often shapes people's horizons in ways powerfully represented in the following interview excerpt.

> Respondent: Millennium [the current NGO] has destroyed our community and must go.
> Interviewer: What will you do if Millennium leaves?
> Resp: We will find a new donor.
> Int: What if there are no new donors?
> Resp: We will surely die.[73]

---

[72]This is admittedly an insufficient portrayal of the sociocultural dynamics in play. A full ethnographic account is given in Haro, L., *The End(s) of the End of Poverty*. PhD Dissertation. The dynamic is particularly intense in Sauri because of its status as the first of twelve model Millennium Villages across Africa, which were established beginning in 2005 as "proof-of-concept" sites to "show the world that poverty can be ended in our time" by following the prescriptions of economist Jeffrey Sachs and the UN Millennium Project.

[73]Haro, Lia. Oral interview 29 June 2009 in Sauri, Kenya.

We began to hold public narrative workshops in that context as a way for community members to dialogue about the challenges and identify collective possibilities that might begin to address those challenges. To make crafting and sharing stories politically meaningful, we drew an unexpectedly resonant set of metaphors from the story of David and Goliath (Daudi and Go-lee-aht in Dholuo).[74] In the workshops and then spontaneously in group settings over the span of the next two years, a few key images in the story served as metaphoric nodes that solicited collective reflection and dialogue: King Saul's armour, David's smooth stones, the lions killed with the slingshot in the past, and Goliath's towering figure. In their retellings, these flexible images could take on different metaphoric attachments but were generally articulated within the following basic storyline: Saul's armour was very good and expensive, like the GMO seeds and chemical fertilizer (or X intervention of present concern) of developers; but, when Daudi put it on, it crushed him under its incredible weight and he could not move. As Daudi thought back on his life, he saw himself successfully killing lions with just his slingshot and stones so he went down to the river and found six small stones. Because he chose to pay attention to his own strengths instead of accepting the ill-fitted armor, Daudi could creatively and successfully respond to the challenge that seemed absolutely impossible to overcome. Over and over, in a myriad of politically-charged contexts, someone would bring up the Daudi story, with its unique Saurian spin, and then tie it metaphorically to the context at hand in a way that invited conversation. The images stirred metaphoric dialogue that centered around the questions: What are our stones? What were our lions in the past? What are our Goliaths now? The images called forth a creative spirit of engagement with the challenges and successes of the past in ways that provided new perspectives on existing community resources and capacities, many of which had been considerably dampened by the donor-supplicant ethos. In the midst of various conflicts and challenges, the metaphoric dialogues framed by the Daudi and Goliath story enabled community members to identify and focus on neglected assets that had been rapidly eroded in the development process including community relationships, indigenous knowledge and traditions of collective survival.[75]

The practice of public narrative sharing in small problem-focused groups and receptive one-on-one relational meetings facilitate the birth of four research-action teams to address four very different Goliaths that had emerged in the dialogues. Over the next two years, the action-research teams

---

[74]Ganz uses the David and Goliath story in his essay on public narrative.

[75]The resonant force of the David and Goliath story, which was largely due to predominance of Christianity and its mythos in the region, also raised our awareness of the strategic necessity of the poetic attitude of tuning in carefully for shared imagery already significant within a specific community.

collaboratively explored their particular challenge by gathering stories and actively experimenting with the actualization of ideas that emerged in them (some of which became quite successful while others blew up or fell flat). To discuss just one example, we can look to the well-organized, publicly exuberant group of widows who formed around their common social exclusion from regular community social, political and economic activity. To see the Sinani[76] women, as they now call themselves, dancing and singing at community events or gathered with male elders in a common circle in which everyone present sits on one of the colorful hand-woven stools that Sinani women now make as a group enterprise, one would never guess that a few short years ago, they each lived in social isolation struggling to support children with very few culturally-sanctioned ways to do so.

In long afternoon gatherings over the course of several months in 2009, circled in a grassy field or in the main room of a mud home, the women shared detailed accounts of the brutality of widowhood and of their various attempts to carve out livable lives for themselves and their dependent children and grandchildren. They listened attentively to one another without losing focus until the sun began to set. In the mainly Luo tribal culture of Sauri, a widowed woman undergoes multiple, ongoing social and political deaths. Traditionally, she had no public existence or voice unless she undergoes widow-inheritance whereby a male relative of the deceased husband, called a Jatero, "marries" her into his existing family and becomes the household decision-maker even if he lives elsewhere and has other wives. A number of strict rules and taboos govern what a widow can and cannot do. For example, she cannot build a new house, refuse sex with her Jatero or sit down in the house of a woman whose husband is living without calling down a deadly curse (bad *chira*) from the deceased, who play an incredibly active role in the world of the living in Luo culture. Additionally, in the AIDS era, widows have become stigmatized as carriers of the disease (which many do have because of the forced sex with Jateros and with their former husbands in the polygamous society). As the women shared their stories of challenge and struggle, these basic contours of social exclusion took on vivid, emotional specificity with few eyes remaining dry throughout an entire story. One woman's house had burnt down but she was not allowed to build a new one, which meant she had to stay in the tiny one room hut that had been her kitchen. Another woman contracted HIV from her Jatero and passed it on to three babies. Another had her livestock and land (an individual's main sources of livelihood in Sauri) taken shortly after her husband's funeral by a brother-in-law who legally claimed that a widowed woman had no property rights. Another woman began picking up men in the *busaa* club (underground bar) in order to

[76]Sinani means resilience and endurance in Dholuo.

bring in some kind of income but she could only afford to send one of her six children to school.

The stories, all wrenching in some way, did not end with the details of immiseration. Instead, the women combed through the details of their lives to identify "stones" that they had successfully used to meet challenges or might begin to use as a group. For example, those who had managed to reject the Jatero marriage or reconfigure the terms of those alliances shared strategies with others. In the course of the conversations, a deep bond formed between the women. They began going as a group to help one another farm and even started planting a collective plot with vegetables they could distribute for feeding children. The sharing of stories had built relational threads to form a very resilient web of social support that had not been previously conceived. As their collective body became stronger so did the voices of the women in public spaces and with community officials, whom they successfully lobbied to pay for their official state registration as a community-based organization. Their exploration of their potential "stones" led them to turn basic weaving abilities into a small-scale collective enterprise that served specific needs that they identified in the community. They began making colorfully-woven twine stools to replace the hard benches that had to be borrowed from a nearby church every time a community meeting was held. Over time, the stools themselves became metaphoric nodes: those who had not been allowed to sit down in the houses of others were now foundationally part of every community meeting in the aesthetic form of their vibrant benches and increasingly as integral, vocal participants as well. If there is a large community event in Sauri these days, count on a musical performance in which the Sinani women make up songs that often retell their collective story and end with them dancing, waving the stools exuberantly over their heads. It is not that the stools have generated so much income. In fact, whatever they generated has been distributed among the women to pay school fees for their children. Rather, they symbolize a Davidic triumph and the ongoing possibility of possibilities already present, like David's stones, in the knowledge and capacities of community members.

What we see in the example of the Sinani widows is the fruitful interplay between capillary arts of receptive relationship building and broader public practices of resonance. We have found that tending to this interplay is also crucial in the organizing in Northern Arizona where a variety of anti-democratic discourses and practices repeatedly instantiate walls of impossibility that dampen emergent enthusiasms and visions. Thus, in addition to practices of receptive relationality, radical democratic alchemy must engender a broader poetics of resonance that can amplify rather diminish attentive and active explorations of "What if?" By "democratic poetics of resonance" we mean both a political movement that is explicitly informed and storied by the metaphor of resonance itself and, in turn, political practices that lead to the creation of the resonant tissues that constitute inter-corporeal bodies of moving democratic initiative—analogous to the way Levertov spoke of poetry as a dynamic body-in-movement. This initiative takes the poetics of energy that Rich and Rukeyser use to give expression to natality and employs it to guide our work.

From the inception of our work in Northern Arizona, we have sought to cultivate political situations and events that generate resonance from the interactions of vast numbers of people: the interplay of diverse constituencies gathered together as never before, the intersections among students and community members doing exemplary work in diverse Action Research Teams (ARTs), the creation of public spaces where such resonant interactions are called forth and celebrated repeatedly, etc. Resonance as a metaphor evokes a sense of deep meaning and affect, which we explicitly construe in relation to scientific theories that refer to how energetic vibrations and frequencies of moving bodies interact in ways that supplement, enrich, intensify and greatly amplify one another.[77]

During the first semester of our initiative at NAU, the students in an ART called WACBAT (Weatherization And Community Building Action Team) organized a public action explicitly to generate resonant "buzz" in order to enhance our community's sense of political possibility for promoting and expanding energy efficiency retrofits—to reduce utility bills, stimulate a green economy, reduce our carbon footprint, build community solidarity, etc. They weatherized a convent that was the home of two beloved and highly esteemed elderly Sisters and worked carefully to organize myriad constituencies who had never before gathered together in the hundreds in this sort of active solidarity: sustainability advocates, Native Americans, Hispanics (both long-time residents and newcomers who had just crossed the border), Black people, White folks of all classes, social movements, NGOs, green businesses, city staff managing a retrofit program, the young and old, people of all faiths, and so forth.

Beneath windy skies, we gathered in the basement of the Chapel of Guadalupe and exchanged information, networked, signed up for retrofit work and gathered in conversation about future possibilities. The energy in the room was kinetic, as the vibrant movement of different networks of folks began to interact in ways that literally began to amplify each other in a manner none could have accomplished alone. A couple of hours into the event two dozen brightly-dressed children unexpectedly moved into the room, energetically dancing to the rhythm of a large drum in a fashion inspired by Aztec and Christian traditions. The crowd in the basement was riveted in awe. I have seen the Guadalupanas (as they call themselves) dance

---

[77]Coles Romand (2011), "The neuropolitical habitus of resonant receptive democracy," *Ethics and Global Politics* Vol. 4 (4): pp. 273–93.

in numerous contexts and they are always wonderful. Yet, the performance intertwined and amplified the energy in the room in a way that was as magnificent as anything I've ever witnessed. In the basement that day, the resonant sound of the drum and the moving feet of the dancers fed upon, made manifest and further intensified the resonances among the different groups gathered in the room. In a manner analogous to how intense vibrations can actually crack mechanical components and structures, one could sense that the resonance in the room literally began to crack the walls of impossibility we had taken for granted and move us toward a new "we" beyond centuries of racism, colonial inequalities and environmental destruction.

This event, and our frequent evocation of it, has continued to inform and inspirit not only WACBAT, but myriad other ARTs and community groups as well. Indeed, the echoes of this story have persistently moved those involved in the larger organizing process to cultivate more opportunities for resonant political events and experiences that, in turn, become part of our animating story. One way we do this is through once-a-semester ARTs Symposiums in which hundreds of students working on initiatives—ranging from grassroots education and community stewardship teams in K–12 schools to immigration issues, alternative food production on and off campus, renewable energy, public space, gender issues, water conservation, indigenous environmental justice, employee-owned cooperatives and so forth—gather to present and witness each other's work. This intermingling and witnessing regularly generates an atmosphere of resonant enthusiasm that is overwhelming to most of those who are present. It functions as a "mountain top" experience which both animates future endeavors and informs the stories we continue to fashion to inform our movement.

These poetic events of political resonance and the poetic narratives and sensibilities that are circularly intertwined with them have shaped our work in numerous ways, one of which concerns our active attention to the creation of spaces where resonant political practice and the poetics of resonance can be experienced with greater frequency. The Green Scene Café at NAU is one such example. The Café was created as the result of a two-year-long ART initiative that envisioned a place where the diverse ARTs meet to do their work, witness and bump into each other, host artistic events, debate public issues and promote sustainable, just dining practices, etc. Within just a few months, this public space is already becoming highly resonant with interaction—a vibrant locus of our expansion of multidimensional political and ecological possibilities.

In a visual expression that echoes the aesthetic interventions of the Guadalupanas and the widows in Sauri, world-famous Navajo artist Shonto Begay, working with students, has created a huge mural in the Café that celebrates and solicits resonant action. Shonto describes his experience of painting, as well as the experience he hopes his paintings will continually evoke, as a kind of "visual drumming." He taps paint onto the canvass, or in this case the wall, in a manner that gives visual expression to the rhythm of things and peoples in intertwined motion and pregnant stillnesses. The Café mural evokes the resonant work of ARTs within a sacred and historic landscape in a manner that vibrates with memories and solicitations of possibilities for an engaged, diverse and flourishing commonwealth among humans and the more-than-human world. Along with the drums and footsteps of the Guadalupanas, the pedagogical interactions in the Café and the poetic visual drumming of the mural reciprocally amplify and vivify a movement for democratic and sustainable communities, which is gathering steam and creativity at a pace no one could have anticipated.

* * * *

We suggested early in this essay that theory is a process of reflective becoming as intimate witness to the agonistic relationship between aesthetics and politics evoked in Rich's discussion of Jacob and the Angel. As the theoretical practice in this essay should have made evident, both the substance and modes of theorizing themselves undergo transformations in this interaction. We want to posit a third figure in the scene of Jacob and the Angel. This third figure, theory, might be envisioned as a dwarf holding a prismatic mirror. The mirror aspect, akin to Baldwin's unsparing mirror, faces the darkness of the present as it is worked on by poetry and politics to create a relentless reflection of the catastrophe as well as faint shimmerings of possibility in suppressed yearnings, dreams and visions. The prismatic aspect condenses and intensifies these shimmerings to powerfully project political possibilities. Energized by this intensification, the dwarf works the mirror and its angles of vision to illuminate resonant possibilities for radical democracy.

As a locus of these reflections, energies and movements, the mouth of the dwarf, which had previously been so prone to "muttering small talk at the wall of impossibility,"[78] begins to speak a language that is profoundly indebted to both politics and poetics while nevertheless remaining distinct. The dwarf's voice is born of a body that, however intimately entangled with the others, remains at just enough distance to hold the prismatic mirror up without being swept into the epicenter of their struggle. As the mirror twists and turns, the dwarf occasionally catches indispensable glimpses of the entwined threesome—Jacob, Angel and Dwarf—and begins to reflect explicitly on the shapes and textures of their relationships most capable of enabling journeys along the farther shorelines of democracy. Such reflection is no small part of theory's task. Yet, as the dwarf can sense, the mirror

[78]Dylan, Bob, "Visions of Johanna in Dylan," in *Bob Dylan Lyrics: 1962–2001* (New York: Simon and Schuster, 2004), p. 196.

informing such theoretical reflection remains attached to situated hands that conceal as well as reveal. Hence, the dwarf's work requires an extraordinary set of ears and a spider-like flexibility.

We call the labor of the dwarf utopian pragmatics, an art of midwifing the birth of new and better possibilities by carefully tending to the intertwinements of aesthetics, politics and theory. This web of intertwinement constitutes a smart-flexible platform, the utopian character of which enables us to sail toward farther shores. Unlike the deadening utopian nostalgias that we discussed at the outset of this paper—narratives that declare the present to be beyond Utopia—utopian pragmatics as a responsive movement of imaginative action is always *beyond* any articulated instantiation. "Beyond" can be read here in the sense evoked by the Old English "begeondan," in which "be" indicates position (as in "by") and "yond" (as in "yonder") signifies a farther side. In this sense, we read the equivocation inherent in the well-known etymological roots of "utopia" (as *eutopos*, good place and *outopos*, no place) to be generative: the good place is no place other than the place where Jacob, the Angel and the dwarf are busy being born.

PART THREE

Receptivity, re-inscription, affirmation

CHAPTER SIX

Recognition and receptivity: Forms of normative response in the lives of the animals we are

Nikolas Kompridis
Institute for Social Justice, Australian Catholic University

> *Our problem is that society can no longer hear its own screams. Our problem, in getting back to beginnings, will not be to find the thing we have always cared about, but to discover whether we have it in us always to care about something.*
>
> —STANLEY CAVELL, "THE AVOIDANCE OF LOVE"[1]

Elizabeth Costello, the protagonist of J. M. Coetzee's tragic fable *The Lives of Animals*, is a difficult and troubled person. The difficulties that trouble her create trouble of one kind or another for all those who encounter her, as characters and as readers. A celebrated Australian writer of literary fiction,

---

Edits to this original essay have been made by Nikolas Kompridis.

[1]Stanley Cavell, *Must We Mean What We Say?* (Cambridge: Cambridge Univ. Press, 1969), 350.

invited to a fictitious American college to deliver a pair of public lectures, one on "The Philosophers and the Animals," the other on "The Poets and the Animals," Costello immediately generates unsettling confusion about what it is that she wants to say, and what she wants to do in saying it. It is clear that there is something she wants from us, that she's calling for a certain kind of response, but it is not altogether clear what, exactly, that something is. Indeed, as we will see, both the characters in the book and readers of the book seem unable to recognize who Costello is, unable to hear exactly what she is saying.

If there is a failure of recognition here, what kind of recognition failure is it? And what would success mean in *this* case, the case of Elizabeth Costello? Can political theories of recognition offer any illumination? After all, much of what has driven recent developments in political theories of recognition has been the attempt to diagnose recognition failures as particularly salient forms of injustice—be they distributive or cultural in form—that plague the deeply diverse, late-capitalist societies in which we live. If we wish to bring literary theory into dialogue with political theory around questions of recognition, as Rita Felski has proposed, perhaps the case of Elizabeth Costello is a particularly good, because particularly difficult, place to start. Not least, because the failure of recognition at issue here is the failure to recognize—in some full-blooded sense of the word—the life and death concerns of a fictional person.[2] What kind of failure is that? Does anything much hang on it? If so, what? What does such a failure tell us about the subject of recognition? What does it tell us about ourselves? What would it tell us about ourselves if this sort of failure, concerning the life of a fictional person, were a failure to which we could be indifferent or unaccountable? Is there something that political theorists can learn about their own concerns from the way they are figured in literature? How must literature *mean* for political theorists if they are to learn from it what they cannot learn from political philosophy or political theory?

Amy Gutmann, one of a distinguished group of scholars invited to respond to Coetzee's text,[3] regards the two lectures comprising *The Lives of Animals* as putting forward "in the frame of fiction ... empirical and philosophical arguments that are relevant to the ethical issue of how human beings should treat animals."[4] Gutmann sees that Costello's fictional

---

[2]See the chapter on "Recognition" in Rita Felski's *Uses of Literature* (London: Blackwell, 2008), 23–50, from which I learned about the importance of self-recognition.

[3]In addition to Amy Gutmann, there are also responses from Wendy Doniger, Marjorie Garber, Peter Singer, and Barbara Smuts. I've chosen to restrict my discussion to *The Lives of Animals*. I do not engage with Coetzee's later (expanded) text, *Elizabeth Costello*, partly because of the dialogue I wanted to initiate with Cora Diamond's essay (below), and partly because I wanted to productively limit the scope of my discussion.

[4]J. M. Coetzee, *The Lives of Animals* (Princeton, NJ: Princeton Univ. Press, 1999), 3 (hereafter cited as *LA*).

audience responds to her as someone "demanding something of them," and believes the something she is demanding is "a radical change in the way they treat animals," a change that her audience thinks "she has no right to demand, and that they have no obligation or desire to deliver" (*LA* 4).

Gutmann is absolutely right: the kind of response Costello is demanding from her audience implies a change of some kind, but because Gutmann is too quick to conclude that these fictional lectures are about the ethical issue of how human beings should treat animals, she misunderstands and misrepresents Costello's concerns, and as a consequence prematurely limits what it is, ultimately, that Costello wants from her audience, from us. Whatever it is that Elizabeth Costello *is* asking of us, it is something demanding, something unsettling, something that would place us in some difficulty in relation to our lives, to what matters to us, the overcoming of which might require some change in us, a change we will be more inclined to resist than to embrace.

One might say that what Gutmann seizes upon as the moral of the story makes her deaf to the storyteller, and to the story she is actually trying to tell. And, as one further consequence of her misreading, Gutmann fails also to notice, let alone explain, the ongoing and thorough perplexity with which Costello's audience, fictional and real, responds to her, and to her lectures. It *seems* that Costello's primary object of concern is the ethical issue of how we should treat animals, but she says things that make her audience unsure about what it is she's really talking about, what it is she really wants—things that unsettle their assumptions about her and about her lectures. They think she's telling a story about the rights of animals (which is not the title of the story or the topic of her lectures), and it is indeed no small part of her struggle to make herself intelligible to others that imposed on the story that she wants to tell is a story about the rights of animals that for her audience or readers is the only story she could intelligibly be telling.

John Bernard, her inexplicably estranged son, a physics professor at the same fictitious college, cannot fathom what it is his mother really wants, either from him or from anyone else. At a crucial, defining moment at the end of the text, his mother breaks down, declaring that she is helplessly lost to herself, unable to speak the words she aches to speak, unable to face what she most fears, unable to avoid a question she can't answer.

> "When I think of the words, they seem best spoken into a pillow or into a hole in the ground, like King Midas."
>
> "I don't follow. What is it you can't say?"
>
> "It's that I no longer know where I am. I seem to move around perfectly easily among people, to have perfectly normal relations with them. Is it possible, I ask myself, that all of them are participants in a crime of stupefying proportions? Am I fantasizing it all? I must be mad!

> … Calm down, I tell myself, you are making a mountain out of a molehill. This is life. Everyone else comes to terms with it. Why can't you? *Why can't you?*"

Once again, he finds himself in the position of not knowing how to respond to her, of not knowing what kind of response she is calling for, what, indeed, her call is about.

> "She turns on him a tearful face. What does she want, he thinks. Does she want me to answer her question for her?" (*LA* 69)

What would it mean for him to answer *that* question for her? Could he even begin to give an answer if he could not first see it as a question to which he must also fashion a response, a question that he has to take on as his own? How else could he begin to understand what the question demands of his mother? Is the injustice that wounds and haunts his mother a mountain or a molehill? Is it something one has to come to terms with or not? How does one do that? What does it mean to do so, what must be done, how is it done? What tells us we are dealing with a molehill rather than a mountain? What is the basis of our self-assurance that we got it right—be it mountain or molehill? At what point do we start to take these questions seriously? What point must we reach?

John Bernard cannot reach that point, wherever or whatever it may be in this case. He cannot reach that point because he can't follow his mother's line of thought. It is a "line of flight" he does not wish to undertake. It is not so much a line of flight, however, as it is a line of descent, a descent into darkness. To follow that line of thought would mean to follow his mother to where she has been thrown, to where one does not know where one is, where one stands. In that place, one is not only displaced, one is also bewildered by the powerlessness of one's words to make oneself intelligible to others, or to oneself. *Ich kenne mich nicht aus*, this common German expression used in various ways in a variety of everyday contexts, also names the state of mind and the circumstance in which, according to Wittgenstein, genuine philosophical questioning begins. "A philosophical problem has the form: I don't know my way about."[5] Put more to the point, more accurately, existentially and epistemologically, "I don't know my way around here," which is to say, I am lost, and, in some urgent sense, I am lost to myself. (Translated literally: "I know me not out here.")

Thus the question Costello's question puts to her son is whether he is even in a position to reply to his mother without recognizing that she has lost her way, *and* that to take her question seriously would mean to risk

[5]Ludwig Wittgenstein, *Philosophical Investigations*, trans. G. E. M. Anscombe (Oxford: Blackwell, 1958), §123.

losing his way too, requiring that he follow her to the place where it first becomes a question that one cannot evade on pain of incoherence, and at the same time, that one cannot confront directly without risk of isolation, even madness. John Bernard is not ready to take on the pain or the risk involved in following his mother down that line of thought. He is not interested in the descent into his mother's darkness. But being unwilling or unable to follow his mother into that dark place means that he will have to abandon her there, which he does at the end, while holding her in his arms in a comforting embrace. In a scene of chilling and devastating irony, he abandons her there where she is exiled and lost, while she is sitting right next to him.

Peter Singer, another invited commentator, is also very puzzled about how he is supposed to respond, either to Elizabeth Costello or to the complex, multilevelled text, which, one could say, she actively haunts. "All I want to know is: how am I supposed to reply to this?" (*LA* 86).

His question, a variation of "I don't know my way around here," has the requisite form of a genuine philosophical problem. It could and should be the form in which the philosophical problem posed by Costello and Coetzee's text is announced, engagement with it initiated. But Singer does not want to follow that line of thought, preferring to attribute the puzzlement and perplexity he feels about how to reply to the shortcomings or peculiarities of the text. He is not sure who is speaking, or to whom he should respond, Coetzee or Costello. Just like Gutmann, Singer thinks he is dealing with a fictionalized set of—not particularly persuasive or cogent or original—arguments. That the *life* of a particular animal is at stake, a life that has reached a point of crisis about how it is to go on, and that what is at stake in the life of this particular animal might also be at stake in the lives of other animals like her, is not a thought that crosses his mind, a thought he is inclined to follow—anywhere. Singer does not acknowledge that the form Costello gives to her concerns, through a variety of discursive and nondiscursive means, is meant principally to be *received* as a normative challenge—a challenge to how and when we *let* ourselves care about something, and to how and when we *fail* to let ourselves care.

In a remarkable and subtle essay, "The Difficulty of Reality and the Difficulty of Philosophy," Cora Diamond suggests that all of the commentators invited to respond to Coetzee's text failed to do justice to Elizabeth Costello, to the difficulties she and the text pose to their audiences. All the commentators took her the wrong way in more senses than one, reproducing in their response to her the same misunderstanding produced by the characters in the text, even those closest to her. In that rather strange but familiar way we readers form an ethical relationship to fictional persons, they also failed Elizabeth Costello. Rather than seeing "a woman haunted by the horror of what we do to animals ... wounded by this knowledge, this horror, and by the knowledge of how unhaunted others are," the commentators saw a fictional device from which they abstracted a discourse on "animal rights," presented by Coetzee, evidently for the sake of convenience, in the form of fictional lectures. Diamond writes, "For none of the commentators does the title of the story have any particular significance in relation to the wounded animal that the story has as its central character. For none of the commentators does the title of the story have any significance in how we might understand the story in relation to our own lives, the lives of the animals we are."[6]

A failure of recognition?

The failure Diamond describes could be treated as a failure of recognition or as a case of misrecognition. It seems to invite such treatment. The failure would seem to be the consequence of misreading *The Lives of Animals* as a text primarily concerned with making a case for the rights of animals through the words of its central character. But what kind of failure is this, really? Is it merely a cognitive failure, the taking of an *x* for a *y*, when it is so obviously a case of *x* and not *y*? In which case, it would not be a recognition failure, strictly speaking, for to speak meaningfully of a recognition failure we would have to be dealing with a situation in which demands were being made of us, demands whose intelligibility and answerability require some form of recognition of the demands these are and of those who are making them.

Clearly, the commentators as much as the characters in the text think Costello is making demands, even if they are mistaken or unsure about what is demanded of and from them. If we reduce the failure of recognition that is involved solely to an instance of misreading, however, we will fail to understand what kind of failure we are dealing with—why five distinguished scholars uniformly read the text as a discourse on the rights of animals. By framing Costello's lectures in this way, the commentators, unintentionally, to be sure, preempt rather than facilitate the kind of conversation into which Costello, and *The Lives of Animals*, invites its audience—a conversation which would have to begin when all parties to it are able to begin it in the right way—which is to say, only after together arriving at the place where they have lost their way, the place where the philosophical problems of the text can first appear. Since the early 1990s, when Charles Taylor pushed the topic of recognition back into the center of moral and political debate to make sense of and to rearticulate the political claims of minority cultures, contemporary political theorists, especially

[6]Cora Diamond, "The Difficulty of Reality and the Difficulty of Philosophy," in *Philosophy and Animal Life*, ed. Carey Wolfe (New York: Columbia Univ. Press, 2008), 48–9.

Axel Honneth and Nancy Fraser, have made recognition *the* key or *a* key dimension of a theory of justice. Honneth, like Taylor, regards recognition as a "vital human need,"[7] revealing a deep-seated *anthropological* fact of the matter about "the intersubjective nature of human beings."[8] We do not only *desire* recognition, we *need* multiple forms of recognition—respect in the political sphere, without which we could not fully exercise our political agency, esteem in the social sphere, without which we could not regard our contributions to social life as worthy, and care in the intimate sphere of the family, without which we could not develop self-reflective and self-confident practical identities. Thus, without the "intersubjective protection"[9] provided by these interlocking and interdependent forms of recognition, we could not become who we want to be, could not realize the kind of life we want for ourselves. The lives we would be living would be *unfree*, since the intersubjective conditions necessary for full human freedom, what Honneth calls "self-realization," have not been met.

Fraser, on the other hand, eschews the thick account of recognition favored by Honneth, proposing instead a far more minimalist (and less grandiose) one. On her account, the good of recognition is not to be understood as instrumental to the hypergood of individual self-realization, but, rather, as instrumental to acquiring full status as an equal partner in social interaction. Recognition, she argues, is best treated as an issue of social status, not as an anthropological constant that provides the necessary (and apparently sufficient) conditions for the formation of "intact" personal identities. We need to focus our critical attention on patterns of cultural value that exclude some individuals and groups, constituting them as inferior or wholly other, rendering them invisible as claimants to full status as equal partners in social interaction. In such cases, misrecognition is a form of "status subordination," the just response to which requires the "deinstitutionalization" of those patterns of cultural value which foster misrecognition and status subordination.[10]

If we rely on what counts as a failure of recognition in light of recent political theory, it is by no means obvious in what sense we can meaningfully speak of a failure of recognition in the case of Elizabeth Costello. We are not dealing with a case of status subordination, certainly not as the kind of marginalization and exclusion with which political theorists are concerned. Nor is it a case of withheld respect, esteem, or care, as Honneth construes

---

[7]Charles Taylor, "The Politics of Recognition," in *Multiculturalism: Examining the Politics of Recognition*, ed. Amy Gutmann (Princeton, NJ: Princeton Univ. Press, 1994), 25.

[8]Nancy Fraser and Axel Honneth, *Redistribution or Recognition? A Political-Philosophical Exchange* (London: Verso, 2003), 145.

[9]Honneth, *The Struggle for Recognition: The Moral Grammar of Social Conflicts*, trans. Joel Anderson (Cambridge, MA: MIT Press, 1996), 174.

[10]Fraser, *Redistribution or Recognition?*, 22

these normative dimensions of recognition. Elizabeth Costello is a very successful writer, controversial, yes, but also very highly regarded, so much so that she gets regular invitations to speak on any subject on which she is inclined to speak. Unquestionably, there are traces of sexism and ageism in the treatment she receives from the other characters in the text, but these are nothing compared to the philosophical condescension with which her "arguments" are viewed, both by the other characters (her son and her daughter-in-law, Norma, a currently unemployed professional philosopher) and by the commentators, above all, Peter Singer. Elizabeth Costello does not meet the criteria for failures of recognition as political theories of recognition construe them. And yet, if Diamond is right, and I think she is, there is something *like* a failure of recognition here, for the life of a particular human being has been rendered invisible, and, indeed, voiceless, in the very struggle to make it visible, to find the words in which to voice it.

Most obviously and most generally, the failure, be it of the characters or of the commentators, is the failure to recognize that Costello is saying something that does not match the assumptions guiding their own listening and reading. Moreover, in spite of their avowed perplexity about what to make of her and of the text in which they encounter her, there is no attempt to put these assumptions into question. One would think that a book whose title points to a concern with the *lives* of animals might check the temptation to treat it strictly as a fictionalized discourse on the rights of nonhuman animals. There is too much in the text, starting from its very title, that resists or repudiates such a reading. Its title should attune us to the numerous and nuanced ways in which the *lives* of the human and nonhuman animals in the text are thematized *as* lives—as lives that can be lived well or badly, as lives that can be exchanged and shortchanged. In thematizing the *lives* of animals, Coetzee and Costello are also inviting renewed reflection on *how* lives should be lived, the question Socrates poses in *The Republic*. Whereas for Socrates and Plato only the lives of human animals are at stake, for Costello and Coetzee the time has come for us to see that the lives of human *and* nonhuman animals are together at stake in how we answer this question.[11]

More justifiably tempting, I think, is to treat a remark of Costello's, made spontaneously while taking questions after her first lecture, as anticipating, indeed, as internalizing in the very construction of *The Lives of Animals*, both the misrecognition from which she suffers and the misreading to which it will be exposed. Costello's remark concerns the limitations of the standard reading of Swift's *A Modest Proposal*: "Whenever there is overwhelming

[11] As Ian Hacking puts it, using the example of one animal very much a part of the eating rituals of human animals: "one is horrified by the insult to animal life when turkeys are bred too big to walk or procreate; we have created a species that cannot have any dignity." Ian Hacking, "Deflections," *Philosophy and Animal Life*, 155.

agreement about how to read a book, I prick up my ears" (*LA* 56). That none of her fictional interlocutors and none of the invited commentators pricked up their ears is certainly telling, for as Cora Diamond suggests, it reveals that none of them *let* themselves become unsettled by Costello's words to the point where they would *let* themselves question their assumptions about what it was she was saying. Overwhelming agreement lets us go on as before, however, and lets us remain where we already are, without having to put ourselves at risk of finding ourselves somewhere where we don't already know our way around, where we might descend into darkness. As John said to Norma on the morning of his mother's departure, "a few hours and she'll be gone, then we can return to normal" (*LA* 68).

The Lives of Animals thus illuminates in its own complex way a phenomenon not unknown either to literary theorists or political theorists: overwhelming (background) agreement about the meaning of a text or practice, about how to interpret a set of claims or arguments, can overwhelm whatever and whomever this agreement is about, leading to failures of understanding and failures of recognition. Of course, this is an altogether commonplace and resilient feature of our politics, particularly when cultural differences turn also on epistemic differences, leading one side to "mistranslate" the claims of the other, as so often happens when a majority political culture consistently "mistranslates" the diverse languages and practices of the minority or indigenous cultures in its midst. (For example, the degree to which the meaning of land for indigenous peoples remains mysterious to the majority of nonindigenous citizens of settler societies, as if it were something mythical, a piece of romantic primitivism out of place and unplaceable in the modern world.) More recently, in the debates over secularism, some political philosophers have conceded that the differences between religious language and the "secular" language of public reason are so great that for *democratic reasons* religious language needs to be translated into secular language in order to insure that religious citizens can participate equally in democratic life in a voice of their own.[12]

Perhaps the case of Elizabeth Costello points to a lacuna in political theories of recognition, a failure to recognize (a class of) recognition failures that fall outside the normal range of injustices with which these theories normally concern themselves. We could call it a failure to recognize an expression of suffering that, as the young Marx famously put it, "lays claim to no particular right, because it is the object of no particular injustice but of injustice in general."[13] The idea that there may be a general kind of

[12]See Jürgen Habermas, "Religion in the Public Sphere: Cognitive Presuppositions for the 'Public Use of Reason' by Secular and Religious Citizens," in *Between Naturalism and Religion: Philosophical Essays*, trans. Ciaran Cronin (Cambridge: Polity Press, 2008), 114–48.
[13]Karl Marx, "Towards a Critique of Hegel's *Philosophy of Right*," in *Karl Marx: Selected Writings*, ed. David McLellan (Oxford: Oxford Univ. Press, 1977), 72.

injustice for which we have no particular name, which cannot be expressed, as such claims must, in the form of a determinate and fully explicit political claim, figures importantly in Stanley Cavell's influential analysis of Ibsen's *A Doll's House*.[14] The point of Cavell's analysis is to reveal how the kind of injustice suffered by its central character, Nora Helmer, cannot appear *as* an injustice within the conceptual framework of John Rawls's *Theory of Justice*. The same may be said about the theories of justice proposed by recognition theorists such as Fraser and Honneth.

For example, in Nancy Fraser's minimal rendering of misrecognition, the burden of proof is placed on claimants to publicly justify their experience of injustice. Misrecognition "is a matter of externally manifest and publicly verifiable impediments to some people's standing as full members of society."[15] It cannot be a matter of inarticulate suffering, of being wounded, or anything of the like, otherwise we would not be able to conceptualize the difference between "what really merits the title of injustice, as opposed to what is merely *experienced* as injustice."[16] For Fraser, feelings of injustice and suffering must be "subject to critical scrutiny in open debate," not "sheltered from public contestation."[17] But what Cavell said of Nora's suffering in *A Doll's House* may equally be said of Elizabeth Costello's, that this too is a case in which "specific wrong may not be claimable; yet the misery is such that, on the other side, right is not assertible; instead something must be shown."[18] But what must be shown? How must it be shown to show *that* which must be shown? And, when shown, must it not also be *seen*? What kind of seeing would that be? What would it require of us, to see now what we could not see before?

Exposed to intelligibility

That the case of Elizabeth Costello is in many ways strongly reminiscent of the case of Nora Helmer cannot be entirely surprising to readers of Stanley Cavell, since in both cases we are dealing with two women who have in common a condition of injustice, are suffering from that condition, a condition in which "words are called for" but "there are no words,"

---

[14]Stanley Cavell, "The Conversation of Justice: Rawls and the Drama of Consent," in *Conditions Handsome and Unhandsome: The Constitution of Emersonian Perfectionism* (Chicago: Univ. of Chicago Press, 1990), 101–26. Cavell cites this passage three times (!) in *Conditions Handsome and Unhandsome*.

[15]Fraser, *Redistribution or Recognition?*, 31

[16]Fraser, *Redistribution or Recognition?*, 205.

[17]Fraser, *Redistribution or Recognition?*, 205.

[18]Cavell, *Conditions Handsome and Unhandsome*, 112.

which drives them both to extremes of expression.[19] The words they are using, the words they are testing, are found to be unintelligible, and when intelligible, are found to be outrageous. Either they are nonsensical, or they can't be taken seriously. When they speak, their speech is found wanting, falling short of standards of intelligibility expected of such speech—be it in the domestic or public realm. Their words and lives are exposed to intelligibility, as is their humanity.[20]

Nora Helmer experiences her marriage as a violation of self, as having violated her to such an extent that she wants to "tear herself to pieces." That destructive urge comes from the realization that she has been giving her consent to an arrangement, to an institution, that has rendered her voiceless. Torvald, her husband, regards her various expressions of moral outrage as instances of childish histrionics, a petulant refusal to understand her place, their place, in the world. "You're ill Nora ..., I almost believe you are out of your senses." He implores her to express herself in a clear way: "a songbird needs a clear voice to sing with." But that's not Nora's voice, not the voice in which she must sing her voicelessness and her oppression, not the voice she is seeking to make her own: Nora has realized that the matter of her liberty has become a matter of her voice. The search for that voice requires a radical new beginning, which may or may not go well. All she knows is that "I must find out which is right—the world or I."[21]

Elizabeth Costello must also confront a world in which her voice is found unintelligible, lacking sense, or lacking a sense of appropriateness. Her interlocutors do not think they are dealing with an adult behaving like a petulant child, but, rather, with a vulnerable old woman who has lost her way, if not her mind. Her daughter-in-law, Norma, trained as a philosopher of mind, finds her "opinions on animals, animal consciousness, and ethical relations with animals ... jejune and sentimental" (17). During the course of Costello's first lecture, Norma lets John know that his mother is "rambling," that she has "lost her thread" (31). At the end of the lecture, an exasperated Norma wants to rebut her mother-in-law's claims, but John seeing nothing but trouble ahead, asks Norma to desist from doing so, which leads to a fraught exchange between them:

> "She shouldn't be allowed to get away with it! She's confused!"
> "She's old, she's my mother. Please!" (36)

The confusion of which Costello is accused is not the confusion of which an old woman's decrepit mind might be accused, although there is some

[19] Cavell, *Conditions Handsome and Unhandsome*, xxxvii.
[20] The link between being exposed to intelligibility and being exposed to one's humanity is suggested in Cavell, *The Claim of Reason*, 438–9.
[21] As quoted in Cavell, *Conditions Handsome and Unhandsome*, 112, 150.

suspicion raised about the condition of her mind in what is unsaid and implied. Rather, the implication is that she is out of her depth, intellectually, confused about what the issues are, confused about what is required to discuss them with the requisite clarity. In short, she doesn't know what she's talking about, and doesn't know how one must talk about such matters if one is to talk about them intelligibly. There is overwhelming agreement about how this is done, which provides Norma with all the reassurance she needs to hold Costello to account, to make sure Costello doesn't get away with doing it the wrong way, her age and all the rest notwithstanding. Her son, attuned to this background agreement concedes that it was strange talk, from beginning to end: "A strange ending ... A strange ending to a strange talk, he thinks, ill gauged, ill argued. Not her métier, argumentation. She should not be here" (37).

In a response that takes the (much too cute) form of a fictionalized dialogue between a well-known animal rights philosopher and his undergraduate daughter, Singer, the well-known animal rights philosopher, construes the character of Norma as a "marvelous device," through which Coetzee can distance himself from Costello's wobbly or outrageous claims. Norma "makes all the usual objections to what Costello is saying" (*LA* 91), making clear that Costello's arguments really are pretty pathetic as *philosophical* arguments, "jejune" as Norma put it, thereby relieving Coetzee of the burden of defending claims to which he is not really committed, or if he is committed to them, not ready or able to defend with persuasive arguments. "Coetzee doesn't even have to worry too much about getting the structure of the lecture right. When he notices that it is starting to ramble, he just has Norma say that Costello is rambling!" (*LA* 91).

Singer's response thus instances the reading of *The Lives of Animals* that Diamond regards as so profoundly wrong, and, indeed, unjust. *All* the characters are treated as mere devices for putting forward philosophical arguments (mostly of dubious cogency), and not just "the woman with the haunted mind and the raw nerves." No one takes seriously the question that Costello needs to answer, needs us to see that it is as much our question as it is hers: how is it possible to *live* in the face of what we do to animals, and "in face of the fact that, for nearly everyone, it is as nothing, as the mere accepted background of life."[22] How *does* one live in the face of such circumstances?

Elizabeth Costello also wants to know which is right—the world or her. "Everyone else comes to terms with it. Why can't you? *Why can't you?*" But she is not as confident as Nora that she will find an answer to that question. Partly, that is because she is a much older woman, older and more conscious of her limitations, of the fact that the years remaining are not so

[22]Diamond, "Difficulty of Reality," 47.

many.[23] Costello is also more in touch with her scepticism about herself, with doubts about her intelligibility to herself that go so far as to threaten her with madness, with a loss of any reliable difference between dreaming and being awake, recalling the skeptical fantasies of the protagonist of Descartes's *Meditations*.[24]

> "Am I fantasizing it all? I must be mad. Yet every day I see the evidences. The very people I suspect produce the evidence, exhibit it, offer it to me. Corpses. Fragments of corpses. That they bought for money.
>
> "It is as if I were to visit friends, and to make some polite remark about the lamp in their living room, and they were to say, 'Yes, it's nice, isn't it? Polish-Jewish skin it's made of, we find that's the best, the skins of young Polish-Jewish virgins.' And then I go to the bathroom and the soap-wrapper says, 'Treblinka—100% human stearate.' Am I dreaming, I say to myself? What kind of house is this?" (*LA* 69).

Like Nora Helmer before her in yet another respect, Elizabeth Costello finds herself intolerably implicated in the injustice she finds so horrific. She too wants to scream, yet, she holds herself back, barely, from screaming as loud and as long as she can. As she says in her first lecture, not without some guile, "I want to find a way of speaking to fellow human beings that will be cool rather than heated" (*LA* 22). Though this way of speaking is to be achieved in the language of philosophy, a language not designed for screaming, she screams nonetheless, but it is as if nobody hears her scream. Perhaps it is too subtle, couched as it is in academic protocols and subtleties. If it is heard, it is ignored. It is as if Elizabeth Costello finds herself in one of those nightmares in which, in the face of some unspeakable terror, one opens one's mouth to scream, but no sound comes out, and no sound will come out. This is the state of mind in which Elizabeth Costello is trying to speak: she might as well be speaking/screaming into her pillow or into a hole in the ground. To say she has lost her voice, become aphonic, is not to say she can't make sounds of some kind; it is to say that her voice cannot utter words, sounds, that can move others, that can help her make herself intelligible to herself.

The panic that arises from her deprivation of voice is inseparable from the extremes of expression to which she succumbs, and nothing is more indicative of such extremes than the comparison she makes between the slaughter of millions of Jews in the Nazi death camps and the daily

---

[23]It goes without saying that the differences in their future possibilities are not only a function of differences in age but also of differences in ages—between living at the end of the nineteenth century and at the start of the twenty-first.

[24]On this, see Stanley Cavell, "Being Odd, Getting Even," in *In Quest of the Ordinary: Lines of Skepticism and Romanticism* (Chicago: Univ. of Chicago Press, 1988), 105–49.

industrialized slaughter of animals for human consumption: "Let me say it openly: we are surrounded by an enterprise of degradation, cruelty, and killing which rivals anything that the Third Reich was capable of, indeed dwarfs it, in that ours is an enterprise without end, self-regenerating, bringing rabbits, rats, poultry, livestock ceaselessly into the world for the purpose of killing them" (*LA* 21).

It is a controversial and, for some, a cheap, unbearable, and even blasphemous comparison (a point made by the character Abraham Stern). Unfortunately, it too easily deflects attention from what underlies it, and with it, the key to making sense of Costello's hauntedness and woundedness. Much too valuable to be lost in the futile exercise of comparing holocausts with one another is what Costello has to say about what happens to the human animal when it begins to lose its humanity, as was the case when a "certain line was crossed" in Nazi Germany, and the human animal falls "into a state we can only call sin" (*LA* 20). "We may not, all of us, believe in pollution, we may not believe in sin, but we do believe in their psychic correlates. We accept without question that the psyche (or soul) touched with guilty knowledge cannot be well" (*LA* 21). From this starting point, Costello raises the possibility that we human animals have crossed a line that puts our humanity at risk in just the same way, such that we might become or have become like those "Germans of a particular generation" who "lost their humanity, in our eyes, because of a certain willed ignorance on their part" (*LA* 20). Right now, in our midst, somewhere, not far away at all, down the street perhaps, are drug-testing laboratories, factory farms, abattoirs. "They are all around us as I speak, only we do not, in a certain sense, know about them" (*LA* 21).

In what sense do we not *know* about them? In the sense not of knowledge but of acknowledgment. "Acknowledgement goes beyond knowledge. (Goes beyond not, so to speak, in the order of knowledge, but in its requirement that I *do* something or reveal something on the basis of that knowledge.)"[25] The distinction introduced by Cavell, between knowing and acknowledging is meant to capture some sense of our *answerability* to others that flows from the acknowledgement or recognition of their suffering. Why? "Because your suffering makes a *claim* upon me. It is not enough that I *know* (am certain) that you suffer—I must do or reveal something (whatever can be done). In a word, I must *acknowledge* it, otherwise I do not know 'what (your or his) being in pain' means. Is."[26]

[25] Cavell, "Knowing and Acknowledging," in *Must We Mean What We Say?* (Cambridge: Cambridge Univ. Press, 1969), 257.
[26] Cavell, "Knowing and Acknowledging," 263.

Recognition or acknowledgment?

In everyday use the difference between recognition and acknowledgment can be a merely terminological difference. However, if we compare Cavell's elucidation of acknowledgment with what Fraser has to say about "suffering" being subject to critical scrutiny and public contestation, then there is a difference that makes a difference: what counts as a case of misrecognition is a matter of knowing rather than of acknowledging. In this respect, treating a claim to suffering as a matter of knowledge rather than acknowledgment is to be working within the picture of knowledge transmitted by the modern epistemological tradition, where what something *is* is a matter of *how* it is known.[27] Thus, the priority of knowing to acknowledgment means that there must be a way of adjudicating recognition claims so that we can know the difference between those claims that merit the title of injustice and those that do not, and it is for this reason that the burden of proof must be placed on the claimants, and that their claims must be made in "externally manifest and publicly verifiable" form as determinate and fully explicit claims. "Inarticulate suffering, in contrast, is by definition sheltered from public contestation."[28] Perhaps, however, there are cases of inarticulate suffering that are not so much sheltered from public contestation as they are made invisible, inaudible, by it. As I have written elsewhere in this connection, "the light of publicity can be blinding as well as illuminating. We may fail to see some morally relevant feature of an issue or conflict *because* of the light publicity sheds—which is why we need continually to adjust the lighting by disclosing what the light of publicity itself obscures."[29]

If we are to make sense of what it is Nora Helmer and Elizabeth Costello are demanding from their audiences, from us, we must recognize that theirs are calls for acknowledgment—calls that call in turn for some change in us we are reluctant, or that we refuse, to answer. "What makes change (supposing it is possible) hard; why does it suggest violence?"[30] But is there not violence in the resistance to change, in its refusal? Why are we more inclined to answer the calls of the Nora Helmers and Elizabeth Costellos with skepticism about other minds than with a change in how we go on from here? Why are questions of knowledge about pain and suffering more pressing than the acknowledgment of pain and suffering? (How do we know that Nora and Elizabeth really are in pain? How

[27]Charles Taylor, "Explanation and Practical Reason," in *Philosophical Arguments* (Cambridge, MA: Harvard Univ. Press, 1995), 34.

[28]Fraser, *Redistribution or Recognition*, 205.

[29]Nikolas Kompridis, "Struggling Over the Meaning of Recognition: A Matter of Identity, Justice, or Freedom?" *European Journal of Political Theory* 6, no. 3 (2007): 282.

[30]Cavell, *Conditions Handsome and Unhandsome*, xxx.

can we be sure that their pain is pain that we should, are bound to, acknowledge?) If "a failure to know" means that there is an ignorance, or absence of something, a "failure to acknowledge" means that there is "the presence of something, a confusion, an indifference, a callousness, an exhaustion, a coldness."[31] And for this reason, it is not surprising that Cavell can arrive at the view (through a host of philosophical, literary, and everyday examples) that "skepticism concerning other minds is not skepticism but is tragedy."[32]

The link between tragedy and skepticism is also made in *The Lives of Animals*, the story it tells is told in the tragic mode, ends in tragedy, as much as it foretells of one. Consider how, at the point when Costello makes the extreme comparison between the Holocaust and the "daily holocaust" of the worldwide human slaughter of nonhuman animals, the story she wants to tell is about what *our* failure of acknowledgment in the case of what we do to animals costs *us*, how it exposes our humanity, not only to our loss of it, but also to a loss of our intelligibility to ourselves, to the risk of losing our way, losing ourselves across a line which we cannot simply cross back again, anymore than Othello can breathe life back into Desdemona, because, in tragedy, the tragedy of such a crossing, it is already too late.

> "The particular horror of the death camps, the horror that convinces us that what went on there was a crime against humanity, is not that despite a humanity shared with their victims, the killers treated them like lice. That is too abstract. The horror is that the killers refused to think themselves into the place of their victims, as did everyone else. They said, 'It is *they* in those cattle-cars rattling past.' They did not say, 'How would it be if it were I in that cattle-car? They did not say, 'It is I who am in that cattle-car?' They said, 'It must be the dead who are being burnt today, making the air stink and falling in ash on my cabbages.' They did not say, 'How would it be if I were burning?' They did not say, 'I am burning. I am falling in ash.'
>
> In other words, they closed their hearts." (*LA* 34)

In the end, the story Costello is telling her audience is not about comparing holocausts but about illuminating the danger that overwhelming agreement about our need of animal flesh poses to our exposed humanity, the possible or actual tragedy, depending on where one stands, that our hearts have closed to a suffering for which only we can be held responsible, and held responsible only by one another.

Now we are in a position to see that Elizabeth Costello is not only

---

[31] Cavell, "Knowing and Acknowledging," 264.

[32] Cavell, *The Claim of Reason*, xxii–xxiii.

"haunted by the horror of what we do to animals ... and by the knowledge of how unhaunted others are." She is also terrified by the thought that *her* heart will close, too. It is this fear that she can't announce to her son, John. She really doesn't "know" which is right—the world or her. She is unsure, doubtful, about how to go on, for, after all, "This is life. Everyone else comes to terms with it. Why can't you? *Why can't you?*" Coming to terms with it would mean, of course, that she must let her heart close. Closing her heart will reopen the world to her, the world of overwhelming agreement from which she is exiled so long as she simply can't come to terms with it. But then, as she knows, she would become so morally compromised she would lose her soul, rendering herself morally contemptible, morally indefensible, in her eyes.[33] Closing her heart would also mean losing the ability to prick up her ears in response to overwhelming agreement—she risks losing her mind, either way.

> "She turns on him a tearful face. What does she want, he thinks. Does she want me to answer her question for her?
> They are not yet on the expressway. He pulls the car over, switches off the engine, takes his mother in his arms. He inhales the smell of cold cream, of old flesh. 'There, there,' he whispers in her ear. 'There, there. It will soon be over.'" (*LA* 69)

The ending is devastating in its irony, as is all tragedy. Costello is struggling to keep her heart open, just as those closest to her have already closed theirs to her. John Bernard, her son, manifests the very incapacity to enter into the life of another that Elizabeth Costello made central to her lectures, and that Coetzee makes the framing device of the entire text. John Bernard can, however, smell on his mother the decaying deathliness of flesh, notice the cold comfort of "cold cream" on the face of "old flesh."[34] A heart must be very closed, indeed, to say, in this circumstance, "There, there. It will soon be over." *What* will be over? And why would it be comforting to say so? It seems that he is saying one (or both) of two things. Either, "You're old. You're dying. I can smell it on you. So don't worry so much, for soon this burden will be lifted from you shoulders. Amen." Or, no less appalling, no less callous and insensitive, "There, there. Your heart will soon close, and your worries will come, finally, to an end. You fought the good fight,

[33]The word "soul" appears fifteen times in the text. I do not have the space to address its significance, but thanks to Ian Hacking for counting

[34]*The Lives of Animals* begins as it ends, with the son being inordinately shocked by how much his mother has aged. We are the animal that is particularly marked out by the marks of aging, and I suppose our markings, our practices of marking, and our typically negative responses to them is also something that Coetzee sees as implicated in our human responses to the lives of animals, human and nonhuman.

but it was futile, as you finally realize. Now we can all be together, in the community of closed hearts and overwhelming agreement. You can have a normal life, again."

All I want to know is: How am I supposed to reply to this?

How *are* we supposed to reply to something or to someone when it is not clear just what it is we are dealing with and what it is that is being asked of us? Can we speak meaningfully about responding rightly or wrongly in cases like this—as readers, as intimates, as citizens, as human beings? What can guide us, normatively speaking? How do we tell what form of response we owe an *other* when that other appears inscrutable to us, and, as in the case of Elizabeth Costello, when the other appears as inscrutable to herself as she appears to us? Where do we begin? What might get in the way of a reply that is just, in every sense of just, not callous, insensitive, indifferent? I would claim that this is the central theme and the organizing principle of *The Lives of Animals*: the question of how we should respond and reply, how we should answer and be answerable to others, the question of human responsiveness or lack of it in the face of suffering.

Peter Singer does not seem to be aware of the proximity of his question to the question at the heart of Coetzee's *The Lives of Animals*, the irony of which is magnified and intensified *by* his reply, which foreshortens the scope of the question and possible reflection on it, especially when he dismisses Costello's suggestion that the only obstacles to thinking our way into the being of other creatures, like and unlike ourselves, real or fictional, are obstacles we put there ourselves: "there is no limit to the extent which we can think ourselves into the being of another. There are no bounds to the sympathetic imagination.... If I can think my way into the existence of a being who has never existed, then I can think my way into the existence of a bat or chimpanzee or an oyster, any being with whom I share the substrate of life" (*LA* 35).

Costello's claim is offered as the conclusion of an unusual and inventive engagement with one of the most discussed papers in the philosophical literature, Thomas Nagel's "What Is It Like to Be a Bat?"[35] Her discussion of Nagel deserves a separate discussion. My interest here is in the specifics of Singer's reply, a reply he puts in the mouth of his daughter, who up to this point had been consigned to the role of playing the straight man to her philosopher-father. "You don't have to be a philosopher to see what's

[35]Thomas Nagel, "What Is It Like to Be a Bat," *The Philosophical Review* LXXXIII, 4 (October 1974): 435–50.

wrong with that. The fact that a character doesn't exist isn't something that makes it hard to imagine yourself as that character. You can imagine someone very like yourself, or like someone else you know. Then it is easy to think your way into the existence of that being. But a bat, or an oyster?" (*LA* 90–91).

In the grip of a picture, a picture of the text as a pair of fictionalized academic lectures, Singer is seemingly blind to his failure to do what he claims to be so *easy*—to sympathetically, imaginatively, enter into the existence of the human being by whose claims he is so perplexed, a being not as unlike himself as a bat or an oyster. Is she not also a possible object of sympathetic imagination of a kind that Singer has declared to be well within reach of human imagination, but for some reason, out of reach of his own? Rather than demonstrating the philosophical weakness of Costello's argument, he performatively enacts the limitations of his own philosophical and moral imagination—at least when it comes to persons that are not real. He can no more *follow* Elizabeth Costello than her son can. But what is at stake in treating persons whom we encounter in literature as mere "devices"? Is Singer's response to the fictional person of Elizabeth Costello a function of the putative form of *The Lives of Animals*—that is, a function of presenting itself as a set of fictional lectures at a fictitious American liberal arts college? Or is it a function of a particular kind of reading, which, as Cora Diamond claims, cuts across the disciplinary differences and intellectual temperaments of all the commentators, a reading in whose grip they all are? "So we have then two quite different ways of seeing the lectures: as centrally concerned with the presenting of a wounded woman, and as centrally concerned with the presenting of a position on the issue of how we should treat animals."[36]

Why is it that the wounded woman reading is not a pressing concern? What impression must *The Lives of Animals* make on a reader for that reading to be compelling? It is as if Costello's audience, fictional and real, actively resists being pressed by resisting any experience of Costello and the text that leaves an impression, some mark that marks us as living lives that have been put in question, that put to us, a call to change how we live. As Costello tells us, we human beings don't engage in this kind of change unless "we press ourselves or are pressed. But we resist being pressed, and rarely press ourselves" (*LA* 32). To use Costello's untrendy, thoroughly unacademic language, the task of opening our heart, and keeping it open, involves enormous struggle—psychological, physical, intellectual, and emotional struggle. The heart is not a tap we can open and close at will.

Among the difficulties that arise when we are pressed in this way is a difficulty that Diamond illuminates, "a difficulty that pushes us beyond

[36]Diamond, "The Difficulty of Reality," 49.

what we can think. To attempt to think it is to feel one's thinking come unhinged. Our concepts, our ordinary life with our concepts, pass by this difficulty as if it were not there ... to appreciate the difficulty is to feel oneself being shouldered out of how one thinks, how one is apparently supposed to think, or to have a sense of the inability of thought to encompass what it is attempting to reach."[37] Who looks for opportunities to "feel one's thinking come unhinged"? But if the difficulty of following Elizabeth Costello's line of thought is "a difficulty that pushes us beyond what we can think," then we cannot say *in advance* of being pushed beyond what we can think whether she is wrong (or right) to demand a change in us. That change, whatever it may be, presupposes that we can enter into and possibly overcome this kind of difficulty, the overcoming of which is also the overcoming of overwhelming agreement about "our ordinary life with our concepts," about our ordinary understanding and application of them (for example, "animal," "human," "reason," "argument," "philosophy," "literature," "life," "flesh").

Understandably, it is a difficulty we are more likely to evade than to embrace. As Diamond points out, drawing from Cavell, one prominent strategy of evasion is *deflection*, deflection *from* a circumstance of appalling suffering to a philosophical problem in the vicinity. We turn away from the suffering to the question of what counts as suffering: whether suffering must be publicly knowable to count as such; whether suffering must be made externally manifest and publicly verifiable if it is to count as injustice. We turn the problem of skepticism about other minds into the problem of skepticism about the mindedness of nonhuman animals (Norma, the specialist in philosophy of mind, believes there is overwhelming agreement to support her skepticism). And, as Diamond has shown, we turn from the difficulty of making sense of Elizabeth Costello's suffering to the difficulty of taking her "arguments" seriously.

Another prominent strategy of evasion is also amply on display in *The Lives of Animals*. In this case we do not have to face the perplexing difficulty of how to respond when we are pushed beyond what we can think: we *already* know how to respond, which is to say, there is nothing more to know, nothing which can unsettle us. I will call this evasive response "knowingness," meaning a "knowing" stance towards the world.[38] Nothing better exemplifies this stance towards Coetzee's text and its protagonist than Marjorie Garber's commentary, in which she makes it clear that she is not fooled by the text and is already in the know, so to speak, when it comes to discerning the metafictional strategies and epistemological ruses

[37]Diamond, "The Difficulty of Reality," 8.

[38]I am inspired to do so by Jonathan Lear's "Knowingness and Abandonment: An Oedipus for Our Time," in *Open-Minded: Working Out the Logic of the Soul* (Cambridge, MA: Harvard Univ. Press, 1998), 33–55.

through which it seeks to realize its ambition to anticipate and incorporate all possible responses to it. The text is *obviously* framed to "insulate ... warring 'ideas' (about animal rights, about consciousness, about death, about the family, about academia) against claims of authorship and authority. They are put in play by characters who—precisely because they are 'academics'—can be relied upon to be unreliable ... 'Sincerity,' assuming it to be a value, cannot be assumed in this contest of the faculties. We don't know whose voice to believe" (*LA* 79).

This kind of "knowing" reading supposes that the logical space of interpretive possibility is closed, that there are only a finite number of moves that can be made in this space. Once one comes to know one's way around in it, one cannot get lost, or come to have doubts about (the reliability of) one's own voice, only doubts about the reliability of the voices of others. Since we cannot know "whose voice to believe," we cannot *know* whether the other makes a claim on us, and, therefore, we cannot *fail* to respond to the other's claims, say, for acknowledgment. Our "knowing" stance shields us from exposure to the possibility that our "knowledge of others may be challenged or overthrown, or that it ought to be."[39] We already know, too well, the response that is called for.

From recognition to receptivity

Theories of recognition have been mainly, indeed, almost exclusively, concerned with the struggle *for* recognition—concerned, that is, with the nature and justifiability of demands for recognition. The *Kampf* has almost always been seen from the side of those demanding recognition, not from the side of those *from* whom it is demanded. Thus, missing from these theories is attention to the struggle *to* acknowledge demands for recognition—which is to say, the struggle to overcome something in ourselves that resists acknowledgment of others—a resistance that we cannot take for granted *as* justifiable. As we have seen, the failures of normative responsiveness that are exemplarily presented in *The Lives of Animals* cannot be captured in the conceptual language of recognition. That is because what we are dealing with are not failures of recognition, but, rather, with *failures of receptivity*. Recognition *presupposes* receptivity, for the struggle to recognize and acknowledge the other is *first of all* a struggle to become *receptive* to the other, particularly when the other's call for acknowledgment appears in an unfamiliar form.

To speak of receptivity here is not to speak of passivity or openness: receptivity is not reducible to either of these. To identify receptivity with

[39] Cavell, *The Claim of Reason*, 439.

passivity or openness is to identify it with mindless submission to anyone or anything that comes along (the usual suspects: Nazis, fascists, etc.). This altogether prevalent and stubborn conception of receptivity is one that makes it synonymous with indiscriminate openness, as though we are equally open to any and all possibilities. A mind that is equally open to any and all possibilities, however, would be a mind that is unminded, a mind rendered incapable of judging anything, precisely because a mind to which everything mattered equally would be a mind to which nothing mattered. In short, nothing we could recognize as a human mind.

I conceive of receptivity as a form of normative responsiveness that is both spontaneous and reflective, which is to say a form of *agency* through which we are responsive to something or someone in an attitude of *answerability*.[40] The spontaneous moment of receptivity is what we commonly refer to when we speak of openness, openness to that which is unfamiliar or unsettling, a spontaneous readiness to follow a line of flight or descent. Conceiving of receptivity in this way allows us to think of our epistemic and normative agency, our mindedness, if you like, as involving and requiring exposure to human vulnerability—the vulnerability of a being that can be marked, struck, impressed by experienced reality, by what and whom it encounters in the world. It involves and requires a willingness to risk self-dispossession, and thus it is not so much about becoming open as it is about becoming *unclosed* to something or someone. Thus, when Elizabeth Costello talks about entering into the being of another, whatever other that may be, she is also presupposing receptivity to that other, for it is only when we allow entry of that other into *our* being—only when we allow ourselves to be marked, struck, impressed by it—that we are able to then enter into its being. That is why I prefer to think of receptivity as an unclosing of oneself. Unlike some abstract, free-floating openness to anyone or anything, unclosing involves struggle, a struggle with ourselves to open up what is now closed, or what has never been open. It is this struggle that the *Lives of Animals* dramatizes so powerfully, and which the commentators missed, because they did not accept the invitation of the text to take on that struggle with themselves, an invitation that comes in the form of the perplexity it produces—the perplexity of not knowing how to reply either to Costello or to the text she haunts.

The failures of responsiveness in and to *The Lives of Animals* are failures to respond to the normative challenges posed by the text and by its central character. Becoming receptive to those challenges entails seeing what is new

---

[40]For a more elaborate and systematic account of my conception of receptivity, see "Receptivity, Possibility and Democratic Politics," in *Ethics & Global Politics* 4, no. 4 (2011): 255–72; "Romanticism," in *Oxford Handbook of Philosophy and Literature*, ed. Richard Eldridge (Oxford: Oxford Univ. Press, 2009), 247–70; and *Critique and Disclosure: Critical Theory between Past and Future* (Cambridge, MA: MIT Press, 2006), 199–223.

in them, seeing that something or someone is calling for a new response, not just any kind of response, but a response that also requires, manifests, a freer relation to ourselves. If the characters in *The Lives of Animals* had responded to Elizabeth Costello neither by deflection nor by knowingness, but by becoming receptive to her calls for acknowledgment, they would not only have been in a position to acknowledge her suffering, they would have been in a position to facilitate its voicing, letting it become a voice they had not allowed themselves to hear before. Becoming receptive in this reflective sense is to become attuned to the selectivity of our reception, attuned to what and to whom we were unable to be receptive, and therefore attuned to the normative demands for change, change we may envision only in an indeterminate and inchoate way, but to which we feel nonetheless obligated to be receptive, answerable. Why? Because it is here, in this gap between who we have been and who we might become, that we see our own freedom is at stake, and where we may "find" it manifested.

Similarly, if the invited readers of *The Lives of Animals* had approached the text and its difficult central character from the stance of receptivity, they may have recognized their own first-order responses in the strategies of deflection and knowingness pursued by those characters instead of reproducing them in their own readings—unknowingly, we might say. This moment of self-recognition would have freed their readings from the premises with which they began. So, for example, rather than seeing in Costello's "arguments" the lack of the requisite métier, they would have noticed that she was quite consciously and quite reflectively refusing to engage in academic forms of argument.[41] Instead of engaging in argument, with the purpose of winning it, she was "manifesting for the other another way,"[42] another way to engage her audience in urgent discussion of the lives of the animals we are. And that too, I believe, is what lies behind the peculiar form of *The Lives of Animals*, both identical and nonidentical with a fictionalized set of lectures, that which makes them seem at once familiar and unsettling.

That same moment of self-recognition would have allowed the invited readers to see that the lives *in question* in *The Lives of Animals* are the lives of human animals, not in any anthropocentric sense, but in the sense of a call to think anew, now from the perspective of the lives of all animals, what makes or ought to make the lives of the animals we are, *human*. Think of it as a call to rethink the mode of our humanity. Responsiveness to *that* call would make receptivity itself central to becoming human again. Since Elizabeth Costello's primary concern is with the loss of our humanity, the closing of the human heart, she would surely agree with Marx, that

---

[41] As Cora Diamond notes, Costello "does not engage with others in argument, in the sense in which philosophers do. Her responses to arguments from others move out from the kind of engagement in argument that might have been expected." ("The Difficulty of Reality," 52).

[42] Cavell, *Conditions Handsome and Unhandsome*, 31.

the "complete loss of humanity.... can only recover itself by a complete redemption of humanity."[43]

Political theorists might thereby learn from encounters with literary texts like *The Lives of Animals*, and difficult characters like Elizabeth Costello, that institutional and constitutional change is not the only change we need. Sometimes we need change that aims at "the cultivation of a new mode of human being, of being human, where the idea is not that this comes later than justice but that it is essential in pursuing the justice of sharing one another's fate without reducing that fate, as it were, to mitigation."[44] Engagement with literature's capacity to manifest for others another way, in ways both complex and ambiguous, might shoulder political theorists out of our assumptions about how best to make sense of things political, making us more alert to the inadequacy of our conceptual vocabularies. It might also make us capaciously less confident about the powers of academic forms of argument and practices of justification, and more sensitively attuned to the need for new ways of thinking and reasoning with others, ways that must themselves be newly cultivated. Perhaps literary theorists need to learn this, too, by becoming receptive to other ways of inhabiting literature, other than as Cartesian skeptics obsessed with methods of interrogation. After all, this is but one very restrictive way to live our skepticism, and it is a question for us, whether we might wish to live it differently, less restrictively.[45]

[43]Marx, "Towards a Critique of Hegel's *Philosophy of Right*," 72.

[44]Cavell, *Conditions Handsome and Unhandsome*, 25.

[45]I want to thank Rita Felski for her valuable comments and suggestions.

CHAPTER SEVEN

For the love of earthly life: Nietzsche and Winnicott between modernism and naturalism

Melissa A. Orlie

For better and worse, our ethical and political judgments are rooted in what we find beautiful and worthy of love. It is in this sense that my essay presumes that political theory has made, or needs, an aesthetic turn.

In many circles, associations between aesthetics and politics are suspect, especially when one's source for making the connection is a figure like Nietzsche, to whom I turn here. Many factors inform such suspicion and it is beyond the reach of this essay to consider them. My own aesthetic turn has little if anything to do Nietzsche's early interest in the aesthetic justification of life, and consciously began with the insights of one of the great ecological thinkers of the twentieth century.

Aldo Leopold is hardly known among political theorists, routinely dismissed by continentally oriented thinkers of the ecological, and oversimplified even by commentators sympathetic to his claims. Although my essay works its way through matters of beauty and love with the aid of Nietzsche and the great psychoanalytic essayist D. W. Winnicott, Leopold's reflections on the vital importance of perception sets its course.

The root of ecological conscience is aesthetic perception, writes Leopold, "the perception of the natural processes by which the land and living things upon it have achieved their characteristic forms (evolution), and by which they maintain their existence (ecology)."[1] Leopold here subtly introduces a perspective which he states more explicitly elsewhere, namely, he calls us to relinquish our judgments and actions as conquerors and consumers of the land and to change ourselves into plain members and citizens of a land community.[2] Leopold enlarges the boundaries of community to include not only all flora and fauna, but all soils and waters as well. All of these elements and their relations, says Leopold, compose a "biotic complex" so "conditioned by interwoven cooperations and competitions that no man can say where utility begins and ends." The only sure conclusion, Leopold asserts, "is that the biota as a whole is useful."[3]

In Leopold's view, the truly creative ecological task is to promote perception and not only because the "outstanding characteristic of perception is that it entails no consumption and no dilution of any resource." When human beings ravage or spoil the land while they claim to be enjoying or improving it, their doing so is dependent not only on the quality of what they see, says Leopold, but on the quality of the "mental eyes" with which they see it. Which is to say that earthly well-being is dependent upon "building receptivity into the still unlovely human mind."[4]

Nietzsche is regarded by many besides Martin Heidegger as the epitome of Western wilfulness gone mad. Yet it hardly has been noticed that Nietzsche took a decisive turn away from his own previously unlovely relationship to earthly life. The crux of Nietzsche's aesthetic turn is to endeavor to find beauty in what is "necessary in things" by "learning to love" what has become of earthly life. The task of my essay is to say what this means and entails, and why and how it matters.

The Nietzsche we need now

When it comes to matters of judgment there are at least two Nietzsches. For many, Nietzsche is a modernist who longs for new inspiring values and calls for the free spirits who are strong enough to overcome any resistance to their creations.[5] For others, Nietzsche is a naturalist who emphasizes what

---

[1]Aldo Leopold, "Conservation Esthetic" in *A Sand County Almanac* (Oxford University Press, 1949), p. 173.

[2]Aldo Leopold, "The Land Ethic" in *A Sand County Almanac*, p. 204.

[3]Aldo Leopold, "Biotic View of the Land" in *The River of the Mother God* (University of Wisconsin, 1991), p. 267.

[4]Leopold, "Land Esthetic," p. 177.

[5]The best, recent exemplar of this tradition of interpretation is Bernard Reginster's *The Affirmation of Life: Nietzsche on Overcoming Nihilism* (Harvard University Press, 2006). Robert Gooding-William's excellent *Zarathustra's Dionysian Modernism* (Stanford, 2001)

is necessary and waits for those with the strength to bear what truly benefits life.[6] There is warrant for both of these figures in Nietzsche's writings. What is less clear is how to reconcile them.

Both modernist and naturalist readers get something truly right about Nietzsche's writings, albeit only partially so. Before we consider what they each get right, I want to emphasize two senses in which both interpretations are too partial. First, both modernist and naturalist readers of Nietzsche usually muster little more than a refusal of the opposing line of interpretation. Mainly, both sides express incredulity at such practiced ignorance of passages that so obviously throw into question the other's reading. However, a second, more important partiality modernist and naturalist readers share is their relative neglect of Nietzsche's most constructive hope. Neither modernists nor naturalists tend to do justice to what Nietzsche calls the "highest formula of affirmation that is at all attainable," an experience Nietzsche pursues by experimenting with the idea of eternal recurrence.[7]

Nietzsche most often represents the idea of eternal return as a thought experiment rather than as a cosmological or causal theory. Still, calling it an experiment should not be taken to lessen its importance. Of what do you become aware, Nietzsche queries, when you engage the idea that, "This life as you now live it and have lived it, you will have to live once more and innumerable times more; and there will be nothing new in it, but every pain and every joy and every thought and sigh and everything unutterably small or great in your life will have to return to you, all in the same succession and sequence...?"[8] Nietzsche calls eternal return the fundamental conception of *Thus Spoke Zarathustra* and, he explains that working through the thought of eternal return is his way of enacting his highest aspiration, namely, to affirm earthly life wholeheartedly, without reservation or resentment (*EH* 297).[9]

If we foreground Nietzsche's most affirmative aspiration, then it is possible to make sense of the textual moments which preoccupy both modernist and naturalist readers of Nietzsche by folding each into an orientation more befitting Nietzsche's most distinctive, and now most needed, line of thinking. This line of thinking, as Nietzsche himself expected, has

---

narrates Nietzsche's crisis of confidence in the promise of modernism, yet sees him as resuscitating it rather than overjoyed to let it go.

[6]An excellent collection of essays exemplifying the naturalist reading of Nietzsche is Brian Leiter and Neil Sinhababu (eds.), *Nietzsche and Morality* (Clarendon Press, 2007).

[7]Friedrich Nietzsche, *Ecce Homo* (Kaufmann trans.) (Vintage, 1989), p. 295 (henceforth cited as *EH* and by page number).

[8]Friedrich Nietzsche, *The Gay Science* (Kaufmann trans.) (Vintage, 1974), number 334 (henceforth cited as *GS* and by aphorism number).

[9]Friedrich Nietzsche, *Thus Spoke Zarathustra* in *The Portable Nietzsche* (Kaufmann trans.) (Penguin, 1976) (henceforth cited as *Z* and by page number).

come meaningfully alive only posthumously. This Nietzschean orientation is impersonal rather than modernist, materialist rather than naturalist.

Yet there is something far more important at issue here than reconciling apparently contradictory strands of Nietzsche's writings. At stake is what Nietzsche calls "wakefulness itself" and upon it hinges nothing less than the habitability of the earth.

Wakefulness itself

Beyond Good and Evil opens with Nietzsche's call to the task of "wakefulness itself."[10] This call to wake up is a call to conscious awareness of an ever-broadening range of affective experience. Broadened awareness of the affective reverberations flowing into our predominate perceptions and intentions, judgments and actions, not only allows us to become more conscious of the roots of our perspectives on life. Such broadening affective awareness also may allow competing perceptions and affects to enter our conscious life and, along with them, divergent possibilities of life, especially in those aspects of life which may evoke our ire and foster our hatred of life. Awakening to fuller affective experience, first facilitates feeling, then taking up the task of affirming, a broader range of earthly life than we are readily inclined toward by birth or habit.

Why does Nietzsche value such efforts to awaken to a fuller range of affective experience? As the journey of *Zarathustra* dramatizes, Nietzsche became convinced that the modernist effort wilfully to remake earthly life is no remedy for nihilism but only deepens resentment at life. Whatever has become of earthly life to which we cannot say "yes" only feeds our wish to take revenge upon all that defies our will and to make it suffer (*Z* 251–3). Overcoming nihilism begins with acknowledging and accepting all that has come to be as it has come to be. To be sure, this is an uncanny thought to meet with in a man who professed to philosophize with a hammer.

Still, at the beginning of *Gay Science Book IV*, Nietzsche announces a decisive turning away from the wilful self-assertion of his previous writings and a critique of which he enacts in *Zarathustra*. In *GS* 276, Nietzsche declares his want "to learn more and more to see as beautiful what is necessary in things." Although Nietzsche still maintains that seeing beauty is a creative activity, his reference to "what is necessary in things" is striking, and is the sort of formulation which naturalist readers find supportive of their interpretations. Yet Nietzsche makes as clear in this passage, and in the next (*GS* 277), that to see beauty is to *make* beautiful and that such

[10]Friedrich Nietzsche, *Beyond Good and Evil*, Preface (Kaufmann trans.) (Vintage, 1989) (henceforth cited as *BGE* and by section number).

activity is a matter of "personal providence" rather than anything simply given in the nature of things. So, here, two strands of Nietzsche's thinking join in a new way. First, he would have us acknowledge that there can be something necessary in things—whatever that can mean to Nietzsche we will need to consider. Second, Nietzsche announces that he will work to find beauty in all that is necessary, which, as he clarifies further in *GS* 334, involves learning to love beyond our usual ken.

The crux of Nietzsche's aesthetic turn, then, is a call to find beauty in "what is necessary in things" by "learning to love" what has become of earthly life.

Beyond morality in the narrower sense

The conscious intentions which have preoccupied so much modern moral thinking Nietzsche calls the concern of "morality in the narrower sense" (*BGE* 32). Our conscious intentions are symptoms of perceptions and judgments of which we are unaware. Nietzsche wants to welcome a new stage in humanity's moral development, a stage he calls "extra-moral" and for which "the decisive value of an action lies precisely in what is *unintentional* in it" (*BGE* 32, emphasis original). The task of wakefulness itself is to discover and work with these hitherto unconscious sources. We can then evaluate the perceptions, interpretations and judgments to which our intentions point. To what bearing toward earthly life do these perceptions, interpretations, judgments and intentions attest? Are they worthy of us and worthy of earthly life? Or is our affective life reactive and resentful, full of perceptions and judgments fueled by a wish for recrimination and revenge?

As naturalist readers emphasize, modernist interpretations of Nietzsche have tended to ignore his naturalist and realist moments, as when, to take another example, Nietzsche explains his commitment to overthrowing idols (which he calls "his word for ideals") to the fact that these ideals have "deprived *reality* of its value, its meaning, its truthfulness" (*EH* 218, emphasis original). The naturalists are right that Nietzsche is some kind of realist, calling us to be truthful about all that has come to be. It is some such reality to which he points in *GS* 276 when he invokes what is necessary in things. At the same time, we cannot deny the modernist's insistence that even in such passages, Nietzsche never abandons his sense that what beauty we find and what love we feel is a creative activity, a matter of invention rather than any simple discovery.

In the *Gay Science*, in *Thus Spoke Zarathustra* and *Beyond Good and Evil*, Nietzsche comes closest to overcoming the sense of either/or that had circumscribed his imagination and still imprisons human living. When Nietzsche inquires whether his and our perceptions, judgments, intentions and actions affirm earthly life, I take him to be asking whether we are creating from whatever we find here anything worthy of love? Are we helping to make beautiful all that is necessary and real?

From the perspective of this most affirmative Nietzsche, our attention and intention should not be, as modernists would have it, to determine which aspects of earthly life we accept and which we reject.[11] Our attention and intention are indeed selective in the love we come to feel as a result of the beauty we can make of what we find here. Yet all of what has become of earthly life, as Nietzsche's naturalist readers rightly point out, he would call necessary and real simply by the fact that it has become or has been. This is a main lesson of *Zarathustra*. If "will is the great liberator," it cannot be in any ordinary or common sense, since anything that is past is a stone the will cannot move (*Z* 251). What naturalists tend to ignore, however, is the modernist's sense, albeit too partially exercised, that our love of this world and the discovery of its beauty depend upon aesthetic judgments and actions that are as much contrary to the ways of nature as they are continuous with it. Let me take a moment to explain this last point because it is decisive.

I have argued more fully elsewhere that Nietzsche is most aptly described as an impersonal materialist.[12] Nietzsche is not sufficiently organicist to imagine matter as a singular being, even as he rejects any of the senses we may have that there is anything other than matter. Ego, soul, self, mind—though we often construe these words to refer to something we call immaterial or spiritual, Nietzsche is persuaded such words refer to thoroughly material realities. That said, Nietzsche's imagination of matter is striated by random variability and singularities, all woven together in an all-inclusive web of causality so complex as to defy our comprehension. Given his causally complex and differentiated, if holistic sense of matter, it obscures as much as it illuminates to call Nietzsche a naturalist.

We begin to see some of the subtleties of Nietzsche's thinking and how it presses upon our customary efforts at classification in a thought experiment he entertains in *BGE* 9. What "if we imagine a being like nature?" In posing his question this way, Nietzsche seems to be saying that nature exists as a singular being only in our imaginations. Regardless, if we undertake this experiment and imagine nature as such, we should imagine it as "wasteful beyond measure, indifferent beyond measure, without purposes and consideration, without mercy and justice, fertile and desolate and uncertain at the same time" (*BGE* 9). This nature includes all, gain and loss, arising and passing away, without reason or judgment.

---

[11]I think the best modernist interpretation of eternal return is still found Alexander Nehamas's *Nietzsche: Life as Literature* (Harvard, 1985).

[12]Melissa A. Orlie, "Impersonal Matter" in *New Materialisms* (Diana Coole & Samantha Frost, eds.) (Duke University Press, 2010), pp. 116–36.

Yet, Nietzsche asks in the same passage, living: "is that not precisely wanting to be other than this nature?". Living is "estimating, preferring, being unjust, being limited, wanting to be different" (*BGE* 9). In a word, as Nietzsche likes to say, living is "will to power."

Modernist and naturalists alike tend to gloss will to power as referring to the strength of our capacity to overcome any resistance to our own becoming, although interpreters construe the sources of this capacity in quite distinct ways. For some time, Nietzsche himself was content to hammer his sense of living as requiring the assertive overcoming of any internal or external resistance to his estimations and preferences. Indeed, Nietzsche never altogether abandons his preoccupation with differentiated judgment and singular action, though, as we saw above, he does announce a decisive redirection of his earlier, modernist imagination of such practices of overcoming.

Further on in the passage we have already discussed, where Nietzsche associates creatively seeing beauty in what is necessary in things, he calls this practice "*Amor fati*." In doing so, Nietzsche engages in a not so subtle critique of some of his previous literary selves: "I do not want to wage war against what is ugly. I do not want to accuse; I do not even want to accuse those who accuse. *Looking away* shall be my only negation" (*GS* 276). Thus, Nietzsche begins a distinctive path in his experimentation with self-overcoming in which becoming who one is has as much to do with Yes-saying as it does with No-saying.

What enables us to say yes to each being and thing and to earthly life as a whole? Nietzsche's vision of affirmation is often pared back by his readers to something much less inclusive and holistic than this aspiration. Typically, he is read as advocating that some beings and things are to be fostered, while the "strong" will work to rid earthly life of what we don't or can't affirm by giving it a quick, firm kick into the abyss. This is the dominant modern attitude, and where and when in his writings this is Nietzsche's teaching, Heidegger's characterization of him as the apotheosis of the willfulness of the western tradition of metaphysics is apt.

However, Nietzsche himself recognized the problem with which Heidegger tries to pin him. He thematized the problem explicitly in *Zarathustra* where the conviction that will is the great liberator is diagnosed to lead to endless desire for revenge and recrimination and to foment the very hatred of earthly life Nietzsche hopes to overcome. *Zarathustra* announces the thought of eternal return as the key to overcoming such resentment, and the working through which Nietzsche wagers can issue in holistic affirmation of earthly life is evident there as well as in *The Gay Science* and *Beyond Good and Evil*.

So, what is necessary, beautiful and worthy of love? At his most inspired and affirmative, Nietzsche answers that everything is to be found beautiful and worthy of love. Everything that has become is necessary since "all things are knotted together" (*Z* 270). This thought of the importance of All is not original to Nietzsche. It is, for instance, a persistent concern of Ralph Waldo Emerson, whom Nietzsche read with more than passing interest. What may be unique to Nietzsche, however, is his rendering of such inclusive, holistic affirmation without sentimentality or rationalization, without surrendering our species's will to power but without deifying it either. This is the Nietzsche we need now. This is the Nietzsche who understands the vital importance of the aesthetic basis of our ethical and political judgments and actions.

How the leonine critic becomes like a child again

Most of us know Nietzsche best as a genealogist, as the lion who slays the great dragon "Thou shalt." By his own admission, the most apparent effect of Nietzsche's hammering philosophical labours and tireless No-saying is to leave us in a world which first appears to be the loneliest of deserts (*Z* 138–9). Many of Nietzsche's readers stop there, satisfied with his essentially negative, critical, genealogical project.

However, if we stop there, then we miss what Nietzsche himself declares the key aspiration of his thinking—to seek the fullest affirmation of earthly life attainable. Nietzsche judges the thought experiment of the eternal return a primary means of working through what stands between us and this most inclusive affirmation. By experimenting with boundless affirmation of all that has become—which is what wrestling with the idea of eternal return is meant to facilitate—Nietzsche imagines that what first appears to us as the loneliest of deserts, we may become able to feel as something more like a beautiful open sea (*GS* 343). Were we able to feel this way, we would have "become a child" again, able to say the "sacred Yes" needed for the "game of creation" (*Z* 139). Still, what does this mean and to what does it point?

Nietzsche is aware of the paradox that arises when we give our attention to the affirmative aspects of his thinking. He sums it up in the following way: "The psychological problem in the type Zarathustra is how he that says No and does No to an unheard-of degree, to everything which one has so far said Yes, can nevertheless be the opposite of a No-saying spirit…" (*EH* 306).

Nietzsche here captures a basic interpretive quandary posed by his writings, namely, how to square his relentless, withering critical spirit with his aspiration to affirm all of earthly life as it has become. The solution is deceptively simple. We are to become able to be affected by what is in such a way that we come to love it, and thereby make it beautiful rather than an object of scorn and resentment. *The Gay Science* develops explicitly the connections between the nature of love and beauty for this most affirmative Nietzsche. What we love appears beautiful to us, perhaps because we thereby animate it, as Emerson says. Yet, Nietzsche realizes, one "must learn to love" (*GS* 334).

What we love does not come naturally or habitually, or at least it should not in Nietzsche's view. If love comes without having to be learned, can it really be called love? Nietzsche thinks not, because we then confound loving with rote reaction. Said differently, love that is habitual rather than learned is usually a matter of projection. Reactive love summons the projections of a fixated self upon a perceptively fixed other, each frozen by a psychic enmeshment of which neither is likely aware. We cannot help but use grammatical conventions that Nietzsche judges obscure as much as they reveal about our ontological condition and enact our problem. So, we must say it this way: both self and other, subject and object are materially entwined, but in ways which always defy definition. Still, the parties' experience is fixed and fixated according to preconceptions which drive intentions of which they are unaware. The fixations of our perceptions of earthly life can be traced back to fantasies of omnipotent and omniscient control by which the separate, let alone differentiated, existence of the other is imaginatively dissolved. If I appear to be imposing a contemporary psychoanalytic frame on Nietzsche's effort to remake psychology as first philosophy, consider Nietzsche's specific formulations in *GS* 334. There Nietzsche explains how he thinks we learn to love something in its differentiated independence, including ourselves. For, although he begins this reflection with an example close to his heart, music, Nietzsche submits that we have learned to love all things that we now love in the way he describes, including learning to love ourselves.

First, we must to learn to apprehend the object in its distinctness, "to detect and distinguish it, to isolate and delimit it as a separate life" (*GS* 334). After we acknowledge its distinct separateness, "then it requires some exertion and good will to tolerate it in spite of its strangeness." The practice of love does not really begin, it seems, until we recognize another's separate, independent existence. What we get in return for this act of generous magnanimity, at least at first Nietzsche says, is at best a sense of its oddness, at worst a trying of our patience. Before we acknowledge the object's independence from ourselves, perhaps its existence had altogether escaped our notice, or perhaps we had ignored its condition and presumed it was already at one with us, wanting and moving as we want and move. Once we acknowledge its separateness, then, at least in some measure, dissonance, even annoyance, is our reward.

Yet there is a greater reward to receive, Nietzsche submits, which cannot be had in any other way than by our allowing and engaging the independence of an object of our attention. That reward is an experience of the beauty of what we have learned to love so thoroughly that we come to feel filled by it as well as joined to the world anew. Nietzsche puts it this way: "In the end we are always rewarded for our good will, our patience, fairmindedness, and gentleness with what is strange; gradually, it sheds its veil and turns out to be a new and indescribable beauty." Our reward arrives when "there comes a moment when we are used to it, when we wait for it, when we sense that we should miss it if it were missing; and now it continues to compel and enchant us relentlessly until we have become its humble and enraptured lovers who desire nothing better for the world than it and only it." Such is the way of love with all things, concludes Nietzsche, at least if they are loved truly. Seeing "new and indescribable beauty" is the object's "*thanks* for our hospitality" (*GS* 334, emphasis original).

The movement from a sense of differentiation to being joined, from strangeness to "humble and enraptured" love, is subtle and fascinating in this passage. First, there is the sense that we must come to recognize whatever we would learn to love as there, such as it is, independent from ourselves. Second, this experience of distinctness and new separation generates annoyance, possibly even aggression. Finally, by learning to love the object as separate, we are rewarded with an experience of its differentiated dependence; what we love becomes at once part of ourselves and something we affirm in and for the world, some sort of bridge connecting the two in some way that remains to be clarified. I will turn to explore these meanings shortly. First let us consider what is becoming of what we know of Nietzsche.

As naturalist interpreters of Nietzsche stress, we must come to terms with those passages where Nietzsche admonishes us to acknowledge and accept all that is necessary and cease to take flight from what is real. From this perspective, modernist interpretations of Nietzsche generally fail to meet this challenge because they read Nietzsche advocating selective approval and appropriation of earthly life. Do we imagine it as some great improvement upon the hateful consequences of Plato's two-world metaphysics if, instead of rejecting earthly life entirely, we instead selectively choose what we find to our liking and refuse the rest? Although there are many such modernist moments in Nietzsche, we may see Nietzsche at least verging on some quite different attitude as he comes to wrestle with the fallout from his own inclination to excise and destroy those aspects of earthly life, past and present, which habitually offend his judgment. Arguably, Nietzsche was among the first to begin to see how modernist assertion threatens to render the earth more uninhabitable than any otherworldly oriented metaphysics because it actively sets out to remake and destroy what it deems without value or expendable. We need only look about us at the fate of exploited mountaintops and toxic rivers, clear cut forests and warming oceans, rusting human communities and daily species' extinctions to doubt the wisdom and sustainability of that approach to earthly life.

That said, naturalist readers of Nietzsche tend to make as little sense of his preoccupation with the creation of beauty and what is worthy of love out of what we find here. Such naturalist readers are right to stress those passages where Nietzsche says we must accept that all is knotted together, that all which exists is necessary, and that he would have us cease to take flight from what is real. However, what the modernists have right, is that loving what is necessary and finding beauty in it is a thoroughly creative activity. If we do it well, Nietzsche acknowledges, we may come to feel a sense of providence in nature (*GS* 277), that is to say: we may be tempted to believe that what we find and our relations to it are determined or fated, law-like or even law-abiding. However, if we make that leap, we ignore not only that nature exists as a singular being only in our imaginations, but also that nature is "wasteful beyond measure, indifferent beyond measure, without purposes and consideration, without mercy and justice, fertile and desolate and uncertain at the same time" (*BGE* 9).

The key challenge, then, is to find this earthly world and life good enough to be loved. We do this in the most affirmative spirit to which Nietzsche aspires, not by selecting what we like and discarding or destroying the rest, but by endeavoring to create beauty and what is worthy of love in all that we find here. That beauty is created out of what is found, that such creative selectivity arises from holding all as demanding acceptance and as acceptable, is surely paradoxical. The psychoanalyst D. W. Winnicott concluded decades later that being able to abide in rather than resolve this paradoxical blend of finding and creating, to which Nietzsche points, may be the key to the capacities for spontaneous action, differentiated judgment and cultural creativity which concerned him as it did Nietzsche before him.

Feeling something there

By invoking what is necessary or real, Nietzsche opens up a question he is generally taken to have closed, namely: is what we deem beautiful and worthy of love found or created? What has happened to Nietzsche so that he speaks more ambiguously about this matter from *The Gay Science* on?

We know that Nietzsche regularly took long daily walks. He tells us also that the thought of eternal return came upon him during one such walk. He suggests that it arose in a moment of broadened affective awareness of the sort he calls for in the beginning of *Beyond Good and Evil*. In moments of wakefulness, when his affective experience is at its broadest and takes him beyond his normal ken, it seems it begins to dawn on Nietzsche that objects may be real and necessary, not merely a bundle of his projections. This is not to say that Nietzsche reverts to some pre-critical apprehension of experience, his longstanding affirmation of Emerson notwithstanding. To be sure, it is still common to presume that beings and things are real and necessary in some simple positivist sense. Not surprisingly, Nietzsche never entertains such a positivist outlook and begins his own distinctive path where the unfolding of German philosophy has left him.

As a post-Kantian, Nietzsche's stock formulations claim that everything is a matter of perspective. Of course, he goes further than Kant apparently does, claiming not only that we cannot gain access to things in themselves, but that there are no such things, that there are no substances. No person or practice is constant or definable because all are the effect of continually changing and never univocal material circumstances.[13]

Like his Romantic predecessors, Nietzsche is not content to be cut off from the sensual world. Like Hegel, he wants to overcome the division of man and nature, mind and body, consciousness and instinct, which is Kant's legacy. Yet, also like Hegel, Nietzsche wants to do all this without forsaking critical mindedness. To be sure, Nietzsche conceives of critical consciousness as thoroughly material whereas Hegel apparently does not. However, the other main difference between Hegel and Nietzsche is that Nietzsche is not a systemic philosopher and for reasons of ontological conviction. Where Hegel sees *Geist* (however construed), Nietzsche sees random, unfathomably complex, fundamentally material relations. In this sense, recent interpreters are right when they stress that Nietzsche may be closer to Darwin than to Hegel, all his criticisms and antipathy toward Darwin notwithstanding.[14]

To be sure, there are interpretations of Nietzsche that take up and develop each of the lines of interpretation I have just cast as *not* Nietzsche. There are moments in Nietzsche's texts that suggest naturalism and Kantianism, Romanticism and even a systemic metaphysics aspiring to rival Hegel's own.[15] However, none of these interpretations, brilliant as some exemplars of them are, seem to me to do justice to the whole of Nietzsche's thinking, a path of thinking he finally concludes is most aptly named joyful wisdom.

What distinguishes the path of joyful wisdom is a certain attitude toward and manner of handling some basic paradoxes of human existence. These are paradoxes which preoccupied Hegel as well, though he preferred to call

---

[13]Friedrich Nietzsche, *On the Genealogy of Morals* (Kaufmann trans.) (Vintage, 1989), Essay II, section 12.

[14]See especially Elizabeth Grosz, *The Nick of Time: Politics, Evolution, and the Untimely* (Duke, 2004), pp. 95–132; also John Richardson, *Nietzsche's New Darwinism* (Oxford University Press, 2004; Dirk R. Johnson, *Nietzsche's Anti-Darwinism* (Cambridge University Press, 2010). Robert Pippin's *Nietzsche, Psychology & First Philosophy* (Chicago University Press, 2010) honors the Nietzsche we need now as well as any current book, though as one would expect, he appreciates Nietzsche through a Hegelian lens.

[15]To the works on Nietzsche I have already cited add John Richardson, *Nietzsche's System* (Oxford University Press, 2002); R. Kevin Hill, *Nietzsche's Critiques: The Kantian Foundations of His Thought* (Oxford University Press, 2003).

them contradictions and sought to resolve them, however much we may read him as tarrying with the negative. By contrast, the wakeful Nietzsche of joyful wisdom arrives at his most promising path in relating to paradox much as D. W. Winnicott advocates some decades later, namely, by living with and keeping alive paradox rather than seeking to resolve it.

Is what we deem beautiful and worthy of love found or created? Should Nietzsche's notion of will to power lead us to understand ourselves as independent or interdependent, as existing separately or inextricably in union with all that has become? The wakeful Nietzsche's practical approach to these questions is illuminated by Winnicott's approach to the same paradoxes.

Paradoxes of finding and creating, separating and union

D. W. Winnicott spent most of his days working with children and adults who were unable to play, who did not feel altogether real or as if they were fully alive. On occasion, things changed for some of them, which sent Winnicott reflecting upon what sort of experiences enabled them to feel otherwise. I will say something about the sort of transitional experiencing and movement from object-relating to object use which Winnicott judges to be decisive to a self's lively sense of "going on being" in a world which feels real. I want to dwell upon Winnicott's sense of how creative living becomes possible and what it involves because I find it illuminates Nietzsche's advice about how to make beautiful and find worthy of love what is necessary in earthly life, including those aspects which we may previously have resented, judged ugly or worthless. It is useful to begin by considering what Winnicott says more generally about the attitude toward paradox we need to abide if our engagement of earthly life is to issue in anything more than a barren house of mirrors.

The paradigmatic modernist fantasy of creativity insists on valuing only the new, what has been self-made or spontaneously created, and positions itself against discovering value dwelling in what is simply found, handed down or given. Of course, it may be that none of us will see ourselves in this modernist fantasy so bluntly drawn. That readers of Nietzsche continue to see in him only variations on this fantasy suggests, however, that the fantasy may be so deeply part of ourselves that we may meet with it only in our projections. Regardless, the irony of this fantasy of new creation and spontaneous action is that it is predicated upon a determination to do away with the paradoxes which Winnicott finds living creatively requires us to inhabit.

To see the vital role of the acceptance of paradox, we need begin with Winnicott's observation that creative living occurs in a third, intermediate space, between inner psychic life and the actual world in which the individual lives, but to which both ultimately contribute.[16] This transitional space is the area where playing first takes place, wherein creativity is rooted, and from which life is found to be worth living because both the world and self are felt to be real and lively. Feeling real, says Winnicott, "is more than existing; it is finding a way to exist as oneself, and relate to objects as oneself, and to have a self into which to retreat for relaxation" (*PR* 117). Winnicott emphasizes the acceptance of a series of paradoxes that enable transitional experiencing to arise. The first paradox we need abide is that in play, as in cultural experience, the object is created, but the object is waiting there to be created (*PR* 89). To this basic paradox, Winnicott adds three others we need tolerate rather than resolve and they are more uncanny than the first. When it comes to matters of separating and union, we need be able to hold, first, that two objects can be both joined and separated at the same time; second, that "with human beings there can be no separation, only the threat of separation"; and third, that there is a manner of union which can become an infinite area of separation filled with play and cultural enjoyment and creativity. In a moment, I will discuss how Winnicott believes abiding with these paradoxes enables creative activity to locate itself in the world.

Importantly, though, these paradoxes are allowed and sustained, Winnicott says, by a quality of attitude transitional phenomena require, namely: to be perceived rather than conceived of, to be felt there rather than only experienced conceptually in the mind. In short, one can accept paradox if one can bear to embody an attitude of "not knowing." By contrast, the drive to resolve paradox is generally accompanied by defensive fantasies of omnipotence and omniscience. As Winnicott once so aptly put it, when the world is not good enough, one has a mind instead. That is to say: the self-enclosed experience of mind becomes our perception of the world in lieu of a fuller somatic living.

I am suggesting that Nietzsche's aspiration to wake up, as well as the ecstatic experiencing evoked by his experiments with the thought of eternal return, represent moments where he is able to relinquish a fantasy of self-knowing mastery and move into transitional experiencing.

Loving by destroying and using the object

We tend to take for granted that we are able to use objects, just as we may presume that all children can play and that all adults can experience and participate in a culture. Of course, Nietzsche makes no such presumptions

[16] D. W. Winnicott, *Playing and Reality* (Routledge, 1989), pp. 2–3, 102–3 (henceforth cited as *PR* and by page number).

and is often judged a misanthrope for it. Winnicott is no misanthrope, but he shares Nietzsche's doubts. Winnicott calls "irksome" the development of the capacity to use objects playfully and creatively. He judges it "perhaps one of the most difficult things in human development" (*PR* 89). Winnicott found that to be able to use an object is not the same as relating to an object. In all but the most deeply psychotic moments of human experience, we can relate to objects. However, to use an object, Winnicott maintains, is not something that is inborn, but a capacity which must be developed and development of which depends upon the facilitating environment (*PR* 89). What makes learning to use an object troublesome comes down to a single decisive factor. Winnicott explains: "This thing that there is in between relating and use is the subject's placing of the object outside the area of the subject's omnipotent control; that is, the subject's perception of the object as an external phenomenon, not as a projective entity, in fact recognition of it as an entity in its own right" (*PR* 89). I take Winnicott to be describing here something like the first moment in Nietzsche's narration of how we learn to love. I also have suggested that the aesthetic turn Nietzsche makes in *The Gay Science* accompanies his coming to feel that there is something there to perceive, not only projections and perspectives to conceive of.

The paradox of object relating and use is that "usage cannot be described except in terms of acceptance of the object's independent existence, its property of having been there all the time" (*PR* 88). So, when we can use an object, we are able create something of our own by using it, but using it first requires that we find it existing independent of our projections of it. To this point, fantasies of the object may have defined our experience of it, as something to which we have related in our minds but not experienced through actual use which engages its independent existence, as it is, in its own right.

A key aspect of the paradox of finding and creating is the way it is askew of our most common use of the terms. Ordinarily, we think of using as exploitative and relating as more mutual or dialogical. However, on Winnicott's account, object use is more open to the other than relating, for object relating habitually entails trading in one's internal projections of the object and can occur without acknowledging the independent existence of the object. Again, Nietzsche's own reflections on learning to love concur with Winnicott's discussion here at every point.

In the case of object use, more mutual experiencing takes place in a transitional space between self and other, subject and object, where the independent existence of the object is at issue and, in time, becomes acknowledged. As Winnicott describes it, the independent existence of the object arises in a paradoxical play of aggression and love, joy and destruction that could only have made Nietzsche smile. We are holding aside for the moment Winnicott's reflections on paradoxes of separating and union, which will prove vital to a fuller understanding of what is involved in the capacity to use an object. At this juncture, suffice to say that the self's aggression toward the object is withstood by the object with an attitude and quality of love that enables the self to experience the opening of a gap between the self's fantasy projections of the object and its independent existence. As Winnicott enigmatically traces the process, "'after subject relates to object' comes 'subject destroys object' (as it becomes external); and then may come '*object survives* destruction by the subject'" (*PR* 90). Describing the upshot somewhat less enigmatically, Winnicott writes: "From now on the subject says: 'Hullo object!' 'I destroyed you.' 'I love you.' 'While I am loving you I am all the time destroying you in (unconscious) *fantasy*.'" (*PR* 90). As Winnicott explains, the subject can now use the object that has survived.

Loving is destructive and destroying because it involves the destroying of unconscious fantasy (*PR* 90). The object becomes more real when it at once evokes and survives this destruction (*PR* 90). Winnicott pauses to emphasize that we can and must say two things about this event. First, we must say that the subject destroys the object, which is to say that it destroys its internalized fantasied projection of the object because it is placed outside of its area of omnipotent control. Second, he says, we must also say that it is this destruction that places the object outside of omnipotent control (*PR* 90). The object becomes available for use, rather than merely fantasy relating, only during surviving destruction. Such survival is manifest in a felt sense that there is something there other than my fantasy. However, the self will only feel the object in this way if that object itself can bear to assume an attitude of not knowing what is or what will happen and, furthermore, can communicate its willingness not to know to the self which is seeking it. We will see more clearly how this is so when I momentarily turn to consider paradoxes of separating and union.

Like Nietzsche, Winnicott revalues aggression. He explicitly leaves aside the presumption that aggression arises in frustrated reaction to reality. Instead, he maintains that aggression paradoxically can evince a love for the world because the destructive drive creates the quality of externality (*PR* 93). Destruction, says Winnicott, is not motivated by anger but by joy at the object's survival: "The object is in fantasy always being destroyed. This quality of 'always being destroyed' makes the reality of the surviving object felt as such, strengthens the feeling tone, and contributes to object constancy" (*PR* 93). This is to say, the play of destruction, joy and love gives rise not only to the object feeling more real to the self, but also to the self feeling more real and alive too.

However, like Nietzsche, Winnicott's sense is that object-relating is what most of us may be doing most of the time, because we can do so without relinquishing our fantasy projections about objects and our cherished treasure with which these projections are enmeshed, our fantasy of ourselves as omnipotent and omniscient subjects of experience. Whether we can risk relinquishing those fantasies has everything to do with paradoxes of separating and union.

A familiar feature of stories about whether we can risk relinquishing our all-knowing, controlling fantasies is whether we experience a world worthy of trust and sufficiently reliable. Hearing that, we may conclude that all is lost, and that our best bet is to hold on tight and fight our way through, rallying whatever sense of knowing control we can muster. However, Winnicott notices that a single factor may define our experience of the world as sufficiently reliable to be trusted, namely, a sense that we are in the presence of someone or something able to tolerate that "love does not only mean meeting dependency needs" or, we may add, cultivating dependency needs (*PR* 108). In Nietzsche's words, we are in the presence of someone who has learned to love or something worthy of love. We must add the last formulation to Winnicott's own for it seems in Nietzsche's case that it was not someone, but ecstatic experiences of earthly life itself that sustained and possibly evoked his own capacity to use an object.

Winnicott's claim that any facilitating environment is sufficiently reliable if one can trust that the move from dependency to autonomy can be tolerated, even encouraged, hardly seems a startling revelation. Yet to benefit fully from his insight, we need to understand why Winnicott believes that when love is truly experienced as genuinely allowing the opportunity for a move from dependency to autonomy, then the space of intermediate experiencing can become "an infinite area of separation, which the baby, child, adolescent, adult may creatively fill with playing, which in time becomes the enjoyment of the cultural heritage" (*PR* 108). We need not only to understand what he means by this phrase, "an infinite area of separation," but why he considers it a good thing. After all, separations are at the very least potentially vexing, especially for infants and children, and Winnicott well knows they can prove traumatic. However, like finding and creating, separating and union exist in a paradoxical relationship. Winnicott deepens the enigma of the paradox with two related formulations proximate to the above passage. We need to be able to tolerate the further paradox that: from the perspective of psychic life as well as intermediate experiencing, two objects can be both joined and separated. Furthermore, Winnicott adds: "It could be said that with human beings there can be no separation, only a threat of separation; and the threat is maximally or minimally traumatic according to the experience of the first separatings" (*PR* 108). Winnicott himself asks what we cannot help but wonder: how does separation of subject and object, parent and child, seem in fact to happen, and so often with profit to all involved, and "this in spite of the impossibility of separation? (The paradox must be tolerated.)" (*PR* 108).

The passage is rich, as are the essays that supply its context, and I cannot hope to do justice to them here. Nor can I feel at all sure I know

Winnicott's meaning. With Nietzsche in mind, however, I make the following suggestion. All that is, human and not human, *is* in fact all knotted together and going on being, whether we perceive and experience it as such or not. What trauma instantiates, whether minimally or maximally experienced, is a conception of separation in this going on being, so that soma and psyche feel a consummation of the threat of separation. When a trauma is maximal, then Winnicott observes traces of the experience in evidence of mortal terror. Still, the separation is in fact only the threat of separation, so long as threat does not result in actual death. The separation remains only a threat rather than actual because the fabric of being remains. However, from the perspective of psychic experience, the threat is hardly an empty one. Winnicott says such experiences involve not frustration but the threat of annihilation.[17]

A likely repercussion of traumatic experiences of the threat of separation is a tendency to have a mind, and only a mind, in lieu of experiencing a good enough world. Which is to say that the likely repercussion of traumatic threats of separation are fantasies of omnipotence and omniscience so entrenched as not to be able to be destroyed. As a consequence, no true object use can ensue, no deeper feelings of being alive and real arise, nor the sort of boundless attachment to the world which, as Nietzsche says, "continues to compel and enchant us relentlessly until we have become its humble and enraptured lovers" (*GS* 334). What is tragic is that such unloved minds may themselves tend to be unlovely and so see and make the world unlovely too. What is promising is that a beautiful world, worthy of love, is still there to be found, only waiting to be created. Nietzsche, although himself utterly alone, found it.

For the love of earthly life

Hardly a handful of Nietzsche's readers appear to have noticed that his fantasy of omnipotent and omniscient self-mastery breaks open.[18] There are moments in his writings where that fantasy has altogether fallen away. For decades, critics have been riven by disagreement about whether Nietzsche's modernist aspiration to redeem earthly life by overcoming resistance and assertively creating the new is estimable or deplorable, advisable or possible, democratic or aristocratic. That such assertive overcoming of

[17]D. W. Winnicott, "Primary Maternal Preoccupation" in *Through Pediatrics to Psycho-Analysis* (Basic Books, 1975), p. 303.

[18]The most outstanding exceptions are Alphonso Lingis and Joan Stambaugh. William E. Connolly's understanding of Nietzsche's receptivity, though salutary, ultimately serves the self rather than breaking it open and apart. My sense is that Gilles Deleuze's Spinoza comes closer to the Nietzsche we need now than his Nietzsche, although the two are surely entangled.

resistance—albeit variously construed—is his aim has been, however, all but taken for granted. One need not look far, indeed one need only consider for a moment the unlovely modes and effects of our ways of earthly life, to make a good guess at why we seem unable to help seeing Nietzsche in any other way.

It is as if we cannot help but imagine that when Nietzsche calls forth Dionysus he envisions Mephistopheles. Admittedly, Nietzsche feeds our fixed perceptions of him, when his writings evince his own fixation by a fantasy of self-knowing mastery, as in his passing infatuation with *Übermensch* as a personification of overcoming. In these, perhaps predominant, modernist moments in his writings, he is apparently mesmerized by a conception of experience, rather than satisfied by passing moments of a more everyday Dionysian ecstasy, premonitions of which must have first attracted him to Emerson's sentences. Yet, compare the image in your mind of what Nietzsche represents and wants, with his portrait of Dionysus toward the end of *Beyond Good and Evil*: "the genius of the heart who silences all that is loud and self-satisfied, teaching it to listen; who smooths rough souls and lets them taste a new desire—to lie still as a mirror, that the deep sky may mirror itself in them—the genius of the heart who teaches the doltish and rash hand to hesitate and reach out more delicately; [….] the genius of the heart from whose touch everyone walks away richer, not having received grace and surprised, not as blessed and oppressed by alien goods, but richer in himself, newer to himself than before, broken open and sounded out by a thawing wind; more uncertain, perhaps; tenderer, more fragile, more broken, but full of hopes that as yet have no name" (*BGE* 295). This is the Nietzsche we need now, beckoning receptivity into the still unlovely human mind. He is waiting there to be found, as is the earthly life, at once necessary, beautiful and worthy of love, he would have us create.

CHAPTER EIGHT

"Writing a Name in the Sky": Rancière, Cavell, and the possibility of egalitarian inscription

Aletta J. Norval
University of Essex

Democratic theory is often portrayed as torn between two moments: that of disruption of rule, and the ordinary, ongoing institutionalization of politics. This dualism also marks contemporary democratic theory. In Jacques Rancière's theory of politics it takes the form of an emphasis on the ruptural qualities of the staging of novel democratic demands and the reconfiguration of the space of political argument. The reconfiguration of existing political imaginaries depends upon a moment of inscription, which remains underdeveloped in Rancière's work. Arguing that the possibility of inscription is indeed thematized in Rancière's more historical writings, but is often ignored by commentators, this article seeks to draw out the implications of a focus on inscription for democratic theory and practice. To flesh out this account, the article draws on Cavell's writings on exemplarity and the role of exemplars in fostering both critical reflection and the imagination of alternatives. The focus on such exemplars and an aversive, nonconformist ethos together

---

Edits to this original essay have been made by Aletta J. Norval.

facilitate a better understanding of what is required for such novel demands to be acknowledged and inscribed into democratic life.

Commenting on recent events in Egypt, Ahmed Badawi described in his blog how one year ago, "street children flocked to Tahrir and other major squares in Egypt and threw their lot in with the revolutionaries." He argues that they felt, perhaps for the first time in their lives, "a sense of comradeship" with the more affluent youth and "found vehicles to vent their anger at a society that had routinely ignored them and, particularly, a police force that had abused them and treated them as animals and criminals." Through staging their protests on Tahrir Square, they became part of the "common cause uniting all Egyptians."[1] Political life today is replete with eruptions of popular protests, which seek to make visible a range of injustices, both familiar and unfamiliar. Whether it is the "Arab Spring" or more local struggles for equality—one need only think here of the ongoing contestation of the demands for same-sex marriages[2]—such struggles foreground deeply felt senses of wrong, thrusting them into visibility. In originary moments such as these, new identities and ways of life that were once invisible and excluded may be "ushered onto the threshold of justice" (Honig 2009, 47). But, as Honig argues, and as we know from experience, there are no guarantees here. These events bring home to us in a particularly forceful manner the difficulty, as well as the high costs, associated with "getting things onto the political agenda."

Such struggles articulate specific claims and demands, while they also invoke alternatives to the existing order. In doing so, they seek to project and inscribe new and unheard-of ways of being and acting, beyond the currently acceptable political languages and norms of our times, onto the political agenda. In this article, I explore this idea of "writing a name in the sky" by engaging with two theorists—Jacques Rancière and Stanley Cavell—who both address issues relating to the processes through which challenges to existing political languages and imaginaries are enacted.[3] These theorists each offer distinctive insights into different aspects of these processes. I focus in particular on one key aspect, namely that of the transition from the initial articulation of democratic demands to their inscription onto a horizon that

---

[1]http://www.transform-egypt.blogspot.com/ (accessed January 30, 2012).

[2]On 3 December 1996, Hawaii became the first U.S. state to recognize same-sex marriage. Since then same-sex marriage has been introduced in six U.S. states, in addition to countries such as Spain, Portugal, South Africa, and the Netherlands, where it is already incorporated on the statute books.

[3]The concept "imaginary" designates a space of representation, which has the function of representing the unity of society in modernity, in the absence of a God-given order (Lefort 1986). Laclau (1990) suggests that a collective political imaginary acts as a horizon on which a multiplicity of demands can be inscribed. Horizons make possible and limit what may appear as relevant subjects and objects of politics. Examples of political imaginaries include, for instance, "the free market," "the welfare state," and "Kemalism."

would allow for their flourishing and extension to other areas of social and political life.[4] This movement captures an important set of issues facing our societies today, while also reflecting wider debates in political theory about the dualism between founding moments and processes of institutionalization.[5] Contemporary societies in transition to democracy, as well as societies in the process of deepening democratic political participation, are faced with the challenge of responding to and harnessing democratic energy, insight, and imagination without, however, immediately subordinating this vitality to the potentially deadening weight of procedures, rules, and institutions. Given these concerns, we need to give attention to precisely how extant systems are affected by the articulation of novel and often challenging demands; what processes contribute to and enable the inscription of demands onto the wider political agenda so that the existing political order is altered as a result; and what sort of political ethos is needed to enable such processes to develop in a democratic direction. I turn to the writings of Rancière and Cavell to think through what is required practically as well as theoretically if we are to respond imaginatively to democratic demands and if we are to learn from and harness the critical insights arising from such demands in the service of deepening democracy.

Two scenarios may be used to frame the issues I seek to address here. These will be familiar to readers of Rancière and Cavell, and they resonate with contemporary political events and struggles. The first relates an ancient event, as told and retold by Livy and a host of others, of the secession of the Roman plebeians on the Aventine Hill. The second is a commentary on Nora's position in Ibsen's *A Doll's House*. On the face of it, these scenarios are very different. Yet, I shall argue, they share an important set of concerns arising in democratic theory today. By juxtaposing and bringing these scenarios and thinkers into conversation with one another, we can enrich our understanding of contemporary debates concerning the relation between the expression of new demands and their articulation into the political life of a community, and of the role of a democratic ethos and political imagination in these processes.

Scenario 1

In *Disagreement* Rancière (1999) draws on Pierre-Simon Ballanche's writings recounting the tale told by Livy of the secession of the Roman

---

[4]The notion of inscription is drawn from Derrida's reading of speech act theory, and it denotes the idea that meaning is constituted, partly, by reference to the specific context in which it is "inscribed" (Derrida 1988). Here I deploy the term in a similar sense in order to indicate both the fact that the meaning of any political demand is shaped by the context in which it is inscribed *and* the fact that novel demands require inscription into wider political imaginaries if they are to become effectively institutionalized.

[5]For a recent treatment of this issue in the work of Weber, Schmitt, and Arendt, see Kalyvas (2008).

plebeians on the Aventine Hill. The plebeians seceded—literally withdrew from the city—as a result of the harsh rule of Appius Claudius (Parmele 2006, 44). In response, the patricians conceded some of their demands and created the offices of the plebeian tribunes. For Rancière, the significance of this retelling of the tale is that Ballanche notes Livy's inability "to think of the event as anything other than a revolt, an uprising caused by poverty and anger and sparking a power play devoid of all meaning" (1999, 23). Livy fails to be able to supply the meaning of the conflict because he does not put it in the right context, that of "a quarrel over the issue of speech itself." Rancière (1999, 23) suggests that Ballanche effectively restages the conflict as one in which the "entire issue at stake involves finding out whether there exists a common stage where plebeians and patricians can debate anything." In Ballanche's view, the relation between plebeians and patricians is structured through patrician domination, which holds that those beings deprived of logos—the plebeians—are not capable of speech; they are beings of no ac/count, capable only of noise, of a sort of "lowing."[6] Not unlike those participating in the Arab Spring, the plebeians faced with this situation establish another order—another division of the sensible—by setting themselves up as speaking beings, "sharing the same properties as those who deny them" the ability to speak (Rancière 1999, 24). They do so by engaging in a number of speech acts "that mimic those of the patricians." Ballanche's rendering of this tale makes visible that what is going on is the "staging of a nonexistent right" (Rancière 1999, 25).

When the Senate's emissary, Menenius, delivers his apologia to the plebs, stating the necessary inequality between the patricians and the plebeians, the plebs are already equals, for they can understand it and, indeed, after listening politely, respond in kind by asking for a treaty.[7] As a result, the Roman Senate concludes that "since the plebs have become creatures of speech, there is nothing left to do but to talk to them" (1999, 26). Hence, they are successful in making the transition from interruption

[6]Rancière suggests that politics concerns a distinction between those who have speech (logos) and those who do not. Possession of speech as logos is exclusive to human beings and allows distinctions to be made between what is just and what is unjust. Having speech signifies enrolment in the city (Rancière 1999, 23). Those who lack speech are capable only of "noise" (phônê). As he puts it, "the difference is marked precisely in the logos that separates the discursive articulation of a grievance from the phonic articulation of a groan" (1999, 2).

[7]Menenius Agrippa delivers his apologia in the form of the fable of the Belly and its Members (Patterson 1991, 4). The fable recounts the attempt made by the members of the body (the hands, eyes, ears, feet, and tongue) to conspire against the belly, which they thought devoured the fruits of their labour. Patterson notes that the fable articulates in symbolic terms "some of the most intransigent problems in political philosophy and practice" relating to the relation between ruler and ruled, with "the image of the human body and its nutritional needs as a symbol of the distribution of wealth in the body politic." This fable, she argues, has historically been open to diverging appropriations, not only those reinforcing hierarchy, but also those making the case of the rebellious members (Patterson 1991, 111–37).

to inscription. I shall argue, however, that Rancière's analysis here moves far too quickly. He fails to explore the Roman Senate's response to the plebeians. Accounting for the role of responsiveness in bringing about change to the extant order is crucial, and stands at the heart of Cavell's work, and of his reading of *A Doll's House*.

Scenario 2

The second scenario is taken from Cavell's discussion of Ibsen's *A Doll's House* and seeks to capture the difficulty of expressing senses of injustice that do not fit the parameters of current moral and political discourse (Cavell 1990).[8] Cavell's reading is aimed at those people within existing democracies, who take themselves to be "above reproach" in response to the resentment expressed by members of society who feel aggrieved.[9] Hence, in contrast to that offered by Rancière, Cavell's focus is on those who are in dominant positions, and more particularly on the question of their responsiveness to, as well as acknowledgment of, the expression of senses of wrong by others. In the play, Nora struggles to express her sense of injustice to Torvald, her husband of eight years. When challenged by him as to why she secretly borrowed money and then skimped on household expenses to repay interest, she emphasizes the fact that although she knows that most people would agree with him, and that he has "warrant for it in books," she cannot "be satisfied any longer with what most people say, and with what's in books." She must have the opportunity to think things out for herself, an opportunity she has thus far been denied. In this, Cavell (1990, 110) suggests, Nora feels herself representative "beyond her personal resentment," thus drawing attention to thousands of women like her. Torvald, in turn, questions her moral sense, and accuses her of "talking like a child," like one who does not understand the world she lives in, thus depriving her, again, of a voice (Cavell 1990, 109). When, at the climax of the story, Torvald tells Nora that he forgives her—instead of begging her forgiveness—Nora leaves him. In so doing she enacts change; she can no longer live in an order that denies her a voice, *her* voice and more, the voice of thousands like her. Through the example of Nora, Cavell captures

---

[8]As Cavell (1990, xxxviii) puts it, "What if there is a cry of justice that expresses a sense not of having *lost* out in an unequal yet fair struggle, but of having from the start been *left* out."

[9]This argument is developed contra Rawls who, Cavell suggests, "in effect claims that my sense of living in a society which in my judgement exhibits a favourable degree of partial compliance is one which, in response to an expression of resentment levelled by an aggrieved member (permanent or impermanent, I believe) of that society, I can say my conduct is above reproach (422). (What 'in effect' means here is critical. Rawls does not explicitly claim what I find him implicitly to claim here." Cavell 2004, 171).

the experience of a sense of injustice that is inexpressible in the terms of prevailing discourse, but where, as he puts it, misery is clearly unmistakable (1990, 112). And the question arises: What does one make of such an experience in a context governed by a democratic grammar? What role does responsiveness, or the lack of it represented by Torvald, play here?

What is at stake for Rancière and Cavell in each of these cases is the possibility of speaking and of being heard, even though they deal in different fashions with the processes and consequences of the acts through which something that was previously excluded is made visible. Rancière tends to refrain from explicitly engaging with the issues that arise after moments of rupture, when previously excluded senses of wrong become visible and alternative ways of doing things need to become institutionalized, and thus inscribed into the current order. This refusal arises from his much remarked upon division between "politics" and the "police order,"[10] as well as the ruptural picture of democracy that accompanies this distinction. Cavell, on the other hand, focuses overtly on questions of responsiveness, a focus that is crucial if one is to elucidate fully, not only the transition from disruption to inscription, but also the character of practices of inscription. What stance, for instance, would facilitate a democratic form of inscription, rather than a mere incorporation of demands?[11] What role does a democratic ethos play here? Despite the differences between these thinkers, I shall suggest that what they share is sufficient to draw them together into a conversation that is potentially mutually enriching. My key claim then is that

[10]Rancière's use of the term "police" should be understood in relation to two sets of doctrine—the "reason of state" and the "theory of the police"—arising with the formation of modern European nation states (Foucault 1988; Habermas 1992, 30). Foucault (1988, 74) notes that the former refers to attempts to "define how the principles and methods of state government differed ... from the way God governed the world, the father his family or a superior his community," whereas the latter refers to "a governmental technology peculiar to the state." Hence, here "police" is not understood as an institution functioning within the state. Rather, it concerns the observation and regulation of all dimensions of life, amongst them morals, health, public safety, labor, and population. Thus, "the police" covers "the whole new field in which centralized and administrative power can intervene" (Foucault 1988, 80). It was encapsulated in the emergence of *Polizeiwissenschaft*—which incorporated the public law, administration, public health, urban planning—in the first half of the eighteenth century in Germany. For a historical overview of the emergence of the reason of state, see Viroli (1992); for a discussion of the emergence of the theory of the police, see Foucault (2007).

[11]The relevant contrast here is between the cooptation of demands (mere incorporation) and an ethos that takes seriously the idea that new demands, if taken on board, require a reworking of the extant order. Rancière's worry is that the extant order will always be able to incorporate new demands. Cavell's writing addresses this issue through the emphasis on responsiveness. Hence, I shall argue, a democratic form of responsiveness is one that works through the consequences for an extant order of new demands, and places a premium on the responsibility to respond, rather than turn away, simply justify the existing ordering of affairs, or attempt to render powerless and make ineffective, new demands.

Rancière does not do enough by way of addressing questions regarding the processes through which democratic challenges find a foothold in existing orders. Given this, a turn to Cavell may be fruitful, for he offers a picture of democratic responsiveness that thematizes precisely those processes. Without addressing the interconnections between the interruption of an existing order by novel demands and their inscription into and change to that order, I shall argue, any account of democratic rupture remains fundamentally flawed.

In both of these scenarios, there are subjects who are to a greater or lesser extent excluded from the extant order, with the result that their claims cannot be heard as claims (at least *not yet*).[12] Yet their actions, Ballanche suggests, consist of "writing a name in the sky" in that they open up new ways of being and acting. How does "writing a name in the sky" facilitate carving out a place in the community of speaking beings, which does not yet exist? In this process of carving out a new space in which something or someone may appear, what is the relationship between speech and that which exceeds speech, insofar as it involves an emphasis on seeing and on staging? What view of subjectivity and of political community does this presuppose?

In seeking to address these questions, I shall suggest that Rancière's characterization of democracy is caught on the horns of a familiar dilemma, which needs to be resolved if convincing answers to these questions are to be provided. In a nutshell, the problem is this. On one hand, democracy is presented as ruptural, as a moment of break from the prevailing order. On the other hand, the democratic experience must be able to intervene in and reconfigure that order, which is possible only if it does not take the form of a rupture or a complete break. This much is made clear by the plebeian case. I shall argue that the resolution of this dilemma lies not in a choice between the two horns, but more in what, in Wittgensteinian fashion, one may call an attempt to dissolve the problem through a careful reconsideration of Rancière's conceptions of political subjectivity, political community, and, with them, his conceptualization of the possibilities and mechanisms of political change. My discussion of these conceptions allows me to attend to the reasons for Rancière's refusal to flesh out these mechanisms. Making these reasons visible is not, however, sufficient. Further reflection is needed on their place in Rancière's writings. In contrast to familiar interpretations of Rancière that present him as a theorist of rupture who is able only to "momentarily expose the injustice at the heart of rule" (Markell 2006, 3), this article makes the case that there

---

[12]This covers many facets of the issue that are not discussed here, including the question of what is required in terms of knowledge, leadership, and processes of formation of collective identities. Here I am concerned less with these general processes than with what is required in a democratic order to enable it to engage with and respond to such demands.

are neglected resources in Rancière's writings that offer some means of addressing the practices of inscription, which would allow expressions of wrong and novel demands to reshape the existing political order. Arguing that the ruptural version rests too heavily on a reading of only a limited number of his more explicitly theoretical writings, this article suggests that his historical writings offer rich resources for understanding *how* these practices operate. Drawing out these insights and reflecting on the work that historical examples do in his writings, it reorients discussion to focus on the role of exemplars in bridging the gap between interruption and inscription. Here historical examples play an important role in making available alternatives with which one can identify and which could act as "catalysts of conversion," as Tocqueville put it (Frank 2011, 386). To flesh out these insights further, I turn to Cavell, whose perfectionist rendering of exemplarity, with its link to an aversive ethos,[13] furnishes us with a way to address some of the remaining shortcomings of Rancière's account. The turn to ethos is controversial from a Rancièrian point of view. Nevertheless, the way it is elaborated in Cavell's writings not only addresses the concerns that he expresses, but also makes available additional resources to extend and deepen the reach of Rancière's insights into ongoing democratic practices of contestation.

Rather than treating these two theorists as engaged in fundamentally divergent enterprises, this article suggests that they could both be argued to contribute to thought that seeks to bridge the division between rupture and inscription that is characteristic of so much democratic theory. Democratic theory is torn between two moments: that of the extraordinary, the moment of founding and of constituent power, and that of the ordinary, the institutional and constituted power. The extraordinary/ordinary couple echoes other forms in which this dichotomy—between revolutionary founding acts and institutional politics—has appeared both in theorizing democracy and in thinking about the nature and character of politics more generally (Laclau 2005; Markell 2006). I think here of the work of constitutional scholars such as Ackerman (1991), who emphasizes the need for popular participation in moments of constitutional innovation, as well as of attempts to reflect upon the conundrums posed by demands for transitional justice and the refounding of states, not ex nihilo, but in the aftermath of sometimes protracted conflicts. In each of these cases, different

[13]The term "aversive ethos" is drawn from Cavell's reading of Emerson (Cavell 1990, 33–63). It emphasizes the role of oppositional thinking in developing a critique of the present state of things, which calls for a transformation of that order and of the self. An aversive ethos is thus closely linked to perfectionism for Cavell, because becoming "averse" to conformity means we need to transform ourselves, aspiring to a better state of self and of society. For an analysis of the South African Truth and Reconciliation Commission as an exemplar of an aversive ethos, see Norval (2007).

aspects of the problem of instituting and maintaining a democratic order are emphasized.

The significance of the interpretation proposed here is that it suggests that instead of concentrating on the horns of the dilemma, a different way of approaching the matter is needed. Rather than remaining fixated on either side of the dichotomy, we need to look at the processes and mechanisms that are available to us for bridging the division. Such a shift may allow us to see the problem in a different way, thus disclosing aspects of it that may allow us to dissolve it.[14] The figure of "writing a name in the sky"—projecting and inscribing new and unheard-of ways of being and acting onto existing political imaginaries—captures and condenses what is at stake here. It shifts our gaze onto the mechanisms through which senses of wrong are inscribed into existing political languages such that they are reconfigured as a result, and to the conditions for doing so. The writings of Rancière and Cavell, when read together, offer a nuanced and novel way of thinking about such mechanisms and practices. Hence, Kalyvas (2008, 4) is correct to suggest that we need to rework the dualism between the extraordinary and the ordinary, and appropriate the extraordinary in order to expand the scope of democratic experience, retaining the energies, freedom, and imagination that are associated with acts of founding. What this reading of Rancière and Cavell offers is a vision of *how* this may be done.

Democracy, visibility, and the staging of wrongs

Rancière's view of "democratic life" seeks to distance itself from what is problematic, if not downright objectionable, in discourses on democracy, both historical and contemporary (2006). These include discourses expressing hatred of democracy, as well as various forms of critique that acknowledge democracy but seek to confine it within certain limits (Rancière 2006, 2).[15] Contemporary expressions of hatred against democracy, he argues, do not call for more "real" democracy; nor do they complain about the

[14]In this, I follow a Wittgensteinian strategy of reading. Wittgenstein argues that in approaching the problems of philosophy, rather than solving them, we need to dissolve them. I take this to mean that we need to approach problems in such a manner that new aspects become visible, and older ones dissolve.

[15]Rancière notes that hatred of democracy is as old as democracy itself. In Ancient Greece the term was one of insult, signifying the government of the multitude that would ruin any legitimate order (Rancière 2006, 2). In our contemporary world, hatred of democracy is often expressed by spokespersons living in democracies. Rancière (2006, 7–8) lists a number of recent writings on democracy, including the Trilateral Commission Report—*The Crisis of Democracy*—as exemplifying the paradox of democracy: "as a social and political form of life, democracy is the reign of excess. This excess signifies the ruin of democratic government and must therefore be repressed by it."

institutions embodying the power of the people. Rather, in these discourses the problem is located in "democratic civilization" itself: Excess is what ruins democracy and hence is what must be controlled by it.[16] The image of democracy as associated with an excess that stands in need of being governed is one that goes back to Plato and it embodies what, for Rancière, is the very (improper) principle of politics itself.[17] Democratic excess, he argues, is simply "the dissolving of any standard by which nature could give its law to communitarian artifice via the relations of authority that structure the social body"; it is government based on nothing other than the "absence of every title to govern." Rancière (2006, 4647) puts it thus:

> [T]he only remaining title is the anarchic title, the title specific to those who have no more title for governing than they have for being governed. This is what of all things democracy means. Democracy is not a type of constitution, nor a form of society. The power of the people is not that of a people gathered together, of the majority, or of the working class. It is simply the power peculiar to those who have no more entitlements to govern than to submit.

In the absence of the power of birth and of wealth, what remains is the power of the people, which is the power of "anyone at all, the equality of capabilities to occupy the position of governors and of the governed." Hence, democracy is marked by the fact that it rests on the absence of a foundation.

Rancière fleshes out his understanding of this absence of foundation that characterizes the beginning of politics in terms of a division of the sensible.[18] The institution of democracy takes place with the creation of a space "made of disconnected places" (Rancière 2006, 46–7), a new topography that redistributes places and reconfigures what is visible and invisible, what can be seen and heard and what cannot be seen and heard. Politics, in this view, is a matter of aesthetics first and foremost, in the sense in that it concerns the *division* between the perceptible and the imperceptible. The logic of the police—the extant order—distributes bodies within the space of visibility; it is challenged by political acts that shift bodies from the places

[16]Rancière (2006, 7–8) notes that the historical remedy for this sort of excess consisted in redirecting "feverish energy activated on the public stage towards other ends" often, as is today also the case, toward the search for material prosperity.

[17]It should be noted that Rancière's "return to the classics" is not one that seeks to affirm the Aristotelian idea that politics is based on a natural disposition to political life. Rather, it is a return that seeks to show that democracy, already in the classical texts, marks the place of those who have no specific properties allowing them to govern.

[18]Rancière (2009a, 277) suggests that the "distribution of the sensible" establishes a link between "being in a specific space and time, performing specific activities, and being endowed with capacities of seeing, saying, and doing that 'fit' those activities."

assigned to them, thus making visible "what had no business being seen." Political activity here takes a particular form. It is concerned with "conflict over the existence of a common stage and over the existence and status of those present on it. It must first be established that the stage exists for the use of an interlocutor who can't see it and who can't see if for good reason *because* it doesn't exist" (1999, 26–7). The plebs on the Aventine Hill and the Tahrir protesters must first establish their right to be counted as parties to the dispute, and they do so through the declaration of a wrong. Rancière (1999, 27) thus argues that

> Parties do not exist prior to the conflict they name and in which they are counted as parties.... Politics exists because those who have no right to be counted as speaking beings make themselves of some account, setting up a community by the fact of placing in common a wrong that is nothing more than this very confrontation.

On this reading democracy does not concern itself with questions of institutional design or a particular "human disposition" that would characterize it. It excludes activities of representation, as well as any concern with regimes or forms of government.[19] In contrast, democracy concerns

> the system of forms of *subjectification* through which any order of distribution of bodies into functions corresponding to their "nature" and places corresponding to their functions is undermined, thrown back on its contingency. (Rancière 1999, 101, emphasis added)

This partition takes place through the articulation of a *wrong*.[20] A wrong is a "mode of subjectification in which the assertion of equality takes its political shape" (Rancière 1999, 39). The protestors in Tahrir Square and the plebs on the Aventine Hill stage such a wrong by conducting themselves like beings with names, as equals to those who have previously dominated them.[21] The staging of a wrong and the verification of equality take effect

---

[19]Rancière suggests that we should not think of representation as a mechanism or system invented to compensate for the growth of populations, nor as a form of adaptation of democracy to vast spaces and modern times. Like Tully, Rancière (2006, 53) notes that the assimilation of democracy to representative government is a recent phenomenon, and one that has been used by elites to exercise power de facto. The term democracy, Tully (2008a, 155–6) argues, came to be associated with "representative democracy" only in the late eighteenth century.

[20]I use the term articulation here in its theoretical sense, as developed by Laclau and Mouffe (1985, 113). In contrast to mediation, it is a process that binds together elements or objects that have no natural or necessary belonging together.

[21]His understanding of equality and its verification is of crucial importance because it distinguishes a political from a nonpolitical wrong (Rancière 1999, 39).

through attempts to refashion and challenge the existing division of the sensible. They occur rarely (1999, 17) and do not "express" pregiven, objective interests. "Speaking out," Rancière suggests, is not "awareness and expression of a self asserting what belongs to it" (1999, 37). Rather, it is a process of *disidentification*, removal from a "natural" place (1999, 36).

It is also through this process that political bonds are created. Political bonds, Rancière suggests, are not created by identification with a victim or his or her cause, but as a result of disidentification from the dominant terms or available subject positions. As a result, political community is not based upon having something positive in common, but rather is a sharing of "what is not given as being in-common," ties that "bind the given to what is not given" (1999, 138–9). On this reading, democracy as a political mode of subjectification has three distinguishing characteristics. First, it is a kind of community that is defined by the appearance of the people, such that it reconfigures the regime of the visible. Second, this space is occupied by a people of a particular kind: It is a unity that superimposes the effectiveness of a part of those that have no part, "floating subjects that deregulate all representation of places and portions" (1999, 99–100). Third, the place where the people appear is a place where a dispute is conducted. Hence its ruptural quality.[22]

Rancière: A theorist of rupture?

Despite the crucial insights Rancière offers, there are serious questions to be raised about this characterization of democracy. Numerous critics have voiced their concern over what variously has been called Rancière's "non-political" understanding of politics (Dillon 2003), the too sharp division posed between politics and the police order, and his emphasis on the spontaneous and interruptive quality of democracy. As the foregoing suggests, there is indeed a deeply ingrained view of democracy as disruption. In this sense, Rancière's work echoes that of other recent theorists of

[22] As Rancière (1995, 49) puts it, "Democracy is the community of sharing, in both senses of the term: a membership in a single world which can only be expressed in adversarial terms, and a coming together which can only occur in conflict. To postulate a world of shared meaning is always transgressive." In the sentence preceding this quotation, Rancière emphasizes the role of rupture and even of violence: "In order to uphold one's correctness other kinds of arguments have always been needed. The affirmation of the right to be correct is dependent on the violence of its inscription. Thus, the reasonable arguments of the strikers of 1833 were audible, their demonstration visible, only because the events of 1830, recalling those of 1789, had torn them from the nether world of inarticulate sounds and ensconced them by a contingent forced-entry in the world of meaning and visibility. The repetition of egalitarian words is a repetition of that forced-entry, which is why the space of shared meaning it opens up is not a space of consensus."

democracy. Laclau, for instance, in his later writings increasingly emphasizes the disruptive quality of politics and of democracy, while denigrating concerns with institutionalization as nonpolitical, the administration of things.[23] A similar position is articulated by Wolin (2004, 603), who contrasts the moment of experience of democracy—"a crystallized response to deeply felt grievances or needs"—to governing understood as "manning and accommodating to bureaucratized institutions" that are inherently "anti-democratic." More recently still, analogous arguments have been developed by Žižek (2011), who argues that "the name of the ultimate enemy today is not capitalism, empire, exploitation or anything of the kind, but democracy: It is the 'democratic illusion', the acceptance of democratic mechanisms as the only legitimate means of change, which prevents a genuine transformation in capitalist relations."[24] Such accounts raise serious questions, not simply about the narrow conceptions that are often associated with the term "democracy," but more importantly, regarding how much we can say of and about democracy other than emphasizing its disruptive qualities.[25]

Readings of Rancière that emphasize the ruptural qualities of his writings, however, often do so at the expense of ignoring the points in his writings where he distances himself from the revolutionary fervor associated with interruptive characterizations. For instance, Rancière (1999, 100) is critical of Lefort's portrayal of modern democracy as occupying the empty space of power precisely on this point, arguing that Lefort's work is too closely associated with "a theatre of sacrifice that originally ties the emergence of democracy to the great specters of the reembodiments staged by terrorism and the totalitarianism of a body torn asunder."[26] He is similarly at pains to argue that democracy is not about setting up a counterpower, a pure site where it exists in isolation from the police. This is suggestive of a more nuanced analysis of democracy that can be teased out from a discussion of Rancière's more historical work, but that needs further deepening and development.

With this in mind, let us turn to two of Rancière's key examples: the secession of the plebs on the Aventine Hill and a revolt of Scythian slaves as recounted by Herodotus. These examples share an emphasis on *staging*

[23]Like other political theorists in this respect, Laclau's work is also marked by ambiguity. His work on hegemony suggests something quite different: not a ruptural view of politics, but one of a war of position in the Gramscian sense.

[24]For a nuanced reading of Žižek's rendering of democracy that situates his critique in the context of his writings, see Dean (2005).

[25]Markell (2006) explores a similar set of questions with regard to Arendt.

[26]Lefort (1989, 304) argues that "Power appears as an empty place and those who exercise it as mere mortals who occupy it only temporarily or who could install themselves in it only by force or cunning." Rancière (2003, para. 13) also further suggests, contra Lefort, that it is not productive to think of politics in terms of a structural void.

in struggles to verify equality.[27] Only the former, however, demonstrates a movement that goes beyond mere interruption. In the case of the Scythian slaves, what initially appears to be a successful demonstration of equality turns out to be of limited effect (Rancière 1999, 12–13). After nearly three decades away battling the Medes, a Scythian army returned home, only to be confronted by a generation of sons, sprung from their own wives and fathered by their slaves. Determined to oppose the army, the slaves started to act as if they were the equals of the warriors. They built trenches and armed themselves in readiness to defend the territory. Initial attempts to reconquer the slaves by force of arms failed; but the warriors then asserted their claim to superiority bearing only horsewhips. This, Herodotus suggests, made the slaves feel that they were, indeed, slaves and not the warriors' equals (Rancière 1999, 12). What the slaves failed to do was to turn a war-generated achievement of equality into political freedom. They did not succeed in inscribing their sense of wrong onto the political horizon, in challenging the existing ordering of hierarchies.

In the case of the Aventine plebs, in contrast, a reconfiguration of the sensible does occur. A successful displacement of "natural" relations is the result of a combination of elements, consisting of the use of words, of argument, poetics, props, and the invention of names. The Aventine plebs do so by engaging in a number of speech acts, mimicking those of the patricians:

> [T]hey pronounce imprecations and apotheoses; they delegate one of their number to go and consult their oracles; they give themselves representatives by rebaptizing them ... Through transgression, they find that they too ... are endowed with speech that does not simply express want, suffering or rage, but intelligence. They write, Ballanche tells us, "a name in the sky": a place in the symbolic order of the community of speaking beings. (Rancière 1999, 24–5)

Through their speech acts they bring into being new positions of speaking and acting. The plebs declare themselves to have standing with the patricians, writing a name in the sky: opening up new worlds, inventing a future that does not (yet) exist.[28]

---

[27]Rancière (1999, 88) maintains, politics is a matter of "interpreting, in the theatrical sense of the word, the gap between a place where the demos exists and a place where it does not ... Politics consist in interpreting this relationship, which means first setting it up as theatre, inventing the argument, in the double logical and dramatic sense of the term, connecting the unconnected." As several commentators have noted, "the artifice of the theatrical scene shares with politics the displacement of 'natural' relations between bodies and places" (Ross 2009, 128; see also Hallward 2006, 113).

[28]The question of opening up new worlds has recently begun to receive systematic treatment (Kompridis 2006). For an insightful rendering of the opening up of new spaces of imagination

Rancière is not alone in his emphasis on the importance of the displacement of the existing division of the sensible and the need to open up new worlds. This is a familiar theme in which the writings of Heidegger and Arendt, in particular, loom large.[29] Honig's (1993, 93) reading of Arendt focuses, for instance, on promising as an action that is unconditioned, that brings something new into being. However, she notes that the sharp division between extraordinary action and the ordinary means that this investigation of promising leaves Arendt "unable to account for how promising *works.*" Zerilli (2005) also draws on Arendt to think through the exigencies of the emergence of the new and its inscription in feminist political imaginaries. Others suggest that the invention of the new is something we should associate with social critics and social movements whose activities could challenge and alter existing frameworks of deliberation (Bohman 1996, 140).[30] Drawing on Heidegger, Spinosa, Flores, and Dreyfus (1997) also suggest that we come to see things differently as a result of activities that bring into the open and articulate experiences that "force recognition."[31] They characterize these activities as "disclosing skills."[32] All of these analyses of forms of world disclosure, of coming to see things anew, emphasize that such practices do not rely exclusively on objective measures (e.g., measuring inequality), on knowledge, and on reasongiving. Even though these may form part of the process, it is important that the emphasis on coming to view things differently is maintained. This is also the case for Rancière. As we have seen earlier, for him the possibility of engendering a new reality is not, in the first instance, an objective process. It is, rather, *subjective* in that it emphasizes

in feminist politics, see Zerilli (2005), who draws on Arendt to develop her argument. See also Frank's reading (2009) of Frederick Douglas' staging of dissensus, and Schaap's exploration (2009) of the Aboriginal tent embassy in Australia.

[29]Kompridis (2006, 188), drawing on Heidegger's treatment of disclosure as a practice that facilitates a new beginning, argues that Heidegger's analysis suffers from two problems, both of which are relevant to our understanding of change and agency. First, he "failed to connect the normativity of disclosure with the normativity of intersubjectivity"; and second, he aligns disclosure too closely to truth.

[30]For Tully (2008b, 308), Gandhi is such an exemplar, as his "ordinary, civic and glocal life continues to move millions of people to begin to act."

[31]As Spinosa, Flores, and Dreyfus (1997, 81) put it, "Discovering that a good friend, a trusted colleague, or a family member is gay brings about the necessary change more surely than any argument about abstract rights."

[32]This includes activities such as constituting organizations that produce clarity on an issue; uncovering a disharmony as a disparity worthy of investigation; determining that the practice that the disparity reveals permeates many domains of life; cross-appropriating practices with people in other disclosive spaces so that they become sensitive to the problem and respond to it in their own domain; proposing a social change in the light of what one is seeing anew; and talking with people who are specialists in making legal changes (Spinosa, Flores, and Dreyfus 1997, 94).

the importance of *seeing* things differently.[33] As he puts it with reference to his discussion of workers in the nineteenth century, it is the framing of a new common sense that allows new forms of political subjectification to be implemented.

This process, and the world that is to come into being, has a paradoxical status. It involves a delicate negotiation of the old and the new, between the extant order and an egalitarian inscription. In his example of striking workers in nineteenth-century France, for instance, Rancière emphasizes that egalitarian inscription is dependent upon the police order and must take its resources, at least in part, from it. As Rancière (2011, 6) puts it elsewhere, politics "does not stem from a place outside of the police.... There is no place outside of the police."[34] Given this, the key question is the one with which I started, namely, how precisely does one explain the movement from interruption to inscription, and what resources does Rancière offer us in this respect? As I have suggested, in his historical writings, as well as in his writings on aesthetics and politics, there are numerous pointers. His portrayal of staging as a making visible of previously unheard-of claims and demands, of naming, and his emphasis on speech acts mimicking dominant orders present some avenues for exploration. To bring the precise contours of the issue into focus we need to recall the link between egalitarian inscription and his understanding of political subjectivity, which foregrounds processes of subjectification and disidentification, and explore whether disidentification is able to do the work he needs it to do. Is a distancing from an extant order sufficient to open up the possibility of "writing a name in the sky"? If not, what else is needed?

---

[33]Wittgenstein's work on aspect dawning is relevant here. The dawning of an aspect involves seeing something differently. Wittgenstein (1989, 46) argues with respect to the interpretation of dreams that "When a dream is interpreted we might say that it is fitted into a context in which it ceases to be puzzling. In a sense the dreamer redreams his dream in surroundings such that its aspect changes.... and the result is that we say: 'Ah, now I see why it is like that, how it all comes to be arranged in that way, and what these various bits are ...' and so on." Likewise, in Rancière, the emphasis on (re)staging plays the role of reconfiguring what he calls the order of the sensible, what appears and what can appear to us.

[34]If, as Rancière notes, there are conflicting ways of dealing with the places that the police order allocates, if there are indeed are better and worse police orders, then we need to interrogate the conditions that would make these distinctions possible. Although Rancière (1999, 31) does gesture in this direction with the statement that the better one is "the one that all the breaking and entering perpetrated by egalitarian logic has most often jolted out of its 'natural' logic," he argues immediately afterward that if "the police is sweet and kind" it does not make it any less the opposite of politics.

Disidentification and the possibility of egalitarian inscription

Rancière, we have seen, suggests that disidentification from the places and subject positions offered by the police is what opens up the possibility of creating political bonds and imagining alternative worlds. Here is the conundrum. New positions of identification (subjectification) have to be produced purely by negative means, through a process of disidentification. These suggestions are clearly not entirely implausible. In this respect, we might note Rancière's example of the bodies of Algerians thrown into the Seine by the French police in October 1961 during the time of the Algerian war. He argues that around those bodies "a political bond was effectively created, made up not of identification with the victims or even with their cause but of a disidentification in relation to the 'French' subject who massacred them." He goes on to say that such politics is the "art of warped deductions and mixed identities" constructing local and singular cases of universality. The singularity of the wrong, for Rancière, must always be distinguished from the "particularization of right attributed to collectivities according to their identity" (1999, 139). But one has to ask why this emphasis on disidentification and a problematization of identification? And what are the consequences of this emphasis?

The problem here arises from Rancière's association of identification with the positions of the extant order, the natural places and hierarchies offered by the police order. For instance, for him rights are not egalitarian inscriptions, but positions that are occupied by subjects within the given order, and they stand in stark contrast to the miscount of the democratic community. Although much of Rancière's (1999, 138) critique of discourses of right and of the political limitations of compassion and good will might well be correct, these criticisms do not suffice to address the difficulties of a negative identification or disidentification as the basis of an egalitarian inscription. Is an exclusive emphasis on disruptive identification—a politics of negation—sufficient to Rancière's account of politics? Could it provide anything other than bonds of a fleeting character?[35] We have seen previously that it is plausible that under certain circumstances a rejection of an order could act as a powerful binding force. This is so particularly under conditions of severe dislocation. But whether the politics of rejection, negation, and disruption are effective in the making of alternative worlds, in the reconfiguration of the sensible, is another matter altogether.

It may be useful here to turn to another of Rancière's examples, namely the trial of the revolutionary Auguste Blanqui in 1832, where there is a clearer explication of the intertwining of the old and the new, which is

---

[35]Rancière (1999, 40) himself does not think this necessarily poses a problem.

necessary if we are to conceptualize a reconfiguration of the sensible. Asked by a magistrate to give his profession, Blanqui responds, "proletarian." The magistrate replies that it is not a profession, to which Blanqui retorts that it is the profession of thirty million Frenchmen "who live off their labor and who are deprived of political rights" (Rancière 1999, 37). The judge then allows "proletarian" to be added to the court's list of professions. Rancière (1999, 38–9), in his analysis of this event, argues that everything turns on the acceptance of a double word, "profession":

> For the prosecutor, embodying police logic, profession means job, trade: the activity that puts a body in its place and function.... But within revolutionary politics, Blanqui gives the same word a different meaning: a profession is a profession of faith, a declaration of a membership of a collective.

This collective, Rancière continues, is not a social group but is part of a process of subjectification: "Proletarian" subjectification defines a subject of wrong, the counting of the uncounted. This clearly is an example of a process establishing a relation between two worlds.

Yet it is not clear that subjectification here involves disidentification. Blanqui rearticulates what it means to be a proletarian and a member of a profession and the judge's response here is not dissimilar to that of the patricians who come to hear the words of the plebs as logos rather than phônê. This does not, however, rest upon a process of disidentification. Moreover, it is also clear that for the term proletariat to become a term that opens up new worlds, much else has to occur. Although this is in part a matter of the specific history and destiny of the term proletariat, the more general question here concerns the import of the inscription of an egalitarian logic. Rancière (1999, 40) acknowledges that such inscriptions might be fragile and fleeting. However, his acknowledgment could be read in two different ways. One could argue, as Rancière repeatedly does, that what matters is the *specific* miscount. As he puts it (2011, 9): "All my historical research has been aimed at ... showing that the history of social emancipation had always been made out of small narratives, particular speech acts, etc." Even so, Rancière *does* seek to offer an account of democracy and egalitarian inscription that *exceeds* the local and the specific miscount, and that provides tools to think critically about democracy beyond the confines of the local and the present. Here lies its strength.

However, if the verification of equality is to take the form of an inscription that resignifies the sensible, then it *has* to have the power to reconfigure. This means that it has to be potentially more than fleeting if reinscription is to have any significance at all. In this light, it is clear that disidentification is not sufficient to the task. We have seen that although it does play a crucial role in opening up new worlds, the very figuring of such new worlds, of alternative possibilities, requires more. The opening up of new worlds presupposes a characterization of subjectification that focuses not only on disidentification, but also on the possibility of reidentifying with an alternative vision. In contrast to his theoretical writings, Rancière is remarkably clear on this in his earlier historical studies. For instance, in *The Nights of Labor*, significantly subtitled *The Workers' Dream in Nineteenth-century France,* he argues (1989, 20) that

> It is the secret of others that the worker needs to define the meaning of his own life and struggle. Not the "secret of the commodity" ... It is not knowledge of exploitation that the worker needs in order "to stand tall in the face of that which is ready to devour him." What he lacks and needs is a knowledge of self that reveals to him a being dedicated to something else besides exploitation, a revelation that comes circuitously by way of the secret of others: that is, those intellectuals and bourgeois people with whom they will later say, and we in turn will repeat, they want to have nothing to do—and especially not with any distinction between the good ones and the bad ones.

Rancière continues his analysis, suggesting that the world of the bourgeoisie divides into two: "those who live a vegetative existence, the rich people so persistently depicted as stretched out indolently on their sofas or feather beds" and those, by contrast, "who desert the domestic cult of Baal to set out in search of the unknown: the inventors, the poets, the lovers of the people and the Republic, the organizers of the cities of the future, and the apostles of new religions" (1989, 20). The worker, he argues, needs all these people, "not to gain scientific or scholarly knowledge of his condition, *but to entertain and maintain his passions and desires for another world*" (1989, 20, emphasis added). Hence, the possibility of entertaining and maintaining passions and desires for another world arises not simply from disidentification, but from "revelation of a different world and the initiation of a new kind of relationship between beings," from other possibilities becoming visible (1989, 116).

In terms of the initiation of new relationships between political subjects, Rancière argues repeatedly that a democratic community must be *both* a community of "interruptions" *and* one in which "intervals constructed between identities, between spaces and places" inaugurate a political "being-together" as "a being-between: between identities, between worlds" (1989, 137).[36] However, there is a gap between discourses of disidentification,

[36] "The democratic process is the process of perpetually bringing into play, of invention of forms of subjectivation, and of cases of verification that counteract the perpetual privatization of public life. Democracy really means, in this sense, the *impurity* of politics" (Rancière 2006, 62).

which often take the form of discourses of purity, and the institution and maintenance of complex new forms of identification capable of sustaining an ethos of egalitarian inscription. Addressing this gap between disidentification and the possibility of reidentification with another way of doing things necessitates a reworking of Rancière's use of the category of identification. I have already noted his association of identification with the extant order, the natural places and hierarchies offered by the police. If, however, this conflation of a theoretical category with a particular politics is questioned, it becomes possible to provide a much more nuanced explication of processes both of disidentification (turning away from) and of reidentification (turning toward), neither of which can be presumed to take a specific, predetermined political form.[37] That is, nothing, in itself, follows from identification as such. All depends on the precise forms of identification and the possibilities opened up or closed down by particular identifications. Significantly it also allows one to address a persistent criticism of Rancière's work, namely the presumed homogeneity of the police order. If attention is directed, as Rancière himself argues, to the specificity and singularity of specific forms of identification, it becomes much more problematic to assume that there is one wholly hegemonic form of identification that dominates the police order and from which there is no escape. This issue is absolutely central, because without it no reconfiguration of the sensible is possible. To put it in different terms: a reconfiguration of the sensible requires, of necessity, the possibility of altering and initiating new relations between beings, and that cannot occur so long as one holds onto the idea of an undifferentiated police order. Let us now turn to an examination of the question of ethos, which addresses, precisely, the relational dispositions between people.

The role of exemplars in egalitarian inscription

I take the characterization of the plebian revolt by Ballanche to foreground the world disclosive character of staging equality. As Rancière himself puts it, "politics is both argument and opening up the world where argument can be received and have an impact" (1999, 56), bringing about a different way of *seeing* things:

> Political invention operates in acts that are at once argumentative and poetic, shows of strength that open again and again, as often as necessary,

[37]Conceptually I would argue that "disidentification" remains a form of identification, albeit one with a negative basis. In this case, it makes sense to deploy the broader category of identification as involving *both* an aspect of distancing oneself from another *and* of drawing on alternatives to produce novel subject positions.

> worlds in which such acts of community are acts of community. That is why the "poetic" is not opposed here to argument. (1999, 59)

Hence, the question is how he conceives of this impact? What must be shifted in order for a dispute to reconfigure the regime of the sensible? I wish to focus on one particular candidate, namely the possibility that such an impact may be felt or conceived through a *shift in ethos*. That is, the writing of names in the sky, if they are to have an impact, will have to have a wider effect, a reconfiguring effect, and this can be thought through the instatement of a different ethos.

However, Rancière consistently objects to a range of possible candidates for this task, arguing that they all fall prey to the order of the police. He objects to the idea that democracy has anything at all to do with a way of being.[38] Ethos, he argues, signifies an abode, a place or location and ethics; it means that one interprets a sphere of experience as the exercise of a property or a faculty possessed in common by all those who belong to a location. But this precisely is where Rancière locates the problem, because the purported commonality of properties such as logos is always already divided.[39] Hence, he argues that politics as a set of practices should not be regulated by "ethics conceived as the instance pronouncing values or principles of action in general" (2011, 4). In contrast, the egalitarian inscription is conceived of as a break with an ethos, as a distancing from it.

Is there a way to conceive of egalitarian inscription that would do the work of disruption and distancing that Rancière has in mind, but that would also, further, be capable of inscribing such distancing into a way of being, an ethos, yet in a manner that would not by definition fall prey to the order of the police? From the foregoing it is clear that the work of such an inscription should be conceived along a series of strictly specified lines. First, it should conceive of political subjectivity in a manner that avoids a given and pure conception of identity in favor of a *critical subjectification*. Second, it should facilitate the possibility of opening up new worlds. This means that it should be *futural* in character (Rancière 1999, 50): It should allow political actors to "write names in the sky"—to imagine unthought of possibilities. Third, it should conceive of political community, not in substantive terms, but in terms that are *attentive* to the inevitable closures

[38] "It is not their ethos, their 'way of being,' that disposes individuals to democracy but a break with this ethos, the gap experienced between the capability of speaking and any 'ethical' harmony of doing, being, and saying" (1999, 101).

[39] As he puts it (2009b, 4): "As is well known, it soon is made apparent that this common property is not shared by everyone; there are human beings who are not entirely human beings. For instance, Aristotle says, the slaves have the *aisthesis* of language (the passive capacity of understanding words), but they don't have the *hexis* of language (the active power of stating and discussing what is just or unjust)."

necessarily accompanying any police order. Taken together, these specifications resonate strongly with a certain contemporary understanding of a democratic ethos, developed in the work of Cavell, conceived of as an aversive ethos, an ethos that is precisely not that of a location or a place, but of an aversion to it. In what follows, I turn to a discussion of the features of such an ethos, arguing that it is capable of providing us with the means to think through crucial aspects of "writing a name in the sky" that remain underemphasized in Rancière's writings. I will focus in particular on the role of the exemplar in constituting a horizon of possibilities, one that adumbrates a conception of democratic subjectivity that foregrounds (critical) responsiveness, thus highlighting the placing of demands on the moral order (or the police order, to put it in Rancière's terms).

To amplify this point, let us return again to the work done by Rancière's examples: Auguste Blanqui, the revolt of the plebs on the Aventine Hill, the disidentification from a certain "French subject" that occurred in the wake of the Algerian war. Most commentators on Rancière's work focus on the disruptive character of each of these examples. However, as we have seen, they have a further role that exceeds that of disruption. Each also acts as *an exemplar* of the possibility of being and acting differently. Like the figure of Nora, they embody claims exceeding existing moral discourse, they "put the social order as such on notice" (Cavell 1990, 109), as well as manifesting for us another way of doing things. The protesters in Tahrir Square not only demanded an extension and deepening of the right to be heard, but also organized themselves in a manner that enacted alternative forms of social arrangement. The much commented-upon organization of teams to provide childcare and to clean the square signifies attentiveness to the position of women and the need for social care.[40] This is the work of egalitarian *inscription*: Opening up a horizon of imagination in which other ways of conceiving political community are kept alive and, importantly, can be (re)inscribed repeatedly.[41] On this reading, reinscription always takes into consideration the precise, local conditions, yet simultaneously acts as a call to open ourselves up to other, foreign possibilities manifested in the declaration of a dispute with the extant order. It is Rancière's attention to the singular character of these examples that leads commentators to overemphasize the ruptural quality of democracy in his writings, and thus to miss the wider significance and power of his historical cases. However, as

---

[40] See, for instance, the reportage in the *New York Post*, February 12, 2011: "Protesters clean up Tahrir Square, as army pledges civilian rule."

[41] This rendering of inscription relies on insights from Derrida's treatment of the possibilities of "grafting" and iteration (Derrida 1988), which emphasizes the complex interaction between change and repetition, such that every repetition or reinscription contains both an element of newness, of break with an extant context, and an element of continuity, which allows it to make sense, to be intelligible.

Rancière suggests, his work may be thought of as "panecastic philosophy" because it deploys "a method for finding in every (*ekaston*) peculiar manifestation" the "whole (*pan*) of its power" (2009a, 281). Hence, his "little narratives" that are extracted from the fabric of social history, where they are "expressions of a certain 'workers' culture,'" may become, instead, "statements on and shifts in the distribution of the sensible" (2009a, 281). The words resound. In doing so, they are concrete enunciations. But they also contain a principle of untimeliness and universalization: "You must also draw the line of escape, the line of universalization" (Rancière 2009a, 282).

Despite this very clear emphasis on the exemplariness of his examples, Rancière refrains from drawing out a generalizable ethos of engagement. The reason for this, as I have argued, arises in part from the specific understanding of ethos as located, signifying a place, and in part from his conceptualization of subjectivity as disidentification. Paradoxically, then, he refrains from thinking through what is required on the side of the extant order, for the exemplar to do its work of inscription. In each of these respects Cavell's work could usefully supplement Rancière's writings.

An emphasis on (re)inscription through the work of the exemplar allows one to retain the importance of singularity and historicity, while not remaining trapped in what is merely fleeting, sporadic, fugitive, and interruptive.[42] Thinking about the exemplarity of the example, enables one to focus on *both* the distancing from the given order, a turning away, *and* the possibility of another way of being and acting—a turning toward—that is inscribed in it. This both–and logic helps to counter the force of much of contemporary democratic theory, which seeks to resolve dilemmas regarding rupture and institution through an exclusive emphasis on one or the other.[43] In contrast, Cavell's Nietzschean rendering of exemplarity captures the double logic that is required here. On one hand, it allows for a certain disidentification (Rancière) or aversion (Cavell) to the given, a critique of conformism that also resonates with Arendt's.[44] On the other, it

---

[42]Melissa Lane (2011) provides a general discussion of the work of historical exemplars in political theorizing. An excellent range of contributions dealing with historical forms of exemplarity are also contained in Gelley (1995).

[43]Here I draw on Derrida, who refuses what he regards as the "blackmail" of either–or arguments, and explores the possibility of thinking one possibility together with another. As already noted, either–or forms of argumentation—either complete break or conservative continuity—occur across the spectrum of democratic theory. However, they also take other forms. Notable examples include what Foucault called "Enlightenment blackmail"—the idea that one has to be either for or against Enlightenment—and the dichotomous division between power and domination-free communication in Habermas. These older debates continue to have an impact on how we think of democracy and of possibilities that are more complex than what the either–or form allows.

[44]Cavell's Emersonian emphasis on aversion clearly resonates with Arendt's critique of conformism. Arendt (1994, 744) depicts it thus: "Morality collapsed into a mere set of

keeps open the possibility of an identification with that which exceeds the current order through a focus on the *demands* these exemplars place upon us; upon everyone, and also upon those who occupy the positions of "the police."

Inherent in Cavell's vision of democracy is the goal of demonstrating to others the partiality of society's arrangements, by offering oneself and one's position as presenting an *alternative* self for those others (Hammer 2002, 132–3). An important part of this work of both making available and keeping open the possibility of another way of doing things is done by such exemplars.[45] As Conant (2001, 193, emphasis added) puts it, "To be an exemplar ... is to be someone whose way of life ... *places a demand* on others to emulate his example in a *non-imitative* fashion." Hence, an exemplar provides a concrete representation of something one aspires to (Conant 2001, 195). Its role is to unsettle us—provoking disidentification, in Rancière's terms—and to open up horizons of imagination not previously available to us. What needs to be shown is how this rendering of exemplarity could contribute to our understanding of the development and fostering of alternative forms of identification and inscription.

Let us now return to Cavell's exemplars in this context. Nora acts as an exemplar in that she manifests another way of being, opening up potential new horizons that do not leave things unchanged: Her departure demands a response at the same time as it stimulates thinking of imaginative ways to "light out from the common ways" (Walker, 2001, 175). Cavell (1990, 111) argues that Nora's taking off her "fancy clothes" upon leaving Torvald at the end of the play is an enactment of inner change. He also argues that how Torvald picks up the pieces "is as morally fateful for him as Nora's leaving is for her" (Cavell, 1990, 113). Torvald can, Cavell notes, persist in his initial view of Nora. That, precisely, is what disturbs Cavell about the idea that we should act to ensure that our conduct is "above reproach," suggesting as it does a rejection of perfectionism (1990, 113). Cavell and Rancière both acknowledge that there are no guarantees here. That is why the political work of the exemplar is so important.

To break out from the common way presupposes not only a sense of dislocation, of dispute and of dissatisfaction, but also the *availability* of an alternative imaginary horizon, something transcending the here and now, disclosing at least the possibility of new worlds. It is here that Rancière's

---

mores—manners, customs, conventions to be changed at will—not with the criminals, but with ordinary people, who, as long as moral standards were socially accepted, never dreamt of doubting what they had been taught to believe in."

[45]Ferrara (2006, 66–7) argues, for instance, that "Alongside the 'force of things'—of what exists, of habits and traditions—and the 'force of ideas'—of what should or ought to be the case—stands the force of the example, which replaces the normativity of a law or principle with the normativity of the example."

historical exemplars come into play and take on their full force. Exemplars "manifest another way," are always singular, yet in their singularity they facilitate the glimpsing of a universal, of another way of doing things. For Cavell (1990, 59), friendship and authorship are paradigm cases of exemplars, allowing us to strive for the next self. He suggests, for instance, that Plato's *Republic* is an obvious candidate to illustrate this work of conversation between friends. The friend, who is also an enemy "contesting my present attainments" (1990, 59), is

> intellectually authoritative because ... his life is somehow exemplary or representative of a life the other(s) are attracted to ... the self finds that it can turn (convert, revolutionize itself) and ... a process of education is undertaken ... in which each self is drawn on a journey of assent to ... a further state of that self, where ... the higher is determined not by natural talent but by seeking to know what you are made of and cultivating the things you are meant to do; it is a transformation of the self which finds expression in ... the imagination of a transformation of society. (Cavell 1990, 6–7)

Every one of us has the inherent capacities needed for this process—there is nothing elitist about this argument. The cultivation of these capacities takes place, among other things, through the work of exemplars that are constituted, not given. The "commonalities" they propose, as Zerilli (1998, 11) puts it, "must be articulated through the interplay of diverse political struggles—rather than discovered and then merely followed, as one follows a rule." Thus, exemplars are products of political struggle: The fact that Nora and Tahrir Square are recognizable to us as exemplars of struggles against inequality is the result of ongoing political struggles that have contributed to the sedimentation and inscription of a certain democratic, egalitarian ethos.[46]

Toward an ethos appropriate to egalitarian inscription

Nevertheless, the work of exemplarity done by Tahrir Square and Nora is not the same. Perhaps one of the pivotal contrasts between Rancière's and Cavell's exemplars concerns their respective renderings of subjectivity. Although Rancière's is limited by his emphasis on disidentification, it has

---

[46] "Sedimentation," a geological metaphor, is drawn from Derrida's reading of Husserlian phenomenology. It suggests the process through which the meaning of a term becomes fixed and its origins forgotten as a result of a process of layering that occurs over time.

the advantage of explicitly dealing with collective forms of identification. In contrast, Cavell's focus on the individual is often taken to suggest that his writings are somehow nonpolitical, and commentators are skeptical as to its potential political import. Shulman (2011), for instance, argues that a focus on the collective is necessary if we are to develop a properly political understanding of ethos in general and an ethos of responsiveness more specifically. He suggests that a "political form of acknowledgment ... requires a compelling counter-narrative that connects private troubles to public causes," and he doubts that Cavell provides this. Others have similarly emphasized the fragility of the first person plural in Cavell. Hammer (2006, 165) notes that "[t]he 'we' in Cavell is a contested, fragile space of individual human voices that are exercised without any communal or metaphysical assurances." Despite skepticism in this regard, there is little doubt that Cavell's focus on conversation, on "speaking together, about matters of common importance," is deeply political (Cavell 2006, 265). The emphasis in his writings on politics as claim-making foregrounds the task of citizenship as one of making and staking claims; of working out, together, through these processes, what we are responsible for, with whom we are in community (Cavell 1982, 23). Norris (2006, 33) puts it succinctly: "I don't have, so to speak, a choice between myself and others, the individual and the community.... The community both gives me a political voice, and can take that voice back from me." Indeed, Cavell's elaboration of exemplarity addresses these issues through its focus on the processes involved in the constitution of claims of the common, what we may call "ours" (Zerilli 2005, 170).

The view of exemplarity is sustained by a conception of subjectivity that starts from the riven character of every identity and moral order. Rather than focusing exclusively on the division of the sensible between the extant order and those excluded, "the part of those who have no part," division is thought of as *running through* the self and through society, between a given, attained self or state of society, and a next or future state of self and society.[47] Despite the focus on the self, it is clear that Cavell breaks decisively with a liberal understanding of the individual as an isolated self, fully constituted before he or she enters into any relation with others. The self, for him, is inherently divided and doubled; any autonomy is always something to be attained, and if attained, always remains threatened and precarious (Mulhall 1994, 292–310). Moreover, it is important that the identity of the self—both attained and next (futural)—requires "the recog-

[47]Cavell (1990, 59) notes in this respect that for Emerson "we are divided not alone between the intellect and sense, for we can say that each of these halves is itself split. We are halved not only horizontally but vertically—as that other myth of the original dividing of the human pictures it—as in Plato's Symposium, the form of it picked up in Freud, each of us seeking that of which we were originally half, with which we were partial."

nition of an other—the acknowledgment of a relationship."[48] The emphasis on relationality, which is necessary to any account of inscription, is constitutive of the human for Cavell. He suggests that

> Whatever Moral Perfectionism knows as the human individual, one who is not everything but is open to the further self, in oneself and in others, which means holding oneself in knowledge of the need for change; which means, *being one who lives in promise* ... which in turn means expecting oneself to be, making oneself intelligible as an inhabitant now also of a further realm—Kant and Mill, and Nora Helmer and Tracy Lord in *The Philadelphia Story*, call this the realm of the human—and to show oneself prepared to recognize others as belonging there ... This is not a particular moral demand, but the condition of democratic morality. (Cavell 1990, 125, emphasis added)

Relationality as constitutive of a democratic ethos avoids the overly individualistic emphasis of which Cavell is often accused and places the self always already in relation to others, as well in relation to his or her society and the demands it places upon him or her. Bates (2003, 42) argues this point thus:

> Hence one must be careful in interpreting the phrase from Emerson's "History" that Cavell quotes—the "unattained but attainable self." This is not a designation of some specific state to be reached ... What perfectionism wants is the possibility of self-transformation according to an ideal that is internal to the self's constitution rather than one that comes from without. However, we need to remember that what is "internal" and what comes from "without" are themselves not fixed and permanent categories. If the transfiguration of any particular state of the self is to be possible, then even these categories will be capable of transformation. Of course, every part of every state of my self is how I relate to the society that has helped to form me.

The nonteleological character of the perfectionism advocated by Cavell (1990, xxxiv) leaves no role for the idea of a true, or indeed a false self. Hence, the transfiguration of the self always occurs in response and in relation to the extant order and it is here that exemplars play a crucial role.

---

[48] Cavell (1990, 31) argues that the working out of any identity can only occur in the context of my relations to others: "Emerson's turn is to make my partiality the sign and incentive of my siding with the next or further self, which means siding against my attained perfection (or conformity), sidings which require the recognition of an other—the acknowledgement of a relationship—in which this sign is manifest."

As we have seen, there are two aspects of this process that are important. The first relates to the process of distancing oneself from the given order. In Rancière, this work is done through a process of disidentification. In Cavell, drawing on Emerson and Nietzsche, it takes the form of a critique of conformism. Cavell (1990, 146) argues in this respect that there are two key aspects shared by his two focal examples of perfectionism, Emerson and Nietzsche: a hatred of moralism/conformity and a disdain for the present state of things "so complete as to require not merely reform, but a transformation of the self." Politically, conformism for him entails a forgetting of the need to define oneself: "The conformist, by failing to estrange himself from prevailing opinion (as well as from himself), lets the community speak for him, yet without interrogating its right to do so" (Hammer 2002, 132). Oppositional, critical thinking, in contrast, consists in the ability to withstand conformism and to develop the resources to respond to the inevitable failures of democracy.[49] Here the visibility of alternatives is crucial.

The advantage of Cavell's emphasis on the critique of conformism and the making visible of alternatives, in contrast to Rancière's, is that he explicitly situates them in relation to the extant (moral) order, as criticism of democracy from within (1990, 56). Let us recall the case of Nora: Her presence and departure place a demand upon the moral order, thus thematizing the issue of responsiveness. As Sparti (2000, 91) suggests, "our responsibility to others lies in our responsiveness to them." Torvald clearly fails to respond to Nora; he cannot hear her demands. What are the demands that we cannot hear today? Those expressing a sense of injustice often find themselves in Nora's position: faced with a society that cannot even begin to comprehend the sense of wrong expressed. This is the case today with a plethora of struggles within societies that regard themselves as democratic, and as otherwise, "above reproach." Here one only needs to think of responses to demands for same-sex marital unions—branded as "madness" and as "grotesque"—that echo Torvald in his unwillingness to engage with Nora and with her struggle to give voice to her sense of exclusion.[50]

Responsiveness plays a crucial role in Cavell and it is precisely what is absent—for structural reasons—from Rancière's depiction of egalitarian

---

[49]Cavell (1990, 56) argues the point thus: "I understand the training and character and friendship that Emerson requires for democracy as preparation to withstand not its rigors, but its failures, character to keep the democratic hope alive in the face of disappointment with it." I take this to mean, amongst other things, that we need to respond to these failures without falling back into cynicism and a crucial part of this process of keeping democratic hope alive is precisely the very character of responsiveness, not turning away saying that we stand "above reproach," as Rawls suggests.

[50]As recently as 4 March 2012, the head of the Scottish Catholic Church, Cardinal O'Brien, in an article for *The Sunday Telegraph*, branded campaigns for same-sex marriage as "madness" and as "grotesque."

inscription. The too sharp division between politics and the police order closes off this possibility for Rancière, leading him to see the matter almost exclusively from the perspective of the part that has no part. If a democratic political community must indeed be conceived of as both a community of "interruptions" and one in which "intervals constructed between identities, between spaces and places" inaugurate a political "being-together" as "a being-between: between identities, between worlds" (Rancière 1999, 137), then the consequences of an egalitarian inscription, *also for those who occupy positions within the extant order*, must be contemplated. Events such as those portrayed in the concrete historical cases discussed by Rancière make us aware of the painful distance from "perfect justice" in the current order, as Cavell (1990, 107) puts it, and demand a response, an examination and possible revision of the dominant position, hence provoking engagement with the claims articulated and disputes declared. Lacking responsiveness and engagement would be a form of aspect-blindness, where one is "unable or unwilling to realize the significance of the other's expressions" (Hammer 2002, 73).[51]

These provocations are significant not only for what they bring about in specific situations, for those miscounted, but also for the horizons of imagination they open up and keep open. Cavell (1990, xxxvi) marks their significance by arguing that the "demand of one's human nature for expression demands the granting of this human demand to others" and conversely, "showing that at some stage the scoundrel, opting out of membership in the intelligible realm, must seek to deprive others of expression, or their voice in choosing principles, or say, ideas, of their lives." From here it becomes possible to think through the demands of a politics of responsiveness, conceived of as the ability and responsibility to respond to the inevitable failures of democracy. These themes clearly intersect with contemporary debates on the nature of a democratic ethos and in particular with the recent turn to questions of responsiveness and receptivity. Much of this work focuses on the need to intensify our receptivity (Kompridis 2006, 209) and develop practices that can foster agonistic respect and critical responsiveness that works on the self in its response to others (Coles 1996; Connolly 1995). As Connolly (1995, xvi) argues, a pluralist culture needs to cultivate such critical responsiveness, because "to become something new is to move the self-recognition and relational standards of judgment endorsed by other constituencies to whom you are connected ... to be white, female,

[51] Cavell comments in this respect upon the case of slave owners, suggesting that although they see slaves as "a certain kind of human being" the slave owner denies his internal relation to these people. Hammer (2002, 74–5) summarizes what is at stake here in the following terms: this and other examples demonstrate "the extent to which we experience something as human depends not on its physical or mental features, but on our relation to it—the quality of our reciprocal stance."

heterosexual ... is to participate in a diverse set of collective identifications ... To alter your recognition of difference, therefore, is to revise your own terms of self-recognition as well." Debates concerning the centrality of a critical ethos to democracy can be traced back to the writings of Foucault and Nietzsche on agonism and can be contrasted with thinkers who either downplay or deny the role of ethos in developing their respective understandings of democracy.[52] More recent writings on deliberative democracy have, however, also sought to articulate a specific ethos commensurate with deliberation. In this respect Laden (2001, 194) suggests that deliberative democracy itself must institute an ethos that is suited to the values of deliberation. Coming close to a Cavell-inspired position that attention needs to be given to the practices through which we come to hold particular dispositions, most of these authors agree that a critical, responsive ethos is an indispensible part of democratic practice.

However, positions clearly still diverge on the role of struggle in such an ethos. Rancière foregrounds struggle and confrontation, whereas Cavell's writings often emphasize the conversational. Nevertheless, although the conversational emphasis in Cavell does not occur at the expense of other practices of "manifesting for another,"[53] the manner in which he conceives of these practices could be supplemented with a more explicit consideration of confrontation and struggle. In a commentary on "Homer's Contest," Owen (2002, 125) argues that what is at stake here is a practical form that the instantiation of this attitude or ethos may take. He suggests that the agon captures this well, being a political culture in which "citizens strive to develop their capacities for self-rule in competition with one another, a culture that honors exemplary democratic citizens as setting standards that we should seek to match and surpass." To work in this fashion, an exemplar should be an excellence that is "attainable," because its educative function depends on its unsettling us, not on our following it in a slavish fashion (Cavell 1990, 6–7). It is notable that this Nietzschean rendering of exemplarity echoes John Stuart Mill's treatment of "originality," which he suggests opens our eyes, "which once fully done" allows one to be original oneself (Conant 2001, 229). These conditions are important because they make it clear that the educative role of the exemplar can only be fulfilled if someone or something is both related, similar to us (exemplarity is a mark of this), and different from us (exemplariness is an indicator of inessential difference). Establishing these similarities and differences, Rancière teaches us, comes about as a result of imaginative engagement in political struggle, a possibility, as Conant and Cavell point out, that is open to everyone.

[52]Bernstein (1998, 291) argues in this respect that Habermas' discourse theory of law and politics presupposes but does not provide an explication of a democratic ethos.

[53]For a discussion of the role of "manifesting for another" in Cavell's writing, see Norval (2011).

Such standard setting involves attending to the "rough ground of politics," including the struggles in and through which exemplary qualities are developed (Honig 2011, 203). Emerson makes this all too clear. The responsiveness required of us is often jarring in character. We need to "affront and reprimand the smooth mediocrity and the squalid contentment of the times" (Emerson [1841] 1977, 147). That includes, for Cavell, confronting and responding to the inevitable failures of democracy. With this insistence on the ever-present possibility of the nonresponsiveness of the extant order, he addresses one of Rancière's key concerns, and goes beyond many theorists of the democratic ethos.[54] These possibilities are precisely the wellsprings of Cavell's construal. Although he shares with Rancière the deep sense that our democracies often disappoint us, he focuses on the cultivation of an aversive ethos that seeks to prepare us for those failures.

"There is nothing left to do but talk to them"

By way of conclusion, let us return to the scenarios with which we started, making visible the value of an account of inscription that explicitly foregrounds an aversive ethos. As I have suggested with the Aventine example, Rancière implicitly highlights what many of his readers focusing exclusively on his more explicitly theoretical later writings miss, namely, the possibility of inscription accompanying the declaration of a wrong. Such inscription involves a range of activities and practices, including the naming of hitherto unnamed subjects; the reclaiming of a given name; the staging of a wrong that seeks to reconfigure the sensible, thus reframing our existing ways of looking at a situation; the imagination of other possibilities; and seeing the universal in the singular. At the core of Rancière's writings, as in Cavell's, we find "a multitude of individuals such as Louis Gauny, Joseph Jacotot, Jeanne Derion" who "by their declarations, their grievances, and their acts transform the distribution of the sensible" (Rockhill and Watts 2009, 4). In reciting these names, Rancière engages in a double gesture, contesting histories written in the names of great men, as well as histories of the longue durée that "erase the possibility of acknowledging the actions of anyone whatever" (Rockhill and Watts 2009, 4).[55] It is an abiding theme of Cavell's writings that they similarly draw on the works of figures whose status as philosophers are contested. Cavell (1995, 12) argues, for instance,

[54]Cavell's work allows one to elaborate a conception of a democratic ethos that goes beyond a focus on the role of critique, and a supplement to relations of antagonism. Its nonteleological perfectionism facilitates a specification of the grammar of relations between citizen subjects that places demands and expectations upon participants in the democratic game.

[55]Rockhill and Watts (2009, 4) note that in doing so Rancière distances his work explicitly from the *Annales* school.

that it is an important part of his project to reappropriate Emerson as a philosophical writer, because from this he could "learn something not only about Emerson, and not only about American culture, but something about philosophy, about what makes it painful." For both of these thinkers, then, invoking such names plays an important, critical role. For Rancière, as we have seen, it is important that these are not names of great men, but of figures hitherto unknown; singular, yet capturing something of the significance of a moment of political challenge and change. In Cavell (1990, 58), the theme of representativeness is also present and is equally linked to presenting "standards," yet in such a way as to emphasize our split nature, between our existing world and self and what we could become, our nextness. Blanqui's remarkable claim to the "profession" of proletarian, Jeanne Deroin's equally striking presentation of herself as a candidate for an election in which women cannot run: Both stage nonexistent rights, constructing a singular, polemical universality (Rancière 1999, 42). As Bosteels (2009, 163) puts it, "the universal exists only in the singular—that is, in the plurality of particular modes, places, and operations."

Yet, despite the presence and explicit acknowledgment of exemplarity in Rancière's work,[56] his analysis of Roman patricians' acceptance of the plebeians' "becoming beings who may very well make promises and draw up contracts" is brief (1999, 25). He notes that from "the moment the plebs could understand Menenius's apologia ... they were already, just as necessarily, equals." The Roman Senate concludes that "since the plebs have become creatures of speech, there is nothing left to do but to talk to them" (Rancière, 1999, 25–6).[57] This brief gesture, I have argued, covers over precisely the question of responsiveness and the need, for the plebeian speech act to become effective, for it to be inscribed in the extant order. The responsiveness in question here is not predetermined. Yet this does not make it any less significant. The patricians accepted the staging of equality by the plebeians; elsewhere, the staging of equality is less successful. The story of the Scythian slaves is a case in point; they fail to turn their war-generated equality into political freedom (Rancière 1999, 13). What this contrast foregrounds is that the gains of struggle need to be defended, beyond their initial staging. This is necessary, not only in cases of the instituting moment of democracy, but also in well-established democratic orders, where we cannot risk thinking ourselves to be "above reproach." Part of this defense consists in cultivating an ethos of aversive responsiveness. Such an ethos, far from affirming a "way of being," alerts us to the necessity to challenge

[56]Rancière (1999, 41) calls Jeanne Deroin's actions "exemplary." For a more extended historical treatment of Deroin, see Scott (1996, chap. 3).

[57]Rancière (1999, 26) contests Ballanche's own view that this acceptance is matter of a "progressive revelation that can be recognized by its own signs," a "determined philosophy," but leaves it at that.

the "squalid contentment" of our age (Emerson 1977, 147) on an ongoing basis. It captures the intertwining of politics and the police order, and shifts the emphasis to a study of the places where they are inscribed in one another, allowing us to focus on the specific historical modalities in which this inscription occurs (Bosteels 2009, 170). This includes, crucially, an emphasis not only on the perspective of the articulators of a wrong, but on their addressees, those occupying privileged positions within the extant order. It requires attention to historical specificity and singularity, just as it calls for an emphasis on the politics of claim-making and the fragile collectivities it brings into being.

I started this reading with the suggestion that Rancière's view of democracy is torn on the horns of a dilemma: between democracy as a staging of equality that interrupts the extant order, and democracy conceived of as an inscription of equality that has the capacity to relocate and reshape it. As we know from much democratic theory, there are advantages to both of these characterizations. In Rancière, as in other theorists, they lead to radically divergent conceptions of democratic practice, each of which is accompanied by an emphasis on different aspects of political community. In the case of the former, the emphasis is on the division between the community and the part of the community that has no part. It makes visible the necessary exclusions accompanying any instituted order. In the latter the focus is on the imbrication and redoubling of names and it is suggestive of the possibilities of not only staging the miscount, but envisioning alternative ways of doing things. The latter is more evident where Rancière discusses his historical examples. As I have suggested, this should give us cause to reflect further on the role and function of such examples. Rancière turned to a detailed examination of the working class intellectual production that thrived in France in the 1830s and 1840s in the wake of his break with Althusser, turning Althusser's privileging of scientific insight over popular delusion on its head. As Hallward (2006, 109) points out, Rancière's writings consistently explore the presumption that everyone shares equal power of speech and thought. Yet, as I have suggested, these historical cases as they appear in his later theoretical writings stop short of working through the consequences of a staging of equality for the relation between the order of the police and the part that has no part. The reasons for this are doubtless multiple and complex, but I have focused attention here on one specific aspect of that larger problem. In considering his conception of subjectivity and the difficult relation between subjectification and disidentification, I have suggested that the latter is still a form of identification, and that it is necessary to move beyond identification understood as a (negative) distancing to address the mechanisms of the egalitarian inscription.

Egalitarian inscription, if it is to mean anything beyond the singular instance, needs to be enacted and conceptualized in a way that makes it possible not only to maintain the insights specific to it, but to extend their reach and impact to a wider domain. Conceptualizing egalitarian inscription in this way can be achieved by thinking more carefully about the role of the exemplar in the constitution of alternative political horizons. Rancière's own historical cases, I have suggested, could be conceived of as exemplars, which would then open up the analysis to consider the work of exemplars in relation to a wider audience—those occupying places in the extant order—and of their responses to the theatre of egalitarian inscription. Such an account is only possible once one problematizes the sharp division between the police order and the moment of politics. Thinking of egalitarian inscription as a moment of bringing the universal into play comes at the price of giving up that sharp division. However, this is not something that should be lamented, for the rethinking of the relation radically opens up the police order for contestation and politicization.

If, finally, one thinks of democracy not as a disruption occurring in rare instances and on the margins of society, but as an aversive practice that could occur anywhere and with consequences for how we think of political community everywhere, it is possible to foreground the central role of responsiveness to such practices. This is not an optional luxury that we can afford to add as an afterthought. It is, rather, a central aspect of democratic subjectivity and practice, without which, in Rancière's own terms, "writing a name in the sky" loses its ability to reconfigure the division of the sensible. This reconfiguration has the potential to dissolve the extraordinary/ordinary division, the dualism that holds much of democratic theory captive, for it provides us with the resources to enjoy the fruits of democratic vitality, yet without too quickly subordinating these energies to legal and institutional procedures. In addition, and this is perhaps its most crucial contribution, it emphasizes the positive, critical, and energizing role of moments of staging a wrong for the extant order. As so many of our contemporary struggles attest, moments of challenge and critique, of the staging of democratic demands, are not important only because they make us aware of and demand that we address existing wrongs. They also are crucial to the deepening and sustaining of a democratic ethos, an ethos that foregrounds democratic responsiveness. The "nextness" that for Cavell characterizes our subjectivity allows us to think of interruption and inscription as ongoing possibilities that place serious normative demands upon democratic orders.

References

Ackerman, Bruce. (1991), *We the People: Foundations*. Cambridge, MA: Harvard University Press.

Arendt, Hannah. (1994), "Some Questions of Moral Philosophy." *Social Research* 61 (4): 739–64.

Bates, Stanley. (2003), "Stanley Cavell and Ethics." In *Stanley Cavell*, ed. Richard Eldridge. Cambridge: Cambridge University Press, 15–47.

Bernstein, Richard. (1998), "The Retrieval of the Democratic Ethos." In *Habermas on Law and Democracy: Critical Exchanges*, eds. Michael Rosenfeld and Andrew Arato. Berkeley: University of California Press, 287–307.

Bohman, James. (1996), *Public Deliberation: Pluralism, Complexity, and Democracy*. Cambridge, MA: MIT Press.

Bosteels, Bruno. (2009), "Rancière's Leftism, or, Politics and Its Discontents." In *Jacques Rancière: History, Politics, Aesthetics*, eds. Gabriel Rockhill and Philip Watts. Durham, NC: Duke University Press, 158–75.

Cavell, Stanley. (1982), *The Claim of Reason: Wittgenstein, Skepticism, Morality, and Tragedy*. Oxford: Oxford University Press.

——(1990), *Conditions Handsome and Unhandsome: The Constitution of Emersonian Perfectionism*. Chicago: Chicago University Press.

——(1995), *Philosophical Passages: Wittgenstein, Emerson, Austin, Derrida*. Oxford: Blackwell.

——(2004), *Cities of Words: Pedagogical Letters on a Register of the Moral Life*. Cambridge, MA: Belknap Press of Harvard University Press.

——(2006), "The Incessance and Absence of the Political." In *The Claim to Community: Essays on Stanley Cavell and Political Philosophy*, ed. Andrew Norris. Stanford, CA: Stanford University Press, 263–318.

Coles, Romand. (1996), "Liberty, Equality, Receptive Generosity: Neo-Nietzschean Reflections on the Ethics and Politics of Coalition." *American Political Science Review* 90 (2): 375–88.

Conant, James. (2001), "Nietzsche's Perfectionism: A Reading of Schopenhauer as Educator." In *Nietzsche's Postmoralism: Essays on Nietzsche's Prelude to Philosophy's Future*, ed. R. Schacht. Cambridge: Cambridge University Press, 181–257.

Connolly, William E. (1995), *The Ethos of Pluralization*. Vol. 1 of *Borderlines*. Minneapolis: University of Minnesota Press.

Dean, Jodi. (2005), "Zizek against Democracy." *Law, Culture, and the Humanities* 1 (2): 154–77.

Derrida, Jacques. (1988), *Limited Inc*. Evanston, IL: Northwestern University Press.

Dillon, Michael. (2003), "(De)void of Politics? A Response to Rancière's Ten Theses on Politics." *Theory and Event* 6 (4). http:// muse.jhu.edu/journals/ theory_and_event/v006/6.4dillon.html (accessed August 3, 2012).

Emerson, Ralph Waldo. [1841] (1977), "Self-reliance." In *The Portable Emerson*, ed. Carl Bode, in collaboration with Malcolm Cowley. Harmondsworth, UK: Penguin Books.

Ferrara, Alessandro. (2008), "Does Kant Share Sancho's Dream? Judgment and Sensus Communis." *Philosophy and Social Criticism* 34 (1/2): 65–81.

Foucault, Michel. (1988), *Politics, Philosophy, Culture: Interviews and Other Writings 1977–1984*. Ed. Lawrence D. Krizman. New York: Routledge.

——(2007), *Security, Territory, Population: Lectures at the Collège de France 1977–1978*. Basingstoke, UK: Palgrave Macmillan.

Frank, Jason. (2009), "Staging Dissensus: Frederick Douglas and 'We, the People.'" In *Law and Agonistic Politics*, ed. Andrew Schaap. Farnham, UK: Ashgate, 87–104.

——(2011), "Standing for Others: Reform and Representation in Emerson's Political Thought." In *A Political Companion to Ralph Waldo Emerson*, eds. Alan M. Levine and Daniel S. Malachuk. Lexington: University Press of Kentucky, 383–414.

Gelley, Alexander, ed. (1995), *Unruly Examples: On the Rhetoric of Exemplarity*. Stanford, CA: Stanford University Press.

Habermas, Jürgen. (1992), *The Structural Transformation of the Public Sphere*. Cambridge: Polity Press.

Hallward, Peter. (2006), "Staging Equality: On Rancière's Theatrocracy." *New Left Review* 37: 109–29.

Hammer, Espen. (2002), *Stanley Cavell: Skepticism, Subjectivity, and the Ordinary*. Cambridge: Polity.

Honig, Bonnie. (1993), *Political Theory and the Displacement of Politics*. Ithaca, NY: Cornell University Press.

——(2009), *Emergency Politics: Paradox, Law, Democracy*. Princeton, NJ: Princeton University Press.

Honig, Bonnie and Marc Stears. (2011), "The New Realism: From Modus Vivendi to Justice." In *Political Philosophy versus History? Contextualism and Real Politics in Contemporary Political Thought*, eds. Jonathan Floyd and Marc Stears, Cambridge: Cambridge University Press, 177–205.

Kalyvas, Andreas. (2008), *Democracy and the Politics of the Extraordinary: Max Weber, Carl Schmitt, and Hannah Arendt*. Cambridge: Cambridge University Press.

Kompridis, Nikolas. (2006), *Critique and Disclosure: Critical Theory between Past and Future*. Cambridge: MIT Press.

Laclau, Ernesto. (1990), *New Reflections on the Revolution of Our Time*. London: Verso.

——(2005), *On Populist Reason*. London: Verso.

Laclau, Ernesto and Chantal Mouffe. (1985), *Hegemony and Socialist Strategy*. London: Verso.

Laden, Anthony. (2001), *Reasonably Radical: Deliberative Liberalism and the Politics of Identity*. Ithaca, NY: Cornell University Press.

Lane, Melissa. (2011), "Constraint, Freedom, and Exemplar: History and Theory without Teleology." In *Political Philosophy versus History? Contextualism and Real Politics in Contemporary Political Thought*, eds. Jonathan Floyd and Marc Stears. Cambridge: Cambridge University Press, 128–50.

Lefort, Claude. (1986), *The Political Forms of Modern Society: Bureaucracy, Democracy, Totalitarianism*. Cambridge: Polity Press.

——(1989), *Democracy and Political Theory*. Minneapolis: University of Minnesota Press.

Markell, Patchen. (2006), "The Rule of the People: Arendt, Archê, and Democracy." *American Political Science Review* 100 (1): 1–14.

Mulhall, Stephen. (1994), *Stanley Cavell: Philosophy's Recounting of the Ordinary*. Oxford: Clarendon Press.

Norris, Andrew. (2006), "Introduction: Stanley Cavell and the Claim to Community." In *The Claim to Community: Essays on Stanley Cavell and Political Philosophy*, ed. Andrew Norris. Stanford, CA: Stanford University Press, 1–18.

Norval, Aletta J. (2007), *Aversive Democracy: Inheritance and Originality in the Democratic Tradition*. Cambridge: Cambridge University Press.
——(2011), "Moral Perfectionism and Democratic Responsiveness." *Ethics and Global Politics* 4 (4): 207–29.
Owen, David. (2002), "Equality, Democracy, and Self-respect: Reflections on Nietzsche's Agonal Perfectionism." *Journal of Nietzsche Studies* 24: 113–31.
Parmele, Mary Platt. (2006), *A Short History of Rome*. New York: Cosimo Classics.
Patterson, Annabel M. (1991), *Fables of Power: Aesopian Writing and Political History*. Durham, NC: Duke University Press.
Rancière, Jacques. (1989), *The Nights of Labor: The Workers' Dream in Nineteenth-century France*. Trans. by John Drury. Philadelphia: Temple University Press.
——(1995), *On the Shores of Politics*.Trans. by Liz Heron. London: Verso.
——(1999), *Disagreement: Politics and Philosophy*. Trans. by Julie Rose. Minneapolis: University of Minnesota Press.
——(2003), "Comment and Responses." *Theory and Event* 6 (4). http://muse.jhu.edu/journals/theory_and_event/v006/6.4Rancière.html (accessed August 3, 2012).
——(2006), *Hatred of Democracy*. Trans. by Steve Corcoran. London: Verso.
——(2009a), "Afterword/The Method of Equality: An Answer to Some Questions." In *Jacques Rancière: History, Politics, Aesthetics*, eds. Gabriel Rockhill and Philip Watts. Durham: Duke University Press, 273–88.
——(2009b), "The Aesthetic Dimension: Aesthetics, Politics, Knowledge." *Critical Inquiry* 36 (1): 1–19.
——(2011), "The Thinking of Dissensus: Politics and Aesthetics." In *Reading Rancière: Critical Dissensus*, eds. Paul Bowman and Richard Stamp. London: Continuum Books, 1–17.
Rockhill, Gabriel and Philip Watts. (2009), "Introduction: Jacques Rancière: *Thinker of Dissensus*." In *Jacques Rancière: History, Politics, Aesthetics*, eds. G. Rockhill and P. Watts. Durham, NC: Duke University Press, 1–12.
Ross, Alison. (2009), "The Aesthetic Fable: Cinema in Jacques Rancière's 'Aesthetic Politics,'" *SubStance* 38 (1): 128–50.
Schaap, Andrew. (2009), "The Absurd Proposition of Aboriginal Sovereignty." In *Law and Agonistic Politics*, ed. Andrew Schaap. Farnham, UK: Ashgate, 209–24.
Scott, Joan Wallach. (1996), *Only Paradoxes to Offer: French Feminists and the Rights of Man*. Cambridge, MA: Harvard University Press.
Shulman, George. (2011), "Acknowledgement and Disavowal as Idiom for Theorizing Politics." *Theory and Event* 14 (1). http:// muse.jhu.edu/journals/theory_and_event/v014/14.1.shulman.html (accessed August 3, 2012)
Sparti, Davide. (2000), "Responsiveness as Responsibility." *Philosophy and Social Criticism* 26: 81–107.
Spinosa, Charles, Fernando Flores, and Hubert L. Dreyfus. (1997), *Disclosing New Worlds: Entrepreneurship, Democratic Action, and the Cultivation of Solidarity*. Cambridge, MA: MIT Press.
Tully, James. (2008a), *Public Philosophy in a New Key*, Volume I. Cambridge: Cambridge University Press.

——(2008b), *Public Philosophy in a New Key*, Volume II. Cambridge: Cambridge University Press.

Viroli, M. (1992), *From Politics to Reason of State: The Acquisition and Transformation of the Language of Politics 1250–1600*. Cambridge: Cambridge University Press.

Walker, Brian. (2001), "Thoreau on Democratic Cultivation," *Political Theory* 29: 155–89.

Wittgenstein, Ludwig. (1989), *Lectures and Conversations on Aesthetics, Psychology and Religious Belief*. Oxford: Basil Blackwell.

Wolin, Sheldon S. (2004), *Politics and Vision: Continuity and Innovation in Western Political Thought*. Princeton, NJ: Princeton University Press.

Zerilli, Linda M. G. (1998), '"This Universalism Which Is Not One': A Review of Ernesto Laclau's *Emancipation(s)*." *Diacritics* 28 (2): 3–20.

——(2005), *Feminism and the Abyss of Freedom*. Chicago: Chicago University Press.

Žižek, Slavoj. (2011), "Democracy Is the Enemy." *LRB Blog*, October 28. http://www.lrb.co.uk/blog/2011/10/28/slavoj-zizek/democracy-is-the-enemy/ (accessed August 3, 2012).

Aletta J. Norval is Professor of Political Theory, Department of Government, University of Essex, Wivenhoe Park, Colchester CO4 3SQ, United Kingdom (alett@essex.ac.uk).

I have incurred many intellectual debts in writing this article. I presented earlier versions of it in the Humanities Centre, Johns Hopkins University, as well as at the Chicago Political Theory Workshop. I thank my hosts, Jane Bennett and William Connolly at Johns Hopkins and Robert Gooding-Williams at Chicago, as well as the participants in those seminars for probing discussion and valuable suggestions. They have helped in developing the final arguments I present here. I also owe a debt of gratitude to others who gave generously of their time in commenting on various versions of this article: David Howarth, David Owen, Davide Panagia, Thomas Dumm, and Hugh Ward. I am grateful to the anonymous *APSR* referees for comments and criticisms that guided me in my final revisions. My deepest gratitude goes to Coeditor Kirstie McClure for her substantive comments and consistent support throughout the publication process.

PART FOUR

Aesthetic "seeing as," politics of the "as if"

CHAPTER NINE

Blankets, screens, and projections: Or, the claim of film

Davide Panagia
Trent University

I go to the movies for the same reason that the "others" go: because I am attracted to Humphrey Bogart or Shelley Winters or Greta Garbo; because I require the absorbing immediacy of the screen; because in some way I take all that nonsense seriously.

ROBERT WARSHOW, "AUTHOR'S PREFACE." *THE IMMEDIATE EXPERIENCE.*

In the following pages I address some concerns for an aesthetics of politics. Specifically, I prompt several lines of comparison and investigation into what I take to be the central problem of aesthetic experience and its relation to an ethics of appearances for contemporary democratic life. I do so by examining some works of Stanley Cavell and, more directly, the implicit though underexplored overlap between his ethical writings in *The Claim of Reason* and his writings on the ontology of film in *The World Viewed.*[1]

---

[1]I should note right off the mark that I have benefited greatly from many excellent works published and influenced by Cavell's writings. Most notably, Stephen Mulhall's comprehensive *Stanley Cavell: Philosophy's Recounting of the Ordinary* (Oxford: Clarendon Press, 1994),

My reading of Cavell's writings begins from the idea that *The Claim of Reason* and *The World Viewed* are very much the same work (the fact that in *The World Viewed* Cavell famously refers to film as "a moving image of skepticism" (p. 188) is a good hint that we may be on the right track). Through exegesis and innuendo I explore the conceptual traits and connections of these two projects so as to arrive at the tenets of what I call an ethics of appearances.

By "ethics of appearances" I am referring to a minoritarian tradition of enlightenment thought that takes as its starting point the relationship between spectator and aesthetic object, variously conceived. Here such issues as aesthetic responsiveness, the shareability of sensation, the development of criteria for the appraisal of value, and—importantly for what I have to say in the subsequent pages—the practices of authoritatively indexing the sources of value in any appearance, are some of the key concerns that an ethics of appearances contends with. These concerns are also central to our reflections about democratic theory: the capacity for citizens to hold a view, the ability to invest our judgments of the good with an authority that extends beyond the privacy of a preference, and

---

William Rothman's and Marian Keane's *Reading Cavell's* The World Viewed: *A Philosophical Perspective on Film* (Detroit, MI: Wayne State University Press, 2000), Andrew Norris's edited collection, *The Claim to Community: Essays on Stanley Cavell's Political Philosophy* (Stanford, CA: Stanford University Press, 2006), and Aletta Norval's *Aversive Democracy* (Cambridge: The University of Cambridge Press, 2007) are excellent resources for anyone interested in Cavell's moral, political and aesthetic writings. But my concern in this essay lies in the fact that in most instances, Cavell's moral, political and aesthetic insights are treated independently of one another. (Though from the above list, Mulhall's study comes closest to addressing the relationship between Cavell's ethical and aesthetic writings, specifically with regards to Cavell's reflections on film as a moving image of scepticism. The relevant chapter here is Chapter 9 entitled "Cinema: Photography, Comedy, Melodrama" (pp. 222–45). Also helpful in this regard are Robert Goodwin-Williams and Thomas Dumm's essays in *The Claim to Community*.) Finally, the one work that is exemplary in showing the connection between Cavell's ontology of film and his moral writings is D. N. Rodowick's *The Virtual Life of Film* (Harvard, 2007). Rodowick's discussion of classical film theory and his treatment of Cavell's "Ethics of cinema" (p. 63) is, for lack of a better word, excellent.

In my own manner, in the following pages I try to show how Cavell's aesthetics of film and his ethical considerations are imbricated one with the other, how they share a genetic resemblance (not just a family resemblance), and how the fact that this is true points to Cavell's participation in the minoritarian tradition of aesthetic and political thought I call an ethics of appearances. I should specify that the genetic resemblance between Cavell's ethical and aesthetic thinking and writing lies in the fact that the central concept of acknowledgement that has become for many readers of Cavell the cornerstone of his philosophical contributions to both moral and political thought is, as he explains, an aesthetic concept that he invokes following Michael Fried's discussion "of the fact of modernist painting as an *acknowledging* of its conditions." (*The World Viewed* (Enlarged Edition). Cambridge, MA: Harvard University Press, 1979, p. 109. Hereafter *WV*). Further relevant in the connection between Cavell's ethical and aesthetic thinking are two essays in *Must We Mean What We Say?*, "Knowing and Acknowledging" and "Aesthetic Problems of Modern Philosophy."

the possibility (or hope) that our senses of the good are shareable and therefore intersubjective remain consistent issues of address in our political theorizings about democratic pluralism. No less is this overlap between aesthetic and political reflection relevant to our thinking about democratic citizenship, which begins with the question of what it means to give admittance to a new subjectivity that appears at our limits? Indeed, much of what I address in the following pages speaks directly to the terms and conditions of reflection for the admittance of an appearance whose ingression marks our finitude.

The ontological relationship between beholder and projected image and the microcultural practices of interface that emerge in a dynamics of beholding will prove vital to my explorations. Specifically, the issue of touching an appearance takes center stage in these reflections. What does it mean to touch or be touched by an appearance and how might such a hapticity be conceived? Asked in this manner, such questions might seem esoteric, the province of a specialized theoretical discourse. But I am actually talking about diurnal experiences like the ones we ordinarily partake in when we express our enthusiasm for things we appreciate and or our distaste for things we disapprove of. Our everyday judgments of appraisal or disapproval are infused with an intention to touch an appearance (e.g. song, image, flavor) as expressed by our expressing our allure to that appearance. When I say "this is delicious," I am at once avowing a judgement and indicating something; I am calling attention to an experience of sensation and what I take to be the reference or source of that experience. If you will, I am indexing the source of my sensation. And yet, such forms of pointing and touching are entirely disappointing because try as I might, I will never be able to assay the source of my sensation with enough accuracy as to make my sensation tangible to others; that is, shareable. There is in aesthetic experience an intangible hapticity – a *noli me tangere*[2]—in my wanting to touch or be/hold the appearance.[3]

---

[2]My reference is to Jean-Luc Nancy's study on the *noli me tangere* of aesthetic experience and the tradition of Biblical iconography he discusses related to the *noli me tangere* scene in the New Testament Gospels, when Jesus exits the tomb on the third day and encounters Mary Magdalen who is in the garden mourning his passing. Astonished by his appearance, Mary lunges towards Jesus while he withdraws from her, uttering the negative injunction "*noli me tangere*" (in Greek, *mê mou haptou*): "do not touch me," or "do not withhold me," or "do not hold me back". The *noli me tangere*, in other words, pictures the intangible hapticity that we lend an advenience, an ungraspable caress that nonetheless reaches out to the appearance as the appearance advenes. Here is how Nancy accounts for this moment of detached attachment: "What is seeing if not a deferred touch? But what is a deferred touch if not a touching that sharpens or concentrates without reserve, up to a necessary excess, the point, the tip, and the instant through which the touch detaches itself from what it touches, at the very moment when it touches? Without this detachment, without this recoil or retreat, the touch would no longer be what it is, and would no longer do what it does (or it would not let itself do what it lets itself do). It would begin to reify itself in a grip, in an adhesion or a sticking, indeed, in

[3] The possibility of touching something as untenable as an appearance emerges as a principal concern in Cavell's aesthetic and ethical writings. My ability to attend to an appearance and bear it attention involves my being able to approach it and to allow myself to touch and be touched by it; that is, to be/hold and be absorbed by it. Cavell articulates his own relationship to film and to the possibility of thinking about films philosophically in this way, as a "coming to attention" so as to provide sufficient tuition to one's experience "so that it is worthy of trust."[4] The entirety of his enterprise as a philosopher of film stems from the absorptive, ungraspable hold that certain projected images have for him (what Robert Warshow, in the epigraph above, refers to as "the absorbing immediacy of the screen"); an untenability that, as we shall see below, is first thematized in terms of inaccurate memories and later developed in his ontology of projection. Hence the importance for Cavell of recalling and engaging an experience rather than requiring of it criteria to satisfy a standard of accuracy; by recalling an experience we curate it, we show a care for it, and make room for it in our lives. In doing so, we afford it—and our sensations of it—authority.

The experience of an intangible hapticity is equally important to Cavell's ethical writings, especially with regard to the problem of sensorial verifiability and the kind of penetrative touching that is expected (in the tradition of modern skepticism that he engages) in order to accept as valid an other's

---

an agglutination that would grasp the touch in the thing and the thing within it, matching and appropriating the one to the other and then the one in the other. There would be identification, fixation, property, immobility. 'Do not hold me back' amounts to saying 'Touch me with a real touch, one that is restrained, nonappropriating and nonidentifying.' Caress me, don't touch me."(Nancy, *Noli me Tangere: On the Raising of the Body*. Fordham, University Press: 2008, pp. 49–50).

[3]A brief note on the potentially clumsy application of the diacritical mark in my spelling of "be/hold": I insert the backslash in "be/holding" to give emphasis to the orientation that an ethics of appearances espouses; namely, that all looking is also a bearing, a having to bear the burden of the advenience of an appearance, and that to be/hold is not merely a passive viewership but is an active participation in the curatorial handling of an appearance's ingression. To be/hold is to look, but it also suggests a holding up to view, or a handling *as a view* of that which bodies forth. In other words, and as I outline below, to be/hold is also to regard: it is to look but also to hold an appearance in regard. The diacritical backslash in be/holding, therefore, signals the *double entendre* of regarding as both a "looking" and a "caring for." But the diacritical backslash also signals the disruption between our desire to touch the source of an other's sensation in order to verify it and the impossibility of ever fulfilling that desire; that is, it signals the discomposition of sensation and reference characteristic of the *noli me tangere* of aesthetic experience. And when we speak of being absorbed by the advenience of an appearance, of being struck and captured by the intensity of conviction it projects, we not only speak of being "taken in" by that appearance but also of absorbing it, or bearing its force upon us. Once again, to be/hold and to absorb the advenience of an appearance refers to an active spectatorship and a curatorial attitude of regard that is a basic concern of an ethics of appearances.

[4]Stanley Cavell, *The Pursuits of Happiness*, p. 12. Hereafter *Pursuits*.

expression of sensation. Here the "perfected automaton" example in *The Claim of Reason* is fruitful for a variety of reasons; but most notably for our purposes because there is an aspectual overlap between Cavell's discussion of an ethics of relation and response vis-à-vis the automaton and his description of film as "a succession of automatic world projections."[5] In Cavell's example, the automaton is in the guise of a human, he is wearing a mask – one might go so far as to say that he is a *persona*, an actor projecting a part—in any case, the automaton projects a world. Importantly, in *The World Viewed* Cavell describes actors as projected on a screen as "a human something ... unlike anything else we know."[6] How we relate to the projected world of film and how we relate to the projection of the human somethingness of an other is, for Cavell, ethically, aesthetically and ontologically the same issue.

I might state the problem I pursue in this essay in this way: because I can never penetrate and verify the source of an other's humanness, the best that I can do is admit that we are all human somethings to one another, like the perfected automaton in the parable, or the filmed actor on the screen is "a human something ... unlike anything else we know" to the be/holder; that is, he or she is an appearance that advenes.[7] Cavell hints at this mode of *seeing as* in an essay written in 1965 when affirming that "objects of art not merely interest and absorb, they move us; we are not merely involved with them, but concerned with them, and care about them; we treat them in special ways, invest them with a value which normal people otherwise reserve only for other people—*and* with the same kind of scorn and outrage."[8]

The basis of my argument for an ethics of appearances begins with the idea that whatever else it may be, a human life is a succession of world projections. That is, living a life involves projecting worlds into the world for others to be/hold.[9] To quote Heidegger, whose influence on Cavell's writings on the ontology of film is not insignificant: "To exist means,

---

[5]Stanley Cavell, *WV*, p. 105.

[6]The relevant passage reads as follows: "It is an incontestable fact that in a motion picture no live human being is up there. But a human *something* is, and something unlike anything else we know." *WV*, p. 26.

[7]A point raised by one of my students, Liam Young, in seminar is worth mentioning: one film where this dynamic between human somethings is explored vividly is *Blade Runner*. The relationship between Deckard and Roy Baty and the final duel between them at the end of the movie is exemplary in this regard, and Stephen Mulhall's account of it in his *On Film* (New York, Routledge, 2002, pp. 37–45) is equally compelling.

[8]Stanley Cavell, "Music Discomposed" in *Must We Mean What We Say?*, p. 198.

[9]I also take this phenomenon of humans projecting, or of holding up a view and the dynamics of frontality and interface that this action implies, to be one of John Rawls's principal concerns in his articulation of political liberalism, especially as it is laid out in the infamous "original position." I discuss Rawls's veil and its relationship to twentieth-century visual culture in an essay entitled "Rawls's Vision (Slight Return)."

among other things, to cast-forth a world, and in fact in such a way that with the thrownness of this projection, with the factical existence of *Dasein*, extant entities are always already uncovered."[10] With this in mind, the central thesis of a politics of appearances affirms that an encounter with the thrownness of a projection (what I call "the advenience of an appearance") calls into relief our capacity and willingness to bear the weight of an appearance by be/holding it. The be/holding of an appearance's advenience is a looking that is not of the nature of a passive viewership. On the contrary, be/holding is also a handling or a holding up to view of that which bodies forth. The nature of such be/holdings speaks of a curatorial mode of attention that sources an ethics of appearances.

A second thesis follows: our handling of the advenience of an appearance projects our handling of one another. Another term we might use to indicate our handling of one another is "practices of governance."[11] Thus, an aesthetics of politics takes aesthetic experience as relevant to political life because our practices of microcultural interface with aesthetic objects source our curatorship and governance of one another. To the extent that we are all advening appearances to one another, the manners, attitudes and forms of handling we enlist to be/hold appearances is of central concern to our understandings of the forces of collectivity that make a political handling-with-others at once thinkable and possible. Such is the theoretical basis that sources an ethics of appearances for contemporary democratic life.

Finally, a third thesis: the *noli me tangere* of aesthetic experience that denies the possibility of sharing sensations also withholds the kind of stability that grounds democratic theory and that marks one of the ambitions of democratic institutions. To Bonnie Honig's analysis of the two central paradoxes of democratic theory, therefore, I would add a third paradox of an intangible sympathy.[12] One of the central contentions of modern democratic thought is the possibility of grounding political stability in shared, intersubjective values. Despite our competing conceptions of the good life, or our individual or collective pluralisms, there remains the furtive belief that intersubjective consensus is achievable or, at the very

---

[10]Martin Heidegger, *The Basic Problems of Phenomenology*. Albert Hofstadter, transl. (Bloomington, IN: Indiana University Press, 1988), p. 168.

[11]I take the term "practices of governance" from James Tully's discussion of public philosophy as a critical activity in *Public Philosophy in a New Key: Volume 1, Democracy and Civic Freedom* (Cambridge: Cambridge University Press, 2008). Here Tully states that "one might take as a provisional field of inquiry 'practices of governance', that is, the forms of reason and organization through which individuals and groups coordinate their various activities and the practices of freedom by which they act within these systems, either following the rules of the game or striving to modify them." (p. 21).

[12]Bonnie Honig, "Between Decision and Deliberation: Political Paradox in Democratic Theory" in *American Political Science Review* (Vol. 101, No. 1 February 2007), 1–17.

least, desirable. Whether we choose to call it an overlapping consensus, or an ideal speech situation, or bi-partisanship, the assumption is that in order to establish strong and sound democratic institutions we must be able to agree upon a set of shared values that ground sovereignty. Therein lies the puzzle: collective values are valued by a disparate collectivity that values collectively shared values. Or, to put it slightly differently, the absolute value of sharing values is the ground for our conceptions of a democratic community. Yet, as I show in my discussion of Cavell's ontology of projection and of his parable of a "striptease of misery"[13] in *The Claim of Reason*, our desire to touch the sources of value of an other is thwarted by an interval of dissension which discomposes our habitudes of referencing the world, interrupting those matters of course that make sensation and reference compatible. Sensation is the experience of an intangible hapticity that disrupts the relata which procure a sensing-in-common. At the heart of democratic life—of the possibility of thinking the *demos* as a collective entity—there lies the aesthetic paradox of an intangible sympathy.[14]

Part One
An aesthetics of politics

The project of an aesthetics of politics involves an exploration of the ways in which our handlings of aesthetic objects mirrors, informs, sustains and disrupts our political lives. Whether watching a television show or a movie, listening to a song, scanning a web page, eating a morsel of food, or simply walking down the street, we participate in microcultural practices of interface with the world that surrounds us. Often, included in such practices are the expression and solicitation of value that take the form of an enthusiastic appraisal, or perhaps a disregard, or even disgust. We point at an image, we turn away from a view, we give emphasis through the enthusiasm we have for the things we love to do, our stomachs churn at a pungent smell, our muscles tense at the screeching sound of an ambulance. To the extent that such events of microcultural interface involve sensorial encounters with an advening world of appearances, these are aesthetic experiences.

They are aesthetic experiences also because they solicit in us a sense

[13]Stanley Cavell, *The Claim of Reason*, New York: Oxford University Press, 1999. p. 404. (Hereafter *Claim.*). This is the expression Cavell divines to describe the perfected automaton parable.

[14]I use "sympathy" in the eighteenth-century sense of the term, which referred to the ability of sharing sensations. I explore the nature of this intangible sympathy with greater care in a book entitled *Impressions of Hume: Cinematic Thinking and the Politics of Discontinuity*. Lanham, MD: Rowman and Littlefield, 2013.

of absoluteness; they are, in short, experiences of conviction. Indeed, one dilemma of aesthetic experience regards how to make sense of the sensation of absolute conviction that arises from the advenience of an appearance – this, despite the fact that there is nothing essential in the appearance that would make for sufficient evidence to justify that conviction. Thus, the sense of absoluteness that characterizes aesthetic conviction is not synonymous with totality, consensus or completeness; on the contrary, grounded as it is in an intangible hapticity, the sensation of aesthetic conviction is an anxious absolute, equivocal and unverifiable.

What is it, for instance, about Hollywood films of the 1930s, 40s, and 50s that make Cavell's conviction of their value plausible? Isn't *The Pursuits of Happiness* at one level simply a book that proclaims a private sensation on the par with Wittgenstein's declaration, "I am in pain"? Is his conviction a correct expression of the value of the aesthetic object in question? Does its correctness matter? Or, we might ask, isn't it the case that the sense of conviction that comes from aesthetic experience procures a disjuncture between our capacities to reference the world and the sensations that result from an advenience – a disjuncture, that is, of the possibility of the in-between itself?

I take the central feature of aesthetic experience to be the interval of disjuncture between sensation and reference that emerges at the event of advenience; and I take one of the tasks of aesthetic criticism to be the forging of new relations between sensation and reference – that is, the forging of relations between a sensation felt from the ingression of an appearance and our giving that sensation a reference by indexing our sense of the appearance's value.[15] As I suggest, an aesthetic experience occurs when an appearance advenes. Though anything can count as an appearance, not all appearances are of the order of an advenience. To be more specific, an advenience is the bodying forth or ingression of a sensorial permanence whose value is yet to be determined. More to the point, an aesthetic experience compels a confrontation with the sense of conviction that arises in the face of the event of advenience. Regardless of form, matter or medium, the advenience of an appearance impacts our sensorial apparatus and procures a temporal interval whereby the set of correspondences between sensation and reference that we conventionally deploy to give sense to our worlds are discomposed. Thus, aesthetic experience is an event of discomposition of the matters of course through which we give value to the world. Paradoxically, the discomposition procured by an advenience sources our sense of conviction regarding the value of an aesthetic object. One might say that the absorptive attraction one has towards an appearance

[15]Though I will not address the dynamics of aesthetic criticism in detail here, I discuss the nature of such an enterprise, and the invention of what I call "anomic affinities," in a paper entitled "Film Blanc: Luminosity and Perspicuity in the Films of Michael Mann."

is itself the marker of conviction; the most approximate definition we can give for an advenience is the intangible and yet punctuated sensation of conviction it procures. The capacity to articulate the terms through and by which such a conviction is made possible is the work of aesthetic criticism.

Stanley Cavell's writings on the ontology of film, his readings of specific films and the ethical positions he articulates in his moral writings stem from the punctual discomposition of an advenience. We might refer to this as a state of absorption; or, as he recounts it, the disruption of a previous absorption—a disruption of what Heidegger, as Cavell explains, accounts for as "the matters of course running among our tools, and the occupations they extend, and the environment which supports these occupations. It is upon the disruption of such matters of course (of a tool, say by its breaking; or of someone's occupation, say because of an injury; or of some absence of material) that the mode of sight brought forth discovers objects in what Heidegger notes as their conspicuousness, their obtrusiveness, and their obstinacy."[16]

Cavell's reference is to Heidegger's discussion of the worldhood of the world in the third chapter of *Being and Time*, and though it would be worthwhile to advance an extended treatment of that discussion here, I forgo such a temptation (or, better put: indulgence). Suffice to say that for Cavell, film and films—in any case, the projected image—occasion the kind of anxious disruption that Heidegger indicates is of the order of a world-disclosing encounter. It is not the case that for Cavell film is the only medium that encourages such events; it is the case, however, that for him film affords as good an occasion as any to experience such anxieties. An ontology of the projected image attempts to account for the anxiety over the break in referential contexts (i.e. a disruption of "the matters of course") that Cavell (via Heidegger) appreciates as part and parcel of aesthetic experience.

The anxiety over broken referential contexts also litters many of Wittgenstein's insights in his *Philosophical Investigations*, a further source of inspiration for Cavell's reflections on films (and, I would add, for his aesthetic theory more generally). In order to be able to see an aspect, to see something *as* something, that previous something's relation to its matters of course must be dislodged and reconfigured. Just think here of the fact that the genre of Hollywood comedies that Cavell invents and collects, the comedies of remarriage, are characterized not simply by an interruption of relations, a disruption of such referential contexts that goes by the name of divorce or separation, but a reconfiguration of the representational structures and criteria of the collectivity that goes by the name of "a married

[16]Stanley Cavell, "What Becomes of Things on Film?" in *Themes Out of School: Effects and Causes*, p. 174. In this essay Cavell is picking up on a similar discussion that appears in the appendix to *The Pursuits of Happiness* entitled "Film in the University."

couple." I take the "re" part of the comedies of remarriage as underscoring Cavell's investigations into the nature of family resemblances, the "queer connexions"[17] that occasion their disruptions, and the kind of disruption of a previous absorption necessary in order to see two disparate human somethings—two individual lives—*as* something (i.e. married).[18]

Here the emphasis is on a capacity for regarding things; that is, not just viewing them, but affording them a curatorial looking, a "regarding" in the sense of caring—or caring enough to turn one's attention and look—marks a further connection between Heidegger and Wittgenstein for Cavell. As Cavell notes in the context of a discussion of Charlie Chaplin's comedic ability to transform a dinner roll into a dance sequence, "to this human capacity for seeing or for treating something *as* something, Wittgenstein attributes our capacity for intimacy in understanding, for what we may call the innerness of the meaning we attach to words and gestures."[19]

At this point, therefore, we may elaborate two further methodological points for an aesthetics of politics: the first is that the discomposition procured by the advenience of an aesthetic object occasions the possibility of a be/holding. It is precisely because referential contexts are not binding that it is possible to see something *as* something, to see a family resemblance. Thus, when it comes to matters of ethics and aesthetics, the intelligibility of objects is not a necessary condition of experience. In fact, one might go so far as to imply—as Cavell does following Heidegger and Wittgenstein—that unintelligibility is of the order of the day. Indeed, for both Heidegger and Wittgenstein the breaking of referentiality gives rise to an alteration in and of our worlds: Heidegger calls this disclosure, Wittgenstein calls it aspect seeing.

The second important point regards the relationship between intimacy and understanding. Aspect seeing is a moment of intimacy that happens to me. I might be able to share it, if my indexical gestures are successful, but I have no guarantees other than that of a potential disappointment. The intimacy of understanding in aspect seeing speaks directly to what Cavell imagines is the ethical risk of modern scepticism (and, I would add, the

[17]The reference here is to Section 38 of the *Philosophical Investigations*: "Naming appears as a *queer* connexion of a word with an object.—And you really get such a queer connexion when the philosopher tries to bring out *the* relation between name and thing by staring at an object in front of him and repeating a name or even the word 'this' innumerable times. For philosophical problems arise when language *goes on holiday*. And *here* we may indeed fancy naming to be some remarkable act of mind, as it were a baptism of an object."

[18]Unable to resist the temptation for further innuendo, I want to say that Cavell's inquiry into the comedies of re-marriage betrays an implicit suggestion that another name for the disruption between sensation and reference characteristic of aesthetic experience and that sources one's capacity for aspect seeing (for seeing something *as* something) is love.

[19]Stanley Cavell, "What Becomes of Things on Film?" in *Themes Out of School: Effects and Causes*, p. 175.

risk that accompanies the democratic paradox of an intangible sympathy), that is: the expectation to make explicit the sources of our sensations in order to validate our expressions of them, as if our affirming the intimacy of our sensations—"I am in pain," "I love you," "What a wonderful film"—is insufficient to making the words count as participants in a shared life.

I raise these connections between Heidegger and Wittgenstein in Cavell's aesthetic ontology and in his ethical writings more generally because it helps set the tone and themes of the discussion that follows.[20] Issues of be/holding, sensation, intimacy, reference, caring, attention, absorption and so forth will reappear in the subsequent pages though in other guises, *as* something else. That something else will include discussions of Cavell's ontology of projection, his attention to candidness (in film acting and in everyday life), his exposition of the nature of photo-genesis as well as the medium specificity of film as "a succession of automatic world projections."[21] But before we get to all that, we might begin by asking "why film?"

Part Two
Thinking film

"Why film?" is, in fact, a question that Cavell repeatedly asks of himself and (often) of his readers and audiences. It is a question that betrays a palpable anxiety in the face of the expectations of professional philosophical thinking. Can film be a subject worthy of philosophical attention and authority? If so (and for Cavell it clearly is), then *how*? In asking this Cavell intends to ask nothing less than what is the nature of experiences such that they capture and express our reflective attentions; that is, our convictions.

But more than that, I believe Cavell to also be making a polemical claim about the nature of professional philosophizing, and specifically professional philosophizing in America. Amidst Cavell's various autobiographical starts that offer a prelude to his theoretical claims regarding one's aesthetic experiences as evidentiary sources of one's intimacy with things in the world,[22] there is also always the more subtle suggestion that

[20]Three other thinkers Cavell references repeatedly are worth mentioning as their insights also set the backdrop of his aesthetic and ethical thinking, though discussing them in any detail would require my writing a different essay. Those three thinkers are André Bazin, Robert Warshow and Walter Benjamin.

[21]*WV*, p. 72.

[22]Consider here the tone of self-declaration in the first line of *The World Viewed*: "Memories of movies are strand over strand with memories of my life." (*WV*, "Preface," xix).

professional philosophy in the American academy has inadvertently (or perhaps even advertently) missed out on something. Something has gone unnoticed, an event was disregarded, avoided.[23]

The period in question is, as Cavell notes, the period between 1935 and 1960, approximately, during which "going to movies was a normal part of my week."[24] We know that his going to movies on a regular basis was not an exception and movie-going was an ordinary part of many Americans' weekly schedule—so ordinary in fact that one might even miss it as a relevant fact about a culture. But Cavell's innuendo that avoiding the relevance of such an ordinary event as going to the movies for a discipline that pretends and demands to give purchase to human motivations, preferences and beliefs, as philosophy does (i.e. a self-professed human discipline), suggests that something has gone terribly awry. In disregarding films philosophy has avoided a human something. That is, what has been avoided is not simply something about humans and specifically, about humans in a particular culture like pre- and post-war America. No. The claim is more subtle and more distressing: in disregarding film, philosophy has refused to confront or interface with a human something.

The impetus here is thus to ask why hadn't American philosophers noted the importance of movies to the cultural and individual landscape of everyday experience? Others had paid attention to it, most notably the popular culture critic and writer, Robert Warshow.[25] More than an impetus, then, I would say it is a charge that helps get at Cavell's own anxiety in writing about movies and asking—perhaps rhetorically, but nonetheless repeatedly—whether film and films merit serious and authoritative philosophical attention.

The period between 1935 and 1960 includes the period that John McCumber, in his study of the development of professional philosophy in America, identifies and documents as the time when there was a concerted effort by professional philosophers and professional philosophical associations, like the American Philosophical Association, to distance themselves from pragmatic social and cultural issues. This, according to McCumber,

---

[23]This, in fact, is a point raised by one of the first reviews published of the book, in 1973, by Frances Ferguson, where she states that the book itself does not encourage a precipitous flight to the theaters to see movies, but rather compels us to think on and about the nature of our experience in film viewing: "It does not move one (or me, at least) to rush to the nearest movie theater for a new immersion in films; rather, it prompts one to reexamine one's own past experiences of films—to see what one was responding to, what one was avoiding, before one read the book." Frances Ferguson, "Stanley Cavell, *The World Viewed: Reflections on the Ontology of Film*." *College English*, Vol. 34 (May 1973), 1145–8.

[24]*WV*, xix.

[25]Robert Warshow. *The Immediate Experience: Movies, Comics, Theatre and Other Aspects of Popular Culture*. Cambridge, MA: Harvard University Press, 2001 (published originally in 1946).

was the result of a quick and easy association between philosophy and communism, an association implied and established by the pervasive culture of McCarthyism.[26] The result was a radical shift in philosophical orientation that is today indentified with the dominance of analytic philosophy in professional philosophy departments. The point here being that what Cavell identifies as a period characterized by philosophy's curious avoidance of film, McCumber identifies as a sociological and historical phenomenon of political and disciplinary significance. More to the point, and implicit in both these engagements, is the implication that part of what is at stake in any pedagogical enterprise is the delimitation of the partitions that make objects, events and things count as intelligible and/or unintelligible. To put it bluntly, by asking the why and how of film, Cavell wants to do nothing other than to ask what it means for us to think, what are the sources of our ideas, and what do we disregard when we avoid attending to certain things.[27] The experience of film, and specifically the experiences of the films one has seen, forces the question of the relation between thinking and caring—or, as Cavell describes it, of trying "to meld the ways of thinking that have invited my conviction with the experiences of film that I have cared about."[28]

The question of thinking about films is inextricably linked to the intimacy of memory, recall and inaccuracy—themes that, as I suggested in my introductory remarks, point to the central problem of aesthetic experience as the problem of not being able to specify with any kind of certainty the referential sources of one's conviction in one's sensations (an experience referred to as the *noli me tangere* of aesthetic experience). Let me rephrase this: for Cavell, the experience of film is bound to memory and therefore to one's intimate relation with the inaccurate "like childhood memories whose treasure no one else appreciates, whose content is nothing compared to their unspeakable importance for me."[29] This experience of an "unspeakable importance" is the same experience that Baudelaire, in

---

[26]My recounting of this history does not do justice to McCumber's detailed and thoroughly well documented intellectual history. See especially "Philosophy's Family Secret" in *Time in the Ditch: American Philosophy and the McCarthy Era*. Northwestern University Press, 2001. For more recent articulations of these concerns, see Alex Abella's *Soldiers of Reason: The RAND Corporation and the Rise of the American Empire* (New York: Harcourt 2008) and S. M. Amadae's *Rationalizing Capitalist Democracy: the Cold War Origins of Rational Choice Liberalism* (University of Chicago Press, 2003); and finally, John McCumber's review of these: "America's State Philosophy?" in *New APPS: Art, Politics, Philosophy, Science* (www.newappsblog.com/2010/09/americas-state-philosophy.html#more), accessed 26 September 2010.

[27]I can put it even more bluntly, echoing Wittgenstein's "A Lecture on Ethics" (1965, *The Philosophical Review*, 74: pp. 3–12), and suggest that Cavell may be asking: what is philosophy for?

[28]*WV*, p. 9.

[29]*WV*, p. 154.

"The Painter of Modern Life," likens to "convalescence" or a return to childhood impressions.[30] Cavell's "conviction with the experiences of film that [he has] cared about" exists because he remembers those experiences as a kind of convalescence—a recovering from a striking event—that evince his sense of conviction regarding the films' successes. Recall that Cavell is writing about film at a time when VHS recorders or DVD players were not available. Perhaps, as he suggests, he has seen these films more than once and one could have, at the time, reverted to published scripts of the movies in question to verify one's accuracy of recall.

But an accuracy of the recall is not the point. That is, accurately reporting on the film does not get at the experience of conviction that is, in the end, the point of Cavell's philosophical investigations into an ontology of film. Rather to treat films as philosophically authoritative objects of inquiry means allowing oneself to occupy a place of inaccurate reflection, a place of misremembering, a place where the correspondences between my sensations and what those sensations may reference is discomposed. To think film and to think cinematically means, for Cavell, to access an interval of active inaccuracy that solicits a "continuous appeal ... to an active memory of the experience"[31] of the film in question and thus, a continuous solicitation of evanescence so as "not to accept any experience as final."[32]

Such infinitude and its accompanying inaccuracy is the promise of aesthetic experience that Cavell will repeatedly return to as a central resource for his reflections on ethical life. One might go so far as to suggest that for Cavell, film is an ethical medium.[33] It is relevant, then, that both *The World Viewed* and *The Pursuits of Happiness*, though importantly different works of and about film, begin with an admission of (mis)recol-

---

[30]I have no doubt that Cavell's likening of the absorption of filmic experience to childhood memories is a direct reference to Baudelaire's discussion of Edgar Allen Poe's "The Man of the Crowd" in "The Painter of Modern Life." The relevant passage is the following: "Now convalescence is like a return towards childhood. The convalescent, like the child, is possessed in the highest degree of the faculty of keenly interesting himself in things, be they apparently of the most trivial. Let us go back, if we can, by a retrospective effort of the imagination, towards our most youthful, our earliest impressions, and we will recognize that they had a strange kinship with those brightly coloured impressions which we were later to receive in the aftermath of a physical illness, always provided that that illness had left our spiritual capacities pure and unharmed. The child sees everything in a state of newness; he is always drunk. Nothing more resembles what we call inspiration than the delight with which a child absorbs form and colour. I am prepared to go even further and assert that inspiration has something in common with a convulsion, and that every sublime thought is accompanied by a more or less violent nervous shock which has its repercussion in the very core of the brain." In *The Painter of Modern Life and Other Essays*. New York: Phaidon Press, 2004, pp. 7–8.

[31]*The Pursuits of Happiness*, p. 11.

[32]*The Pursuits of Happiness*, p. 12.

[33]This is, in fact, D. N. Rodowick's claim in his reading of Cavell in *The Virtual Life of Film* where he asserts that "Cavell, along with Gilles Deleuze in recent scholarship, proposes not just an ontology but an ethics of cinema." (p. 63).

lection that betrays Cavell's curatorial sentiments vis-à-vis the experiences of advenience that his viewings of film recommend. He wants to write about films because his viewings of films at a specific point in his life represent a category of experience that he remembers and recalls. Moreover, those same experiences generate in him a series of thoughts that would be unavailable without having seen those films that matter to him.

But most importantly, at stake here is the making of experience matter and the making of what matters (as evinced through the datum of memory) count *as* a something of reflection. Not, that is, that we need philosophy in order to think about one's experiences in general, or one's experiences of film in particular. But for Cavell, the calling of attention to one's experiences and the sensations that such a recollection affords is what philosophy is; it is a curatorial handling of objects that we collect and that make up our worlds. And this collection and recollection of things is also what the medium of film is: the recollection and assembly of things that is the nature of handling in film (let us call it manufacture, or film production) as much as it is the nature of ethical and aesthetic handling too. Film collects things—images, appearances, frames, reels, actors, faces, views, shots, etc.—and gathers them, makes them partial to a sensorial collectivity. At a personal level, we do the same with our recollections and rememberings of experiences—those moments of punctuality that compose our diurnal lives. At an interpersonal level, we do it with one another—we pay attention or disregard one another, turn our heads and our attentions. The handling that is the medium of film mirrors our handling of one another.

The curatorial timbre that scores Cavell's reflections on film engages the expectations of accuracy and intelligibility when accounting for one's experiences. The inaccurate pointing characteristic of one's engagement with one's sensorial life is a handling filled with potential disappointment if one expects of one's indexical gestures the finality of verifiability. There is something of the therapeutic here, as if the coming to attention with the intimacy of one's sensorial life betrays the need to confront the unlivable expectations we hold for ourselves and one another; as if the grasp of the "how do I *really* know?" that is the expectation of accuracy regarding our interactive ways of being, sensing and living needs to be loosened by admitting to the intangibility of a be/holding that can never withhold that which touches us because what touches can never be grasped. The *noli me tangere* of aesthetic experience punctures the expectation to penetrate the sources of our sensations and make them available for our circumspection and verification; it compels us to admit of a human residence in the intangibility of unintelligibility, in the interval between sensation and reference. This is what it means to give voice to the no-part of sensorial experience and make it a part of our ethical lives, to give it an authority worthy of one's trust. If I can trust the evanescence of my sensations, then why can't you?

"Why, then, film?" Because one of the things that film affords is a conviction of candidness, an absorptive be/holding that neither touches nor withholds.

Part Three
Candidness and aesthetic conviction

What might I mean by this? Recall that one of my objectives in this essay is to show how Cavell's ethical writings and his considerations of an ontology of film stem from a similar set of aesthetic concerns regarding our relationship to our sensations and the possibility of sharing those sensations with one another. I have also suggested that these concerns are central to democratic theory (most recognizably articulated in terms of the possibility of a common conception of the good, or theories of shared values in pluralist democratic societies, of an "overlapping consensus" as John Rawls calls it). I have gone on to affirm that the main thesis for an aesthetics of politics regards the central problem of aesthetic experience: the fact that the advenience of an appearance discomposes our common ways of thinking about the relationship between sensation and reference and that the project of an ethics of appearances is to come to terms with this disjuncture. Thus, what I have referred to as our ability and willingness to be/hold and bear the weight of an advenience marks the basis for an ethics of appearances for contemporary democratic life.

One of the themes that appears and reappears in Cavell's discussions of both film and everyday interaction is candidness: candidness in acting and the candidness of our claim-making. What, he often asks, are the conditions of candidness and how might we respond to these? First off, it's necessary to admit of a temptation to confirm candidness when confronting the expression of individual experience: "One may say that nothing came between a person's experience and his expression of it as a way of saying that his expression was genuine, uncontrived, candid."[34] One may say this, but this is a wrong picture of what candidness is. The problem, of course, is that our inner lives have no manifestation other than through outward expressions and this makes such expressions feel as if they mediate our experiences; that is, it makes us feel as if expression intervenes between our experiences and their source thereby tainting the experience. Hence doubt and the need to verify expression's mediation of experience in the face of the "temptation to want to penetrate the other, to see inside and ... of comparing what the other shows with what is actually going on in him."[35]

[34] *Claim*, p. 341.
[35] *Claim*, p. 381.

Here the temptation of candidness is figured in terms of an unveiling, of taking off a guise or a mask, of stripping the other of their adornments or of their persona, so as to verify trust in their expression. In contrast, what Cavell will try to show is how an aesthetic conception of candidness does not rely on our having to confirm trust in an appearance's accuracy; rather, aesthetic experience affords conviction without ground, candidness without confirmation.[36]

In film, candidness is most easily felt through the photogenic transubstantiation of human into star (i.e. of human being into human something, of thing into appearance). Cavell's example of "Bogart" comes to mind here—the fact that Bogart does not exist (i.e. has no presence) other than through his filmic presence. Bogart, Cavell asserts, "is who he is, not merely in the sense that a photograph of an event is that event; but in the sense that if those films did not exist, Bogart would not exist, the name 'Bogart' would not mean what it does. The figure it names is not only in our presence, we are in his, in the only sense we could ever be. That is all the 'presence' he has."[37]

The insight is complicated, and perhaps also implausible; but plausibility is not Cavell's point because he is wanting to register a conviction that is not of the order of a belief. To assay the insight regarding "Bogart's" photogenic presence, we must take for granted the fact that filmic actors differ from stage actors: the stage actor yields to the character and thus projects that character. A man or a woman is projecting a character on a stage and the possibility of being absorbed by a stage performance rests on the fact that we retain the distinction between actor and character. But the screen performer is projected. This is the prestige of photogenesis and of the medium of photography as the ontological basis of film. On the screen we don't have the sense of an actor occupying a role; all we have is the role. We might recognize a human physiognomy, but that physiognomy is a screened something and whatever it is, it is not fully human; or at least it is not fully

[36]A further point is worth elaborating here: for Cavell the possibility of candidness is a central concern to the kind of modernist aesthetic that Cavell invokes and adopts throughout *The World Viewed*, and specifically to questions regarding the quality of presentness in a work. Presentness is what Courbet and Manet sought, Cavell tells us (*WV*, pp. 41–2. Cavell borrows the term presentness from Michael Fried's discussion of art in his seminal "Art and Object"—see *WV* p. 22, footnote 12); and it is also what film seeks to the extent that as an artistic medium film forgoes traditional themes and myths. Or, as Cavell puts it, familiar Hollywood cycles and plots "no longer naturally establish conviction in our presentness to the world." (*WV*, p. 60.) Whether this claim of criticism is accurate or not, Cavell nonetheless relies on the idea of presentness as a condition for establishing a conviction in the world. To acknowledge the claim of an other is thus to admit of the other's presentness to us in the same way that to regard a film with conviction is also to admit of its presentness. Candidness, I want to say, is a shorthand for the desire to establish conviction of our presentness to the world.

[37]*WV*, p. 28. I should point out that in these passages there seems to be an equivalence in Cavell's use of the terms "presence" and "presentness."

human in the way in which our matters of course allow us to think of it as fully human.

What it is, actually, is a transcription of something real. This is the theoretical point that sources Cavell's insights into the medium of film and that helps explain the nature of photogenesis and film's transubstantiation of humans into human somethings.[38] Recall that for Cavell the basis of film is a sequence of individual photographic stills, "a succession of automatic world projections." Early in *The World Viewed*, Cavell reinforces this claim by making an important distinction between a representation of reality and a transcription of it; a distinction that parallels the difference between a painting and a photograph. At stake in this difference is the issue of likeness, as Stephen Mulhall explains: "To say that a photographed object is not present to someone looking at the photograph as it once was to the camera, or to the person using that camera, is just to say that the photograph of Garbo is not Garbo in the flesh; to say that, none the less, the photographed object is present in the photograph is to say that when we look at a photograph of an object, we see that object (that particular real thing, the original item present to the camera) and not some surrogate for it, some aspect or apparition or likeness of it."[39] That a photograph is not a likeness of an object but a transcription of it means that photography offers an object up to view in such a way that human subjectivity is entirely absent from the presentation of the object; that is, the mechanical basis of photography eliminates the human hand by no longer making the manufacture of the image apparent. Here is Cavell: "Photography overcame subjectivity in a way undreamed of by painting, a way that could not satisfy painting, one which does not so much defeat the act of painting as escape it altogether: by automatism, by removing the human agent from the task of reproduction."[40]

Another way of stating this is that photography overcame painting because it accomplished painting's fantasy of defeating mannerism, and it did so by ensuring mannerism's defeat through the automaticity of the medium. If, as Cavell iterates, modernist painting since Manet wanted to "forgo likeness ... because the illusions it had learned to create did not

---

[38]Cinema's transubstantiation of humans into human somethings through photogenic transcription is the medium-specific feature of film that allows Cavell to affirm that films are a moving image of scepticism. In other words, what film does is project the experience of not being able to access the source of an other's experience and therefore not being able to know if the other is human or not. Cavell's conclusion, which I get to later on in the essay, is that we are all human somethings to one another. My claim that the ability to relate to the inaccuracy of that something—to bear and be/hold it, if you will—is the kernel of insight of Cavell's ethics of appearances.

[39]Mulhall, *Stanley Cavell: Philosophy's Recounting of the Ordinary*, p. 224.

[40]*WV*, p. 23.

provide the conviction in reality, the connection with reality, it craved,"[41] then the transcriptural power of photography was able to assure the forgoing of likeness by automatically capturing objects upon the filmic patina. The automatic nature of photography is such that there is no mediation between picture and real world in the way in which there is in painting via the presence of the painter's hand (visible in the brushstrokes, for instance). This is not to say that a picture is an objective representation of the real world; rather, it is to say that it is a transcription of it.

By describing the photogenic transcription of reality characteristic of the medium of film in this way Cavell wants to emphasize a bifurcated feature of modern art; that is, art's twofold commitment in maintaining conviction in our connection with the world and with one another.[42] To put the point slightly differently, the aesthetic project of art in the modern period is to establish a conviction of our presence in the world by guaranteeing our facingness of it, of having to face up to it, and have views of it; that is, of be/holding it. And I take this to be the ethical point of Cavell's insistence on the relationship between filmic and everyday candidness. To the extent that film is a modernist art that compels conviction, we cannot separate that desire or ambition from our own similar desires and ambitions for accessing the conviction of others. And the fact remains that film isolates those desires and ambitions not as a problem that needs to be overcome but as a fact that needs to be admitted and faced up to. That is, to the extent that when we watch a film we are facing a screen, the fact of film compels our having to also face the fact that we are interfacing with a photogenic presence, a projected image; and that try as we might, we cannot overpass or transpose and transgress the limits of that projection. The candidness of acting, in other words, is the candidness and frontality of facingness; that is, the candidness of having to face a presence whose limit qua projection cannot be transgressed; not, that is, because there is a normative injunction against such forms of transgression, but simply because the medium of a projection is such that it cannot be penetrated. How might we access the presentness of a Bogart, or a Monroe or a Brangelina other than through their projection? Those who try are usually called stalkers.

Stalkers might also characterize the psychological makeup of those whose desire for the verifiability of human somethings wants to transgress the limits of a projection by refusing to face up to the immediacy of candidness. "When I felt I had to get to the other's sensation apart from his giving expression to it (as if that were the way to insure certainty, or as if the way to insure his candidness was to prevent *his* playing any role in his

---

[41] *WV*, p. 21.

[42] This is one way to understand an otherwise cryptic remark that Cavell makes in the first chapter of *The World Viewed*: namely, that "Art now exists in the condition of philosophy." (*WV*, p. 14).

expression)" Cavell affirms, "my wish was to penetrate his behavior with my reference to his sensation, it order to reach the same spot *his* reference to himself occupies *before*, so to speak, the sensation gets expressed."[43] My wish, in other words, is to touch or to withhold, to index and indicate, the source of the sensation before it even gets articulated; that is, in its purity, unmediated by language. Not unlike the doubting Thomas who declares that he must thrust his hands into the wounds of Christ in order to believe, the sceptic's refusal to accept the projection of candidness as sufficient to the conditions for facing an other's presence makes the other qua human something a problem. Cavell's sceptic is a star-stalker (the analogy is mine, not his) who is unable to forgo the desire to touch and to admit that the expression isn't a representation of the sensation but, rather, *is* it. That is, Cavell's conception of candidness makes available the fact that there is no distinction between expression and sensation; that an expression doesn't reference or mediate or represent a sensation, but transcribes it.

"What is the problem of the other," Cavell asks, "if it is not a problem of certainty?"[44] That is, if there isn't the desire to penetrate the other's behavior with my reference to her sensation, is there a problem of the other? Is the other a problem? The condition of candidness vis-à-vis film actors sidesteps the issue all together because the medium of film as a succession of world projections *on a screen* is such that it mechanically interrupts the desire to penetrate the source of the other's projection. This, as I will suggest shortly, *is* what the silver screen screens. But why is it that we don't want to forgo accessing such conditions of certainty in everyday encounters? Why is it, in other words, that the other *is* a problem for us? Or, to put it slightly differently, why is it that we refuse to regard human somethings and want to know them instead?

Our modern condition is such that a pictured soul does not satisfy our cravings for certain knowledge in the face of an other. Alienation, we might say, is another name for that sense of dissatisfaction with pictures. But the filmic advenience *is* a picture of a soul that—if Cavell (and Warshow, amongst many) is right about the nature of one's experience of film—does afford conviction in the face of a projected candidness. One is convinced by the human something despite our not being able to verify the identity of that something. When viewing a movie the projected picture of a soul—the advenience of an appearance—might provide us with uncertainty or anxiety, but not doubt. To doubt and to be unsure are not the same thing: to be unsure is an invitation to move about; to doubt is a warning that it is better to stand still. And if there is one thing that a moving picture does is that it affords occasions to move about. As a succession of world projections, the condition of film is motility. What is it, then, that makes

[43] *Claim*, p. 342.
[44] *Claim*, p. 353.

conviction possible in the face of a projected advenience and that we resist in our everyday encounters with one another?

There is a sense in which I am unsure of how to answer the question simply because I am convinced that we are all human somethings to one another. I can't tell you how I know,[45] in other words; such is the nature of aesthetic conviction. And yet, I search for words that express a sensation and that make my conviction more palpable, more authoritative, even to myself. I can't tell you how I know because in my expressing an experience I am conveying what I sense, I am throwing a projection of my human somethingness at you. I can't tell you how I know because my voiced expressions can only register an experience of sensation, not evince its source. I can convey only the what of an experience, in other words, not the how of my coming to awareness of that experience. The latter is an inhuman expectation that only someone like Jesus might have been able to satisfy for Thomas by appearing to him with his open wounds, after raising from the dead.[46]

But I am not an inhuman divinity; I am a human something.

Part Four
Blankets, screens, and projections

As a human something, one of the things that I do is project a world and in doing so I body forth a presentness of the order of an appearance that advenes. I screen myself to you, if you will, and the screening of my projection, as Cavell states, "already puts a seam in human experience."[47] The seam of projection is the seam of the screen that bears or be/holds the advenience of an appearance. The screen's seam is also the dividing line between intelligible and unintelligible entities. Cavell's query of what becomes of things on film—the title of an essay already cited—might lead us here: filmic photogenesis is a mode of becoming that transubstantiates screened things into unintelligible somethings; not irrational or insensible somethings, but objects whose sensibility is not of the order of intelligibility. I might put the point this way: By projecting a picture of a human somethingness (or soul) I hold up a view, I bear it, for you to be/hold.

---

[45]Cavell, *Claim*, p. 358.

[46]I remain hesitant and say "might have" because, as Glenn Most's study of the iconography and exegesis of the Doubting Thomas shows, there is nothing in the Biblical passage that suggests that Thomas actually took Jesus up on his offer to penetrate his wounds. The only evidence we have of this impossible touch is the iconographic tradition associated with the Biblical passage. See *Doubting Thomas*. Cambridge, MA: Harvard University Press, 2005 (especially pp. 28–73 and 155–214).

[47]*Claim*, p. 425.

In a section entitled "Projecting a Word" of *The Claim of Reason*, Cavell describes how one of the complexities surrounding ordinary language—the language we use on a diurnal basis to express ourselves—is its capacity (and our capacity) to handle inaccuracy by inserting words in situations that are not of their matter of course. We say that we can "feed the monkey" but we also say that we "feed the meter"; and so we project the word "feed" into diverse contexts.[48] Though we might be able to explain such practices in terms of the metaphorical power of language, this does not get at what Cavell might mean by "projecting a word." The difference between a projection and a metaphor is the difference between the metaphorical power of transference and the ingressional power of a projectile. The *metapherein* of metaphor does something extraordinary or "unnatural":[49] it transfers a meaning from one pole to another. In doing so, an intelligibility is established. The projection of a word does not transfer a meaning but throws the word into new contexts; there is a different order of movement here that bequeaths a different mode of response. A metaphor commands comprehension, a projection commends be/holding.

In the example that Cavell gives of "feeding the meter," we could just as easily say "put money in the meter," thus applying a more general verb to the sentence which gets us just as far with communicating our intention or meaning. But to do so would be to refuse a projection, to not want to hold it up, or to want to deprive ourselves of a certain manner of be/holding. For Cavell we are always in a position to either admit or refuse a projection:

> An object or activity or event onto or into which a concept is projected, must *invite* or *allow* that projection; in the way in which, for an object to be (called) an art object, it must allow or invite the experience and behavior which are appropriate or necessary to our concepts of the appreciation or contemplation or absorption ... of an art object. What kind of object will allow or invite or be fit for that contemplation, etc. is no more accidental or arbitrary than what kind of object will be fit to serve as (what we call) a "shoe."[50]

There is an indirect correlation for Cavell between our capacities to admit a projection of a concept—to look and see it—and our abilities to be receptive to a work of art. That connection, I want to argue, is akin to the affinity that develops between projected image and screen: one of the things that a screen does is allow or admit a projection—the screen holds it in place, if you will, handles it, or concerns itself with it. For us to invite or allow a projection indicates a microcultural practice of interface with an advening

---

[48] *Claim*, pp. 180–90.
[49] *Claim*, p. 190.
[50] *Claim*, p. 183.

world; it indicates that our ethical practices project certain aesthetic sensibilities, and vice versa. Here the words "invite" and "allow" work hard to express the plurivalent sensibilities of admittance that one invokes in microcultural practices of aesthetic receptivity. It is just as easy for us to disregard an appearance is it is to be/hold it, and just because something is projected does not mean that that projectile will accede—not every surface is as effective as a screen. An art object, on this account, has nothing specific about it other than a capacity to call our attention, to call us to attend to it. Cavell insists in a very discreet manner that projection is not the property of an object just as no one particular kind of object—say a photograph—is necessarily an art object. An object's capacity to project regards a set of interrelated handlings between spectator and object that mirror the relationship between projection and screen. To admit an appearance—to invite or allow a projection—is to act like a screen does, it means to bear the weight of what appears in the most delicate and discriminating manner.

Here I am reminded of another of Cavell's screens in his treatment of Frank Capra's '*It Happened One Night*' (1934)—a discussion that focuses on a blanket that, Cavell wants to say, is a certain kind of barrier that screens the two protagonists of the movie. The scene of the movie in question involves Clark Gable and Claudette Colbert who are unmarried, on the run, and hiding out for the night in a motel room with two beds. Bed-time is upon them. Clark Gable's character devises the use of a blanket as a barrier between the two beds to create a space of intimacy that screens one half of the room from the other: "behold the Walls of Jericho!". The exclamation is an innuendo: the Walls of Jericho were blown down by a horn and the fact that 1934 is also the year that Hollywood accepted the Production Code (as Cavell points out) and thus self-censoring makes the sexual innuendo unflappable. But the innuendo, though relevant, is not the point.

The issue of the essay is the Kantian problem of knowledge and how "there is between me and this realm of reason also something that may present itself as a barrier—the fact that I cannot reach this realm *alone*."[51] The suggestion is that perhaps our not wanting to be alone is the result of our inability or unwillingness to bear this "not-knowing." But there is also the suggestion that our inabilities to know are conditioned by those same somethings that screen me from you. In the case of '*It Happened One Night*' those somethings are the individual human bodies photogenically occupied by Colbert and Gable. In other words, the desire for knowing is conditioned and impeded by the presence of others. I can begin to know what it means to know because the presence of others occasions the

[51] Cavell, *Pursuits*, p. 79.

expression of my experiences; but it is precisely the limits set by a body that guarantees the uknowability of an other.

This Kantian dilemma is projected by the prop of the barrier-blanket that Gable fashions in order to separate the two halves of the room and that "works—blocking a literal view of the figure, but receiving physical impressions from it, and activating our imagination of that real figure as we watch in the dark—as a movie screen works."[52] The blanket in this case is not only a barrier between human bodies; it also projects a metaphysical barrier that signifies the impenetrability of other people, of a certain inaccessibility of the other to me, despite their appearing before me—there, standing in front of me, screened, if you will. Everything hinges on our sense of admittance of this screened projection and—ultimately—of my admittance of the fact that I cannot penetrate an other's behavior so as to access the source of her sensations, that I cannot know an other in that way, nor can I generate criteria that will allow me to know whether her ability to reference an experience—to give voice and project a sensation of suffering, or joy, or humiliation, or grief—is accurate or not.

And the point here is that the medium-specific relation of projection and screen is itself a projection of how we relate to the advenience of appearances. The screen invites a projection but it also creates a seam, a blocked or cropped view: Gable can't see Colbert undressing, though he is painfully aware of her presence when the blanket is dented and rippled by her movements as she disrobes; just as the audience can only see impressions on filmic patina projected on a screen. The barrier-blanket is a prop that reminds us how our inclination to relate our experiences to others in a knowing manner is screened (i.e. veiled or impeded somehow); what would it mean here to know the blanket? At best, we can relate our experience of the blanket's foldings and its sensorial affinities. But once we have done that, have we related a knowledge? Rather than knowing an other's identity, I want to say, we admit their advenience as a screen admits a projection.

Cavell had already worked out some of the ethical, aesthetic and ontological implications of the relationship between projection, screen and knowledge in *The World Viewed*. There, in a short but incisive chapter entitled "Photograph and Screen," he claims the following:

> The world of a moving picture is screened. The screen is not a support, not like a canvas; there is nothing to support, that way. It holds a projection, as light as light. A screen is a barrier. What does the silver screen screen? It screens me from the world it holds – that is, makes me invisible. And it screens that world from me. That the projected world does not exist (now) is its only difference from reality. (There

[52] Cavell, *Pursuits*, p. 82.

> is no feature, or set of features, in which it differs. Existence is not a predicate.) Because it is the field of a photograph, the screen has no frame; that is to say, no border. Its limits are not so much the edges of a given shape as they are the limitations, or capacity, of a container. The screen *is* a frame; the frame is the whole field of the screen – as a frame of film is the whole field of a photograph, like the frame of the loom or a house. In this sense, the screen-frame is a mold, or form. (*WV*, pp. 24–5)

The screen bears a projection—it handles it by supporting its radiance. This is one sense of how a movie pictures something screened: it is light projected upon a smooth surface. But a screen is also a limit, or a blanket. In order to see the projected light, the spectator must be screened from the projection—one could say, here, that the be/holder or viewer does not count to the projection, she is made invisible to it. The light does not shine on the viewer; rather, the shining of the projected light upon the screen obscures the be/holder. This is a necessary condition for viewing a projected image. And it is only through this projection onto the screen that the appearance of the image can advene. That is, in order for the appearance to advene, I must be obscured; my *I* that is me—my subjectivity in light of this light, with all its expectations and desires to touch, to hold, or to grasp the appearance in a knowing way—must be darkened, withdrawn, absorbed. This is the significance of the screen's capacity to screen me from the projected world, to render me invisible to it. The "I" is absorbed, obscured—or, better yet, it is discomposed—when the projection is projected. And this screening also screens that world from me. The two worlds cannot touch because screened from one another: "existence is not a predicate." The presentness of a projection is not predicated on my having to be present, to be visible, to be there to touch it. The appearance advenes and the best that I can do is admit the projection once it is screened; but to do so is not to touch it, or to penetrate it, or to expose the image. If we expose the image, the appearance vanishes; just as if we were to let ambient light into a room where an image is being projected, the image would no longer be visible. There is nothing we can do to penetrate the appearance and anything we might do risks disturbing or destroying it. This is the lightness of the projection that advenes but does not admit illumination. We must be very careful in a curatorial kind of way when we be/hold projections. The screen is a limit to our knowing and to our being able to handle the world in a knowing manner—to our wanting to contain the world by knowing it. The screen thus has no frame (as might a canvas) but is said *to be* the frame that holds the projection. But what is the nature of this holding and how can one hold something as light as light?

One holds it by attending to it; by turning our attentions to it, by allowing ourselves to be absorbed or be/held by it, by admitting it. In his account of the ontological relation between screen and projection I see Cavell making an ethical claim about our aesthetic ways of relating to one another that indicates a curatorial handling of appearances: here Cavell projects "projection" by throwing the idea of film as a succession of automatic world projections into his reflections on our ethical handlings of one another. This is what I meant when, some pages ago, I suggested that for Cavell film is an ethical medium: the medium specificity of film as "a succession of automatic world projections"[53] speaks to his insistence that as human somethings we, ourselves, automatically and successively project worlds to and at one another. It also speaks to his declaration that "film is a moving image of scepticism." Here the function of the barrier-screen is crucial because "in screening reality, film screens its givenness from us; it holds reality from us, it holds reality before us, i.e. withholds reality before us."[54]

Film holds and withholds reality by projecting it and the barrier-screen supports and withholds that projection. Projection is thus a kind of filmic handling of everyday life; it is the handling of a luminosity that is as light as light and that touches as light might, but that also invites a kind of touch that cannot penetrate. What would it mean to penetrate light? At best, we could cast a shadow, or create another, superimposed projection. Here I am taken by Cavell's expression of a world held by the screen. To the extent that the world is a collection of projected appearances, it is a world of surfaces whose depths cannot be plunged and plundered. And yet, it is not merely superficial either. There is a profundity of surface here that calls for a different order of hapticity—for the kind of handling that is attentive to the adventitious dimensions of appearances.

It is this mode of be/holding that sources a politics of appearances. The standing forth of an appearance projects a luminosity that calls our attention. "Early in its history the cinema discovered the possibility of *calling* attention to persons and parts of persons and objects"; Cavell explains; and then adds, "but it is equally a possibility of the medium not to call attention to them but, rather, to let the world happen, to let its parts draw attention to themselves according to their natural weight."[55] Such is the nature of cinematic absorption. Attending to the natural weight of an advenience—by which I mean bearing its weight, be/holding it as a screen bears and holds the light of a projection—requires a willingness to care for that which stands forth and a manner of curatorship that resists the temptation to touch the image in order to expose and relate it.

---

[53] *WV*, p. 72.
[54] *WV*, p. 189.
[55] *WV*, p. 25.

Part Five
A striptease of misery

Capra's blanket doesn't merely work as a barrier because it represents the threshold of what we can or cannot know, it also expresses the idea that there are things about ourselves which are visible and others which are not, and that one of the most common of human practices is to adorn our lives with visibilities and invisibilites that intimate our presentness. This is, perhaps, also the lesson of Wittgenstein's famous declaration that, "the human body is the best picture of the human soul,"[56] which, in turn, sources Cavell's discussion of the perfected automaton in *The Claim of Reason*. The emphasis here is on picturing and the fact that a body qua picture doesn't hide anything. That is, it's not like the body hides the soul and that we must find ways to break through to what's been hidden. Rather, "the mythology according to which the body is a picture implies that the soul may be hidden not because the body essentially conceals it but because it essentially reveals it. The soul may be invisible to us the way something absolutely present may be invisible to us."[57] Another way of stating this is that the soul may be invisible because it is apparent; it is invisible despite its appearance and what makes its invisibility relevant is not the body's obstruction but rather our unwillingness to be/hold its advenience—to look and see it, or come face to face with its conspicuousness, obtrusiveness, or obstinacy; that is, it's not a question of unveiling or uncovering a body so as to get to the soul, but of admitting of our anxiety in the face of its presentness.

Recall, as I did a few paragraphs ago, that Cavell's ontology of film declares film to be a succession of automatic world projections. The medium-specificity of film (via the camera and the spooling projector) guarantees that automaticity. Moreover, the automaticity of world projections that is the spooling of an imprinted patina of film also helps explain how film is a moving image of scepticism: we do not see the projector; though apparent, it remains unavailable to us—it is part of the unthought of what film affords thinking. Gilles Deleuze describes the automaticity of film thusly: "And it is precisely the automaton, petrified in this way, that thought seizes from the outside, as the unthinkable in thought. This question is very different from that of distancing; it is the question of properly cinematographic automatism, and its consequences. It is the material automatism of images which produces from the outside

[56] Ludwig Wittgenstein, *Philosophical Investigations, Part II*, p. 178.

[57] *Claim*, p. 369. Once again, and at the risk of repeating myself *ad nauseum*, I want to mark Cavell's emphasis in this passage on absolute presence as an experience of conviction and the fact that the idea of "absolute presence" is not at all synonymous with totality.

a thought which it imposes, as the unthinkable in our intellectual automatism."[58]

Now, far from wanting to suggest that Deleuze and Cavell are arguing the same point, I do want to emphasize how Deleuze's insights about the relationship between cinematographic automatism and the unthought share a conspicuous connection with Cavell's petrifying parable of the perfected automaton and the conditions of the unthought that score that tale. For, to be able to see the automaton as a human something (the way in which we see actors projected on a screen as human somethings and the way in which—ultimately—we can only bear witness to each other *as* human somethings) we must be willing to occupy what Deleuze is describing as the interstice of the unthought. For Cavell, the unthought is pictured as a "strip-tease of misery"[59]—the experience of horror and dread—that describes the dismantling of the automaton by the craftsman and the interaction between the automaton and the first person narrator of the parable. Or better put, the unthought is the interval of arrested absorption between sensation and reference (i.e. the sensation of pain and the uncertainty as to whether the body of the perfected automaton is the reference of pain or not).[60]

Without rehearsing the parable here, we recall that it is a story of a man (the narrator) who is shown by a master craftsman his latest invention, what might at first telling best be described as a cyborg. The question of the cyborg's humanness is at issue throughout the parable and is made evident by the master craftsman's desire to put on display the cyborg's authenticity by prying his chest cavity open with a knife. At first encounter, the cyborg doesn't make a sound; but by the third encounter, the cyborg exclaims: "No more. It hurts, it hurts too much. I'm sick of being a human guinea pig, I mean a guinea pig human."

The parable is compelling on many levels but the points most relevant for our purposes are, first of all, that it is episodic in structure in the way that a succession of world projections is serial. This matters not simply because the seriality of the parable further links it to Cavell's insights about modernist art and the automatic nature of film;[61] but also because seriality makes explicit the in-betweenness of film images. Cavell's parable is discontinuous, and we don't know—have no way of knowing, don't know how to know—what happens in between takes, so to speak. That is, we don't know what the craftsman does in order to make the automaton appear more astonishingly real.

---

[58] Gilles Deleuze. *Cinema 2: The Time-Image*. Hugh Tomlinson and Robert Galeta trans. Minnesota, MN: The University of Minnesota Press, 1997, pp. 178–9.
[59] *Claim*, p. 404.
[60] The relevant page numbers are *Claim* pp. 403–11.
[61] The relevant section here is "Excursus: Some Modernist Painting" in *The World Viewed*, pp. 108–18.

"Do I intervene?" is the interrogative that punctuates the end of each episode and Cavell uses it to mark the experience of the unthought in the face of being struck by that aspect of the automaton that allows the narrator to see his physiognomy as human. It is a question addressed to the reader that works like an irrational cut in film: that is, it doesn't expect an answer but forces the question of how much likeness we need in order to accept a human something as forming a picture of humanness. The episodic nature of the parable punctuated by the question of intervention marks the interstice of the unthought.

A second relevant feature: the seriality of the parable relates to the seriality of film. By this I don't mean to suggest that all films are related as if they are all part of a series; rather, I mean to suggest that to the extent that the medium of film deploys the interrelated flow of individual stills, the automaticity of film is itself of the nature of the unthought. Here Deleuze is once again helpful when discussing the in-betweenness of film: "Between two actions, between two affections, between two perceptions, between two visual images, between two sound images, between the sound and the visible: make the indiscernible, that is the frontier, visible."[62] It is a madness that is projected by Cavell's picture of the perfected automaton who—interestingly enough—is portrayed or said to stand between the narrator and the craftsman. The perfected automaton is a picture of the untenable/ungraspable/untouchable in-between where criteria disappoint.

But the parable of the perfected automaton relates to Cavell's ontology of film in one further way (actually, there are many more, but I'll stop here). It is a projection of the body as a picture of a human soul. The automaton is a human something, he is an interval between human and inhuman, but he is also a picture of a human soul. Not, that is, because there is something inherently other-worldly about the parable—on the contrary, there is nothing here that makes one think of anything other than our worldly lives (that is Cavell's point). The body of the automaton is a picture of a human soul because nothing of his body will give us a final, authoritative clue as to whether and if he is fully human in the way in which our matters of course recommend what it means to be fully human. In the same way, nothing about an individual body will ever satisfy the conditions of absolute knowledge about humanness despite the fact that there is nothing other than a body that projects humanness. The automaton is an artificial body, a persona, a something in a human guise.[63] I might put the matter this way: between our projections of our humanness there exists an interval that makes explicit our human somethingness; at this interval the *metapherein*

[62] *Cinema–2*, p. 180.

[63] Needless to add, there is a kinship here to Hobbes's treatment of artificial persons. See my elaboration of the aesthetic dimensions of Hobbes's theory of representation in *Leviathan* in my *The Poetics of Political Thinking* (Duke University Press, 2006).

of inference—the metaphorical power of transitivity that allows transport from picture to identity—is unavailable.

Thus the irrelevance of the question, "how do I know?" (irrelevant because I can never settle it). I don't know if the perfected automaton is really human because my anxiety over whether or not I should intervene speaks to the anxiety of the unthought that appears in-between the picture of a human body and the soul—that interval of discomposition of the matters of course that guarantee a correspondence of sensation and reference, between expression and accuracy.

I take the tuition of Cavell's parable to be the following: that the capacity to be punctured by an aspect of humanness, in the way that we may be struck by an aspect of color or line in a painting, is characteristic of the advenience of an appearance; that being struck by an advenience is a sufficient condition for the admittance of human somethings in our lives; that we are all human somethings to one another; that our refusal to admit of the advenience of an appearance is tied to our anxiety over verifiability in the face of the unthought; and finally, that such a refusal is a disregard or a non-acceptance of what other human somethings offer up to view as potentially human, as an unfinished (or perhaps even new) aspect of human. As I have outlined it thus far, Cavell's view of appearances portrays a conviction of the infinitude of human somethingness.

Three final points before I bring these remarks to a close: the ability to admit of an advenience—to be/hold or bear its weight—regards our forgoing of the demands of interpretation and understanding. To admit that "the body is the best picture of the human soul" asks of our admittance of the sufficiency of immediacy, that what I see is what I get, and that my relation to an other does not require my penetrating into the depths of her soul in order to establish the veracity of her candidness. I might say that the signification is inconsequential to my admittance of the automaton.

To get a better sense of what I mean here, we might return to Cavell's considerations of candidness, this time with reference to some modernist painters (the relevant artists here are Morris Louis, Kenneth Noland, Jules Olitski, Frank Stella). Referring to the kind of availability or "openness" that modernist painting avails, Cavell affirms "the quality I have in mind might be expressed as openness achieved through instantaneousness—which is a way of characterizing the *candid*. The candid has a reverse feature as well: that it must occur independently of me or any audience, that it must be complete without me, in that sense *closed* to me." The perfected automaton qua human something satisfies both these opposing criteria: he is open to the narrator because affronting him but also because he is being opened up and put on display by the craftsman's knife-wielding hand, prying his chest open for the narrator to see his insides. And the automaton is closed to the narrator because regardless of his being put on display, he is complete without him. The instantaneous simultaneity of openness and closedness suggests that the automaton is what it is regardless of my justifying him as such, regardless of my confirming his or her significance. Candidness withstands verification.

The second point: all of the requirements of justifying criteria for acceptance in the face of the advenience of an appearance result from the anxiety that comes with the *noli me tangere* of aesthetic experience. The advenience of an appearance, in other words, ushers into our life experiences an interval of the unthought that, as I have argued, discomposes our composed trajectories of sensation and reference. I take this to be the lesson of Cavell's reliance on Heidegger's discussions of conspicuousness, obtrusiveness and obstinacy of things in the world. The perfected automaton capitulates all of these markers of anxiety as it punctures our picture of humanness.

Finally, a few words about my use of the language of the *punctum*. The reference is, of course, to Roland Barthes's little book on photography, *Camera Lucida*. As I remarked in my introductory comments, I read Cavell's aesthetic and ethical writings as overlapping (recall that I stated forthrightly that *The Claim of Reason* and *The World Viewed* are, in fact, the same work). In doing so, I want to situate Cavell's insights within the context of what I have called an ethics of appearances: a tradition of reflection that takes as its starting point the experience of the advenience of an appearance and the discomposition of the relationship between sensation and reference that such an experience occasions. Cavell's reliance on Wittgenstein's discussion of aspect dawning and his referring to this discussion as being "struck by an aspect"[64] is evidence of his commitment to the kind of experience that Barthes's *punctum* expresses and that I have characterized as the experience of advenience characteristic of an ethics of appearances. The strikingness of an appearance, in other words, ushers the problem of candidness—that the appearance is wholly there and that there is nothing else hiding about—precisely because the sensation that it solicits is one of conviction without banisters or criteria of judgment; it is a *punctum* that strikes us, punctures us, wounds us.

I take this to be most compelling aspect of the perfected automaton parable to the extent that it reiterates and rehearses the relationship between advenience and candidness. The narrator's repeated astonishment (one might, at this point, even say his being struck or absorbed) in the face of the striptease of misery is a marker of a having to face up to the immediacy of an interval of the unthought when our abilities to rely on established criteria to appraise an event, thing or subject are discomposed.

To put this slightly differently, Cavell's indebtedness to a tradition of an ethics of appearances makes explicit the tension between meaning and

---

[64] *Claim*, p. 357.

immediacy when facing an other. It also makes explicit how our microcultural practices of interface come into tension with our expectations of justification and verifiability. Our capacity to be/hold an advenience that appears is rooted in our ability to forgo the tensions between meaning and immediacy, and to forgo the expectations of profundity when affronted with the picture of a soul. There is, here, a curatorial mood at play that makes the anxieties of undecidedness and uncertainty (of inaccuracy and intangibility) worth regarding; that is, worth looking at, bearing, and holding up to view.

Conclusion

I take as central to Cavell's ethical reflections and writings the insight that the events of absorption in our lives bespeak our attitudes of regard of one another: that our capacities to see aspects informs our willingness to see human somethings *as* human; that our willingness to regard an other requires our admittance that we can never get at what is fully human in an other and that the best we can do is to see a human *as* a human something. Yet another way of stating this is that our microcultural practices of handling and be/holding of the advenience of an appearance speaks to our willingness to handle and be/hold the appearance of human somethings. Hence the importance of film to Cavell as a medium for ethical reflection. What film does—in spades—is make the be/holding of appearances its principal activity; the art of film, I might say, is the art of handling appearances. Projection is another name we might give to such an art.

Philosophy's avoidance of film at the height of the professionalization of the discipline in the American academy is a thorn in Cavell's side. He seems stupefied by this omission, especially given the fact that American culture was (and is) so taken with cinema. Therein lies the starting point for his aesthetic and ethical investigations into an ontology of projection. The point here is that in disregarding film, the discipline has disregarded the ontological question of what occasions reflection: in light of what (under what light) does reflection begin, if at all?

For Cavell, this is a central issue not so much of "first philosophy" but of the relationship between reflection and human experience, and of the place of the unthought in our reflections. One might say that for Cavell the unthought of aesthetic experience—with all its uncertainties and intangibilities—curates our thinking about our relationships with one another. This is why the medium of film is so important to his ethical reflections: an ontology of projection insists upon the intangible hapticity of the *noli me tangere* making it so that what appears on film, on the screen-barrier, are human somethings and collected things about whose relationship to reality we cannot really have access, like we cannot have access to our expressions of sensation and their correspondence with reality. Film, in other words, offers a succession of automatic world projections in the same way that life affords encounters with a series of perfected automatons; that is, life affords everyday encounters with others whose humanness I cannot guarantee and need not guarantee, just like I cannot guarantee my humanness to others (and should not have to do so). To live a life means to project our human somethings (our voices, our appearances, our *personas*, etc.) to one another. Our capacity to bear and be/hold those projections as does the barrier-screen of cinema means a willingness to admit of the anxieties of the unthought as constitutive of our human something and as constitutive of our relations with other human somethings.

Recall that the engine that makes the perfected automaton example work is that through time, at various episodes, the automaton starts to feel more and more like a real human, more authentic, less like something human and more like a human something. This is the master craftman's prestige; his conjuring trick. The narrator doesn't know why or how the automaton seems more "really human," though he is convinced that he is. That something can be experienced as convincingly real without a ground for that sensation is another way of describing the sensation of conviction that arises from aesthetic experience. Art's prestige—its conjuring trick—is conviction without ground. This is the great discovery of modern aesthetics that Cavell projects into his ethical thinking (and, *ceteris paribus*, into his reading of Wittgenstein). It is in this way, and for the reasons outlined above, that I have argued that Cavell is a carrier of a minoritarian tradition of ethical reflection I call an ethics of appearances. The capacity and willingness to make the event of the advenience of an appearance count as the uncertain ground of ethical reflection is one of that tradition's key features.

From these insights some implications arise: that a human life is a series of automatic world projections; that our capacity to be/hold an advenience speaks to our capacities to bear the candidness of one another's presentness; that we regularly engage in microcultural practices of interface which source our curatorial attitudes of be/holding; that be/holding an advenience regards an intangible hapticity and a forgoing of our desire to penetrate the source of an appearance's advenience so as to possess a more authentic or accurate knowledge of it (that is, so as to confirm that its intimacy is grounded in something real); that the experience of advenience is an experience of absorption that discomposes those matters of course that guarantee a correspondence between sensation and reference; and, finally (for now), that our expressions of value in reaction to our absorptive be/holdings express a curatorial mood that forms those matters of course that an advenience discomposes. These are the central tenets of an ethics of appearances that are of concern to an aesthetics of politics.

References

Baudelaire, C. (2004), *The Painter of Modern Life and Other Essays*. New York: Phaidon Press.

Cavell, S. (1979), *The World Viewed* (Enlarged Edition). Cambridge, MA: Harvard University Press.

——(1981), *The Pursuits of Happiness*. Cambridge, MA: Harvard University Press.

——(1984), *Themes Out of School: Effects and Causes*. Chicago, IL: University of Chicago.

——(1999), *The Claim of Reason*. New York: Oxford University Press.

——(2002), *Must We Mean What We Say?* Cambridge, UK: University of Cambridge.

Deleuze, G. (1997), *Cinema 2: The Time-Image*. Translated by Hugh Tomlinson and Robert Galeta. Minnesota, MN: The University of Minnesota Press.

Heidegger, M. (1988), *The Basic Problems of Phenomenology*. Translated by Albert Hofstadter. Bloomington, IN: Indiana University Press.

Honig, B. (February 2007), "Between Decision and Deliberation: Political Paradox in Democratic Theory," *American Political Science Review* 101, No. 1.

McCumber, J. (2001), "Philosophy's Family Secret" in *Time in the Ditch: American Philosophy and the McCarthy Era*. Evanston, IL: Northwestern University Press.

Most, G. (2005), *Doubting Thomas*. Cambridge, MA: Harvard University Press.

Mulhall, S. (1994), *Stanley Cavell: Philosophy's Recounting of the Ordinary*. New York: Oxford University Press.

——(2002), *On Film*. New York: Routledge.

Nancy, J.-L. (2008), *Noli me tangere: On the Raising of the Body*. Translated by Sarah Clift, Pascale-Anne Brault, Michael Naas. New York, NY: Fordham University Press.

Norris, A. ed. (2006), *The Claim to Community: Essays on Stanley Cavell's Political Philosophy*. Stanford, CA: Stanford University Press.

Panagia, D. (2006), *The Poetics of Political Thinking*. Durham, NC: Duke University Press.

Rodowick, D. N. (2007), *The Virtual Life of Film*. Cambridge, MA: Harvard University Press.

Rothman, W. and Keane, M. (2000), *Reading Cavell's The World Viewed: A Philosophical Perspective on Film*. Detroit, MI: Wayne State University Press.

Warshow, R. (2001), *The Immediate Experience: Movies, Comics, Theatre and Other Aspects of Popular Culture*. Cambridge, MA: Harvard University Press.

Wittgenstein, L. (1958), *Philosophical Investigations: Third Edition*. Translated by G. E. M. Anscombe. Englewood Cliffs, NJ: Prentice Hall.

——(1965), "A Lecture on Ethics," *The Philosophical Review*, 74 pp. 3–12.

CHAPTER TEN

The aesthetic dimension: Aesthetics, politics, knowledge

Jacques Rancière
University of Paris-VIII

How should we understand the syntagm of my title? Obviously it is not a question of claiming that politics or knowledge must take on an aesthetic dimension or that they have to be grounded in sense, sensation, or sensibility. It is not even a question of stating that they are grounded in the sensible or that the sensible is political as such. What aesthetics refers to is not the sensible. Rather, it is a certain modality, a certain distribution of the sensible. This expression can be understood, at least initially, by turning to the text that has framed the space of aesthetics, though the term was never used there as a substantive. I mean, of course, Kant's *Critique of Judgment,* which I will use as a guiding thread in the construction of a tentatively more comprehensive concept of aesthetics. For now I only wish to draw from this text the three basic elements that make up what I call a distribution of the sensible. First, there is something given, a form that is provided by sense—for instance, the form of a palace as described in section two of Kant's text. Second, the apprehension of this form is not only a matter of sense; rather, sense itself is doubled. The apprehension puts into play a certain relation between what Kant calls faculties: between a faculty that offers the given and a faculty that makes something out of it. For these two faculties the Greek language has only one name, *aesthesis*, the faculty of sense, the capacity to both perceive a given and make sense of it.

Making sense of a sense given, Kant tells us, can be done in three ways. Two of the three ways define a hierarchical order. In the first of these, the faculty of signification rules over the faculty that conveys sensations; the understanding enlists the services of imagination in order to subordinate the sense given. This is the order of knowledge. This order defines a certain view of the palace; the palace is seen as the achievement of an idea imposed on space and on raw materials, as in a plan drafted by an architect. This plan itself is appreciated according to its suitability for the ends of the building. In the second way of making sense, in contrast, the faculty of sensation takes command over the faculty of knowledge. This is the law of desire. This law views the palace as an object of pride, jealousy, or disdain. There is a third way of looking at the palace, a way that sees it and appreciates it neither as an object of knowledge nor as an object of desire. In this case, neither faculty rules over the other; the either/or no longer works. The two faculties agree with each other without any kind of subordination. The spectator may think that the magnificence of the palace is sheer futility; he may oppose its pomp and vanity to the misery of the poor or the sweat of the workers who built it for low wages. But this is not the point. What is at stake here is the specificity of a distribution of the sensible that escapes the hierarchical relationship between a high faculty and a low faculty, that is, escapes in the form of a *positive* neither/nor.

Let us summarize the three points. First, a distribution of the sensible means a certain configuration of the given. Second, this configuration of the given entails a certain relation of sense and sense. That may be conjunctive or disjunctive. The relation is conjunctive when it obeys a certain order of subordination between faculties, a certain manner of playing the game according to established rules. It is disjunctive when the relationship between faculties has no rule. Third, the conjunction or disjunction is also a matter of hierarchy. Either there is a hierarchy between the faculties, which may be overturned, or there is no hierarchy, in which case there is a faculty whose proper power stems from the rejection of the hierarchical relation. This rejection of the hierarchical relation between the faculties that make sense involves a certain neutralization of the social hierarchy. This is suggested in the second section of *Critique of Judgment* through the example of the palace. It is underlined later in the sixtieth section, which attributes to the aesthetic *sensus communis* a power of reconciliation between principles and classes. It is also spelled out a few years later in Schiller's political interpretation of the aesthetic experience as the neutralization of the opposition between the formal drive and the sensible drive. By translating the play between the faculties into a tension between drives, Schiller reminds Kant's readers of what is at stake. Before becoming faculties that cooperate to form judgments, *understanding* and sensibility designated parts of the soul, the better part, the leading part of intelligence that has the power to measure, and the subordinated or rebellious part of sensibility that knows only the shock of sensation and the stimuli of desire. As Plato emphasized, the partitioning of the individual soul was a partition of the collective soul, which also was a partition of the classes in the city; there was the class of intelligence and measure that was destined to rule and the class of sensation, desire, and unlimitedness that is naturally rebellious toward the order of intelligence that it must be subjected to. The aesthetic experience is a supplementation of this partition—a third term that cannot be described as a part but as an activity of redistribution, an activity that takes the form of a neutralization.

What I call the aesthetic dimension is this: the count of a supplement to the parts that cannot be described as a part itself. It is another kind of relation between sense and sense, a supplement that both reveals and neutralizes the division at the heart of the sensible. Let us call it a *dissensus*. A dissensus is not a conflict; it is a perturbation of the normal relation between sense and sense. The normal relation, in Platonic terms, is the domination of the better over the worse. Within the game it is the distribution of two complementary and opposite powers in such a way that the only possible perturbation is the struggle of the worse against the better—for instance, the rebellion of the democratic class of desire against the aristocratic class of intelligence. In this case there is no dissensus, no perturbation of the game. There is a dissensus only when the opposition itself is neutralized.

This means that *neutralization* is not at all tantamount to *pacification*. On the contrary, the neutralization of the opposition between the faculties, the parts of the soul, or the classes of the population is the staging of an excess, a supplement that brings about a more radical way of seeing the conflict. But there are two ways of understanding this excess. Just as there are two ways to think of matters of conflict—a consensual one and a dissensual one—there are also two ways of thinking the nature of dissensus and the relationship between consensus and dissensus. This point is decisive. There are two ways of interpreting matters of consensus and dissensus, an ethical one and an aesthetic one.

The *ethical* must be understood from the original sense of *ethos*. *Ethos* first meant *abode* before it meant the way of being that suits an abode. The ethical law first is the law that is predicated on a location. An ethical relation itself can be understood in two different ways, depending on whether you consider the inner determination of the location or its relation to its outside. Let us start from the inside. The law of the inside is doubled. *Ethical* in the first instance means that you interpret a sphere of experience as the sphere of the exercise of a property or a faculty possessed in common by all those who belong to a location. There is poetry, Aristotle tells us, because men differ from animals by their higher sense of imitation; all men are able to imitate and take pleasure in imitation. In the same way, there is politics because men not only share the animal property of the voice that expresses pleasure or pain but also the specific power of the logos that allows them to reveal and discuss what is useful and what is harmful and thus also what is just and what is unjust.

As is well known, it soon is made apparent that this common property is not shared by everyone; there are human beings who are not entirely human beings. For instance, Aristotle says, the slaves have the *aisthesis* of language (the passive capacity of understanding words), but they don't have the *hexis* of language (the active power of stating and discussing what is just or unjust). More generally, it is always debatable whether a sequence of sounds produced by a mouth is articulated speech or the animalistic expression of pleasure or pain. In such a way, the ethical universal is usually doubled by an ethical principle of discrimination. The common location includes in its topography different locations that entail different ways of being; the workplace, according to Plato, is a place where work does not wait, which means that the artisan has no time to be elsewhere. Since he has no place to be elsewhere, he has no capacity to understand the relation between the different places that make up a community, which means that he has no political intelligence. This relation can be turned around; insofar as the artisan is a man of need and desire he has no sense of the common measure and therefore cannot be anywhere other than the place where the objects of desire and consumption are produced. This is the ethical circle that ties together a location, an occupation, and the aptitude—the sensory equipment—that is geared toward them. The ethical law thus is a law of differentiation between the class of sensation and the class of intelligence.

To summarize, the ethical law, considered as the law of the inside, is a distribution of the sensible that combines—according to different forms of proportionality—the sharing of a common capacity and the distribution of alternative capacities.

But the law of the ethos can also be set up as the law of the outside. After Aristotle's analysis of the basic human community and before his statement on the political animal in *Politics,* he briefly conjures up and dismisses the figure of a subject that is without polis; this is a being that is inferior or superior to man—a monster or a divinity perhaps—a being that is *azux*, that cannot be in relation with any being like it, which is necessary in war. But what Aristotle briefly describes as the figure of an outsider can be turned around as the figure of the immeasurable or the unsubstitutable from which all that is measurable or substitutable, connected according to a law of distribution, has to take its law at the risk of being cancelled by it. As we know, such a figure has been revived over the last few decades in different forms: the law of the Other, the Thing, the sublime, and so on.

This is what I call the ethical interpretation of the matters of consensus and dissensus, the ethical interpretation of the common and its supplement. The aesthetic dimension is another interpretation of this, an interpretation that dismisses both the inner law of distribution and the law of an immeasurable outside. The aesthetic dimension brings about a dismantling of ethical legality, that is, a dismantling of the ethical complementarity of the three terms: the rule of the common ethos, the rule of the distribution of the alternative parts, and the power of the monster that is outside of the rule. It could also be described as the ethical distribution of the same, the different, and the Other. In opposition to that distribution, the general form of the aesthetic configuration could be described that is not the Other, the immeasurable, but rather the redistribution of the same and the different, the division of the same and the dismissal of difference. The aesthetic configuration replays the terms of the difference in such a way as to neutralize them and to make that neutralization the staging of a conflict that is in excess of consensual distribution. Such an excess cannot be counted according to the consensual rules of distribution but nevertheless does not obey the rule of an immeasurable otherness. The difference between these two excesses is the difference between ethical heteronomy and aesthetic heterotopy.

Let me try to illustrate these statements by describing what I have called the politics of aesthetics, the aesthetics of politics, and the aesthetics of knowledge. In each of these fields it is possible to differentiate the aesthetic approach from the two forms of an ethical approach. Let us start from what I call the politics of aesthetics, which means the way in which the aesthetic experience—as a refiguration of the forms of visibility and intelligibility of artistic practice and reception—intervenes in the distribution of the sensible. In order to understand this, let us return to my starting point, that is, to Kant's analysis of the beautiful as the expression of a neither/nor. The object of aesthetic judgment is neither an object of knowledge nor an object of desire. In the political translation made by Schiller this neither/nor was interpreted as the dismissal of the ethical opposition between the class of those who know and the class of those who desire. This way of framing a politics of aesthetics has been contested by two forms of ethical criticism. On the one hand, there is the sociological criticism that saw an ignorance of the social law of the ethos. Pierre Bourdieu's work epitomizes this type of criticism, namely, arguing that the view of aesthetic judgment as a judgment independent of all interest amounts to an illusion or a mystification. The disinterested aesthetic judgment is the privilege of only those who can abstract themselves—or who believe that they can abstract themselves—from the sociological law that accords to each class of society the judgments of taste corresponding to their ethos, that is, to the manner of being and of feeling that their condition imposes upon them. Disinterested judgment of the formal beauty of the palace is in fact reserved for those who are neither the owners of the palace nor its builders. It is the judgment of the petit-bourgeois intellectual who, free from the worries of work or capital, indulges him- or herself by adopting the position of universal thought and disinterested taste. Their exception therefore confirms the rule according to which judgments of taste are in fact incorporated social judgments that translate a socially determined ethos. Such judgments are also part of the mystification that hides the reality of social determinism and helps prevent victims of the system from gaining access to the knowledge that could liberate them.

The opposite form of ethical criticism has been voiced by Jean-François Lyotard. For Lyotard, too, disinterested judgment is a philosophical illusion. It is a logical monster, he argues, that tries to translate into terms of classical harmony the loss of any form of correspondence between the norms of the beautiful and a socially determined public of art connoisseurs. This monstrous replastering of a lost world of harmony conceals the true essence of modern art, which is nevertheless spelled out in Kant's critique: the modern work of art obeys the law of the sublime. The law of the sublime is the law of a disproportion, of an absence of any common measure between the intelligible and the sensible. In a first stage, Lyotard identifies this disproportion with the overwhelming power of the matter of sensation: the singular, incomparable quality of a tone or a color, of "the grain of a skin or a piece of wood, the fragrance of an aroma." But in a second stage he erases all those sensuous differences. "All these terms," he says, "are interchangeable. They all designate the event of a passion, a passibility for which the mind will not have been prepared, which will have unsettled it, and of which it conserves only the feeling—anguish and jubilation—of an obscure debt."[1] All the differences of art add up to one and the same thing: the dependency of the mind on the event of an untameable sensuous shock. And this sensuous shock in turn appears as the sign of radical servitude, the sign of the mind's infinite indebtedness to a law of the Other that may be the commandment of God or the power of the unconscious. Elsewhere I have tried to analyze this ethical turn that put the sublime in the place of aesthetic neutralization and to show that this supposed a complete overturning of the Kantian concept of the sublime. I will not resume that analysis here. What I would like to focus on is the core of the operation: Lyotard dismisses the heterotopy of the beautiful in favor of the heteronomy of the sublime. The result of this operation is the same as that of the sociological critique, though it is made from a very different angle; in both cases the political potential of the heterotopy is boiled down to a sheer illusion that conceals the reality of a subjection.

The political potential of the aesthetic heterotopy can be illustrated by an example. During the French Revolution of 1848, there was a brief blossoming of workers' newspapers. One of those newspapers, *Le Tocsin des travailleurs* (The Workers' Tocsin), published a series of articles in which a joiner describes a fellow joiner's day at work, either in the workshop or in the house where he is laying the floor. He presents it as a kind of diary. For us, however, it appears more akin to a personalized paraphrase of *Critique of Judgment* and more peculiarly of the second paragraph that spells out the disinterestedness of aesthetic judgment. Kant documented disinterestedness with the example of the palace that must be looked at and appreciated without considering its social use and signification. This is how the joiner translates it in his own narration: "Believing himself at home,

[1]Jean-François Lyotard, "After the Sublime, the State of Aesthetics," *The Inhuman: Reflections on Time*, trans. Geoffrey Bennington and Rachel Bowlby (Stanford, Calif., 1991), p. 141.

he loves the arrangement of a room so long as he has not finished laying the floor. If the window opens out onto a garden or commands a view of a picturesque horizon, he stops his arms a moment and glides in imagination towards the spacious view to enjoy it better than the possessors of the neighbouring residences."[2] This text seems to depict exactly what Bourdieu describes as the aesthetic illusion. And the joiner himself acknowledges this when he speaks of belief and imagination and opposes their enjoyment to the reality of possessions. But it is not by accident that this text appears in a revolutionary workers' newspaper, where aesthetic belief or imagination means something very precise: the disconnection between the activity of the hands and that of the gaze. The perspectival gaze has long been associated with mastery and majesty. But in this case it is reappropriated as a means of disrupting the adequation of a body and an ethos. This is what disinterestedness or indifference entails: the dismantling of a certain body of experience that was deemed appropriate to a specific ethos, the ethos of the artisan who knows that work does not wait and whose senses are geared to this lack of time. Ignoring to whom the palace actually belongs, the vanity of the nobles, and the sweat of the people incorporated in the palace are the conditions of aesthetic judgment. This ignorance is by no means the illusion that conceals the reality of possession. Rather, it is the means for building a new sensible world, which is a world of equality within the world of possession and inequality. This aesthetic description is in its proper place in a revolutionary newspaper because this dismantling of the worker's body of experience is the condition for a worker's political voice.

Aesthetic ignorance thus neutralizes the ethical distribution insofar as it splits up the simple alternative laid down by the sociologist that claims you are either ignorant and subjugated or have knowledge and are free. This alternative remains trapped in the Platonic circle, the ethical circle according to which those who have the sensible equipment suitable for the work that does not wait are unable to gain the knowledge of the social machine. The break away from this circle can only be aesthetic. It consists in the disjunction between sensible equipment and the ends that it must serve. The joiner agrees with Kant on a decisive point: the singularity of the aesthetic experience is the singularity of an as if. The aesthetic judgment acts as if the palace were not an object of possession and domination. The joiner acts as if he possessed the perspective. This as if is no illusion. It is a redistribution of the sensible, a redistribution of the parts supposedly played by the higher and the lower faculties, the higher and the lower classes. As such it is the answer to another as if: the ethical order of the city, according to Plato, must be viewed as if God had put gold in the souls

[2]Louis Gabriel Gauny, "Le Travail à la tache," quoted in Jacques Rancière, *The Nights of Labor: The Workers' Dream in Nineteenth-Century France*, trans. John Drury (Philadelphia, 1989), p. 81.

of the men who were destined to rule and iron in the souls of those who were destined to work and be ruled. It was a matter of belief. Obviously Plato did not demand that the workers acquire the inner conviction that a deity truly mixed iron in their souls and gold in the souls of the rulers. It was enough that they sensed it, that is, that they used their arms, their eyes, and their minds as if this were true. And they did so even more as this lie about fitting actually fit the reality of their condition. The ethical ordering of social occupations ultimately occurs in the mode of an as if. The aesthetic rupture breaks this order by constructing another as if.

This brief analysis brings us to what I call the aesthetics of politics. Here too the alternative is between an ethical and an aesthetic perspective. The reason for the alternative is simple: politics is not primarily a matter of laws and constitutions. Rather, it is a matter of configuring the sensible texture of the community for which those laws and constitutions make sense. What objects are common? What subjects are included in the community? Which subjects are able to see and voice what is common? What arguments and practices are considered political arguments and practices? And so on.

Let us consider the most common political notion in our world, the notion of democracy. There is a consensual ethical view of democracy. It is the view of democracy as a system of government grounded in a form of life, the form of freedom determined by the free market. The view that sees a correspondence between a form of economic life, a system of institutions, and a set of values has been favored as long as democracy has been opposed to totalitarianism. As we know, that favor has drastically decreased over the last decade. On the one hand, governments and statesmen complain that democracy is ungovernable, that it is threatened by an enemy that is none other than democracy itself. At the same time, intellectuals complain that democracy is the power of individual consumers indifferent to the common good, a power that not only threatens good government but civilization and human filiation more generally. We are not obliged to take those contentions at face value. What matters is that as they explode the consensual view of democracy by opposing democratic government to a democratic society they urge us to consider a disjunction at the heart of democracy and that such a disjunction is possibly the characteristic not of a bad political regime but of politics itself.

In other words, the current criticism of democracy points to a dissensus at the heart of politics. Dissensus is more than the conflict between a part and another part—between the rich and the poor or the rulers and those who are ruled. Rather, it is a supplement to the simple consensual game of domination and rebellion. How should we understand this supplement? Once more, it can be understood either from an aesthetic or from an ethical point of view.

To understand dissensus from an aesthetic point of view is to understand it from a point of view that neutralizes the ethical rule of the distribution of power. As I mentioned earlier the ethical rule is actually doubled; the common property is doubled by alternative capacities. According to this rule, power is the exercising of a certain qualification of some over those who don't possess it; those who exercise power are entitled to do so because they are the priests of God, the descendants of the founders, the eldest, the best of kin, the wisest, the most virtuous, and so on. This is what I have called the circle of the *arkhè*, the logic according to which the exercise of power is anticipated in the capacity to exercise it, and this capacity in turn is verified by its exercise. I have claimed that the democratic supplement is the neutralization of that logic, the dismissal of any dissymmetry of positions. This is what the notion of a power of the demos means. The demos is not the population. Nor is it the majority or the lower classes. It is made up of those who have no particular qualification, no aptitude attached to their location or occupation, no aptitude to rule rather than be ruled, no reason to be ruled rather than to rule. Democracy is this astounding principle: those who rule do so on the grounds that there is no reason why some persons should rule over others except for the fact that there is no reason. This is the anarchic principle of democracy, which is the disjunctive junction of power and the demos. The paradox is that that anarchic principle of democracy turns out to be the only ground for the existence of something like a political community and political power. There are a variety of ethical powers that work at the level of the social: in families, tribes, schools, workshops, and so on; parents over children, the older over the younger, the rich over the poor, teachers over pupils, and so on. But as long as the community is made from the conjunction of those powers and as long as it is ruled on the whole according to one or a combination of those powers it is not yet political. In order for any community to be a political one there must be one more principle, one more entitlement, that grounds all of the others. But there is only one principle in excess of all the others: the democratic principle or entitlement, the qualification of those who have no qualification.

This is my understanding of the democratic supplement: the demos is a supplement to the collection of social differentiations. It is the supplementary part made of those who have no qualification, who are not counted as units in its count. I have called it the part of those without part, which does not mean the underdogs but means anyone. The power of the demos is the power of whoever. It is the principle of infinite substitutability or indifference to difference, of the denial of any principle of dissymmetry as the ground of the community. The demos is the subject of politics inasmuch as it is heterogeneous to the count of the parts of a society. It is a *heteron*, but a *heteron* of a specific kind since its heterogeneity is tantamount to substitutability. Its specific difference is the indifference to difference, the indifference to the multiplicity of differences—which means inequalities—that make up a social order. Democratic heterogeneity means the disjunctive junction of two logics. What is usually designated as the political is made of two antagonistic logics. On the one hand, there are men who rule over others because they are—or they play the part of—the older, the richer, the wiser, and so on because they are entitled to rule over those who do not have their status or competence. There are patterns and procedures of rule predicated on a certain distribution of place and competence. This is what I call the rule of the police. But, on the other hand, that power has to be supplemented by an additional power. To the extent that a power is political, the rulers rule on the ultimate ground that there is no reason why they should rule. Their power rests on its own absence of legitimacy. This is what the power of the people means: the democratic supplement is that which makes politics exist as such.

Some consequences can be drawn from this regarding the mode of existence of the demos. On the one hand, the power of the demos is nothing but the inner difference that both legitimizes and delegitimizes any state institution or practice of power. As such it is a vanishing difference that is ceaselessly annulled by the oligarchic functioning of institutions. This is why, on the other hand, this power must be continuously reenacted by political subjects. A political subject is a subject constituted through a process of enunciation and manifestation that plays the part of the demos. What does it mean to play the part of the demos? It means to challenge the distribution of parts, places, and competences by linking a particular wrong done to a specific group with the wrong done to anyone by the police distribution—the police's denial of the capacity of the anyone. This is what a political dissensus means. A dissensus puts two worlds—two heterogeneous logics—on the same stage, in the same world. It is a commensurability of incommensurables. This also means that the political subject acts in the mode of the as if; it acts as if it were the demos, that is, as the whole made by those who are not countable as qualified parts of the community. This is the aesthetic dimension of politics: the staging of a dissensus—of a conflict of sensory worlds—by subjects who act as if they were the people, which is made of the uncountable count of the anyone. When a small group of protesters takes to the streets under the banner We Are the People, as they did in Leipzig in 1989, they know that they are not the people. They create the open collective of those who are not the people that is incorporated in the state and located in its offices. They play the role of the uncountable collection of those who have no specific capacity to rule or to be ruled.

This is what I call the aesthetic understanding of the democratic supplement, which amounts to a political understanding. I think that we can oppose it to the ethical view of the supplement, which is epitomized in Derrida's concept of democracy to come. My observations should not be misinterpreted. I am aware that Derrida was also concerned with the elaboration of a concept of democracy that would break the consensual-ethical view of democracy as the way of governing and the way of being of wealthier countries. I am also aware that his search for a new concept of democracy was part of a commitment to a number of struggles against various forms of oppression throughout the world. I acknowledge this theoretical and practical commitment to the main issues of democracy. Nevertheless I think that it can be said that the concept of democracy to come is not a political but an ethical concept. Democracy to come is not, for Derrida, the aesthetic supplement that makes politics possible. It is a supplement to politics. And it is because Derrida's democracy actually is a democracy without demos. What is absent in his view of politics is the idea of the political subject, of the political capacity. The reason for this is simple. There is something that Derrida cannot endorse, namely, the idea of neutralization (or substitutability)—the indifference to difference or the equivalence of the same and the other. Consistently, what he cannot accept is the democratic play of the as if. From his point of view there can be only one alternative: either the law of the same, the law of autonomy, or the law of the other, the law of heteronomy.

What I call the law of the same can be epitomized by two notions that Derrida uses to characterize the consensual view of politics: sovereignty and brotherhood. Derrida endorses without discussion a widely accepted idea that the essence of politics is sovereignty, which is a concept of theological descent. Sovereignty in fact reaches back to the almighty God. God gave it to the kings. The democratic people got it, in turn, when they beheaded the kings. Political concepts are theological concepts that have hardly been secularized. According to this view the concept of the demos cannot have any specificity. It comes down to the concept of a sovereign, self-determined subject who is homogeneous to the logic of sovereignty that sustains the power of nation-states. Therefore the force of the democracy to come cannot be that of the demos. What comes under suspicion thus is not only the figure of the demos; it is the notion of a political subject itself and the idea of politics as the exercise of the capacity of anyone. Just as he identifies the concept of politics with the concept of sovereignty, Derrida equates the notion of the political subject with the notion of brotherhood. From his point of view there is no break between familial power and political power. Just as the nation-state is a sovereign father, the political subject is in fact a brother. Even the concept of citizen—which has so often been used and misused in French political discourse of the last twenty years—has no relevance in his conceptualization. *Citizen* is just another name for brother. We cannot but be struck by the force of Derrida's polemics against brotherhood or fraternity, which include even a critique of parity—as if an equal woman, a substitutable woman, a "calculable" woman still was a brother, a member of the sovereign family. As he conceives of it, a brother is anyone who can be substituted for another, anyone who bears a trait of substitutability.

Democracy to come thus cannot be a community of substitutable persons. In other words, what the democracy to come can oppose to the practice of nation-states is not the action of political subjects playing the part of the anyone. It is the commitment to an absolute other, an other that can never become the same as us, that cannot be substituted—or, we can add, an other that cannot stage his or her otherness, that cannot stage the relationship between his or her inclusion and his or her exclusion. Democracy to come is a democracy without a demos, with no possibility for a subject to perform the *kratos* of the demos.

Such a democracy implies another status of the *heteron*: the *heteron* as the outside, the distant, the asymmetric, the nonsubstitutable. Derrida's notion of hospitality implies much more than the obligation to overstep the borders of nation-states in order to deal with what he calls the "ten plagues" of the International Order.[3] What the *hospes* goes beyond is above all the border that allows reciprocity or substitutability. In this sense, the *hospes* is the strict opposite of the demos. The character of the *hospes* opens up an irreconcilable gap between the stage of the possible or the calculable and the stage of the unconditional, the impossible, or the incalculable. What this precludes is the aesthetic performance of the as if. The *hospes* erases the heterotopy of the demos as he creates a radical gap between the sphere of political compromise and the sphere of the unconditional, between the calculable of the law and the incalculable of justice. What is dismissed by this opposition is the performance of those who play the part of the demos that they are not. When protesters say in the streets that "this is just" or "this is unjust," their "is" is not the deployment of a determinant concept subsuming its object. It is the clash of two justices, the clash of two worlds. This is what a political dissensus or heterotopy means. But it is the kind of justice that Derrida rules out. In his view there can only be either the normal, consensual application of the rule operating as a machine or the law of unconditional justice. This is what the "to come" means. The ethical to come is the opposite of the aesthetic as if. It means that democracy cannot be presented, even in the dissensual figure of the demos, that is, of the subject that acts as if it were the demos. There can be no substitution of the whole by the part, no subject performing the equivalence between sameness and otherness. The heterotopy of the demos is substituted by two forms of irreducible heterogeneity: the temporal heterogeneity of the to come and the spatial heterogeneity of the *hospes*. These two forms are combined in the figure of the first-comer and the newcomer. The *hospes* or the newcomer is the other that cannot come to the place of the same, the other whose part cannot be played by an other. This dissymmetry is clearly spelled out by Derrida in *Rogues* when he identifies the anyone that is at the heart of

[3]Jacques Derrida, *Specters of Marx: The State of the Debt, the Work of Mourning, and the New International*, trans. Peggy Kamuf (New York, 1994), p. 86.

the democracy to come. This anyone is not the subject of a dissensus, the subject who affirms the capacity of those who have no capacity. It is the object of a concern. Derrida gives to the "first to happen by [*le premier venu*]," a term he borrows from Jean Paulhan, a quite significant meaning; it is, he says, "anyone, no matter who, at the permeable limit between 'who' and 'what,' the living being, the cadaver, and the ghost."[4] The anyone thus becomes the exact contrary of what appeared first; it is the absolute singularity of the figure that Aristotle conjured up at the beginning of *Politics*, the being that is less or more than the human being—less insofar as it is the animal, the cadaver, or the ghost that is entrusted to our care (*à revoir*). The other, in that sense, is whoever or whatever that requires that I answer for him, her, or it. This is what responsibility is: the commitment to an other that is entrusted to me, for whom or for which I must answer.

But, on the other hand, the other is whoever or whatever has a power over me without reciprocity. This is demonstrated in *Specters of Marx*, for instance, by the analysis of the visor effect or helmet effect. The ghost or the thing looks at us in a way that rules out any symmetry. We cannot cross its gaze. Derrida adds that it is from that visor effect that we first receive the law—not justice but the law, the justice of which is tantamount to our ignorance, to our incapacity to check the truth of its words: "The one who says 'I am thy Father's spirit' can only be taken at his word. An essentially blind submission to his secret, to the secret of his origin: this is a first obedience to the injunction. It will condition all the others."[5] In order to understand what is at stake in that matter of obedience, we must have in mind another scene between father and son for which the confrontation between Hamlet and the ghost has obviously been substituted. Hamlet is in the place of Abraham, and the ghost in the place of the God who orders him to kill his son. As Derrida puts it in *Rogues*, when emphasizing the principle of heteronomy that is at the heart of this relationship: "It is a question ... of a heteronomy, of a law come from the other, of a responsibility and decision of the other—of the other in me, an other greater and older than I am."[6]

At this point, Derrida offers us, with the help of Kierkegaard, a theoretical *coup de théâtre*: the God who commands Abraham to kill Isaac does ask him to obey his order. As Derrida puts it in *Donner la mort*, he says: you have to obey me unconditionally. But what he wants Abraham to understand is you have to choose unconditionally between betraying your wife and son or betraying me, and you have no reason to choose me rather than Sarah and Isaac.[7] Sacrifice only means choice, and the choice

---

[4]Derrida, "The Reason of the Strongest (Are There Rogue States?)," *Rogues: Two Essays on Reason*, trans. Pascale-Anne Brault and Michael Naas (Stanford, Calif., 2005), p. 86.
[5]Derrida, *Specters of Marx*, p. 7.
[6]Derrida, "The Reason of the Strongest (Are There Rogue States?)," p. 84.
[7]See Derrida, *The Gift of Death*, trans. David Wills (Chicago, 1995), pp. 58–9.

between the absolute Other and the member of the family is no different than the choice I have to make whenever I enter a relation with any other, which obliges me to sacrifice all the others. To obey the law of the absolute Other is to feel the equivalence of any other with any other. *Tout autre est tout autre* (any other is wholly other): this is the formula of the identity of contraries, the formula of the identity between absolute inequality and absolute equality. Anyone can play the part of the any other that is wholly other. Thanks to the God of Abraham, anyone can play the role of the God of Abraham.

So the formula of radical heteronomy turns out to be equivalent to the formula of political equality; the ethical anyone is equivalent to the political anyone. But it is so only by the self-negation or self-betrayal of the ethical law of heteronomy, which means, in my view, that the whole construction of ethical heteronomy has to be self-cancelled in order to make a politics of the anyone possible.

As stated earlier, I am not willing to say that my notion of democracy is more appropriate than Derrida's democracy. I am just trying to outline the difference between an aesthetic and an ethical understanding of politics. And Derrida's democracy to come is all the more significant in this respect since it makes the radical difference between the two approaches appear in the closest proximity, at the very limit of the indiscernible.

In order to underscore the politics of aesthetics and the aesthetics of politics, a certain kind of discourse has to be set to work, a kind of discourse that implies an aesthetics of knowledge. What does this expression mean? First it is a discursive practice that gives its full signification to the apparently innocuous definition of the aesthetic judgment as elaborated by Kant, namely, that aesthetic judgment implies a certain ignorance; we must ignore the way in which the palace has been built and the ends that it serves in order to appreciate it aesthetically. As I have argued, such ignorance or suspension is not a mere omission. In fact it is a division of both knowledge and ignorance. The ignorance of the possession and destination of a building produces the disjunction between two types of knowledge for the joiner: the know-how of his job and the social awareness of his condition as the condition shared with those who don't care for the pleasures of perspective. It produces a new belief. A belief is not an illusion in opposition to knowledge. It is the articulation between two knowledges, the form of balance between those forms of knowledge and the forms of ignorance they are coupled with. As Plato claimed, articulation or balance has to be believed. The economy of knowledge has to be predicated on a story. This does not mean an illusion or a lie. It means it is predicated on an operation that weaves the fabric within which the articulation of the knowledges can be believed, within which it can operate. From the Platonic point of view, technical knowledge has to be submitted to a knowledge of ends. Unfortunately this science, which provides a foundation for the distribution of knowledges and positions, is itself without a demonstrable foundation. It must be presupposed, and in order to do so a story must be recounted and believed. Knowledge requires stories because it is, in fact, always double. Once more there are two ways of dealing with this necessity: an ethical one and an aesthetic one.

Everything revolves around the status of the as if. Plato formulated it in a provocative way: ethical necessity is a fiction. A fiction is not an illusion; it is the operation that creates a topos, a space and a rule for the relation between sense and sense. Modern "human" and social sciences refuse this provocation. They affirm that science cannot admit fiction. Nevertheless they want to reap its benefits; they want to keep the topography of the distribution of the souls, as in the form of a distinction between those who are destined to know and those who are destined to provide the objects of knowledge. I mentioned Bourdieu's sociology earlier because it is the purest form of disavowed or hidden Platonism that animates modern social knowledge. His polemic against the aesthetic illusion is not the idea of one particular sociologist. It is structural. Aesthetics means that the eyes of the worker can be disconnected from his hands, that his belief can be disconnected from his condition. This is what must be ruled out if sociology is to exist. That is, an ethos must define an ethos; an abode must determine a way of being that in turn determines a way of thinking. Of course this is not only the case for sociology. History, for example, has its own particular way of constructing modes of being and thinking as the expressions of different periods of time. Such is the case for disciplines in general or for what can be called disciplinary thinking. A discipline, in effect, is first of all not the exploitation of a territory and the definition of a set of methods appropriate to a certain domain or a certain type of object. It is primarily the very constitution of this object as an object of thought, the demonstration of a certain idea of knowledge—in other words, a certain idea of the rapport between knowledge and a distribution of positions, a regulation of the rapport between two forms of knowledge (*savoir*) and two forms of ignorance. It is a way of defining an idea of the thinkable, an idea of what the objects of knowledge themselves can think and know.

Disciplines delineate their territory by cutting through the common fabric of language and thought. They thereby draw a line of partition between what the joiner, for example, says and what his phrases mean, between their raw materiality and the materiality of the social conditions that they express. They engage in a war against aesthetic ignorance, which means aesthetic disjunction. In other words, they must engage in a war against the war that the worker is himself fighting. They want the bodies that compose society to have the ethos—the perceptions, sensations, and thoughts that correspond to their ethos—proper to their situation and occupation. The point is that this correspondence is perpetually disturbed. There are words and discourses that freely circulate, without a master, and divert bodies from their destinations. For the joiner and his brothers those words may be *the people*, *liberty*, or *equality*. They may be *passion*, *felicity*, or *ecstasy* for their distant sister Emma Bovary. There are spectacles that disassociate the gaze from the hand and transform the worker into an aesthete. Disciplinary thought must ceaselessly stop this hemorrhage in order to establish stable relations between bodily states and the modes of perception and signification that correspond to them. It must ceaselessly pursue war but pursue it as a pacifying operation.

To speak of an aesthetics of knowledge thus is not an occasion to get closer to the sensuous experience. It is an instance to speak of that silent battle, to restage the context of the war—what Foucault called the "distant roar of the battle."[8] In order to do so, an aesthetics of knowledge must practice a certain ignorance. It must ignore disciplinary boundaries in order to restore their status as weapons in a struggle. This is what I have done, for example, in taking the phrases of the joiner out of their normal context, that of social history, which treats them as expressions of the worker's condition. I have taken a different path; these phrases do not describe a lived situation but reinvent the relation between a situation and the forms of visibility and capacities of thought that are attached to it. Put differently, this narrative (*récit*) is a myth in the Platonic sense; it is an anti-Platonic myth, a counterstory of destiny. The Platonic myth prescribes a relationship of reciprocal confirmation between a condition and a thought. The countermyth of the joiner breaks the circle. In order to create the textual and signifying space for which this relation of myth to myth is visible and thinkable, we must initiate a form of "indisciplinary" thinking. We must create a space without boundaries that is also a space of equality, in which the narrative of the joiner's life enters into dialogue with the philosophical narrative of the organized distribution of competencies and destinies.

This implies another practice—an indisciplinary practice—of philosophy and its relation to the social sciences. Classically, philosophy has been considered a sort of superdiscipline that reflects on the methods of the social sciences or provides them with their foundation. Of course these sciences can object to this status, treat it as an illusion, and pose themselves as the true bearers of knowledge about philosophical illusion. This is another hierarchy, another way of putting discourses in their place. But there is a third way of proceeding that seizes the moment in which the philosophical pretension to found the order of discourse is reversed, becoming the declaration, in the egalitarian language of the narrative, of the arbitrary nature of this order. This is what I have tried to do by connecting the narrative of the joiner with the Platonic myth.

---

[8]Michel Foucault, *Surveiller et punir* (Paris, 1975), p. 315; my trans.

The specificity of the Platonic myth is constituted by the way in which it inverts the reasons of knowledge (*savoir*) with the purely arbitrary insistence on the story (*conte*). While the historian and the sociologist show us how a certain life produces a certain thought expressing a life, the myth of the philosopher refers this necessity to an arbitrary, beautiful lie that, at the same time, is the reality of life for the greatest number of people. This identity of necessity and contingency—the reality of the lie—cannot be rationalized in the form of a discourse that separates truth from illusion. It can only be recounted, that is, stated in a discursive form that suspends the distinction and the hierarchy of discourse.

It is here, Plato claims in *Phaedrus*, that we must speak the truth (*vrai*) there where we speak of truth (*vérité*). It is here also that he has recourse to the most radical story, that of the plain of truth, of the divine charioteer, and of the fall that transforms some into men of silver and others into gymnasts, artisans, or poets. In other words, taking things the other way around, at the moment when he most implacably states the organized distribution of conditions, Plato has recourse to what most radically denies this distribution: the power of the story and the common language that abolishes the hierarchy of discourse and the hierarchies that this underwrites. The foundation of the foundation is a story, an aesthetic affair. From this we can imagine a practice of philosophy that points to the story that is implied in each of the methods that define how a certain ethos produces a certain form of thinking. The point is not to claim that the disciplines are false sciences or that what they actually do is in fact a form of literature. Nor is it to annul them from the point of view of some figure of the other or the outside: the traumatic revelation of the real, the shock of the event, the horizon of the messianic promise, and so on.

The point is neither to reverse the order of dependence inside the ethical consensus nor to refer to the subversive power of the wholly Other. If an aesthetic practice of philosophy means something, it means the subversion of those distributions. All territories are topoi predicated on a singular form of the distribution of the sensible. A topography of the thinkable is always the topography of a theater of operations. There is no specific territory of thought. Thought is everywhere. Its space has no periphery, and its inner divisions are always provisory forms of the distribution of the thinkable. A topography of the thinkable is a topography of singular combinations of sense and sense, of provisory knots and gaps. An aesthetics of knowledge creates forms of supplementation that allow us to redistribute the configuration of the topoi, the places of the same and the different, the balance of knowledge and ignorance. It implies a practice of discourse that reinscribes the force of descriptions and arguments in the war of discourses in which no definite border separates the voice of the object of science from the logos of the science that takes it as its object. It means that it reinscribes them in the equality of a common language and the common capacity to invent objects, stories, and arguments. If this practice is named philosophy, this means that philosophy is not the name of a discipline or a territory. It is the name of a practice; it is a performance that sends the specificities of the territories back to the common sharing of the capacity of thinking. In this sense the aesthetic practice of philosophy can also be called a method of equality.

INDEX

Lightning Source UK Ltd.
Milton Keynes UK
UKHW020336161122
412220UK00016B/367